Managing Fashion

The fashion industry is a multibillion-dollar global industry with a variety of organizational structures and a multitude of challenges. Such scope triggered the recent rise in management programs in the U.S. and Europe aiming to produce and train young managers to meet such global and diverse challenges.

Managing Fashion covers the fashion business with a twist – *a management* twist. Its goal is to tackle the topics from a fashion manager perspective referencing relevant management concepts and theories, thus offering a deeper and more practical dimension to the issues addressed. It offers a balanced mix of fashion and management, theory and application, as well as creating an opportunity for analysis and critical thinking.

Discussions throughout the book are supported by specially developed case studies and relevant examples taken from the fashion industry. It is an opportunity to expose the fashion student or reader, as well as aspiring fashion managers, to a more practical approach to fashion theories and issues. *Managing Fashion* will serve as a core text for Fashion Studies, Fashion Entrepreneurship, and Fashion Merchandising majors as well as for special business degrees and management certificates targeting the fashion industry.

Kaled K. Hameide is a tenured Associate Professor in the College of the Arts at Montclair State University, United States.

T0384279

Managing Fashion

A Management Perspective

Kaled K. Hameide

Routledge
Taylor & Francis Group

NEW YORK AND LONDON

Fourth edition published 2021
by Routledge
52 Vanderbilt Avenue, New York, NY 10017

and by Routledge
2 Park Square, Milton Park, Abingdon, Oxon, OX14 4RN

Routledge is an imprint of the Taylor & Francis Group, an informa business

Library of Congress Cataloging-in-Publication Data
Names: Hameide, Kaled K., author.
Title: Managing fashion: a management perspective / Kaled K. Hameide.
Description: New York, NY: Routledge, 2021. | Includes bibliographical
references and index.
Identifiers: LCCN 2020024963 (print) | LCCN 2020024964 (ebook) |
ISBN 9780815386919 (hardback) | ISBN 9780815364757 (paperback) |
ISBN 9781351106856 (ebook)
Subjects: LCSH: Fashion merchandising–Management. | Clothing
trade–Management. | Strategic planning.
Classification: LCC HD9940.A2 H35 2021 (print) | LCC HD9940.A2 (ebook) |
DDC 746.9/2068–dc23
LC record available at https://lccn.loc.gov/2020024963
LC ebook record available at https://lccn.loc.gov/2020024964

ISBN: 978-0-8153-8691-9 (hbk)
ISBN: 978-0-8153-6475-7 (pbk)
ISBN: 978-1-351-10685-6 (ebk)

Typeset in Joanna
by Deanta Global Publishing Services, Chennai, India

Contents

List of illustrations   viii
List of case studies   x
Preface   xi

1   **Understanding Management**   1
    Learning Outcomes   1
    What is Management?   1
    Who is a "Manager"?   2
    Levels of Management   3
    Functions of the Management Process   5
    Strategic Management   28
    Chapter Questions   38
    Case Study: Under Armour: A Strategic Management Perspective   38
    Notes   43
    Bibliography   44

2   **Managing the Fashion Supply Chain: How the Fashion**
    Industry Works   49
    Learning Outcomes   49
    Levels of The Fashion Industry   49
    Supply Chain Management (SCM)   56
    Value Chain Management (VCM)   60
    Significant Fashion Models Impacting the Supply and Value Chains   63
    Chapter Questions   71
    Case Study: Uniqlo: Global LifeWear   71
    Notes   75
    Bibliography   75

3   **Managing the Fashion Brand**   78
    Learning Outcomes   78
    What is a Brand?   78
    The Branding Process   96
    Chapter Questions   107
    Case Study: Longchamp: The Subtle Brand   108
    Notes   112
    Bibliography   113

4   **Managing Fashion Brand Extensions**   **115**
    Learning Outcomes   115
    Why Grow?   115
    Growth Strategies   115
    Smart Growth   122
    Growth Through Brand Extensions   123
    Growth and Risk Management   135
    Chapter Questions   138
    Case Study: Halston: A Tragic Fashion Epic   138
    Notes   141
    Bibliography   142

5   **Managing Fashion Licensing**   **144**
    Learning Outcomes   144
    The State of Licensing   144
    Role of the Licensing Agent   145
    What to License?   146
    Advantages and Challenges of Licensing   147
    The Licensing Agreement   151
    Franchising (Retail Licensing)   160
    Franchising vs. Licensing   161
    Franchise Categories   162
    Advantages and Challenges of Franchising   162
    The Franchising Agreement   166
    Chapter Questions   173
    Case Study: Benetton: Franchising 2.0   173
    Notes   177
    Bibliography   178

6   **Managing Fashion Global Growth**   **181**
    Learning Outcomes   181
    The Global Market   181
    International vs. Global   181
    Why Go Global?   182
    Internal and External Analysis   183
    Entering a Foreign Market   185
    The Export Decision   190
    The Export Process   193
    Common Export Documents   196
    Terms of Payment by Importers   196
    How Can Organizations Finance Their Exports?   202
    Important Issues to Consider as an Exporter   204
    Trade Agreements and Preferential Programs   209
    Free Trade Zones   211
    Chapter Questions   211
    Case Study: CROCS: Managing Supply Chain for Global Growth   212
    Notes   216
    Bibliography   216

7	**Ethics and Other Fashion Management Issues**	**218**
	Learning Outcomes	218
	Issue 1: Ethics and Management	218
	Issue 2: Fashion and Labor Issues	225
	Issue 3: Intellectual Property and Copyrights	230
	Issue 4: Counterfeits	240
	Chapter Questions	243
	Case Study: Brunello Cucinelli: The Humanistic Capitalist	244
	Notes	246
	Bibliography	247
	Index	251

Illustrations

Figures

1.1	Levels of Management	3
1.2	Types of Organizational Structures	15
1.3	Gap Inc. Hybrid Organizational Structure	17
1.4	Porter's Five Forces of Competition	32
1.5	Under Armour Products and Store	43
2.1	Apparel Supply Chain	57
2.2	Porter's Value Chain	62
2.3	Fashion Value Chain	63
3.1	Brand's Dynamic Pyramid	87
3.2	The Loyalty Matrix	88
3.3	The Brand/Asset Valuator (BAV) Model	93
3.4	Positioning Map Example	99
3.5	Longchamp Le Pliage Bag	111
4.1	Ansoff Matrix	118
4.2	The BCG Matrix	119
5.1	Excerpts from a License Agreement Sample	152
5.2	Excerpts from a Franchise Agreement Sample	167
5.3	Benetton New Redesigned Store	176
6.1	Examples of Common Export Price Quotes	195
6.2	Letter of Credit Payment Process	199
7.1	Gucci vs. Guess	238
7.2	Counterfeit Luxury Bags	241

Tables

3.1	Brand Valuation Methods	92
4.1	PEST Analysis Example	121
4.2	Calvin Klein Brands	125
5.1	Examples of Calvin Klein Licensing Partners	150
5.2	Examples of Ralph Lauren Licensing Partners	160
5.3	Franchise vs. License	161
5.4	Franchise Categories Pros and Cons	163
6.1	Examples of Tariffs	209

Boxes

1.1	Zappos and the "Holacracy" Organization Structure	18
1.2	Nike SWOT Analysis	29
1.3	Examples of Management Positions Within the Fashion Industry	34
2.1	Segments in the Fashion Industry Based on Price	52
2.2	See Now, Buy Now (SNBN) Successes and Failures	69
3.1	Disruptive Positioning	84
3.2	Branding and Influencer Marketing	100
3.3	Raf Simons at Calvin Klein: A Failed Revitalization	106
4.1	Pierre Cardin: The Fall of the Licensing King	126
4.2	Diesel: The Rebel Brand	131
4.3	Tom Ford: An Unorthodox Approach to Licensing	134
5.1	Calvin Klein: The Ups and Downs of Licensing	149
5.2	Ralph Lauren Licensing Business Overview	159
5.3	Plato's Closet Franchise Model	171
6.1	Leading International Fashion Trade Fairs	192
6.2	Sources of Assistance to Exporters	204
6.3	NAFTA 2.0	210
7.1	LVMH CSR Strategy	224
7.2	Nike Corporate Social Responsibility and Sustainable Innovation	229
7.3	The Battle of the Gs: Gucci vs. Guess	236

Case Studies

Under Armour: A Strategic Management Perspective   38
Uniqlo: Global LifeWear   71
Longchamp: The Subtle Brand   108
Halston: A Tragic Fashion Epic   138
Benetton: Franchising 2.0   173
CROCS: Managing Supply Chain for Global Growth   212
Brunello Cucinelli: The Humanistic Capitalist   244

Preface

Why this book? The fashion industry is a multibillion-dollar global industry with a variety of organizational structures and a multitude of challenges. Such impactful scope has triggered the recent rise in management programs in the U.S., Europe and around the world aiming to produce and train young fashion managers to meet such global and diverse challenges as well as realize the immense opportunities. However, such a rise in fashion management programs was not matched with the required amount of literature that addresses management theories from a fashion perspective. Thus, it has been the norm for fashion students and industry professionals to rely on general business management books commonly used by business schools to learn the fundamental management theories and other issues of concern. While thorough and informative, such books lack the fashion context. Hence, this book. This project aims to address and introduce the principles of management with both the fashion manager and the fashion student in mind. Its goal is to offer a balanced mix of management theory and fashion application while creating an opportunity for analysis and critical thinking. Accordingly, this book should be approached as a book of management with a fashion focus and not as a Fashion Marketing or a Business of Fashion one.

Based on the above, the book could roughly be divided into four major sections that complement, and build on, each other while offering a logical progression of gained knowledge. Starting with an overview of the basic principles of management and how the fashion industry works, the chapters progress to explore specific areas of interest to any fashion manager such as: organizational structure, the apparel supply chain, understanding and managing the fashion brand, exploring growth options and opportunities, as well as other issues of concern such as ethics, copyright and labor issues. These four sections could be defined as:

- Principles of management: Chapter 1
- Managing the fashion organization: Chapters 1, 2, 5, 6, 7
- Managing the fashion brand and product: Chapters 2, 3, 4, 5, 6, 7
- Managing growth: Chapters 4, 5, 6, 7

It is also important to note that while most chapters are independent and written in a manner that would allow the reader to understand the relevant topic if he/she decides to skip through them, it is highly recommended that the book be read in the sequence of chapters proposed since there is a certain logical build-up to the topics covered.

Discussions throughout the book are supported by case studies that were specifically created for this project. Each case study addresses an apparel brand from a certain angle that reflects issues raised and discussed throughout the relevant chapter. The text boxes included could be viewed as miniature cases and supporting examples that are meant to complement and/or explore specific chapter-relevant topics even further. Finally, questions at the end of each chapter or case study are designed to instigate critical thinking and the desire to conduct further research in order to gain a better understanding of the issues raised. Enjoy the journey.

CHAPTER ONE
Understanding Management

Learning Outcomes

- Understand the concept and process of management
- Assess the differences between a leader and a manager
- Identify the principles of strategic management
- Implement the decision-making process

What is Management?

Humans have known and practiced management since the early days of civilization. Every major ancient structure from the Egyptian pyramids to the Great Wall of China and beyond represents a major project that involved thousands of workers and a variety of specializations that necessitated plans, allocation of resources, set time frames, and division of labor as well as some measures of performance evaluation and reward systems. That is to say they were projects that needed to be *managed* in order to get them done. Our understanding of management today is not much different than such practices. However, it is much more structured and supported with effective and tested theories and principles. Accordingly, we can simply define management as *the process of getting things done effectively and efficiently, through and with other people.*[1]

While simple, the definition effectively highlights three key elements of management which are: *process – efficiency – effectiveness.*

Process

Management is indeed a process which is built on a series of activities that, if performed successfully (i.e. efficiently and effectively), will yield positive results and get the job done. As these activities represent different stages within the process, each of the activities and steps are meant to assist the manager in achieving specific roles or "functions" based on the stage of the process. We can group the main stages and steps of the management process into four main functions: planning, organizing, leading, and controlling.

- *Planning*: This function involves establishing the overall goals for the organization and developing a strategy to achieve them.
- *Organizing*: This function refers to the process by which managers create an organization's structure and system that would enable employees to do their work both effectively and efficiently.

- *Leading*: This function stresses the manager's ability to motivate individuals and teams as they work to accomplish the organization's goals.

- *Control*: This function refers to the monitoring and evaluation process and measures taken to determine whether things are going as planned or not.

Efficiency

Any task is about utilizing certain inputs to deliver desired outputs. Efficiency thus means doing this right and achieving the best possible relationship between the inputs and outputs. Management is always concerned with minimizing the costs of inputs to achieve the best desired outputs and that is what efficiency really means.

Effectiveness

While efficiency is about doing the task right, effectiveness refers to doing or choosing the right task. This in return means that the manager has succeeded in achieving the organization's stated goals. So basically, a manager needs to know what is needed to be done and what is that task he needs to target (effectiveness) and then work on doing it right in the most efficient and cost-effective way (efficiency). Indeed, good management is concerned with both the attainment of goals (effectiveness) and the efficiency of the process.

Who is a "Manager"?

So far, we have used the term *manager* repeatedly and it is obvious that he/she is that person who is responsible for directing the management process. However, it is extremely important to remember that managers do not fulfill tasks, complete the process, or achieve the desired goals solely by themselves. On the contrary, management is a process that involves many people within a department or an organization. Hence, a fundamental element of the manager's role is to direct and "manage" other people throughout the process in order to achieve desired goals. As a matter of fact, the difference between managers and non-managers is the fact that managers have employees who report directly to them. Thus, simply defined, a manager is *that person who directs the activities of other people in the organization to achieve the organization's goals.*

While the details of the manager's job will differ from one organization to the other, they all share some common roles and characteristics. For example:

- *Interpersonal role*. Managers are figureheads and in order to manage and coordinate activities among different employees they also fulfill the role of a liaison between individuals and parties.

- *Informational role*. A manager cannot achieve results and desired outputs without being able to receive, collect, process, and disseminate information. By doing so they also fulfill the role of a mentor and a group spokesperson,

- *Decisional role*. Handling inputs and resources also means possessing an ability to allocate, negotiate, and distribute these resources to where they could be used efficiently and effectively, as stated earlier. As such, a manager is also a negotiator and in many ways an entrepreneur,

And to fulfill these three important roles, a manager must possess the following three essential skills:

- *Technical skills*. A manager must possess some knowledge or proficiency in a certain specialized field. This becomes even more necessary with managers who deal directly with employees doing the work of the organization as is common with lower level managers (more on this later) who are directly involved with hands-on employees such as factory workers and salespeople, etc.

- *Human skills.* In order to successfully fulfill the interpersonal role, a manager must have the ability to work with other people both individually and as a group.

- *Conceptual skills.* In order to transform inputs to outputs and make the necessary decisions to do so, a manager must have the ability to think and conceptualize abstract and complex situations.

It is through these roles and with these skills that a manager is capable of overseeing the four major functions of *planning, organizing, leading, and controlling,* that are the building bricks of the management process.

LEVELS OF MANAGEMENT

There are three levels of management that represent a hierarchy of authority, each with a different set of tasks to perform (Figure 1.1). These levels are:

1. Top Level of Management (or an Administrative level)

2. Middle Level of Management (or an Executive level)

3. Lower Level of Management (or a Supervisory level)

Top-Level Managers

These managers are responsible for overseeing the entire organization. They develop goals, strategic plans, and company policies as well as make decisions on the direction of the business. They also play a crucial role in the mobilization of outside resources.

Managers at this level include members of the boards of directors, presidents, vice presidents, as well as the chief executive officer (CEO). Top-level managers are accountable to shareholders and the general public.

Figure 1.1 Levels of Management.
Created by Author.

The roles of this level of managers are strategic and long term (i.e. big picture) in nature and include:

- Determining the objectives, policies and plans of the organization.

- Mobilizing available resources which include assembling and bringing them together.

- Spending the majority of time in thinking, planning, organizing, and deciding which explains why this level of managers is also referred to as the administrative level or, as some would describe it, the *brain* of the organization.

- Preparing long-term plans of the organization, which are plans generally made for five to 20 years ahead.

- Having maximum and final authority and responsibility in the organization, they are directly responsible to the shareholders, government entities, and the general public. In many ways the success or failure of the organization largely depends on their efficiency and decisions.

Of the three major skills mentioned earlier, they require **more conceptual skills** *and* **fewer technical skills.**

Mid-Level Managers

Mid-level managers spend more time on organizational and directional functions than top-level managers do. They have limited authority and responsibility, but they are intermediaries between top and lower management and part of their job is to define, discuss, and convey information and policies from top management to lower management. Accordingly, they are accountable to top-level managers and are directly responsible to the CEO and board of directors, etc.

Examples of managers at this level include general managers, branch managers, and department managers, etc.

The roles and tasks of mid-level managers may include:

- Communicating and giving recommendations to top-level management.

- Executing and implementing organizational plans and policies in adherence with company policies and objectives placed by top-level managers.

- Preparing short-term plans for their departments (usually 1–5 years).

- Coordinating and monitoring group-level performance indicators and measures,

- Inspiring and providing guidance to low-level managers.

- Helping low-level managers achieve better performance through designing and implementing effective group and intergroup work environment and systems.

- Diagnosing and resolving problems within work groups.

- Designing and implementing an effective reward system that supports cooperative work.

Of the three major skills mentioned earlier, they require **more technical skills** *and* **fewer conceptual skills.**

Low-Level Managers

Low-level managers are selected by mid-level managers. They primarily play a supervisory role; hence this level is sometimes referred to as the operative, supervisory, or first line of management. Examples of low-level managers include directors and supervisors.

The roles and tasks of low-level managers may include:

- Directing employees and workers and assigning different tasks to them.

- Supervising day-to-day activities and boosting general morale among workers.

- Establishing and maintaining a link and communication channel between middle-level management and workers.

- While they may have limited authority compared to higher levels of management, they do have the important responsibility of getting work done and ensuring that quality as well as quantity of production meets the organization's goals.

- While their main job is directing employees and controlling outcomes rather than planning and strategy, they are still involved in short-term planning by making daily, weekly, and monthly plans.

- Reporting directly to middle-level management.

*Of the three major skills mentioned earlier, they require **technical and strong human skills (communications)** and **fewer conceptual skills**.*

FUNCTIONS OF THE MANAGEMENT PROCESS

As mentioned earlier, the four functions or stages of the management process are: *planning – organizing – leading – controlling.*

We have already briefly explained what is meant by each function. We will now take a closer look at the possible tools available to achieve and perform these functions in an effective and efficient way as discussed.

Planning

Planning involves defining the organization's goals as well as establishing an overall strategy that will help achieve these goals. In the process, planning also involves developing a comprehensive set of plans to coordinate and integrate the organizational work involved in the process. That is to say that planning is about the *WHAT* is to be done and the *HOW* it will be done.

It is thus clear that for planning to happen a lot of decisions will have to be made in the process. Decisions that help in choosing between a number of alternatives. Thus, the purpose of planning could be summed up as:

- Setting goals and providing direction

- Reducing uncertainty

- Minimizing waste and redundancy

- Setting the standards for controlling

SETTING GOALS

Goals need to be specific and challenging to provide a target for which to aim and a standard against which to measure success. Traditionally, setting goals has the following characteristics:

- Broad goals are set at the top of the organization.

- Assumes that top management knows best because they can see the "big picture".

- Goals are intended to direct, guide, and constrain from above.

- Goals are then broken into sub-goals for each organizational level.
- Goals may sometimes lose clarity and focus as lower-level managers attempt to interpret and define the goals for their areas of responsibility.

Top management's general organizational goals are usually ambiguous and hard to turn into departmental and team goals. Thus, there has been a number of models to ensure that these goals are effective and realistic. A simple yet popular such model is the SMART model.

SMART MODEL OF SETTING GOALS

A SMART goal incorporates criteria to help focus the manager's efforts and increase the chances of achieving that goal. Thus, based on this model a goal needs to be:

Specific – Measurable – Attainable – Realistic (or Relevant) – Timely.

Specific: A SMART goal needs to be well defined, clear, and unambiguous.

To make a goal specific, the five "W" questions must be addressed:

- *Who*: Who is involved in this goal?
- *What*: What do I want to accomplish?
- *Where*: Where is this goal to be achieved?
- *When*: When do I want to achieve this goal?
- *Why*: Why do I want to achieve this goal?

Example:

Imagine that you are currently a marketing executive, and you would like to become head of the marketing department. A general goal is *"I want to be the future Marketing Manager"*. The specific goal could be, *"I want to gain the skills and experience necessary to become head of marketing within my organization in five years, so that I can build my career and lead a successful team."*

Measurable: A SMART goal must have criteria for measuring progress. If there are no criteria, you will not be able to determine your progress and if you are on track to reach your goal. To make a goal measurable, ask yourself:

- How many/much?
- How do I know if I have reached my goal?
- What is my indicator of progress?

Example:

You might measure your goal of acquiring the skills to become head of marketing by determining that you will have completed the necessary training courses and gained the relevant experience within five years.

Achievable: A SMART goal must be achievable and attainable. This will help you figure out ways that allow you to realize that goal and work towards it. The achievability of the goal should be stretched to make you feel challenged but defined well enough that you can actually achieve it. Ask yourself:

- Do I have the resources and capabilities to achieve the goal? If not, what am I missing?
- Have others done it successfully before?

Example:

You might need to ask yourself whether developing the skills required to become head of marketing is realistic, based on your existing experience and qualifications. For example, do you have the time to complete the required training effectively? Are the necessary resources available to you? Can you afford to do it?

It is also important to avoid setting goals that someone else has power over. For example, *"Get that promotion!"* depends on who else applies, and on the recruiter's decision. But *"Get the experience and training that I need to be considered for that promotion"* is entirely down to you.

Realistic: A SMART goal must be realistically achieved given the available resources and time and thus can be accomplished. Ask yourself:

- Is the goal realistic and within reach?
- Is the goal reachable given the time and resources?
- Am I able to commit to achieving the goal?

Example:

You might want to gain the skills to become head of marketing within your organization, but is it the right time to undertake the required training, or work toward additional qualifications? Are you sure that you are the right person for the head of marketing role?

Timely: A SMART goal must be time-bound in that it has a start and finish date. If the goal is not time constrained, there will be no sense of urgency and motivation to achieve the goal. Ask yourself:

- Does my goal have a deadline?
- By when do I want to achieve the goal?

Example:

Gaining the skills to become head of marketing may require additional training or experience, as we have mentioned earlier. How long will it take you to acquire these skills? Do you need further training, so that you're eligible for certain exams or qualifications? It's important to give yourself a realistic timeframe for accomplishing the smaller goals that are necessary to achieving your final objective.

While the examples given above are of a personal nature the same principle can be applied to any organizational goal-setting process such as: entering a new market, entering into a business partnership, adopting a new IT infrastructure, etc.

DECISION-MAKING PROCESS

Everyone within any organization has to make some decisions at one point or another which requires assessing and choosing between a number of alternatives.

As mentioned, top-level managers are generally concerned with the big picture and have a more strategic approach. And thus, they make decisions that are long-term and relate to the organization's overall goals such as where to allocate manufacturing facilities or what products to produce, etc. On the other hand, middle and lower managers make short term and specific decisions such as weekly or monthly schedules or production-related issues, etc.

No matter what decisions need to be made, in order to make rational decisions there are generally eight steps to follow:[2]

1. *Identifying a problem.* Any problem is basically a discrepancy between an existing and a desired state of affairs. For example, a garment factory is not satisfied with its current level and quality of

production and it realizes that its sewing operation needs new sewing machines to achieve the targeted production levels and quality. Thus, a discrepancy has been noted and a problem identified. There is a need to buy new machines.

2. *Identifying decision criteria.* Now that a need for buying new machines is identified, the next move is to determine the criteria and factors that are relevant and should be considered in making the choice for buying the new sewing machines. For example, price, size, speed, warranty, ease of use and technology, reliability, available accessories, maintenance, etc.

3. *Allocating weights to the criteria.* The determined and listed buying criteria need to be prioritized by assigning weight to each one of them. A weight of 1 to 10 could be used whereby a factor with a weight of 10 is twice as important and urgent as a factor with a weight of 5 and so on. For example, machine reliability could be given a weight of 10, size of machine 8, affordability 7, warranty 6 and so on.

4. *Developing alternatives.* Now that we know what we need and the priorities of the criteria we look for, it is time to examine the available alternatives that could solve our identified problem. Thus, for example, and based on our preferred criteria, we can determine that two machine brands (e.g. Singer and Brother) are the best alternatives for us.

5. *Analyzing alternatives.* Each of the alternatives identified will need to be analyzed and appraised against the weighted criteria we have established earlier. Both brands will be compared, and their offerings examined.

6. *Selecting an alternative.* Based on our analysis of the alternatives we choose the best that would solve our problem (e.g. Brother Model X machine).

7. *Implementing the alternative.* Implementing and choosing the alternative is an indication of the success of the decision process. We buy the machine.

8. *Evaluating the decision effectiveness.* The evaluation stage is an integral part of the decision-making process. The process does not end by implementing the choice, but is completed with evaluating the decision and the choices made (e.g. was buying Brother Model X machine the right choice and did it fulfill our need?).

It is important to remember that any research and alternative analysis is always based on two sources of information: INTERNAL and EXTERNAL. *External* refers to all and any external resources we have, such as consumer reviews, market analysis, word of mouth, etc. On the other hand, *Internal* sources stem from our own personal experiences whereby feedback and evaluations of previous purchases and implementations are the core.

FORMAL VS. INFORMAL PLANNING

Formal planning indicates specific goals covering a defined period of years. These goals are written down and shared with everyone within the organization. And thus, specific action programs are set to achieve these goals which means that managers have a clearly defined path to take them from where they are to where they want to be.

On the other hand, informal planning is when nothing is written down and there is little or no sharing of specific goals with others in the organization. While this type of planning could exist in large organizations it is more common in a small business environment where the owner, who is also the manager, has a vision of where he/she would want the business to go and how to get there. It is his/her dream and clear vision which is not necessarily stated in writing.

MANAGEMENT BY OBJECTIVES (MBO)

Management by Objectives (MBO) is a form of short-term planning process in which managers and subordinates at all levels in a company sit down together to jointly set goals, share information, and discuss strategies that could lead to goal achievement, and then regularly meet to review progress toward accomplishment of those goals. Thus, MBO is based on *goals, participation, and feedback*. While this approach has a lot of supporters, its critics indicate that:

- It may not be as effective in dynamic environments that require constant resetting of goals.

- Overemphasis on individual accomplishment may create problems with teamwork.

- The MBO program may become an occasional paperwork headache.

STRATEGIC VS. FINANCIAL GOALS

Whether formal or informal, any planning is about achieving goals. These goals could differ in range and nature, and while the economic goal of making profit might seem to be the first that comes to mind, it is not the only possible goal. As a matter of fact, goals could be financial or non-financial but still strategic in nature and could also differ with the different stage of the organization's life.

Examples of non-financial strategic goals:

- It is common for a new organization to be in a stage where it is aiming for market penetration and an increase in market share even if it means lowering prices and initially sacrificing profit maximization.

- Maintaining the status quo. More common with an older organization which faces competition from newcomers and thus aims to maintain its market position and not lose market share.

- Focusing on superior customer service.

- Aiming for higher recognition.

- Aiming at lowering costs to achieve competitive advantage.

Examples of financial goals:

- Higher profits or wider profit margins

- Higher dividends for shareholders

- Bigger cash flows

- Stable earnings

STRATEGIC VS. OPERATIONAL PLANS

Formal planning is more common than informal, especially as the organization gets bigger and includes more employees and departments. In that sense plans are written documents that outline how the above-listed goals (strategic or financial) are going to be met, what resources will be allocated, and what schedules will be set to achieve these goals. It is the manager's role to develop both the goals and the necessary relevant plans. Accordingly plans could also be categorized as either *strategic* or *operational*. Let us take a closer look at the differences in focus and scope of each.

Strategic Plans. By now we should have learned that the word "strategic" whenever and wherever is applied usually means two things: *long term impact* as well as *inclusive of all aspects of operations*. Accordingly, strategic plans are ones that apply to the entire organization and aim to establish the origination's overall goals. Thus, they cover a bigger and broader view of the organization and are also long-term in nature, which means they are plans for three to five years ahead.

Operational Plans. On the other hand, operational plans specify the details of how the overall goals stated in the strategic plans will eventually be achieved. Accordingly, these plans tend to cover a short period of time. They are a series of short-term plans that build up to achieve the long-term goals. Short term plans are usually less than a year and could be monthly, weekly, or even on a daily basis.

SPECIFIC VS. DIRECTIONAL PLANS

Plans could also be defined as specific or directional.

Specific plans, as the name implies, are clearly defined plans that leave no room for interpretation.

Directional plans, on the other hand, are more about general guidelines and thus they are more flexible. And while they still could be somewhat focused, they do not lock managers into a specific course of action.

MISSION VS. VISION STATEMENTS

Since planning is meant to set the tone and path the organization will be taking in the days and years to come, it is thus of the utmost importance that the organization and everyone within it understands from the inception of the business what it is all about, why the organization exists, where it is heading and what it envisions its long-term impact to be.

These thoughts are usually clearly stated early on in two important statements known as the mission and vision statements. Most organizations will have them clearly written, posted, and understood by their employees, as they set the direction and tone of the organization and thus impact every decision to be made.

Vision Statement

A vision statement has an outside focus targeting the outside world. It expresses the general direction of the organization and its long-term goal and vision. It has a general overview perspective.

Example:

Nike's Vision Statement: "to remain the most authentic, connected, and distinctive brand."

Nike's vision clearly indicates maintaining its leadership as the most innovative and consumer-centric brand in its industry.

Mission Statement

A mission statement states the purpose of the organization's existence. It answers the questions, "Why do we exist?" and "What business are we in?". It is thus meant primarily for an internal audience and for putting everyone within the organization on the same page and with the same focus.

Example:

Nike Mission Statement: "to bring inspiration and innovation to every athlete in the world." It stems from a statement made by its founder Bill Bowerman: "If you have a body, you are an athlete."

Nike's corporate mission statement defines the fundamental objectives of the business, to inspire and empower consumers by consistently offering innovative athletic products and solutions they cannot find somewhere else.

CORPORATE CULTURE

A Corporate culture refers to the shared values, attitudes, standards, and learned beliefs that characterize members of an organization and define its nature. Corporate culture is rooted in an organization's goals, strategies, structure, and approaches to labor, customers, investors, and the greater community.[3]

This idea of culture has been particularly useful for understanding and differentiating among organizations and the behavior of people in them. In a way, it defines and differentiates one organization's "personality" from another. Clearly, employees take their cues from the messages sent by the organizational leadership. Another important outcome of culture is creating a structure that defines the roles and responsibilities of individuals within an organization. We will take a closer look at the different possible organizational structures and their impacts later in the chapter.

Organizational cultures thus differ by organization and can be categorized in a number of possible forms or styles.

FORMS OF ORGANIZATIONAL CULTURE

Forms of organizational culture include:[4]

1. *Team-First Corporate Culture aka "the Comrade"*: Team-oriented companies hire for culture fit first, skills and experience second. A company with a team-first corporate culture makes employees' happiness its top priority. Frequent team outings, opportunities to provide meaningful feedback, and flexibility to accommodate employees' family lives are common markers of a team-first culture. It's a great culture for any customer service-focused company to embody, because employees are more likely to be satisfied with their work and eager to show their gratitude by going the extra mile for customers.

   Zappos is famous for its fun and nurturing culture, as well as its stellar customer service. As their CEO once famously said: "the way to keep employees satisfied with their job is by ... giving employees the autonomy to help customers the way they see fit, rather than following strict guidelines and scripts."

   Possible challenges:

   The larger the company, the more difficult it is to maintain this type of culture. That is why having a team member dedicated to cultivating culture is a great strategy for any company.

2. *Elite Corporate Culture aka "the Athlete"*: Companies with elite cultures are often out to change the world by untested means. An elite corporate culture hires only the best because it's always pushing the envelope and needs employees to not merely keep up but lead the way. Innovative and sometimes daring, companies with an elite culture hire confident, capable, competitive candidates. The result? Fast growth and making big splashes in the market.

   Possible Challenges:

   Such intensity can lead to competition between employees and people feeling always under pressure. Perks like team outings, peer recognition programs, and health initiatives can combat this.

3. *Horizontal Corporate Culture aka "the Free Spirit"*: Horizontal corporate culture is common among startups because it makes for a collaborative, everyone-pitch-in mindset. These, typically younger, companies have a product or service they're striving to provide yet are more flexible and able to change based on market research or customer feedback. Though a smaller team size might limit their customer service capabilities, they do whatever they can to keep the customer happy, as their success depends on it. Titles don't mean much in horizontal cultures,

where communication between the CEO and office assistant typically happens through conversations across their desks to one another rather than e-mail or memos.

Possible Challenges:

Horizontal cultures can suffer from a lack of direction and accountability. It is important to try to encourage collaboration while still maintaining clearly defined goals and a knowledge of who's primarily responsible for what could be challenging. Horizontal structure shouldn't mean no structure.

4. *Conventional Corporate Culture aka "the Traditionalist":* Traditional companies have clearly defined hierarchies and are still fighting with the learning curve for communicating through new mediums. Companies where a tie and/or slacks are expected are, most likely, of the conventional sort. In fact, any dress code at all is indicative of a more traditional culture, as are a numbers-focused approach and risk-averse decision making. The customer, while crucial, is not necessarily always right, the bottom line takes precedence.

The digital age, which has brought about new forms of communication through social media and software, etc. has led traditional companies to communicate through new mediums that can blur those formal lines.

Possible Challenges:

This very cut-and-dried approach leaves little room for inspiration or experimentation, which can result in a lack of passion or resentment from employees for being micromanaged. Getting employees to understand the company's larger mission and putting more trust in employees to work toward it, can combat that.

5. *Progressive Corporate Culture aka "the Nomad":* Mergers, acquisitions, or sudden changes in the market can all contribute to a progressive culture. Uncertainty is the definitive trait of a progressive culture because employees often do not know what to expect next. Customers are often separate from the company's audience, because these companies usually have investors or advertisers to answer to.

Yet, a major transition can also be a great chance to get clarity on the company's shifted goals or mission and answer employees' most pressing questions. Change can be scary, but it can also be good.

Possible Challenges:

Progressive culture can instill fear in employees for obvious reasons. Any change in management or ownership, even if it's a good thing for the company, isn't always seen as a good thing. Communication is crucial in easing these fears. It's also a good opportunity to hear feedback and concerns from employees and keep top talent engaged.

WHAT MAKES A CULTURE?

As we've seen, each culture is unique and many factors go into creating one. However, we can determine that there are at least six common components of great cultures:[5]

1. *Vision:* A great culture starts with a vision or mission statement, as mentioned. These guide a company's values and provide it with purpose which in turn, orients every decision employees make, as well as help orient customers, suppliers, and other stakeholders.

2. *Values:* A company's values are the core of its culture. While a vision articulates a company's purpose, values offer a set of guidelines on the behaviors and mindsets needed to achieve that vision. And

while many companies find their values revolve around a few simple topics (employees, clients, professionalism, etc.), the originality of those values is less important than their authenticity.

3. *Practices:* Of course, values are of little importance unless they are enshrined in a company's practices. If an organization professes, "people are our greatest asset", it should also be ready to invest in people in visible ways. Whatever an organization's values, they must be reinforced in review criteria and promotion policies and woven into the operating principles of daily life in the firm.

4. *People:* No company can build a coherent culture without people who either share its core values or possess the willingness and ability to embrace those values. That's why the greatest firms in the world also have some of the most stringent recruitment policies. People stick with cultures they like and bringing on the right "culture carriers" reinforces the culture an organization already has.

5. *Narrative:* Any organization has a unique history and a unique story and the ability to unearth that history and craft it into a narrative is a core element of culture creation. The elements of that narrative can be formal, like *Burberry's,* or informal *(a personal story).*

6. *Place:* Place shapes culture. A design studio for instance, is more conducive to certain office behaviors, like collaboration. On the other hand, certain cities and countries have local cultures that may reinforce or contradict the culture a firm is trying to create. Place, whether geography, architecture, or aesthetic design, impacts the values and behaviors of people in a workplace (e.g. Tom Ford adopts an open working space in his design studios whereby different design teams such as shoes, menswear, etc. feed off each other's ideas).

Organizing

Organizing is the second stage or function of the management process. It defines the process by which managers create an organization's structure that allows employees to do their work effectively and efficiently. Now that the goals have been established in the planning stage, tasks to be done are to be determined as well as by whom they will be executed, how they will be grouped, who reports to whom and where decisions are to be made. Accordingly, the organizational structure needed is basically a framework by which tasks are divided, grouped, and coordinated.

ELEMENTS OF ORGANIZATIONAL DESIGN

In order to develop an effective organizational structure, managers are involved in what is called organizational design which is a process that is built on six main elements:[6]

1. *Work specialization.* This refers to the degree to which tasks in an organization are divided into separate jobs (e.g. creative, assembly, marketing, sales etc.).

2. *Departmentalization.* Once jobs are divided up through specialization, they have to be grouped together so that common tasks can be coordinated. This process is referred to as departmentalization. For example, under the "production" department there are different jobs or functions that need to be done such as creative, assembly, finishing, etc. This is an example of functional departmentalization (i.e. a department based on activities or functions).

Departmentalization does not always have to be based on function. For instance, it could be based on product. A product department groups all jobs and functions that relate to a specific product line (e.g. men's dress shirts or denim pants, etc.). We could also have geographic departments (North America vs. Asia) or one that is based on similar consumer needs (e.g. joggers vs. swimmers, etc.). In a large organization we could notice the utilization of more than one form of departmentalization. For example, they could start by departmentalizing based on functions (production, marketing, design, etc.) and then within each of these departments (e.g. production) another level of departmentalization takes place in the form of functions while within another department (e.g. sales) the division could be geography based (east vs. west coast) and so on.

3. *Chain of command.* This is defined as the continuous line of authority that extends from upper organizational levels to the lowest levels and clarifies who reports to whom. The word authority is key here as it defines the inherent rights in each managerial position that allow managers to tell people what to do.

4. *Span of control.* This refers to how many employees can a manager manage both efficiently and effectively. Accordingly, it determines the number of managers an organization will end up having. The appropriate number of employees to be managed by each manager is determined by many factors such as his/her skills and ability as well as the employees' level of training and experience. Managers can manage a higher number of well-trained employees. A wider range, if suitable, could lead to a faster decision-making process, increase in flexibility, and a possible closer relation to customers.

5. *Centralization vs. decentralization.* Some organizations tend to be more centralized in their decision-making process than others, whereby all decisions are made by top-level managers and passed to lower-level managers and employees to implement. Other organizations are very decentralized, whereby the decision making is left to the managers who are closest to the direct situations. There has been a tendency lately towards decentralized structures as they create more flexibility and quicker responsiveness. However, centralized structures could lead to a certain level of control and stability and could also be necessary in situations where lower-level managers are not very experienced, the decisions are significant, the company is too large, or the organization is in a critical phase or facing a crisis, etc.

6. *Formalization.* This refers to the degree to which jobs within the organization are standardized and the extent to which employee behavior is guided by rules and procedures with little freedom to use discretion over what is to be done. With high formalization the job description is explicit, and responsibilities are clearly defined while jobs are less structured with low formalization. The level of formalization could differ from within the same organization. While certain jobs (e.g. design or IT) have the freedom to work according to their own schedule or work from home, etc., other departments (e.g. accounting) may not have such freedom.

TYPES OF ORGANIZATIONAL DESIGNS

There are many different styles of organizational designs, each of which is meant to accommodate different levels and styles of interaction and share of information amongst departments and functions (Figure 1.2).

The most common types of structures are:

1. *Simple Structure.* Most organizations start as a small entrepreneurial business venture with the simple structure of an owner as the manager and with a few employees. It's a structure with a small number of departments and smaller number of managers which also means a wide span of control, little formalization, and the owner is usually where the authority is centralized. However, as the business grows the organization hires more employees adding more duties and the need for specialization which in turn leads to more formalization, etc. becomes evident, and thus, the structure of the organization will have to change, most likely to a traditional functional one.

2. *Traditional/Hierarchical Structure.* Organizations that use a traditional/hierarchical structure rely on a vertical chain of command as the prime method of organizing employees and their responsibilities. Usually, very large organizations use a hierarchy to determine the level of control employees have over their work, as well as their rank relative to others. A centralized organization often houses its primary decision makers or executives in a central headquarters with offices and meeting areas for leaders to discuss business. There are many types and forms of hierarchical structures. These types of traditional hierarchical organization generally have a centralized setup featuring multiple layers of management in which most power and critical decision-making responsibilities are concentrated with a few key leaders.

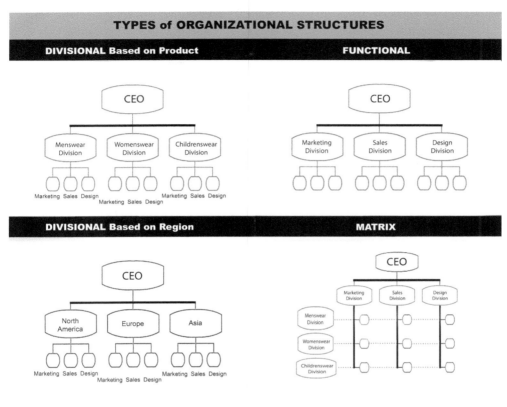

Figure 1.2 Types of Organizational Structures.
Created by Author.

Hierarchical organizations can come in different forms, based on their size and activities, such as:

A. *Functional.* Functional organizational structures are the most common. A structure of this type groups individuals by specific functions performed and related specialties together. Common departments such as human resources, accounting, and purchasing are organized by separating each of these areas and managing them independently of the others, thus leading to the departmentalization of the whole organization. For example, managers of different functional areas all report to one director or vice president who has responsibility for all of the operational areas.

Advantages: Offers a high level of specialization and employees are highly motivated as they clearly see their career path within the functional units.

Challenges: The process is more bureaucratic, and the lack of inter-departmental coordination and communication tends to make decisions take longer.

B. *Divisional.* A divisional structure is made up of separate divisions or units whereby each division has relatively limited autonomy with a divisional manager in charge and responsible for performance and who has strategic and operational authority over his unit. Under this structure, each division essentially operates as its own company, controlling its own resources and how much money it spends on certain projects or aspects of the division. The parent organization still acts as an external overseer to coordinate and control various divisions. This structure allows for much more autonomy among groups within the organization. Organizational division could be based on many criteria such as:

- *Divisional – Product Based.* Organized by a specific product type falling under an executive who oversees everything related to that particular product line. For example, an executive over CK Jeans products would be responsible for every product under that label only.

- *Divisional – Market/Brand Based.* Divisions are made on the basis of a targeted market or brands with different market focus. For example, PVH which operates three business groups: Calvin Klein, Tommy Hilfiger, and Heritage Brands (includes a number of brands such as Arrow and Van Heusen), adopts a mixed divisional geographic- and brand-based structure. Under a centralized corporate and executive leadership, the senior level leaders head divisions that are defined by brands and regions, e.g. Calvin Klein International, Calvin Klein Americas, Heritage Brands, Tommy Hilfiger International & PVH Europe, Tommy Hilfiger Americas, etc.

- *Divisional – Customer Based.* Certain industries are organized by customer type. This is done in an effort to ensure specific customer expectations are met by a customized service approach. (e.g. online vs. store customers, regular vs. top tier loyalty program customers, etc.)

- *Divisional – Geographic Based.* For organizations that cover a span of geographic regions, it sometimes makes sense to organize by region where each region reports up to a central oversight person. This is done to better support logistical demands and differences in geographic customer needs. For example, Nike adopts a geographic divisional structure based on a mix of a global corporate leadership to facilitate control of the organization and semi-autonomous geographic divisions such as North America, Greater China, Japan, etc. in order to adapt the unique conditions of each regional market. Also, until 1993 Macy's operated under two divisions, Macy's East covering New York and the east coast region and Macy's West covering the west coast region.

Advantages: Allows for a more autonomous method of operation and the division's focus allows for the building of a common culture and high level of specialization.

Challenges: Divisions may become concerned with meeting their own objectives instead of those of the organization as a whole. In addition, employees do not communicate across divisions may instead compete over resources, allowing for office politics.

3. *Flat Organization (Horizontal Organization).* A flat organization, or *horizontal organization*, is known for wide spans of control, decentralization, low specialization, and loose departmentalization, where it has fewer levels of supervisors with individual managers taking on a greater amount of responsibility and control. Employees are responsible for making decisions on their parts of the project and report directly to high-level supervisors.

Advantages: More empowerment and freedom given to employees. Fewer layers of management improve coordination, transparency, and decision making. May also eliminate roles and salaries of middle management and reduces an organization's budget costs.

Challenges: Lack of a specific boss to report to, may create confusion and can make accountability and reliability (and even promotion) harder. Large organizations usually struggle to adapt to the flat structure, unless the company divides into smaller, more manageable units.

4. *Matrix Structure.* The matrix organizational structure combines elements of the functional and divisional models in which they group employees based on what they do, their similar skills along with what project they're working on. Thus, while in a flat organization, employees work together on one project and each employee has a role, in a matrix, employees could work on multiple projects at one time, based on their skills. For example, all engineers may be in one engineering department and report to an engineering manager. These same engineers may be assigned to different projects and might be reporting to those project managers as well. Usually, the project manager has the authority over functional or department members. While decisions such as promotions, salary, or annual review, etc. remain the responsibility of the functional or department manager.

Advantages: A more dynamic organization with open communication and sharing of resources such as skilled employees across functions. Thus, it is an environment that facilitates learning and growth. It also offers some flexibility over the constraining traditional hierarchical structures.

Challenges: It is a complex structure that takes a lot of planning and may result in confusion and conflicts between teams as managers compete over employees. Having more people in managerial positions may have a financial impact as well.

5. *Virtual (and Network) Organization (The Modern Organization).* The virtual organization is also rather flat in structure. It relies on distant collaborations among team members. It mainly exists and operates online through the internet by e-mail, real-time conferencing, etc., all of which result in geographic flexibility and responsiveness, as well as lower costs. A network organization, on the other hand, is basically any organization that is very well connected and relies heavily on communication through the internet, etc. but it is not necessarily totally virtual or dispersed geographically.

Advantages: High level of employee satisfaction as they are able to work from home leading to higher retention. They also have lower overhead cost and in the case of startups hiring workers remotely enables them to access a larger pool of talent as well as tap into new markets.

Challenges: Hard to instill a company culture and sense of camaraderie. And, as employees may be spread out all over the world spanning time zones, it becomes almost impossible to gather the entire group together at the same time. Moreover, some potential customers may not take the company as seriously.

6. *Hybrid Organization.* A hybrid structure is a combination of two of the previously described structures. This is very common with larger organizations that oversee a range of businesses. A good example is Gap Inc. which integrates certain elements of divisional and hierarchical organizational structures. Gap's organizational structure is divided into five divisions with each division representing a separate brand and headed by a president. At the same time, the organizational structure within each division is highly hierarchical and there are multiple levels of management between the president of the division and a shop floor assistant for instance (Figure 1.3).

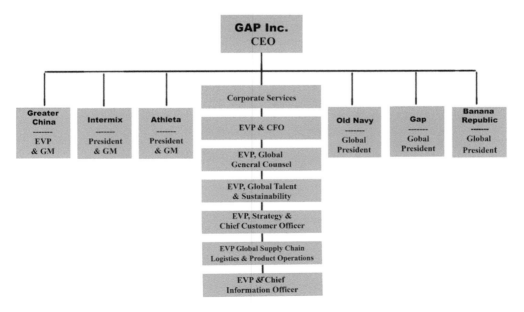

Figure 1.3 Gap Inc. Hybrid Organizational Structure.
Created by Author.

Box 1.1 Zappos and the "Holacracy" Organization Structure

In 2014, Zappos announced that it was implementing a new model of organization structure known as Holacracy which it believed will allow it to cultivate a startup culture in spite of its growing size and age. Indeed, as the company grew, it became slower to sense and respond to customer feedback, because of the layers of employees it needed to go through to get things done. Holacracy, on the other hand, is a model designed to allow every employee to quickly act on customer feedback and in doing so allow the company to continue providing its WOW service.

What is Holacracy?

Holacracy is a term introduced by software engineer Brian Robertson who aimed at introducing a model that would eliminate the ways in which our humanity interferes with productivity. It is a structure about self-organizing, so instead of waiting around for a boss to tell you what to do, you take the reigns as an employee, or as a team, and jump right into projects and collaborations. The thinking is that the more empowered employees feel in their own careers, the more they will want to see the business grow and succeed. Thus, the model is basically built on the concepts of circles and roles. A marketing circle, for example, can contain roles like social media, advertising, web marketing, and brand development. Every role comes with agreed-upon accountabilities. If a role's responsibilities become too much for just one person to take care of, then it can expand into a new sub-circle with its own roles. It is important to note that a role is not representative of a person, a single employee can have many roles, and roles are always subject to change.

Role Marketplace

One of the major elements of the Holacracy model is the *Role Marketplace*. The *Role Marketplace* is basically an internal job board with specific roles and jobs that other departments need completed, along with the percentage of time they estimate it will take out of a person's schedule. That way, if one team needs something completed that they feel will take five percent (or points) of someone's time, they can go ahead and list it and wait to see if anyone is interested.

Thus, an employee comes in the morning and if he/she is not already busy in a role would look at the *Role Marketplace*, examine the posted work and with whom they could be working, and thus pitch themselves for the role they are interested in. Since more than one person could express interest in the same role, the Lead Link (who leads the team responsible for this task/role) will go over the candidates and pick the best fit. Teams determine when and how often they need to meet.

Obviously, for every job posted, there are certain qualifications that limit who can take on the role or side project. Thus, lead links create what is called "badges". These badges equate to skills, so theoretically, you could set your sights on a specific job, figure out the requirements, and earn those badges to make for an easier future transfer. Badges make it easy for others to identify your skills showing you are qualified for similar new projects. A lot of times a lead link will have a role available that they want to open up to the entire company instead of to people with certain badges.

It is important to note that the model does not totally eliminate the need for management or leadership, especially in cases related to raises and firings. Just because an employee is in charge of his/her own direction within the company, does not mean he/she can simply grant themselves raises or fire people at will. Rather than going through their direct boss for compensation, they go up in front of a circle of individuals defending or making a case for the compensation.

Challenges of the Model

* The idea of "no bosses" might sound appealing to some people, but the fact is that plenty of Zappos employees were not that excited about having to define their own job and indeed some decided to quit.
* When dealing with outside organizations and clients, employees at Zappos still need some way to designate their role, even though the company got rid of titles.
* In spite of the flexibility of moving across roles and tasks, the need remained for jobs or circles to be more dedicated and stable than others such as circles for hiring, firing, and deciding on raises, which are dedicated circles and not specific to one department, but serve the entire organization. Customer service has also proven to be a very stable circle due to its day to day, ongoing, routine nature of answering phones, etc. which is attractive to those who prefer such stable area.

Yet in spite of the challenges, Zappos remains a big advocate of the model and a case study on its implementation. Zappos believes that the model has opened up lines of communication between teams and made employees feel more connected to the company, which makes them more invested in their careers. Harvard Prof. Ethan Bernstein explained that by adopting this model, Zappos had basically replaced the traditional organizational chart by creating a work chart instead.

Sources

1. Bernstein, Ethan, John Bunch, Niki Canner and Michael Lee. "Beyond the Holacracy Hype". *Harvard Business Review*. August 2016. https://hbr.org/2016/07/beyond-the-holacracy-hype
2. Dunsmoor, Matt. "An Inside Perspective on the Changes at Zappos.com". Holcracy. Org. September 14, 2015. https://blog.holacracy.org/thanks-for-all-of-your-concern-but-f9c6a86bb332
3. Holacracy. "Holacracy Constitution v.4". Holacracy.Org. June 2015. https://www.holacracy.org/constitution
4. Luenendonk, Martin. "Complete Guide to Holocracy: Example of Zappos". *Cleverism*. March 4, 2016. https://www.cleverism.com/complete-guide-to-holocracy-example-of-zappos/
5. Majchrzak, Piotr. "Our Holacracy Experience What It Is and Why It Works". March 5, 2018. https://medium.com/@piotrmajchrzak/our-holacracy-experience-what-it-is-and-why-it-works-564a36bdfbd7
6. www.zappos.com

FASHION AND ORGANIZATIONAL STRUCTURE

The fashion industry is roughly divided into two major arms or categories: luxury and mass-market. Within each of these categories, companies vary greatly in size, focus, and the segments (e.g. moderate, better, bridge, etc.) they target. (*We will be discussing various fashion segments in more detail in the next chapter.*) Accordingly, the number of organizational structures within each segment is as diverse as the number of companies in them. Indeed, the scope and size of the fashion industry ranges from an entrepreneurial one man/woman business, a traditional functional operation, a network or virtual organization, to large conglomerates such as LVMH which carries a wide range of brands under its umbrella.

However, by looking at the two major arms of the industry (luxury and mass-market) we can conclude some clear differences in how they function and in return how they may need to be structured:

On the Mass-Market Side

- Mass-market organizations are generally fashion followers or at best fast responders to trends. Design is commonly handled by a team of young unknown design talents who could be working under a creative director (or not as in the case of Gap which abolished this position). All these functions could be grouped under the umbrella of marketing and merchandising departments, where they fall under the close supervision of a product or brand manager who imposes price and fashion constraints and where design is basically following rigid commercial plans. This arrangement clearly highlights how design is perceived as more of a merchandising and marketing decision and function rather than a creative one in these organizations.

- While mass-market organizations are lagging in creativity compared to luxury, their strengths lie in production and commercial knowhow. They also have more freedom in their production and sourcing decisions. Mass-market brands, especially at the moderate level where they are very cost conscious, aim for volume rather than margins, and thus they work hard on finding ways to cut costs, one of which is through outsourcing and overseas production.

- Mass-market organizations' willingness to outsource activities means that they are not usually as integrated in production and retail as luxury organizations are, which in return tend to operate and own most of the functions within the process. Mass-market organizations on the other hand, manage a large network of external supplier and distribution channels while rigorously controlling the brand concept. Service provided by fast and continuous deliveries and replenishment times to market is key to success in the business model of higher sub-segments of mass-market (e.g. premium) brands.

- Accordingly, mass-market organizations tend to be more traditional in nature with basic departments and function divisions. Such as product-related departments including merchandising, sourcing, etc., communication and marketing-related departments including PR, advertising, etc. as well we other departments such as accounting, etc.

On the Luxury Side

- Luxury brands such as Dior, Balenciaga, Chanel, etc. are trendsetters with a sense of heritage and roots in haute couture and craftsmanship where creativity and aesthetics are key to their business model. Creativity is commonly handled by a superstar designer (e.g. the late Karl Lagerfeld, Raf Simons, or Alessandro Michele). These designers or creative directors, have almost full control of the design aesthetics and design decisions whereas the CEO and top management have little power or say in the creativity aspect and primarily play a supportive role in terms of general management and financial support. The sides may even rarely meet except when the collection is revealed.

- Thus, the role of creative directors is extremely important in the luxury segment. They create more than designs, they create overall vision and brand aesthetic that takes into account the marketing and advertising strategy, the retail environments, the format of the catwalk presentations, the lifestyle that their label is selling, etc. Thus, it is a high-risk appointment that can transform the whole direction of the brand (e.g. Tom Ford for Gucci, Elbaz for Lanvin, etc.). For this reason, many luxury brands do not have brand managers, as the task is among those carried out by these creative directors.

- In addition to exclusivity, luxury brands are also known for high quality products and small productions. Accordingly, a lot of them still work out of workshops located in Europe in order to monitor quality. For that matter, luxury brands also tend to be vertically integrated both in terms of retail and manufacturing. They strictly control every step and activity of their value chain. French luxury brand Hermès for example, traditionally sells its products through its owned and self-operated boutiques worldwide with a tight control over production phases within its internal facilities. Brunello Cuccinelli produces 100% of his products in his hometown and neighboring villages in Italy. This is why luxury brands tend to have brand extensions rather than brand creations or line extensions (*we will discuss this in more details in a future chapter*). Hermès, Chanel, and most luxury brands do not offer cheaper alternative lines but extend their signature brand into new categories such as perfume and accessories, etc.

- Luxury brands rely heavily on communication to reinforce the brand heritage, iconic products, and brand lifestyle. Hence, they usually spend more than mass market brands on advertising and marketing and thus the role of the marketing department is equally prominent as its creative one.

DEPARTMENTS WITHIN A FASHION ORGANIZATION

The fashion industry is quite diverse, ranging from a small fashion company with three or four people and no formal chart or structure to large conglomerates with multi-brands under one umbrella. It is also very common for fashion organizations to be structured based on function, product, or regional divisions. With this in mind, in addition to corporate governance represented in shareholders, a board of directors and a CEO/president, some possible functions in a fashion organization may include:

- *Finance and Accounting.* The accounting function pays the bills, communicates with each individual department, and allocates money to achieve the overall goals and projections. They also work closely with the CEO/president to develop the top-down budget.

- *Sales and Marketing.* This department is key to promote and establish a business in its niche based on the products and services the business is offering. Public Relations (PR) plays an essential role in promoting a positive image of the organization and its role in the society.

- *Fashion Merchandising.* In retail, merchandisers with their team of buyers predict trends, forecast sales, buy products, and develop displays among many other tasks. In manufacturing, it is very common in a mass-market organization that the merchandising manager also oversees the design and marketing functions since design decisions are more of a merchandising and styling nature. In a luxury organization it is usually a separate function concerned with supplying retail outlets including their own chain of global units with the right mix of merchandise.

- *Design and Product Development.* The design department relies on information developed by the sales and marketing teams. It develops new ideas and concepts through functional areas such as trend forecasting and product development. They are also responsible for the development of "tech packs" (technical package identifying all aspects of the product to be produced, including yarn size and type, dyeing and finishing requirement, as well as all trims and packaging and shipping methods, etc.). The product development functions differ from one company to the other. It could either be a standalone department or part of the design function.

- *Sourcing and Production*. This department can be composed of several subsets: logistics, quality assurance, corporate social responsibility (CSR)/sustainability, and legal/security, all of which are key departments that interact with the supply chain. Sourcing is most often defined as the process of finding suppliers of goods or services. Production, on the other hand, is defined as the processes and methods used to transform tangible inputs (raw materials, semi-finished goods, subassemblies) into goods and services. Once an order is taken by retail buyers, the organization's sourcing and production department sources for a factory to handle the order. Logistics must get involved to ensure that the goods can be shipped in a timely manner to meet the customer needs. Quality assurance plays a major role in providing confidence in the finished product in the factory prior to release of the shipment from the producer and upon receipt at the warehouse. Cost and timing of delivery are important implications as well.

- *Wholesale (and Receiving and Distribution)*. The wholesale department has the responsibility to sell to other retailers and the organization's own outlet stores if available. It affects the production process by placing orders for merchandise that has already been approved in the fashion line or by potentially working with retail buyers to develop a new product for their store, in which case, the department will communicate with the product development or design team to create the requested item. The receiving and distribution function *receives* merchandise in warehouses or drop-ships directly to customers. If receipt is in the organization's own warehouse, they check to ascertain that the product meets all specifications before shipping to customers.

- *Business Development*. This department has a significant impact in redefining and redirecting the company. A fashion company that focuses on one aspect of the fashion industry might create a brand extension by adding a new line of products or introducing accessories, etc. Larger organizations may consider expansions through acquisitions or vertically branching into new functions within the supply chain, such as a manufacturer getting into retailing and opening its own store.

- *IT (Information Technology)*. Apart from the responsibilities of developing and maintaining electronic communication channels within the organizations through developing internet and intranet networks, servicing computers, etc. The IT department has the ability to reduce the amount of time and energy spent on various functions better suited to new technologies. For example, *radio frequency identification* (RFID) has been highly utilized in automatically tracking products and managing inventory while the cloud allows the sharing of reports, etc.

- *Human Resources (HR)*. This is a critical function in the process as it ensures that the right people are in the right positions at the right time and for the right cost.

- *Investor Relations*. This department only exists in publicly traded companies and has the responsibility to provide information and services to shareholders. It also works with the PR department to help shape public opinion of the company by providing positive news stories.

Leading

The manager's job is to work with and through people to accomplish organizational goals. This requires leadership. An ability to motivate others, influence individuals or teams as they work, select the most effective communication channel, and deal in any way with behavior issues.

MANAGERS VS. LEADERS

By definition, the role of a manager is to plan, organize, monitor, and obtain results, i.e. getting things done and achieving goals through others. Leaders are different: they are entrusted with providing vision, inspiring, and setting out the future through strategies that enable goals to be reached by their managers, in short, making others *want* to do things and reach desired results.

Managers' ability to influence stems from their position in which they were appointed. On the other hand, leaders may either be appointed, or they could organically emerge from within the group or team. Thus, leaders are able to influence others to perform beyond the actions dictated by formal authority. A leader may be able to motivate people but not necessarily possess the technical skills or able to fulfill the other three management functions of planning, organizing, and controlling.

In our discussion we will be focusing on leaders who also have managerial authority.

TYPES OF LEADERSHIP STYLES

There are five different types of leadership styles:[7]

Laissez-Faire. A laissez-faire leader lacks direct supervision of employees and thus does not provide regular feedback to those under his supervision. Usually highly experienced and trained employees requiring little supervision fall under the laissez-faire leadership style. This leadership style may hinder the production of employees needing supervision and can lead to poor production, lack of control, and increasing costs.

Autocratic. The autocratic leadership style allows managers to make decisions alone without the input of others. Managers possess total authority and impose their will on employees. No one challenges the decisions of autocratic leaders. This leadership style benefits employees who require close supervision but may constrain creative employees who thrive in group functions.

Participative. Often called the democratic leadership style, participative leadership values the input of team members and peers, but the responsibility of making the final decision rests with the participative leader. Participative leadership boosts employees' morale because employees make contributions to the decision-making process. The participative leadership style helps employees accept changes easily because they play a role in the process. However, this style meets challenges when companies need to make a decision in a short period.

Transactional. Managers using the transactional leadership style receive certain tasks to perform and provide rewards or punishments to team members based on performance results. Managers and team members set predetermined goals together, and employees agree to follow the direction and leadership of the manager to accomplish those goals. The manager possesses power to review results and train or correct employees when team members fail to meet goals. Employees receive rewards, such as bonuses, when they accomplish goals.

Transformational. The transformational leadership style depends on high levels of communication from management to meet goals. Leaders motivate employees and enhance productivity and efficiency through communication and high visibility. This style of leadership requires the involvement of management to meet goals. Leaders focus on the big picture within an organization and delegate smaller tasks to the team to accomplish goals.

LEADERS' SOURCES OF POWER

In general, a leader's source of power could stem from five main sources:

- *Legitimate Power:* This is power as a result of the leader's authority position in the organization.

- *Coercive Power:* The leader's ability to punish or penalize such as to fire employees.

- *Reward Power:* The leader's ability to reward and give positive benefits such as appraisals, promotions, bonuses, etc.

- *Expert Power:* Individuals who hold a certain level of expertise, specialization, or skills possess a certain level of power and have the ability to influence and be heard.

- *Referent Power:* This is a result of a person's desirable resources or personal traits. People you admire or look up to like celebrities or role models possess and exercise such power.

LEADERSHIP AND CULTURE

No one style of leadership is suitable for all situations and both the situation and working environment dictate the suitable type of leadership. In addition, cultural styles within an organization may differ due to the general societal cultural differences. For example, in cultures with steep hierarchies (e.g. Arab and Latin American nations) a leader is expected to show strength. As a matter of fact, workers would be puzzled if their boss asked them for feedback. They could assume the boss was somehow lacking information, or they could feel uncomfortable with the idea of having to criticize a superior. Thus, a democratic and egalitarian leadership approach preferred in western societies may be viewed in these hierarchical cultures where authority is not questioned, and where leaders are seen as dominant, as a weakness. In addition, in many Western cultures effective leaders are often risk-takers who act independently. They are flexible and ambitious, while in countries where the culture is more collaborative, like China, leaders tend to be more risk-averse and rely on consensus.

Different cultures also expect different emotional qualities from their leaders. In the U.S., for example, leaders are admired if they are charismatic and passionate and it is acceptable to display emotion. In Japan, leaders are expected to keep a lid on their feelings. Being overenthusiastic, or readily expressing anger or sadness are signs that you are not in control.

Moreover, some cultures require a leader to be a diplomat. In the Middle East and parts of Asia where people have a strong sense of "face", a leader is expected to think before criticizing, and to consider the honor and reputation of others in every transaction. The U.S. or UK are much more "straight talking" cultures, where a leader can freely give colleagues feedback, even if it is negative.

Controlling

After setting goals the plans are formulated (*planning*), the structural arrangements are determined (*organizing*), and the people hired trained and motivated (*leading*), there has to be some evaluation of whether things are going as planned or not. To ensure this, managers must monitor and evaluate performance and compare results with previously set goals. It is a managers' job to get work performance back on track. This process of monitoring, comparing, and correcting to ensure that the activities have been accomplished without significant deviations is what is meant by *controlling*.

THE CONTROL PROCESS

The control process is a three-stage process that allows the manager to measure performance and compare it to accepted standards and finally take managerial action to correct any deviation noticed. The three stages are:

- Measuring
- Comparing
- Taking Managerial Action

Measuring

In order for the manager to determine whether performance is on track and meets accepted standards or not they must be able to find a way to measure the current performance in order to make such judgment. Managers can achieve this through a number of tools and options such as personal observations, oral reports, written reports, or statistical reports.

Personal Observation: This provides information that is not filtered and gives the manager a first-hand knowledge of what is happening. It also allows for direct interaction with employees which is always a valuable tool. However, this approach clearly requires time and effort but most importantly it does not produce quality quantitative data as other forms may do.

Computers and Dedicated Software: They have made statistical reports readily available and very popular. Data analysis, graphs, and charts, etc. are commonly used to assess performance and reach effective conclusions. However, it usually deals with aggregates of facts and does not deal with individual items, and as such it does not depict the entire story. More importantly, if data is not collected properly, the results will end up being biased and misleading.

Oral/Written Reports: Oral reports could be gathered in meetings, conferences including video conferencing, or one-on-one conversations. This is one of the best tools to keep on track with performance as the information is fast, allows for immediate feedback through language and tone used. However, like personal observations one of the problems is difficulty documenting the content of these conversations. Written reports are slower than oral reports but are indeed more formal. They tend to be more comprehensive and concise than oral reports. In addition, they are easier to save, file, and retrieve.

Comparing

In this stage managers determine the degree of variation between actual performance and the accepted standards. However, from a practical perspective some variation in performance can be expected and accepted. Thus, the first task is to determine the acceptable range of variation by the manager. For example, every fashion retailer will have monthly sales targets. Accordingly, actual sales results will have to be compared with the standard or planned sales goal to determine if sales results are on target or whether the deviation was significant. For example, the acceptable sales deviation could be 5% (higher or lower than target) and so if actual sales are much lower or even higher, then an assessment needs to be done. If sales are higher it could mean that the original stated target could have been unrealistic or that the deviation is due to a specific external factor that needs to be determined and understood. Obviously, if it is lower, then the cause will also have to be determined, whether it is an issue with the merchandise mix, lack of advertising, or rather aggressive advertising by competitors, etc.

Taking Managerial Action

Based on the above analysis and the results achieved, managers will be ready to take relevant actions. There are three possible courses of action to take.

- Do nothing
- Correct the actual performance
- Revise the standards

Do nothing: If performance matches standards and outcomes match goals then managers will most likely do not need to take any further action but to secure that this level of performance is sustained.

Correct actual performance: If results indicate deviation from standards and goals then managers should analyze the results and determine the required corrective action measures. Managers will need to decide on whether these measures need to be immediate or not.

Revise standards: Analysis of deviation may indicate that the problem lies in the goals and standards being unrealistically too low or too high in which case the problem lies with the goals not the performance per se. In the case of higher sales achieved than target, the results could be either an outlier external factor that could not have been anticipated and is an anomaly and thus should not affect the plan (e.g. Michelle Obama wearing that dress from White House/Black Market which could not have been anticipated and should not be relied on as a recurring factor) or the initial goals were unrealistically low in the first place. It is very common for managers who do not meet their target sales or other standards to blame the lack of results on the goals and standards themselves. Thus, managers need to be fair and objective in their assessment.

BUSINESS POLICY AND BUSINESS STRATEGY

In management the terms "policy" and "strategy" are widely and commonly used. Hence, it is essential to understand what each stands for and truly means as they are not interchangeable terms.

What Is a Policy?

A policy is a set of principles and rules which directs the decisions of the organization. Policies are framed by the top-level management of the organization to serve as a guideline for operational decision making. It is helpful in highlighting the rules, values, and beliefs of the organization and thus acts as a basis for guiding actions. Policies are designed by taking the opinion and general view of a number of people in the organization regarding any situation. They are made from the experiences and basic understandings. In this way, the people who come under the range of such policy will completely agree upon its implementation. As policies help the management of an organization to determine what is to be done in a particular situation, they have to be consistently applied over a long period to avoid discrepancies and overlapping.

What Is Business Policy, then?

Accordingly, business policies are the guidelines developed by an organization to govern its actions. They define the limits within which decisions must be made. Thus, it permits the lower-level management to deal with the problems and issues without consulting top-level management every time for decisions. Business policy also deals with the acquisition of resources (who gets what) with which organizational goals can be achieved.

Features of Business Policy

An effective business policy must have following features:

1. *Specific.* Policy should be specific/definite. If it is uncertain, then the implementation will become difficult.

2. *Clear.* Policy must be unambiguous. It should avoid the use of jargon and connotations. There should be no misunderstandings in following the policy.

3. *Reliable/Uniform.* Policy must be uniform enough so that it can be efficiently followed by the subordinates.

4. *Appropriate.* Policy should be appropriate to the present organizational goal.

5. *Simple.* A policy should be simple and easily understood by all in the organization.

6. *Inclusive/Comprehensive.* In order to have a wide scope, a policy must be comprehensive.

7. *Flexible.* Policy should be flexible in operation/application. This does not imply that a policy should always be altered, but it should be wide in scope so as to ensure that the line managers use them in repetitive/routine scenarios.

8. *Stable.* Policy should be stable otherwise it will lead to indecisiveness and uncertainty in the minds of those who look into it for guidance.

What is a Strategy?

Strategy refers to top management plans to develop and sustain competitive advantage which is a state whereby a firm's successful strategies cannot be easily duplicated by its competitors so that the organization's mission is fulfilled. Thus, it is a game plan, chosen to achieve the organizational objectives, gain customers' trust, attain competitive advantage, and to acquire a market position. The following are the features of a strategy:

- It should be formulated from the top-level management. However, sub-strategies can be made by middle-level management.

- It should have a long-range perspective.

- It should be dynamic in nature.

- The main purpose is to overcome uncertain situations.

- It should be made in such a way to make the best possible use of scarce resources.

Difference between Policy and Strategy

The term "policy" should not be considered as synonymous with the term "strategy". There are major differences between the two terms which could be summarized as follows:

1. Policy is a set of rules or guiding principles that help the organization make logical decisions, while a strategy is a comprehensive plan to accomplish the organization's goals.

2. Policy formulation is the responsibility of top-level management, while strategy formulation is the responsibility of both top-level management and middle-level management.

3. Policy deals with routine/daily activities essential for the effective and efficient running of an organization, while strategy deals with strategic decisions.

4. Policy is concerned with both thought and actions (action principles), while strategy is concerned mostly with action.

5. A policy is what is, or what is not done, while a strategy is the methodology used to achieve a target as prescribed by a policy.

6. A strategy is more flexible than a policy.

What are Strategic Decisions?

Based on the above we can now distinguish between "strategic" decisions and common management decisions. In general, strategic decisions are marked by four key distinctions:

1. They are based on a systematic, comprehensive analysis of internal attributes and factors external to the organization. Decisions that address only part of the organization, perhaps a single functional area, are usually not considered to be strategic decisions.

2. They are long-term and future-oriented but are built on knowledge about the past and present. Most agree that "long-term" could range anywhere from several years in duration, as mentioned earlier, to more than a decade.

3. They seek to capitalize on favorable situations outside the organization. This means taking advantage of opportunities that exist for the firm, as well as taking measures to minimize the effects of external threats.

4. They involve choices and most involve some degree of trade-off between alternatives, at least in the short run. For example, raising salaries to retain a skilled workforce can increase wages and adding product features or enhancing quality can increase the cost of production. However, such trade-offs may diminish in the long run, as a more skilled, higher-paid workforce may be more productive than a typical workforce, and sales of a higher-quality product may increase, thereby raising sales and potentially profits, etc.

Because of these distinctions, strategic decision-making is generally reserved for the top executive and members of the top management team. The CEO is the individual ultimately responsible (and generally held responsible) for the organization's strategic management, but he or she rarely acts alone except in the smallest companies.

CORPORATE GOVERNANCE

Another commonly used management concept is that of corporate governance. It refers to the board of directors, institutional investors (e.g. banks, etc.), and large shareholders who monitor firms' strategies to ensure effective management. Boards of directors and institutional investors are generally the most influential in the governance systems as they may own more than half of the shares of a publicly traded organization.

Boards of directors often include both inside (i.e. a firm's executives) and outside directors. Insiders bring company-specific knowledge to the board whereas outsiders bring independence and an external perspective which allows board members to oversee managerial decisions more effectively.

STRATEGIC MANAGEMENT

Strategic management is a broader term than *strategy* and is a process that includes top management's analysis of the environment in which the organization operates prior to formulating a strategy, as well as the plan for implementation and control of the strategy. The difference between a strategy and the strategic management process as a whole, is that the latter considers what must be done before a strategy is formulated through assessing whether or not an already implemented strategy was successful.

Accordingly, Strategic Management is a long-term approach to management and is best described as *a set of managerial decisions and actions that determine long-term performance of an organization*. It is also concerned with the character and direction of the organization as a whole. It includes the same four management functions described earlier (*planning, organizing, leading, controlling*) but from a long-term and holistic perspective and thus it is involved with most of the decisions made by managers.

The strategic management process can be summarized in five steps:

1. *External Analysis*: Analyze the opportunities and threats, or constraints, that exist in the organization's external environment, including industry and other forces.

2. *Internal Analysis*: Analyze the organization's strengths and weaknesses in its internal environment. Consider the context of managerial ethics and corporate social responsibility.

3. *Strategy Formulation*: Formulate strategies that build and sustain competitive advantage by matching the organization's strengths and weaknesses with the environment's opportunities and threats.

4. *Strategy Execution*: Implement the strategies that have been developed.

5. *Strategic Control*: Measure success and make corrections when the strategies are not producing the desired outcomes.

SWOT Analysis

The two levels of analysis (internal and external) needed as the basis of strategy formulation and strategic management are commonly conducted by what is known as the SWOT analysis. The SWOT Analysis is a model devised to evaluate the following criteria:

- *Strengths (S)*. These are *internal* attributes of the organization that are helpful to the achievement of objectives. These are attributes you would like to figure out how to *"use"*.

  Examples are: Talented employees, patents, knowhow, iconic products, strong supplier relationships, etc.

- *Weaknesses (W).* These are *internal* attributes of the organization that are harmful to the achievement of objectives. These are attributes you would like to figure out how to "*stop or overcome*".

  Examples are: Lack of experience, declining sales.

- *Opportunities (O).* These are *external* conditions that are helpful to the achievement of objectives. These are attributes you would like to figure out how to "*exploit*".

  Examples are: Lack of competition, celebrity endorsement, lower taxes, etc.

- *Threats (T).* These are *external* conditions that are harmful to the achievement of objectives. These are attributes you would like to figure out how to "*defend against and avoid*".

  Examples are: Competitors, high taxes, cost of labor, etc.

Note that the Strengths and Weaknesses take an *internal* perspective within the organization while Opportunities and Threats examine *external* factors that surround the organization.

Thus, a SWOT analysis offers four possible strategies to implement:

- *Strength-Opportunity strategies.* Leverage your business strengths to maximize industry opportunities.

- *Strength-Threats strategies.*Leverage your business strengths to minimize industry threats.

- *Weakness-Opportunity strategies.* Minimize your business weaknesses to maximize industry opportunities.

- *Weakness-Threats strategies.* Minimize your business weaknesses to minimize industry threats.

Box 1.2 Nike SWOT Analysis

Nike, is a global brand that specializes in sportswear, including shoes, clothing, and accessories. It is listed on the NYSE and has offices all over the world, and contracts with shops on a global basis as well as factories throughout developing economies like China, India, Vietnam, and the Philippines.

Strengths

- Nike's brand equity in terms of recognition and appeal around the world tied to its status among celebrities and sports professionals.
- Its ongoing sponsorship of events also has built brand recognition for the company, including being known for quality, performance, reliability, and innovative style.
- It has a recognizable tag line of "Just Do It," which continues to inspire consumers.
- The company is highly profitable due to its strategy to outsource all of its production overseas to keep manufacturing costs low while focusing on design, research, and development in the U.S.
- Technology adoption. Nike was among the first brands to offer product customization and integration with electronic devices.

Weaknesses

- Nike has been linked to sweatshops, low wages, and child workers in its overseas manufacturing facilities, which has tarnished some of its brand image.
- Nike is too focused on its footwear business, which can be risky considering that market trends change, and most companies sustain themselves through a product diversification strategy.
- Because the company chooses to do business with retailers that also stock their competitors' brands, there is a loss of exclusivity and the risk that consumers may opt for the other brand based on price and selection.
- The overall high prices of Nike products often position it as a premium brand that is out of reach for many.

Opportunities

- The company can enhance its brand image as a socially responsible manufacturer of retail products by encouraging recycling programs and helping local communities where its manufacturing facilities are to improve their economy.
- Nike can continue to focus on emerging markets such as India where consumers are getting more disposable income and interest is growing in Western brands. This can include increasing sponsorships of local sports stars and celebrities.
- Nike should continue to look at accessories and other clothing products to further diversify its product portfolio as well as continue to look for brand extensions and partnerships.
- Expand technological application and integration.
- Brand extensions at more affordable prices without diluting the brand's existing attributes.

Threats

- International trade practices, labor strikes, currency fluctuations, unethical practices, and other issues related to doing business in an international setting, including the implementation of its entire supply chain.
- Economic conditions such as recessions whereby consumers seek out lower-priced brands and this may lead to a price-cutting war.

Sources

1. Kissinger, Daniel. "Nike Inc. SWOT Analysis & Recommendations". *Panmore*. February 7, 2017. http://panmore.com/nike-inc-swot-analysis-recommendations
2. Mithson, Nathaniel. "Nike Inc.'s Mission Statement & Vision Statement (An Analysis)". *Panmore*. June 23, 2019. http://panmore.com/nike-inc-vision-statement-mission-statement
3. "SWOT Analysis of Nike, Business Teacher". Business Teacher. https://businessteacher.org.uk/swot/nike.php
4. Thompson, Andrew. "Nike Inc. Organizational Structure Characteristics (Analysis)". *Panmore*. Updated February 15, 2019. http://panmore.com/nike-inc-organizational-structure-characteristics-analysis
5. www.Nike.com

The Core Competency Theory and Strategy

As mentioned, one of the big advantages of SWOT analysis is its ability to help managers identify the organization's core competencies through understanding its weakness and strengths. The concept of *core competency* states that firms must play to their strengths or those areas or functions in which they have competencies. Hence, the core competency theory is the theory of strategy that prescribes actions to be taken by firms to achieve competitive advantage in the marketplace.

The aim is to define what forms a core competency as being that thing that is not easy for competitors to imitate. Some core competencies that firms might have include technical superiority, its customer relationship management, and processes that are vastly efficient. Each firm usually has a specific area in which it does well relative to its competitors, this area of excellence can be reused by the firm in other markets and products, and in return, this area of strength adds value to the consumer. Thus, companies must orient their strategies to tap into the core competencies which are the fundamental basis for the value added by the firm.

WHAT DEFINES A CORE COMPETENCY?

- A core competency can lead to the development of new products and services and must provide potential access to a wide variety of markets.

- It must make a significant contribution to the perceived benefits of the end-product.

- It should be difficult for competitors to imitate. In many industries, such competencies are likely to be unique.

The implications for real-world practice are that core competencies must be nurtured, and the business model built around them instead of focusing too much on areas where the firm does not have competency. This is not to say that other competencies must be neglected or ignored. Rather, the idea behind the concept is that firms must leverage upon their core strengths and play them to their advantage.

Competitive Advantage vs. Core Competency

The two terms are closely related to one another, as they help in achieving a greater share of the market, satisfying customers, building brand loyalty, and delivering high-quality products to the customers. However, the two terms are not exactly the same.

Competitive Advantage can be described as *something that the competing firms are not able to do, or it is something owned by the firm that the rival firms wish to have (and can eventually imitate)*. On the other hand, a **Core Competency** refers to the specific skills, knowledge, and expertise which differentiates a company from others. It is the distinct proficiency of the company, which cannot be easily imitated by its rivals. It may include a unique combination of resources or knowledge, etc. It provides one or more lasting competitive advantages to the company in creating and delivering perceived benefits to the customers.

Thus, while a core competency is unique to a particular business entity, a competitive advantage can be easily imitated by the rivals. Thus, we can say that a core competency helps in the creation of continuous competitive advantages and also helps the firm to enter into new markets as mentioned earlier.

For example: As a fashion brand Zara had the competitive advantage of offering trendy fashion at a reasonable price compared to designer brands which offered similar styles at high prices. This competitive advantage is what would make customers choose Zara instead of competitors. This advantage was quickly copied and imitated by other brands which aimed at competing with Zara.

On the other hand, Italian luxury brand Missoni, famous for its tight-knit zigzag designs, had revolutionized knitwear by discovering a way to make the zigzag pattern by using Raschel knitting machines. The unique technique allowed the fashion house to use knits to create any shape of garment, and cut and sew material without loosening the threads, etc. That technique was their core competency as it allowed them to do something different and do it very well, which in return put them in a league by themselves for a long time. Thus, their core competency (what made them unique and better than others) was the innovative technique (i.e. Missoni's technical and aesthetic innovation) which allowed them to create unique, attractive designs and sweaters. These unique and attractive sweaters became its competitive advantage among competing fashion brands.

So, Missoni's unique technique and innovations (what they excelled in) allowed them to produce a product that is different and competitive, thus giving them an advantage in the market. These sweaters may eventually be copied and mimicked by competitors. However, by harnessing their technical competency and strength they will continue to innovate and produce new and competitive products.

How to Create a Competitive Advantage

A competitive advantage is an essential and valuable thing for a brand to compete and survive. It is basically based on the following:

- *Benefit.* What is the real benefit your product provides? It must be something that your customers truly need. It must also offer real value. You must know your product's features, its advantages, and how they benefit your customers. You must stay up to date on the new trends that affect your product. This includes new technology.

- *Target market.* Who are your customers? What are their needs? You have got to know exactly who buys from you and how you can make their life better. That is how you create demand, the driver of all economic growth.

- *Competition.* Have you identified your real competitors? They are not just similar companies or products. They also include anything else your customer could do to meet the need you can fulfill.

Porter's Model of the Five Forces of Competition

In this model, Porter theorized that understanding both the competitive forces at play and the overall industry structure are crucial for effective, strategic decision-making, and developing a compelling competitive strategy for the future.

PORTER'S FIVE FORCES

Figure 1.4 Porter's Five Forces of Competition.
Created by Author.

According to this Porter model (Figure 1.4), the five forces that shape an industry competition are:

1. *Competitive rivalry.* This force examines how intense the competition is in the marketplace. It considers the number of existing competitors and what each one can do. Rivalry competition is high when there are just a few businesses selling a product or service, when the industry is growing, and consumers can easily switch to a competitor's offering for little cost. When rivalry competition is high, advertising and price wars ensue, which can hurt a business's bottom line.

2. *The bargaining power of suppliers.* This force analyzes how much power a business's supplier has and how much control it has over the potential to raise its prices, which, in turn, lowers a business's profitability. It also assesses the number of suppliers of raw materials and other resources that are available. The fewer suppliers there are, the more power they have. Businesses are in a better position when there are multiple suppliers.

3. *The bargaining power of buyers.* This force examines the power of the consumers, and their effect on pricing and quality. Consumers have power when they are fewer in number but there are plentiful sellers and it is easy for consumers to switch or when they are price sensitive.

4. *The threat of new entrants.* This force considers how easy or difficult it is for competitors to join the marketplace. The easier it is for a new competitor to gain entry, the greater the risk is of an established business's market share being depleted. Barriers to entry include absolute cost advantages, access to inputs, economies of scale and strong brand identity (e.g. it is harder to start a new luxury brand than a mass-market one).

5. *The threat of substitute products or services.* This force studies how easy it is for consumers to switch from a business's product or service to that of a competitor. It examines the number of competitors, how their prices and quality compare to the business being examined, and how much of a profit those competitors are earning, which would determine if they can lower their costs even more. The threat of substitutes is informed by switching costs, both immediate and long-term, as well as consumers' inclination to change.

PORTER'S MODEL VS. SWOT ANALYSIS

Using Porter's Five Forces in conjunction with a SWOT analysis will help you understand where your company or business fits in the industry landscape. Porter's Five Forces is considered a macro tool in business analytics – it looks at the industry's economy as a whole, while a SWOT analysis is a microanalytical tool, focusing on a specific company's data and analysis. Thus, they clearly complement each other.

PORTER'S MODEL OF COMPETITIVE STRATEGIES

This Porter model builds on the understanding of the five forces of competition discussed earlier by outlining three main strategies organizations can pursue to achieve a sustainable advantage:

1. *Cost Leadership Strategy.* Seeking to attain the lowest total overall costs relative to other industry competitors. Firms do this by continuously improving operational efficiency. Others take advantage of cheap or unskilled labor surpluses.

2. *Differentiation Strategy.* Attempting to create a unique and distinctive product or service for which customers will pay a premium. Companies typically achieve differentiation with innovation, quality, or customer service. A firm can provide a unique or high-quality product (e.g. Missoni). Another method is to deliver it faster (e.g. Zara). A third is to market in a way that reaches customers better (e.g. Amazon or Nordstrom). A company with a differentiation strategy can charge a premium price. That means it usually has a higher profit margin.

3. *Focus Strategy.* Using a cost or differentiation advantage to exploit a particular market segment rather than a larger market. Thus, the key to a successful focus strategy lies in choosing a very specific target market and be a leader in it (e.g. Harley Davidson).

Finally, an organization that is capable of outperforming its competitors over a long period of time is said to have a sustainable competitive advantage, which is a strong and covetable market position.

Box 1.3 Examples of Management Positions Within the Fashion Industry

There are many career paths and growth opportunities within the diverse apparel industry within its diverse segments. Below are a few examples of management positions within the industry.

Fashion Director (FD)

A FD in a textile organization is primarily interested in identifying the most important fashion trends for their companies and communicating these trends to textile designers, production managers, and customers. FDs often work with trend forecasting firms to determine trend possibilities in color, form, theme, and fabric needs for each season. The majority of FDs move up the ladder from within ranks as many of them were textile designers, product developers' buyers, or assistant fashion directors.

Challenges of the post:

- FD are expected to have a strong foundation of work experience in the industry.
- There is a great pressure to be right about color, pattern, style, and theme trends.
- FD must collaborate successfully with a wide variety of people such as designers, production personnel, and clients. It takes a person with a solid educational foundation in textiles, a well-balanced personality, and excellent communication skills to work effectively with so many people.

Licensing Director (LD)

LD is responsible for overseeing the look, quality, labeling, delivery, and distribution of their companies' product lines. Sourcing is an integral part of this job as they work with the foreign and domestic manufacturers of various product lines known as "the licensees", to make certain that the products are branded correctly. Also licensing directors make sure product lines meet quality expectations and fit within the design concepts of their company's primary line for greater sales and better visual presence on the retail floor.

Challenges of the post:

- The need to stay up to date and have knowledge in various areas such as design and product development, product specifications, as well as trade laws.
- Coordinating the work of many manufacturers located around the world that produce a range of product types is a tremendous task and responsibility.

Product Manager (PM)

PM or product design manager may be responsible for all products within a company's product line in a small firm or a specific product category in a line for a large company. PMs often work in the *creative* and *production* part of the business where they monitor market and fashion trends related to their assigned product lines. PD is also responsible for comparison shopping the lines of competitors. They also shop merchandise lines outside of their product categories making certain that their product line will blend in terms of the color style and fabric trends being shown for the season in all departments.

On the *production side*, PM works with sourcing personnel, production managers, and quality control directors among other departments involved with the manufacturing of the product lines for which they are responsible as they monitor the manufacturing of their product line(s) from start to finish

Challenges of the post:

- Many small companies do not employ PM, instead designers are responsible for evaluating competitors and determining fashion trends for the line. Thus, this position is limited to mid-large firms.
- PM are under pressure to be correct on the fashion color, styling, and themes that will be featured in product lines. Thus, they must conduct detailed research to make accurate decisions.
- PM face great challenges with manufacturing products abroad in terms of quality, fit, and deadlines.
- They require curiosity, observation, and creativity as well as strong skills in communication, organization, and presentation.

Production Manager (Prod. M)

Prod. M are also referred to as *plant managers* and are responsible for all of the operations at production facilities, whether domestic or overseas and contracted or company owned. The responsibilities include supervising, completing the estimation of production and employee costs, scheduling workflow in factories, ensuring product quality control, hiring and training employees, selecting facilities, determining materials, etc. They are also responsible for delivering goods, following up, and executing improvements to the process. Prod. M must possess an ability to work independently, have good communication skills, an ability to speak foreign languages, and appreciate cultural diversity

Challenges of the post:

- They encounter a large number of employees, tasks, and potential problems associated with various aspects of production.
- Tight deadlines that are highly impacted by external factors.
- Manufacturing equipment breakdowns, delayed textile shipments, defective zippers or thread in the wrong color are types of problems that can impact workflow and cause manufacturer to miss shipping commitments.

Quality Control Manager (QM)

QM develop specifications for the products that will be manufactured. They are responsible to see that those standards are met during all phases of production, identifying quality problems and working with manufacturing personnel to correct them. The QM works with such issues as fit, fabric, performance, construction difficulties, packaging and shipping needs, and production pace. QM travels to overseas factories and collaborates with personnel in various company divisions from the design staff to plant employees. Thus, they need to have organizational abilities, effective time-management skills, and communication skills.

Challenges of the post:

- Communicate with so many and diverse people in different locations and time zones.

- Superior organizational abilities.
- Must maintain excellent standards and oversee every detail of production from beginning to conclusion. It can be a high-pressure job with little recognition.

Director of Product Development (DPD)

DPD is responsible for the strategic planning of the division specifying exactly what the company will make and market, as well as when it will do it. After selecting a product category such as junior T-shirts, the director of product development must narrow the focus (e.g. Vintage T-shirts in XS–XL etc.). A key product segmentation decision is specifying the target market niche, which can only happen by knowing the customer well. DPD will also work with the staff to build a brand by creating an image or personality for the line. There could be two approaches a DPD can take toward building a line:

1. *Design driven brand*: led by a designer who is expressing a personal artistic vision and sense of taste, more original and creative.
2. *Merchandising-driven brands*: these brands search for a void in the market or an underserved customer and create a product to fill that void. Styling decisions are based on careful monitoring of past sales, success, and failures in conjunction with customer desires.

A DPD must be able to research and coordinate all phases of the development process, set up costing sheets and communicate with vendors, and research market for innovations in materials and fabrics etc.

Challenges of the post:

- Strong vision to manage a team of executives.
- A lot of research and superior communication skills.
- Excellent consumer knowledge especially if working for a retailer.
- Maintaining strengths while building expertise in weak areas.

Marketing Managers *(various roles)*

Marketing offers a wide range of managerial positions within the fashion industry both in retail and manufacturing.

A *Marketing Director (MD)* is responsible for developing a marketing plan whereby he/she translates the company objectives into marketing strategies to support it and its brands. An MD's responsibilities include overseeing the marketing team and managing the marketing budget (a position known as Chief Marketing Officer (CMO) may exist in larger organizations). In many fashion organizations especially in the mass-market segment which focuses on styling and merchandising than on trend-setting designs, the MD may oversee merchandising and design activities as well.

A *Product Marketing Manager (PPM)*'s goal is to ensure the new product is introduced during the early life cycle of the product when sales are strong and profit margins are high.

A *Brand Marketing Manager (BMM)* develops and executes a multichannel marketing and promotional program in order to drive brand awareness and increase sales. In some organizations a PPM could hold this task as well.

A *Digital Marketing Manager (DMM)* focuses on the organization's digital marketing presence. He/she is responsible for managing online campaigns to increase traffic and sales.

Public Relations (PR) and Advertising Directors (AD) are responsible for cost effective ways to effectively promote the designer or company they represent. They develop and produce fashion shows, book signings, parties, and other events that raise awareness and boost the brand's image. Some PR companies specialize in fashion and represent designer and manufacturer clients. On the other hand, some designer firms such as Gucci and Ferragamo have their own in-house PR staff.

Challenges of the marketing posts "in general":

- They need to be great salespeople with exceptional writing and oral communication skills.
- Stay positive and enthusiastic and be prepared for rejection.
- Face tough competition for the same publications and channels targeted by their competitors.
- Find creative and cost-effective ways to pitch stories and build relationships.
- They must be comfortable with numbers.

Merchandising Managers (Merch. M)

Merchandising is an area that exists both in a retail organization as well as in a manufacturing one. The scope and focus of each position do indicate both resemblance and differences.

In Retail, a *General Merchandising Manager (GMM)* is the boss of buyers. He/she leads and manages the buyers of all divisions. They set the overall strategy and merchandise direction and develop the buying and selling strategy that would maximize business performance and profitability. They ensure that the pricing decision, promotional strategies, and marketing activities support the financial objectives of the merchandising team. Thus, they need to understand their competitors' strength, weakness, strategies in addition to consumers' demographics, wants, and needs and merchandise trends for all departments under him/her.

A *Divisional Merchandising Manager (DMM)* works under the GMM and manages the buying team of a specific division or group of related departments such as menswear.

In Manufacturing, the position of a merchandiser or merchandise planner is usually not a management level position. It is still a very important position as they work in liaison among the design production and sales teams from showroom to factory. One of their primary responsibilities is to develop a merchandise line plan by month and by piece count or by stock keeping unit (SKU) (a type of identification data for a single product). In addition, they need to shop the market and competition to present a merchandising strategy for the design team.

Challenges of the merchandising posts "in general":

- Understand all merchandise classifications.
- Lead a group of diverse buyers working in various departments.
- Be accountable for accuracy of numbers and forecasted sales and inventories.
- Be able to respond quickly to market and consumer needs.
- Be aware of fashion trends and competitors.

Sources

1. Londrigan, Michael L. and Jacqueline M. Jenkins. *Fashion Supply Chain Management* (New York: Fairchild Books, 2018).
2. Ranger, Michelle M. *The Fashion Industry and Its Careers: An Introduction*, 2 ed. (New York: Fairchild Books, 2015).

CHAPTER QUESTIONS

1. Research a fashion organization of your choice and identify the following:

   a. The organizational structure and its various departments.

   b. The hierarchy and decision-making flow between its departments.

   c. Your assessment of the advantages and challenges that this particular organization may face due to its adopted structure in reference to its segment and competitors.

2. Whenever a famous fashion designer passes away (e.g. Alexander McQueen, Karl Lagerfeld) or retires (e.g. Valentino) questions and doubts about the future of the fashion house start to rise in spite of the solid history of the brand and its market position.

   a. Why do these doubts arise?

   b. What does this tell us about the role of the designer in a fashion organization?

   c. How does the role of the fashion designer differ between a mass-market organization and a luxury organization?

3. Porter's model outlines three main organizational strategies.

   a. Identify each of the three strategies.

   b. Give an example of one fashion organization to match each of these strategies (one for each) other than the examples listed above. Explain and justify your answer.

Case Study
Under Armour: A Strategic Management Perspective

Overview

Under Armour (UA) started in 1996 by Kevin Plank. As a former member of the Maryland University football program he started experimenting in his grandmother's basement to create a T-shirt with a moisture-wicking fabric that would help to regulate temperature and enhance body performance. Within two years, UA became the official supplier of performance apparel for the National Football League (NFL) in Europe and by 2005, the year the brand went public, they were supplying clothing for the teams of Major Leagues of soccer, lacrosse, national hockey, the U.S. ski and baseball teams as well as 30 NFL teams and more.

In 2009, the brand made a significant move in introducing its line of performance footwear. In 2011, another milestone came when the brand surpassed $1 billion in annual sales. Since then, the company continued on its quest to introduce innovative products and fabrics such as introducing "charged cotton" a fabric that aims to dry faster than regular cotton yet feels as soft and comfortable, the "Armour Bra" targeting female athletes by offering a product that fits perfectly and comfortably, and the thermo-conductive "Coldgear Infrared" insulation system which is a lining insulator meant to absorb and retain body heat to keep athletes warmer longer with no bulky material.

UA moved into the digital sphere with full force by 2016 when it acquired a number of fitness app companies such as MapMyRun and Endomondo in order to build the world's largest digital fitness and wellness community. In addition, the company continued expanding and innovating its footwear segment by introducing its first smart shoe known as SpeedForm Gemini 2 Record-Equipped with a built-in sensor technology that stores data such as time, duration, distance, etc. In 2017, the company introduced its sleepwear line that it claims to be inspired by Tom Brad's training routine and uses the body's energy to power faster recovery and promote better sleep.

Currently, the brand has around 41 offices globally, a supply chain of over 300 global partners and factories, and close to 250 million connected fitness community members as stated on its site.

Mission and Vision

According to UA its vision and mission statements are stated as:

Vision: Empower Athletes Everywhere.

Mission: To make all athletes better through passion, design, and the relentless pursuit of innovation.

Major Competition

UA, being among the newcomers in the athletic wear arena, faces tough competition from the biggest and well-established brands, especially Adidas and Nike.

ADIDAS

Compared to UA, the German company has a more established market in European countries and has managed to secure a lifetime sponsorship with soccer superstar Lionel Messi. The Adidas Group also owns two other widely recognized names in athletics: Reebok and TaylorMade. While Adidas was initially known as a soccer brand, its ownership of these other brand names established it as a diversified player in athletic apparel and goods. Adidas also plans to create further growth through investments intended to increase the speed of new products to market thus allowing the company to adapt more quickly to market demand. Finally, the company intends to invest strategically in marketing to growing urban populations across the globe.

NIKE

Nike is the largest brand of the three and the one with the most brand recognition. The brand dominates globally especially in the athletic apparel industry where it maintains the largest market share. Nike markets most of its products under the Nike name, but it also owns smaller niche brands such as Jordan and Converse. It also intends to significantly increase its direct sales

---

and e-commerce revenues in developed markets. The company also sees significant growth opportunities in China and in its women-focused product lines.

Strategic Analysis

Applying Porter's Five Forces model and developing a SWOT analysis for the brand may help us better understand where the company stands in the market as well as assess its competitiveness.

UA AND PORTER'S FIVE FORCES

The ultimate goal of applying Porter's Five Forces is to identify the opportunities and threats that could impact a business. Stock analysis firm Trefis used the model to examine how Under Armour fits into the athletic footwear and apparel industry. Among their findings:

1. *Competitive rivalry.* Under Armour faces intense competition from Nike and Adidas as mentioned earlier as well as from newer players. Nike and Adidas specifically, have considerably larger resources at their disposal and are making a play within the performance apparel market to gain market share. On the other hand, UA does not hold any major patents to use as leverage or to protect its product portfolio from being copied in the future.

2. *Bargaining power of suppliers.* Under Armour's products are produced by dozens of manufacturers based in multiple countries. Such a diverse supplier base provides an advantage by diminishing suppliers' leverage as it limits supplier bargaining power.

3. *Bargaining power of customers.* Under Armour's customers include wholesale customers and end-user customers. Wholesale customers, like Dick's Sporting Goods, hold a certain degree of bargaining leverage, as they could substitute UA's products with those of its competitors to gain higher margins. On the other hand, the bargaining power of end-user customers is lower as UA enjoys strong brand recognition and customer loyalty.

4. *Threat of new entrants.* Large capital costs are required for branding, advertising, and creating product demand, which limits the entry of newer players into the sports apparel market. However, existing companies in the sports apparel industry could enter the performance apparel market in the future and create a further threat.

5. *Threat of substitute products.* The demand for performance apparel, sports footwear, and accessories is expected to continue to grow. Therefore, this force may not threaten UA in the foreseeable future.

UA SWOT ANALYSIS

Conducting a SWOT analysis for UA reveals the following:

Strengths

- A loyal customer base
- Having some influential celebrities linked to it
- Brand is known for innovation and new ideas
- Acquired several fitness app companies helping to integrate mobile technologies to bolster its brand
- Footwear, a big source of potential growth for the company

Weakness

- UA requires high capital and large investments in order to compete and grow.

- While growing, the footwear segment still seems to be a challenge for the company.

- UA is the youngest amongst most of its competitors which are market leaders with a stronger market presence and following.

- UA seems to have major challenges in the North American market as indicated by a decline in sales by 3.2% during the fiscal second quarter 2019 reflecting weakness in Under Armour's direct-to-consumer store business whereby about 90% of which are at outlet centers, selling discounted goods.

- No patents.

- The brand has not been able to break out of the gym and connect with the casual wearers who make up most sneaker buyers.

Threats

- Tough competition from rivals such as Nike, Adidas, Lululemon, and others which have been in business longer than UA. Many of these brands may offer more fashionable and colorful athletic apparel that seem to be in higher demand.

- Lack of strong collaborations that strongly support the brand. For instance, Nike is doing collaborations with designer icon Virgil Abloh. Adidas has singer Beyoncé designing shoes and clothes. Puma has Selena Gomez wearing its brand and posting about it on her Instagram account, while Lululemon is teaming up with fitness studios like Barry's Bootcamp, making its leggings a staple in many women's closets today.

- U.S. shoppers appear to be favoring "athleisure" for daily errands or exercise classes over UA's functional products such as its sweat-wicking performance gear that is more popular amongst athletes, and thus the brand does not seem to make enough new products with wider market appeal.

- Low traffic to its outlet stores, and fewer of the people visiting its e-commerce site actually making purchases.

Opportunities

- UA is an innovative brand.

- It tends to appeal to younger market segments who may also show signs of favoring smaller brands and more transparently sourced goods that they can obtain easily through online shopping.

- It is able to price its products at a premium due to the perceived quality of its innovative materials and designs.

- Compared to Nike's size and other bigger brands, UA appears to have substantial room to grow and potentially steal market share away from Nike and others.

- UA projects substantial growth in footwear sales.

- Additional income streams from more sales directly to consumers.

- Potential to continue entering new markets. For example, UA recently hired a talented team to initiate a plan to enter the outdoor performance apparel market.

Corporate Strategy Initiatives

UA believes that it has reached a point where it has a stable foundation and is ready to be more competitive, and thus more capable to meet those challenges and overcome its weaknesses. While building on its strengths and exploring its opportunities, UA has put in place a number of strategic goals and clear steps to promote its market presence and propel its growth. These strategies include:

- Diversify its products while continuing innovation. They have already added the footwear as mentioned earlier and have increased the product offerings for women.

- Diversify their distribution channel while focusing on their direct-to-consumer channels such as their own outlets, specialty stores, and online presence. At the same time, they aim to open more standalone UA stores in the U.S., a strategy that it hopes will help boost its direct-to-consumer segment.

- UA plans to pull more merchandise out of off-price channels and outlets and sell more at full price. Scaling back discounted products hurts in the short term, but is necessary to reinstating UA as a premium, "full price" brand.

- UA plans more product innovation.

- UA plans to be a "louder" brand by investing heavily in marketing, to put the brand and its products in the spotlight.

- Their strategy to expand internationally also includes opening new stores in places like China as well as more sponsorship agreement such as the one they did with English Premier League club Tottenham Hotspur.

- The company recently announced a project to design and produce the "technical spacewear" for Virgin Galactic, Richard Branson's space-tourism company. All the technologies it is developing to create the spacesuits will be used in products that Under Armour will have commercially available.

Finally, according to its founder and CEO, the company will focus more on making sure shoppers know that every Under Armour product does something to make them perform better (Figure 1.5). According to Plank, "That's what makes us and gives us our DNA and gives us our reason for being."

Case Study Questions

1. Pick a direct competitor to UA other than Nike (e.g. Adidas) research the organization and determine the following:

    a. Develop a SWOT analysis for the organization.

    b. Identify its core competency and competitive advantage.

    c. Assess and compare its corporate strategy in reference to UA.

2. Both Nike and UA seem to target "athletes" as their core market. In your assessment how does each organization differ in approach and strategy?

Figure 1.5 Under Armour Products and Store.

Case Study Sources

1. http://www.underarmour.com

2. Loris, Anthony, Charee Kittling and Daniel J. Gomez. *Under Armour: Empowering Athletes Everywhere* (CreateSpace Independent Publishing Platform, 2015).

3. Mwendwa, Hillary. *Strategic Plan of an Athletic Apparel Label: Under Armour* (Nordersteft: GRIN, 2011).

4. Palmer, Barclay. "Adidas vs. Nike vs. Under Armour: Which is a Better Investment for 2019". *Investopedia*. August 29, 2019. https://www.investopedia.com/articles/markets/012616/adidas-vs-nike-vs-under-armour-which-2016-nkeua.asp

5. Sonenshine, Jacob. "Under Armour's Losing Market Share, and it Risks Falling Behind New Balance (UA)". *Business Insider*. April 18, 2018. https://markets.businessinsider.com/news/stocks/under-armour-stock-price-market-share-risks-losing-new-balance-2018-4-10 21521315

Notes

1. Robbins, Stephen A., and Mary Coutler. *Mangement*, 7th ed. (NewJersey: Prentice Hall, 2002), 6.
2. Ibid., 150.
3. Lin Grensing-Pophal. "4 Distinct Types of Corporate Culture, Which Is Yours?". *HR Daily Advisor*. April 12, 2018. https://hrdailyadvisor.blr.com/2018/04/12/4-distinct-types-corporate-culture/.

4. Cassie Paton. "5 Types of Corporate Culture: Which One Is Your Company?", September 15, 2016. https://blog.enplug.com/corporate-culture.
5. Coleman, John. "Six Components of a Great Corporate Culture". *Harvard Business Review*. May 6, 2013. https://hbr.org/2013/05/six-components-of-culture.
6. Robbins, *Management*, 7th ed., 256.
7. Lazzari, Zach. "5 Different Types of Leadership Styles". *SmallBusiness*. August 14, 2018. http://smallbusiness.chron.com/5-different-types-leadership-styles-17584.html.

Bibliography

Books

Burns, Leslie D., Kathy K. Mullet and Nancy O. Bryant. *The Business of Fashion*, 4th ed. (New York: Fairchild, 2011).

Chevalier, Michel and Gerald Mazzalovo. *Luxury Brand Management: A World of Privilege* (Singapore: John Wiley and Sons (Asia), 2008).

Choi, Tsan-Ming and Bin Shen. *Luxury Fashion Retail Management* (Singapore: Springer, 2017).

Corbellini, Erica and Stefania Saviolo. *Managing Fashion and Luxury Companies* (Firenze: Rizzoli ETAS, 2012).

David, Fred R. *Strategic Management: Concepts and Cases*, 13th ed. (Upper Saddle River: Pearson, 2011).

Decenzo, David and Stephen P. Robbins. *Fundamentals of Human Resource Management* (Hoboken: John Wiley and Sons, 2010).

Hosking, Dian M. H., Peter Dachler and Kenneth J. Gergen. *Management and Organization: Relational Alternatives to Individualism* (Chagrin Falls: Taos Institute Publications, 2013).

Keller, Kevin L. *Strategic Brand Management*, 4th ed. (Upper Saddle River: Pearson, 2013).

Loris, Anthony, Charee Kittling and Daniel J. Goelz. Under Armour: Empowering Athletes Everywhere (Middleton: CreateSpace Independent Publishing Platform, 2016).

Merson, Rupert. *Growing a Business; Strategies for Leaders and Entrepreneurs* (New York: Economist, 2016).

Morden, Tony. *Principles of Strategic Management*, 3rd ed. (Hampshire: Ashgate Publishing Limited, 2007).

Mwendwa, Hillary. *Strategic Plan of an Athletic Apparel Label: Under Armour* (Norderstedt: Grin, 2011).

Pinnington, Ashly, Rob Macklin and Tom Campbell. *Human Resource Management: Ethics and Employment* (New York: Oxford University Press, 2007).

Robbins, Stephan P. and Mary Coulter. *Management*, 7th ed. (Upper Saddle River: Prentice Hall, 2001).

Schramme, Annick, Turi Moerkerke and Karinna Nobbs. *Fashion Management* (Leuven: Lannoo, 2013).

Sherman, Gerald J. and Sar S. Perlman. *The Real World Guide to Fashion Selling and Management*, 2nd ed. (New York: Fairchild, 2015).

Thomas, Neil. *The John Adair Handbook of Management and Leadership* (London: Thorogood, 2004).

Varley, Rosemary, et al. *Fashion Management* (London: Red Globe Press, 2019).

Wheelen, Thomas L. and J. David Hunger. *Strategic Management and Business Policy: Toward Global Sustainability*, 3rd ed. (Upper Saddle River: Pearson, 2012).

White, Nicola and Ian Griffiths. *The Fashion Business: Theory, Practice, Image* (New York: Berg, 2000).

Other Sources

"4 Types of Organizational Structures". Pointpark University. February 15, 2018. https://online.pointpark.edu/business/types-of-organizational-structures/

"5 Challenges of Flat Organizations (and 5 Solutions to Flat Organizations). Status. Accessed November 24, 2018. https://status.net/articles/flat-organization-structure/

"5 Ways to Manage Risk". DBP Management. http://www.dbpmanagement.com/15/5-ways-to-manage-risk

"Core Competencies". SHRM Foundation. Accessed May 16, 2018. https://www.shrm.org/resourcesandtools/tools-and-samples/hr-qa/pages/corecompetencies.aspx

"Core Competency Theory of Strategy". Management Study Guide. June 16, 2018. https://www.managementstudyguide.com/core-competency-theory-of-strategy.htm

"Holacracy Constitution version 4.1". Holacracy. Accessed April 24, 2018. https://www.holacracy.org/constitution

"Main Advantages of Functional Organization Structure". ORG Charting. http://www.orgcharting.com/functional-organization-structure-advantages/

"Managing Risk". Info Entrepreneurs. Accessed May 16, 2018. https://www.infoentrepreneurs.org/en/guides/manage-risk/

"National Culture". Hofstede Insights. Accessed. September 12, 2018. https://www.hofstede-insights.com/models/national-culture/

"Nike Mission Statement and Vision Statement in a Nutshell". Four Weeks MBA. Accessed July 12, 2019. https://fourweekmba.com/nike-vision-statement-mission-statement/

"Porter's Five Forces of Competitive Position Analysis". CGMA. June 11, 2013. https://www.cgma.org/resources/tools/essential-tools/porters-five-forces.html

"Porter's Five Forces: A Model for Industry Analysis. Quick MBA. http://www.quickmba.com/strategy/porter.shtml

"Porter's Five Forces". Expert Program Management". Expert Program Management. Accessed July 3, 2019. https://expertprogrammanagement.com/2011/05/porters-five-forces/

"Strategy Explained". Harvard Business School. Accessed April 6, 2018. https://www.isc.hbs.edu/strategy/Pages/strategy-explained.aspx

"SWOT Analysis of Nike". Business Teacher. Accessed September 15, 2018. https://businessteacher.org.uk/swot/nike.php

"The Advantages and Disadvantages if Virtual Organization Design in Startups". Organimi. December 12, 2018. https://www.organimi.com/the-advantages-and-disadvantages-of-virtual-organization-design-in-startups/

"The Five Forces". Harvard Business School. Accessed April 7, 2018. https://www.isc.hbs.edu/strategy/business-strategy/Pages/the-five-forces.aspx

"Types of Business Organizational Structures". Pingboard. May 24, 2019. https://pingboard.com/blog/types-business-organizational-structures/

"Types of Organizational Charts (Organizational Structure Types) for Different Scenarios". Creately. June 12, 2019. https://creately.com/blog/diagrams/types-of-organizational-charts/

"Virtual Organizations". Reference for Business. Accessed May 24, 2018. https://www.referenceforbusiness.com/management/Tr-Z/Virtual-Organizations.html

"What are the 5 Risk Management Steps in a Sound Risk Management Process?". Continuing Professional Development. Accessed June 24, 2018. https://continuingprofessionaldevelopment.org/risk-management-steps-in-risk-management-process/

"What is a Strategic Product Planning Process?". Aha. Accessed November 2, 2018. https://www.aha.io/roadmapping/guide/product-strategy/what-is-a-strategic-product-planning-process

"What is SWOT Analysis?". British Library. Accessed October 22, 2018. https://www.bl.uk/business-and-ip-centre/articles/what-is-swot-analysis

Amadeo, Kimberly. "What is Competitive Advantage? Three Strategies That Work". Balance. Updated December 14, 2019. https://www.thebalance.com/what-is-competitive-advantage-3-strategies-that-work-3305828

Bagal, Sanjeev. "The Differences Between Strategies and Policies". Linedin. February 26, 2016. https://www.linkedin.com/pulse/differences-between-strategies-policies-sanjeev

Bain, Marc. "In the Age of Athleisure, Under Armour is Doubting Down on Performance". Quartz. February 12, 2019. https://qz.com/quartzy/1548515/in-the-age-of-athleisure-under-armour-is-doubling-down-on-performance/

Bain, Marc. "Under Armour Has Fallen. Can it Get Back UP?". Quartz. November 4, 2019. https://qz.com/1741607/can-under-armour-still-turn-its-business-around/

Benincasa, Robyn. "6 Leadership Styles and When You Should Use Them. Fast Company. May 29, 2012. http://www.fastcompany.com/1838481/6-leadership-styles-and-when-you-should-use-them

Bernstein, Ethan, et al. "Beyond Holacracy the Hype". *Harvard Business Review*, August 2016. https://hbr.org/2016/07/beyond-the-holacracy-hype

Bryant, Sue. "8 Tips on How to Impress Senior Leaders Across Cultures". June 26, 2018. https://countrynavigator.com/blog/global-talent/leaders-across-cultures/

Coleman, John. "Six Components of Six Great Cultures. *Harvard Business Review*. May 6, 2013. https://hbr.org/2013/05/six-components-of-culture

Devaney, Erik. "9 Types of Organizational Structure Every Company Should Consider". *Hubspot*. October 12, 2018. https://blog.hubspot.com/marketing/team-structure-diagrams

Dudovskiy, John "Gap Inc. organizational Structure, a Hybrid Structure that is Expected to Change". *Research Methodology*. October 24, 2016. https://research-methodology.net/gap-inc-organizational-structure-a-hybrid-structure-that-is-expected-to-change/

Dudovskiy, John. "Gap Inc. SWOT Analysis: Declining Sales and Profits Despite Strong Brand Portfolio". *Research Methodology*. October 25, 2016. https://research-methodology.net/gap-inc-swot-analysis/

Duggan, Tara. "The Advantages of Team-based Structure". *Small Business*. Accessed December 12, 2018. https://smallbusiness.chron.com/advantages-teambased-structure-55624.html

Dunsmoor, Matt. "An Inside Perspective on the Changes at Zappos.com" *Holacracy*. September 14, 2015. https://blog.holacracy.org/thanks-for-all-of-your-concern-but-f9c6a86bb332

Erickson, Amanda. "What is the Difference Between a Flat Organization and a Matrixed Organization?" *Small Business*. Accessed December 14, 2018. https://smallbusiness.chron.com/difference-between-flat-organization-matrixed-organization-57295.html

Forrester, Kemal. "What's a Creative Director's Job in the Fashion Industry?" *Quora*. May 17, 2106. https://www.quora.com/Whats-a-creative-directors-job-in-the-fashion-industry

Giang, Vivian. "What Kind of Leadership is Needed in Flat hierarchies?". *Fast Company*. May 19, 2015. https://www.fastcompany.com/3046371/what-kind-of-leadership-is-needed-in-flat-hierarchies

Gillikin, Jason. "Advantages and Disadvantages of Divisional Organizational Structure". *Small Business*. Updated January 25, 2019. https://smallbusiness.chron.com/advantages-disadvantages-divisional-organizational-structure-611.html

Gleeson, Patrick. "Benefits and Disadvantages of a Functional Organizational Structure". *Small Business*. January 25, 2109. https://smallbusiness.chron.com/benefits-disadvantages-functional-organizational-structure-11944.html

Grensing-Pophal, Lin. "4 Distinct of Corporate Culture, Which Is Yours?". *HR Daily Advisor*. April 12, 2018. https://hrdailyadvisor.blr.com/2018/04/12/4-distinct-types-corporate-culture/

https://www.managementstudyhq.com/levels-of-management-and-functions.html

Hunt, Bill. "The Myth of the Flat Organization". *Medium*. June 12, 2017. https://medium.com/@krues8dr/the-myth-of-the-flat-organization-b522529bc24a

Kaplan, Robert S. and Anette Mikes. "Managing Risks, a New Framework". *Harvard Business Review*. June 2012. https://hbr.org/2012/06/managing-risks-a-new-framework

Khan, Mohammad A. and Laurie Smith Law. "The Role of National Cultures in Shaping the Corporate Management Cultures: A Three-Country Theoretical Analysis. *IntechOpen*. November 5, 2018. https://www.intechopen.com/books/organizational-culture/the-role-of-national-cultures-in-shaping-the-corporate-management-cultures-a-three-country-theoretic

Lazzari, Zach. "5 Different Types of Leadership Styles". *Small Business*. August 14, 2018. http://smallbusiness.chron.com/5-different-types-leadership-styles-17584.html

Lucidchart team. "The 5 Steps of the Strategic Planning Process". *Lucidchart*. June 24, 2018. https://www.lucidchart.com/blog/the-4-steps-of-the-strategic-planning-process

Luenendonk, Martin. "Complete Guide to Holacracy: Example of Zappos". *Cleverism*. March 26, 2016. https://www.cleverism.com/complete-guide-to-holacracy-example-of-zappos/

Majchrzak, Poitr. "Our Holacracy Experience, What it is and Why it Works". *Medium*. March 5, 2018. https://medium.com/@piotrmajchrzak/our-holacracy-experience-what-it-is-and-why-it-works-564a36bdfbd7

Mar, Anna. "65 Business Risks". *Simplicable*. Accessed June 17, 2016. https://business.simplicable.com/business/new/65-business-risks-list

McIntyre, Marie G. "Don't Knock Amazon's Corporate Culture". *CNBC*. August 18, 2015. http://www.cnbc.com/2015/08/18/dont-knock-amazons-corporate-culture-commentary.html

Merritt, Cam. "Why Are Royalties Based on Net Sales and Not Net Profits?" Accessed October 28, 2018. https://smallbusiness.chron.com/royalties-based-net-sales-not-profits-74386.html

Mind Tools Team. "Hofstede's Cultural Dimensions: Understanding Different Countries". *Mind Tools*. Accessed June 4, 2018. https://www.mindtools.com/pages/article/newLDR_66.htm

Mind Tools Team. "Leadership Styles: Choosing the Right Approach for the Situation". *Mind Tools*. Accessed June 5, 2018. https://www.mindtools.com/pages/article/newLDR_84.htm

Mind Tools Team. "OGSM Frameworks Making Your Strategy a Reality". *Mind Tools*. Accessed June 5, 2018. https://www.mindtools.com/pages/article/ogsm-frameworks.htm

Mind Tools Team. 'PEST Analysis: Identifying "Big Picture" Opportunities and Threats". *Mind Tools*. Accessed June 4, 2018. https://www.mindtools.com/pages/article/newTMC_09.htm

Mind Tools Team. "SMART Goals: How to Make Your Goals Achievable". *Mind Tools*. Accessed June 6, 2018. https://www.mindtools.com/pages/article/smart-goals.htm

Mind Tools Team. "The Ansoff Matrix: Understanding the Risks of Different Options". *Mind Tools*. Accessed June 5, 2018. https://www.mindtools.com/pages/article/newTMC_90.htm

Morgan, Jacob. "The 5 Types of Organizational Structures; Part 1, The Hierarchy". *Forbes*. July 6, 2015. https://www.forbes.com/sites/jacobmorgan/2015/07/06/the-5-types-of-organizational-structures-part-1-the-hierarchy/#6fd236625252

Murray, La Toya J. "Introduction to Organizational Structure". *Small Business*. Accessed December 12, 2018. https://smallbusiness.chron.com/introduction-organizational-structure-2774.html

Palmer, Barclay. "Adidas vs. Nike vs. Under Armour: Which is a Better Investment for 2019?". *Investopedia*. August 29, 2019. https://www.investopedia.com/articles/markets/012616/adidas-vs-nike-vs-under-armour-which-2016-nkeua.asp

Quain, Sampson. "Advantages and Disadvantages of Team-Based Organizations". *Small Business*. Updated January 28, 2019. https://smallbusiness.chron.com/advantages-disadvantages-teambased-organizations-25370.html

Rathle, Marika P. "Leadership in the Retail, Fashion and Luxury Sector". *SpenceStuart*. January 2018. https://www.spencerstuart.com/research-and-insight/leadership-in-the-retail-fashion-and-luxury-sector

Root, George N. "Keys to Managing Virtual Organizations". *Small Business*. Accessed December 13, 2018. https://smallbusiness.chron.com/keys-managing-virtual-organizations-21001.html

Smithson, Nathaniel. "Nike Inc.'s Mission Statement and Vision Statement (An Analysis)". *Panmore*. June 23, 2019. http://panmore.com/nike-inc-vision-statement-mission-statement

Som, Ashok. "What Luxury brands Look in Their Managers". *Knowledge Essec*. September 10, 2017. http://knowledge.essec.edu/en/leadership/what-luxury-brands-are-looking-their-managers.html

Sonenshine, Jacob. "Under Armour's Losing Market Share, and it Risks Falling Behind New Balance (UA)". *Business Insider*. April 18, 2018. https://markets.businessinsider.com/news/stocks/under-armour-stock-price-market-share-risks-losing-new-balance-2018-4-1021521315

Sullivan, Janie. "Four Elements of Organizational Structure". *Small Business*. February 12, 2019. https://smallbusiness.chron.com/four-basic-elements-organizational-structure-288.html

Surbhi, S. "Difference Between Competitive Advantage and Core Competence". *Key Differences*. June 20, 2017. https://keydifferences.com/difference-between-competitive-advantage-and-core-competence.html

Surbhi, S. "Difference Between Strategy and Policy". *Key Differences*. December 19, 2019. https://keydifferences.com/difference-between-strategy-and-policy.html

Tamosiunaite, Ruta. "Organization Virtual or Networked?". *ResearchGate*. August 2011. https://www.researchgate.net/publication/267394518_Organization_Virtual_or_Networked

Thomas, Lauren. "Under Armour's North America Problem Hasn't Gone Away". *CNBC*. July 30, 2019 https://www.cnbc.com/2019/07/30/under-armours-north-america-problem-hasnt-gone-away.html

Thomson, Andrew. "Nike Inc. Organizational Structure Characteristics (Analysis)". *Panmore*. February 15, 2019. http://panmore.com/nike-inc-organizational-structure-characteristics-analysis

Vembar, Kaarin. "United Colors of Benetton Tests a US Comeback". *Retaildive*. October 23, 2019. https://www.retaildive.com/news/united-colors-of-benetton-tests-a-us-comeback/565510/

Wilkinson, Jim. "Porter's Five Forces of Competition". *The Strategic CFO*. July 24, 2013. https://strategiccfo.com/porters-five-forces-of-competition/

CHAPTER TWO

Managing the Fashion Supply Chain

How the Fashion Industry Works

LEARNING OUTCOMES

. . . .

- Become familiarized with the dynamics of the fashion industry and its levels of production.

- Understand the Fashion Supply Chain and how it works.

- Identify differences between Supply and Value Chains.

- Assess the role and impact of fashion models such as Fast Fashion and SNBN.

LEVELS OF THE FASHION INDUSTRY

. . . .

In general, the fashion industry can be divided into four major divisions or levels: *Textile – Apparel Manufacturing – Retail* in addition to the *Auxiliary* division which includes activities that complement the creation and production stages of the product, such as marketing and communication activities. These levels or stages exist in a sequence whereby each one builds on the outcome of the stage before it and feeds into the next stage, adding to what was accomplished and forwarding the outcome to the players at the next level to add more to it and so on. Thus, each one of these stages includes a number of players or organizations that perform an activity to add something to the product until a finished product is produced and is ready to be sold at the retail stage and eventually be promoted to the world through the auxiliary organizations. This path and sequence of events the product goes through from one organization (or supplier) to the other which takes a fashion idea from being a sketch through progressive stages of buildups and layers of activities until it is a finished product, is what we refer to as the *Supply Chain*.

To understand it better, let us take a closer look at the different levels[1] that construct the fashion industry and provide the different players that constitute its supply chain.

Level One: The Textile Segment

Fabrics are made from yarns, which in return are made from either natural fiber (e.g. cotton and wool) or man-made fibers produced by chemical companies such as DuPont or Monsanto (e.g. nylon and polyester). The yarn producers buy natural or man-made fibers and spin them into yarns of different sizes and characters, which fabric manufacturers then weave or knit to produce a fabric.

Companies that own the necessary equipment and use it to produce fabrics are called *mills*. The first form of colorless (or beige-like) fabric, before being processed further, is known as *griege* (or gray) goods. Color is next added to these griege, or unfinished, goods by printing or dyeing (called piece-dyeing). Fabrics may instead be constructed of already dyed yarns; thus, once woven or knitted this *yarn-dyed* cloth is already colored and will not usually be dyed or printed again. *Finishing* is the final process before the textile is used, it removes excess dye, sets the color, and also fluffs the yarns that make up the fabric to complete its structural aspect. If desired, special finishing processes may be used to soften or stiffen the *hand*, make the fabric stain resistant, or add a sheen to it. Many large mills perform all of these processes themselves, but in most cases these functions are performed by small print plants, dye plants, and finishers on a commission basis.

Large mills can do all these stated functions and more such as selling fabric directly to clothes and furniture manufacturers. Thus, these mills' activities extend beyond this first level of production and supply to more advanced levels as well. These mills are then called vertical, or vertically integrated operations (such as Burlington, J. P. Stevens, Milliken, and Dan River). *Vertical integration* is when an organization performs functions at different stages of the supply chain, e.g. a manufacturer which also owns its retail outlet which is an activity at a subsequent stage of the chain (i.e. comes after production) and commonly carried on by a different type of organization, e.g. retailers.

In addition to mills there are other players or organizations at this level that are equally instrumental in the industry and contribute to the production process such as:

CONVERTERS

Mills may also sell fabric to *converters*. A converter buys griege goods and *converts* them into finished fabrics according to their own specifications by having them dyed, printed, and finished on commission by a third company. Large manufacturers could specify to mills certain colors or finishes they need. However, mills can only accommodate these requests made by major and large manufactures purchasing large yarns from mills. Hence, converters become very helpful for smaller manufacturers working with smaller quantities or last-minute requests.

Whereas a mill owns specific equipment, which must be kept in operation to maintain profitability, the fact that a converter does not own any equipment allows broad flexibility in the types of fabric they can deal with. Convertors usually have a good understanding of customer preferences and thus if they have an idea for a new fabric that they believe they can sell the converter has the option of finding a new resource to produce the new item in advance. A mill, on the other hand, has all operations under its own roof, thereby maintaining more complete control.

Accordingly, textile converters are characterized in the following ways:

- Converters are generally experts in color forecasting, fiber content, fabric construction, and various aesthetic and performance fabric finishes. They often contract with dyers, printers, and finishers to create fabrics that they market to apparel and home fashion manufacturers, jobbers, and retailers.

- They usually focus on *aesthetic* finishes such as glazing, crinkling, etc. or *performance* finishes such as colorfast, stain resistance, water resistance, permanent press, etc.

- Some converters specialize in certain types of fabrics while others may work on several types of fabrics.

- Most converters that print fabrics use a rotary printing process. Digital printing is also becoming more widespread.

- Because the fabric is finished close to the time when consumers will be purchasing the end-use product, converters play an important role in analyzing and responding to changing consumer preferences.

Textile mills or converters place their fabric samples in textile showrooms to be marketed to designers and apparel manufacturers. Thus, they follow designers' seasonal calendars by showing their fabrics and often by color themes, in fall/winter (shown in October/November) and spring/summer (shown in March/April). They also participate in international textile trade shows such as: Interstoff (Hong Kong), Intertextile (Beijing), Texworld (New York City), and Premiere Vision (Paris) where manufacturers can place orders for samples (awaiting final orders from retailers) or large final quantities.

JOBBERS

Fabrics are produced by the *piece*, which usually ranges from 30 to 80 yards of fabric depending on the weight and difficulty in production of the goods. Piece lengths of 60 to 70 yards are most common. Mills and converters sell by the piece to manufacturers of clothing and furniture as well as to large retail stores, which in return sell fabrics to consumers for home sewing purposes.

Both mills and converters can also sell to *jobbers*. A jobber buys a product in quantity and, without changing the product, sells it in smaller quantities to new customers. Accordingly, a jobber may be seen as an intermediary who buys overruns and close-out lots from manufacturers and sells them to retail stores or smaller manufacturers. As a matter of fact, most of the well-known fabric houses that sell expensive fabric to interior designers, for instance, are called jobbers. Jobbers also cater to apparel manufacturers.

At this level, a company may fall into more than one of these classifications. For example, a domestic mill produces its own fabrics, but may also convert a fabric from a foreign mill that is complementary to its domestically produced line but is uneconomical for the mill to manufacture itself. A jobber may buy fabric from converters but go directly to mills to convert other types of goods. Some jobbers even own small mills that produce a portion of their lines. Thus, a textile company is usually labeled by the function for which it is primarily known to its suppliers and customers.

The apparel industry is obviously a large consumer of textile products. Therefore, a textile company may orient its products toward manufacturers of women's dresses, men's sportswear, active wear, dance wear, hosiery, or other apparel markets. A mill, converter, or jobber may concentrate on any combination of these areas. Fabric sources could also be categorized by the price range of their product. Companies selling expensive fabric are called high end, upper end, or, in the field of interior textiles, uptown (because these companies are usually uptown in New York City).

In addition, the size of the mill's design staff depends on the company's size, but it usually consists of one design director, a stylist for each division, and several artists.

- A *stylist* handles the development of the company's fabric lines, which is the group of fabrics designed, developed, and edited to be shown and sold to the market each season. The stylist initiates the line, organizes and directs the artists in the development and coloration of intended designs, coordinates with manufacturing personnel to have the samples produced that will be shown to customers, and then edits and finalizes the group of designs to be shown for the season.

- The *artists* who work in the studio of a textile mill do the actual artwork on paper in preparation for production of textiles. These artists may be designers who do complete textile designs, repeat artists who put designs into the size and repeat appropriate for the specific company's needs, or colorists who do the actual renderings and try different color looks for every design.

- *Design directors*, in the case of jobbers for instance, would usually choose the group of fabrics that the jobber should carry since jobbers do not produce their own fabric. In small jobbers, this selection is often made by the president or owner of the company.

TIMING IN THE TEXTILE INDUSTRY

Every segment of the textile-related industries plans and produces products well ahead of retail selling seasons. At a minimum, however, textiles are designed a year and a half ahead of the retail selling season (i.e. *design of fabric for fall next year clothing must begin in spring of this year*). Major changes, such as development of a completely new type of fabric for a mill, will take even longer to produce.

Textiles for apparel are shown to clothing manufacturers in two main selling seasons: spring (April and May) and fall (October and November) a year ahead of the retail spring for which the fabric is intended. Fall is sometimes broken into Fall I and Fall II. Other seasons such as, holiday and resort are smaller seasons that follow fall while the summer season follows spring.

Level Two: The Manufacturing Segment

While the word *manufacturing* implies that these organizations produce their own garments in their own factories, in reality most of them do not and they use contractors. Hence, we can say that we have generally two types of manufacturers: manufacturers who own their own factories (such as Zara) which will also be considered vertically integrated as defined earlier , and manufacturers with no factories (the majority of fashion producers, such as Tommy Hilfiger, Rag & Bone, etc.).

FASHION DESIGN AND MANUFACTURING

Aside from the big designer names of the industry such as Michael Kors, Tom Ford, etc. the vast majority of designers are unknown and working as part of design teams for manufacturers adapting trending styles into marketable garments for average consumers. Designers draw inspiration from a wide range of sources, including art, film, and street styles, etc. For most designers, the use of computer aided design (CAD) software, such as Lectra Systems, has replaced traditional design methods, such as paper sketches or hand draping fabric on mannequins. These software and digital tools allow designers to rapidly make changes to a proposed design's silhouette, fabric, trimmings, and other elements as well as give them the ability to instantaneously share the proposed changes with others who may be located in a factory across the world. It is only a small number of designers and manufacturers that produce innovative trendsetting high-fashion apparel, and an even smaller number (mostly in Paris) that still produces haute couture (i.e. high fashion) anymore. Most manufacturers belong to the mass-market segment which is a segment divided into various sub-segments each with their own price and market profile.

Box 2.1 Segments in the Fashion Industry Based on Price

The Mass-Market Segments

In general, mass-market sub-segments are indeed trend followers and not trendsetters. The main difference is that the highest levels in price and creativity such as Bridge and Premium tend to be more trend-responsive to fashion trends than the other segments. Being trend followers, design decisions for most of these segments are merchandising and styling decisions that are highly sensitive to the price to value ratios. Thus, as we move up the ladder starting from the cheapest *Budget* segment, we expect two things to happen: Prices go up and the level of creativity and response to trends goes up as well. Segments are:

- *Budget.* Lowest prices, national distribution, sensitive to cost, basic styles, least trendy, and/or rely heavily on copying trends (e.g. Wrangler, Forever 21).
- *Moderate.* Generally, sportswear brands aim to offer trendier styles at still affordable prices (e.g. Gap, Uniqlo).
- *Better.* Could be well-known brands with designer (or designer-like) names (e.g. Tommy Hilfiger, Nautica) that offer a mix of staples and semi-trendy styles.

- *Contemporary.* This is a unique category that may sometimes overlap in price range with the better segment, however, it is characterized with trendy, avant- garde styles targeting mainly young fashion-forward consumers (e.g. Betsy Johnson, young designer lines).
- *Bridge.* This segment "bridges" the gap between better and designer labels, mostly sold in specialty stores or private chains in malls (e.g. Lauren by Ralph Lauren and DKNY).
- *Premium.* This is a rather new level of segmentation that gained attention due to its growth in size and impact. It could be regarded as the highest layer of the bridge segment, which makes it the closest to the designer segment. Being at the top edge of mass-market it shares a lot of characteristics of both luxury and mass-market. It is the highest in price among mass-market segments and the most creative. It is not as a trendsetter or limited in distribution as designer yet the most responsive to the trends they set (e.g. Coach, Diesel).

The luxury sub-segments

The luxury segment is the trendsetter and thus is the one that produces superstar designers.

- *Designer.* This is the ready to wear (pret-a-porter) business arm of luxury brands. These are trendsetting aspirational lifestyle brands mostly sold in exclusive boutiques or high-end specialty department stores (e.g. Dolce & Gabbana, Issey Miyake, Tom Ford).
- *Haute Couture (a.k.a. High Fashion).* Technically, for a brand to be considered an haute couture house it has to meet a set of criteria such as having clients who buy made-to-measure pieces produced in workshops, and the designer (couturier) is a member of the *Chambre Syndicale de la Haute Couture* (syndicate of couture designers), all of which are hard to fulfill today. Thus, it is a shrinking segment as the number of real *couturiers* (designers such as Christian Dior, Yves Saint Laurent, Emanuel Ungaro), workshop seamstresses, and most importantly, haute couture clients across the world is rapidly declining.

Other segments to note:

There has been some occasional references to other segments such as "Mastige" (Mass + Prestige) which is credited for democratizing fashion by offering trendy styles at affordable prices (e.g. Zara) catering to the masses of young professionals across the world who are fashion conscious and share knowledge of new trends through social media and the internet and may not be able to afford expensive designer labels.

Along with designers, a number of important roles take place within this level such as: Sample Makers and Pattern Makers. Whatever the size, the pattern, whether drawn on paper or is a set of computer instructions, determines how fabric is cut into the pieces that will be joined to make a garment. Except for the most expensive clothing, fabric cutting is commonly done by computer-guided knives or high-intensity lasers that can cut many layers of fabric at once. This production stage is followed by the assembly of the garment. Here too, technological innovation, including the development of computer-guided machinery, results in the automation of some stages of garment assembly. Nevertheless, the fundamental process of sewing remains labor-intensive. This puts high pressure on clothing manufacturers to seek out low-wage locations for their factories or contractors, such as developing countries in Asia, Africa, and Latin America. Assembled garments then go through the stage known as finishing. Finishing includes various processes such as adding decorative elements (embroidery, beading) buttons and buttonholes, hooks and eyes, snaps, zippers, and other fasteners; hems and cuffs; and brand-name labels and other legally required labels (e.g. care labels) specifying fiber content, laundry instructions, and country of manufacture. Finally, finished garments are then pressed and packed for shipment. It is important to remember that, although usually not considered part of the apparel industry for trade and statistical purposes, the manufacturing and sale of accessories, such as shoes and handbags, as well as underwear, are closely allied with the fashion industry. As with garments, the production of accessories ranges from very expensive luxury goods to inexpensive mass-produced items. Also, like apparel manufacturing, accessory production tends to be located in low-wage locations.

Level Three: Fashion Retailers

Once the clothes have been designed and manufactured, they need to be sold through a retail outlet. Traditionally, retailers make initial purchases for resale three to six months before the customer is able to buy the clothes in-store. Retailers also come in different types, categories, and levels.

Retail categories:

- *Specialty stores.* Could be single free-standing or chain stores available in major streets, malls, or shopping centers. These may sell one or multiple brands, yet the focus is on a segment or a category such as women's ready to wear, lingerie, etc. *Flagship stores* are usually the biggest and most impressive of the chain and mainly located at the brand's headquarters city or in major centers of the world. A specialty store may also include:

  - *Category killers:* Another form of specialty store that offers the largest range of a specific category and at competitive prices. They offer both breadth and depth of merchandise assortment, including stores such as Bed, Bath & Beyond and The Home Depot.

  - *Boutiques:* Smaller specialty stores with a niche market, more focused and trendy merchandise, and higher prices.

- *In-store boutiques (shops-in-shops).* Fully individualized stores located inside department stores, which can be either a space rented by the brand or run and managed by the department store itself with employees picked and trained by the brand.

- *Department stores.* Brands and their products are ordered and managed by the store and are among other brands displayed. Technically, a department store is a retailer that sells both soft goods (e.g. apparel) and hard goods (appliances and furniture). Thus, while Macy's is a department store, Neiman Marcus would be classified as a specialty store or a specialty department store.

- *Discount stores.* Stores that sell known brands discounted below market prices. They are no frills stores that offer minimal services and in-store experiences in return for cutting their costs and passing part of these savings on to customers by adopting a low margin/high volume policy. Discount stores in return come in different formats:

  - *Off-price discounters:* Such as Ross, TJ Maxx, and Marshalls.

  - *Factory outlets:* Owned and managed by specialty retailers and used as an alternative to selling off-season and broken sizes merchandise at a discount. On some occasions, the retailer may purchase merchandise especially for their outlets. These outlets are usually located in suburban areas where they offer shoppers great bargains. Examples include Nordstrom Rack, Off-Saks, and Ralph Lauren Polo outlets, among many others.

  - *Membership clubs:* Examples like Sam's and Costco offer merchandise at close to wholesale prices for member customers. Popular for large quantity purchases of household merchandise at great discounts, many of these chains offer their own brands as well.

  - *Mass merchants and hyper-stores:* The major distinction between these stores and other department stores is that in addition to a mix of hard and soft merchandise they sell groceries as well. As a discounter, they are value-oriented with a wide range of inexpensive product, centralized checkout points, and self-service.

- *Online shopping.* E-tailing offers various models and formats that either complement the physical store's operations or stand on its own. Store sites, shopping portals, luxury rentals, and apps are now readily available and integral parts of our shopping experiences.

- *Pop-up stores.* Refers to the opening of short-term sales spaces (e.g. sample day sales).

- *Other options.* TV shopping channels such as QVC and catalogs are still viable channels for merchandise distribution.

FASHION MERCHANDISING AND RETAILING

Merchandising is an integral function of retailing. It involves *selling the right product, at the right price, at the right time and place, to the right customers.* Fashion merchandisers must thus utilize marketers' information about customer preferences as the basis for decisions about such things as stocking appropriate merchandise in adequate but not excessive quantities, offering items for sale at attractive but still profitable prices, and discounting overstocked goods. Merchandising also involves presenting goods attractively and accessibly through the use of store windows (i.e. visual merchandising), in-store displays, and special promotional events. Merchandising specialists must be able to respond to surges in demand by rapidly acquiring new stocks of the favored product. An inventory-tracking computer program in a department store in New York, for example, can trigger an automatic order to a production facility in Shanghai for a certain quantity of garments of a specified type and size to be delivered in a matter of days. In today's world the internet has opened up new opportunities for merchandisers such as giving them the ability to provide customers with shopping opportunities 24 hours per day and easy access to those in rural areas or overseas.

Merchandising, whether from retailer or manufacturer perspectives is all about choosing the right assortment (or merchandise mix) which is influenced by the following elements:

- *Breadth.* The assortment or the number of brands or lines (e.g. womenswear, menswear or jackets, pants, and shirts, etc.).

- *Depth.* The number of styles, sizes, and color within each brand, or what is referred to as the SKUs (stock-keeping units) within each line (e.g. offering all colors and sizes within a line of shirts).

Level Four: The Auxiliaries (e.g. Marketing)

Fashion marketing commonly refers to more than promotion and communication activities. It is the process of managing the flow of merchandise from the initial selection of designs to be produced to the presentation of products to retail customers, with the goal of maximizing a company's sales and profitability. Successful fashion marketing depends on understanding consumer desire and responding with appropriate products. Marketers use sales tracking data, attention to media coverage, focus groups, and other means of ascertaining consumer preferences to provide feedback to designers and manufacturers about the type and quantity of goods to be produced. Marketers are thus responsible for identifying and defining a fashion producer's target customers and for responding to the preferences of those customers.

Marketing operates at both the wholesale and retail levels. Companies that do not sell their own products at their own retail outlets must place those products at wholesale prices in the hands of retailers, such as boutiques, department stores, and online e-commerce sites. They use fashion shows, catalogs, and a salesforce armed with sample products to find a close fit between the manufacturer's products and the retailer's customers. On the other hand, marketers for companies that do sell their own products at retail are primarily concerned with matching products to their own customer base.

At both the wholesale and retail levels, marketing also involves promotional activities such as print and other media advertising aimed at establishing brand recognition and brand reputation for diverse reasons such as quality, low price, or trendiness. There are many marketing channels to utilize to promote the fashion product which will be addressed in a later chapter. However, throughout many decades, an important promotional feature of fashion has always been the runway fashion shows.[2]

THE ROLE OF FASHION SHOWS

Fashion designers and manufacturers promote their clothes not only to retailers (such as fashion buyers) but also to the media (fashion journalists) and directly to customers. In the late twentieth and early twenty-first centuries, fashion shows became a regular and essential part of the fashion calendar. The couture shows, held twice a year in Paris (in January and July) by the official syndicate of couture designers (comprising the most exclusive and expensive fashion houses), present outfits that might be ordered by potential clients but which often are intended more to showcase the designers' ideas about fashion trends and brand image. Ready-to-wear fashion shows, separately presenting both women's and menswear, are held during spring and fall "Fashion Weeks", of which the most important take place in fashion capitals such as Paris, Milan, New York, and London. These shows, of much greater commercial importance than the couture shows, are aimed primarily at fashion journalists and at buyers for department stores, wholesalers, and other major markets. Extensively covered in the media, fashion shows both reflect and advance the direction of fashion change. Photographs and videos of fashion shows are instantaneously transmitted to mass-market producers who produce inexpensive clothing copied from or inspired by the runway designs. As a result of the media impact and public relations (PR) importance of fashion shows, they became more elaborate and theatrical, held in larger venues with specially constructed elevated runways ("catwalks") for celebrity supermodels to showcase the new designs. In recent years, doubts were raised regarding the role and impact of fashion shows as an instrument of marketing, intrigue, and PR strategies in the age of the internet, social media, and live streams. However, fashion shows remain an integral part of the structure of the fashion industry at least for now.

SUPPLY CHAIN MANAGEMENT (SCM)

As we have seen, the creation of a fashion product is a chain of steps and activities that involve many players whereby each produces and supplies a component of the product that the following in the chain can add to, in what we now understand is called the supply chain (Figure 2.1). Thus, in order to make sure the product goes through these stages in an efficient, timely, and cost-effective manner the whole process and progression of steps needs to be monitored and managed. Hence, the need for supply chain management (SCM).

Accordingly, while supply chain is the flow of products from suppliers to consumers, SCM could be defined as *the process of managing the flow of goods and the production process from design and ideation until the final product is created and reaches the final customer*. In that respect, SCM could be seen as a practice under *operations management* as it focuses on the logistics of operations and accounts for all of the people, companies and processes involved in making, marketing, selling, storing, and delivering the product or service. In today's world, SCM software solutions are utilized by many organizations to ensure effective monitoring of the distribution channels.

Based on the above, SCM could be seen as consisting of five main elements or stages:

1. The first and early stage of planning and designing a product to meet consumer demand

2. Sourcing the materials or components needed to produce the goods

3. Manufacturing the product

4. Delivering the product to the buyer

5. Accepting returns of defective products

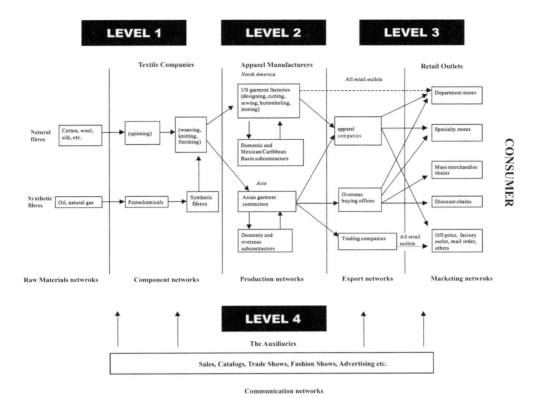

Figure 2.1 Apparel Supply Chain.

Created by Author.

Benefits of SCM

As mentioned, the main purpose of the SCM is to ensure that the product goes through the supply and production chain smoothly and efficiently while managing cost throughout the process and ensuring that it reaches the customer on time as planned. By doing so, SCM ensures a number of benefits:

- Time management. The less time it takes for goods to reach the end customer, the more efficient the product flows. SCM enables working strategies that can accelerate time-to-market and optimize business speed, while ensuring high level of product quality.

- Improves product flow through accurate demand and sales forecasting and also improves inventory management.

- Effective SCM requires the integration of information flows in the supply chain which in return enables accurate, timely, complete, and relevant information flow to avoid missed opportunities, bottlenecks, and possible risks.

- Enables better management of cash flow which is necessary given the number of parties involved in the supply chain.

- By optimizing product, information, and financial flow, companies can proactively create and seize new market opportunities and mitigate risks that can negatively impact their entire business.

- SCM provides a way to develop a competitive advantage without having to lower prices. For instance, by developing a more efficient supply chain, you can deliver orders faster to customers.

- Efficient SCM has other cost benefits such as eliminating redundant steps and saving salary costs by ensuring workers don't waste time on unnecessary procedures.

- Increases your negotiating power with partner businesses, such as suppliers and retailers, which also stand to benefit from you doing business faster. For example, a retail business that carries your products might be more willing to offer you favorable terms if it knows your company always delivers products on schedule.

Challenges of SCM

- As the process is built on a chain of events, it only takes one step of the supply chain to break down to hold up your ability to deliver products and thus, make money. For example, if you can't get supplies, a machine breaks down, your sales website crashes, you can't locate inventory in your warehouse or your delivery truck breaks down, your entire operation might have to shut down to prevent bottlenecks.

- If the business outsources one part of its supply chain, such as materials, production, sales, or shipping, that vendor can easily disrupt its business, either accidentally, when it is struggling, or by holding the goods for payments not yet made or a price increase the vendor demands.

Steps to ensure a more effective SCM process:

- SCM decisions should coincide with company goals so that supply chain goals end up being more valuable to the company's overall success. Thus, before supply chain managers begin developing vendor relations, delivery times, warehousing staffing, and other procedures, they should spend time meeting with senior managers from all the departments within the company to formulate overall company strategies. By aligning supply chain plans with all departments, the supply chain manager earns the support of sales, company executives, and customers.

- When creating the supply chain plans, it is important to identify all the areas the supply chain manager controls. Transportation to and from the plant or warehouse, staffing and structure of the warehouse, and inventory management are vital components of the in-house supply chain that must be addressed. Consider customer needs, procurement processes, supplier pricing, and vendor relationships. SCM must also address environmental arenas involved in all of the areas and include measures to meet regulatory requirements and company environmental policies.

- As mentioned, SCM software is widely available in a variety of applications and choosing the right systems for the company is vital to supply performance and success. And one of the most difficult steps in devising a SCM strategy is deciding how to best implement the plan and ensure that all steps along the way are integrated and communicated effectively. It's also important to make sure that frontline supervisors and employees utilize the tools and applications properly so that no information is lost along the supply chain. Internet-based supply chain applications are also becoming increasingly effective, because they can be made available to every stakeholder in the supply chain, including top management in the company.

- Managers should take into account the various parts of the supply chain process that will affect performance. Those areas include technical improvements the company plans to initiate, an analysis of the competition, what customers need and want and what trends may affect the supply chain in the future. Research can be performed in-house or through an outside consultant and include best-practice ideas from industry sources.

SCM and the Fashion Industry

For the most part apparel production is a low skill and labor-intensive operation. This is why apparel is a leading industry in most developing countries where you can find a large pool of unskilled labor who, with little training, can perform most basic production tasks of apparel manufacturing. As a result, outsourcing is a common practice in the industry whereby manufacturers pass certain activities to other factories or businesses to complete the needed tasks. This in return, leads to a variety of formats and ways in which fashion products are produced which may include the following options:[3]

CUT, MAKE, AND TRIM (CMT)

This is the process of hiring contractors to perform the apparel manufacturing functions of *cutting, making,* and *trimming.* It is usually the entry level by many countries in the production field as it has the lowest entry barriers such as capital and talent constraints. It is also the area with the least amount of return as many of these functions are done using new tools such as laser cutters with increased efficiency and accuracy.

As understood, *cut* refers to the stage of cutting fabrics based on supplied patterns. This process is commonly done using laser cutters operated by a single operator.

Make refers to sewing and assembling the cut pieces together, in low-skill production lines workers usually do not put together the whole garment, instead they work on a piece of the garment and then pass it to the next point and so on. This repetitive process improves their efficiency.

Trim refers to garment finishings and trimmings used as final embellishments and touches before the garment is packed and shipped such as zippers, buttons, etc.

It is worth noting that the CMT model often occurs in the export processing zones (EPZ) which are designated economic zones in developing countries that are designed to attract foreign investment and production by offering expedited permits, minimal customs regulations, and duty-free tax incentives, etc. Materials are brought into EPZ for production and the final products are exported directly to international manufacturing clients in the U.S. and other countries without entering the markets of the producing country.

ORIGINAL EQUIPMENT MANUFACTURING (OEM)

An OEM product is a product made entirely according to the buyer's product specification. For example, any product with a customized design, material, dimensions, functions, or even colors can be classified as OEM. Thus, this model involves the sourcing of raw materials and production of the item. Because the sourcing, production, and distribution at the OEM level is more involved than CMT manufacturing, there is also a need for management talent to support production, supervision, logistics, and procurement during this stage. Thus, this is a level up the value chain from CMT and requires a slightly more advanced level of talent.

ORIGINAL DESIGN MANUFACTURING (ODM)

This level encompasses CMT and OEM while also assuming the responsibilities of garment design. Thus, while OEM necessitates producing the design supplied by the buyer, ODM products are primarily the result of the supplier's own design or R&D team. However, they do not sell directly to the market.

The design aspect of production is one of the more profitable tasks. It requires that the ODM factory has access to talent with technical design skills and some knowledge of market trends and forecasting. A good example of ODM products are private labels created by independent suppliers and manufacturers for clients such as fashion retailers.

ORIGINAL BRAND MANUFACTURING (OBM)

At this level it is a company that retails its own branded products that are either the entire products or component parts produced by a second company. Factories take on the functions of design, assembly, finishing, distribution, planning, and general management as well as selling the goods under their own brand name in order to add value. This is the highest value-added segment of the apparel manufacturing chain.

VALUE CHAIN MANAGEMENT (VCM)

Value chain (VC) and VCM are two other terms that are sometimes confused with supply chain (SC) and SCM and are occasionally used interchangeably. However, it is best to see both processes as parallels and concurrent with different perspectives rather than being interchangeable. The supply chain generally looks at the parts or materials that go into a product, as it is manufactured, and the transportation logistics of getting it from one factory to the other and then to the store. On the other hand, the value chain takes into consideration *contributions* such as product design, research and development, advertising, and marketing activities which add value to what is being produced from the consumer perspective. Even the work of lawyers, bankers, accountants, and IT experts who help make a product possible could be part of the VC. Thus, the key element in VCM is *"value creation"* to the end-user who is the consumer and the main purpose of the VC is to create value that exceeds the cost of providing the product or service and generates a profit margin.

This is why many see VC as a process moving in an opposite track than SC. To clarify, assume that we start the garment production process from point A on the left side of a spectrum where we start with a design and then move step by step, stage by stage until the product is complete at point Z on the right side of the spectrum where it is ready to get sold to the consumer. Following the garment process from point A where it was a sketch to point Z where it is a completed garment ready to be sold is the SC focus and approach. However, from a VC perspective, when you look at the process you start from point Z meaning you first examine what represents value to the consumer, what he/she needs, what makes him/her happy and thus willing to pay for the product. By identifying what is of value to the consumer you can then trace the process as it builds up and determines which activities would help generate this value while the product is moving across the SC (i.e. you examine what needs to be done while the product is moving through the supply chain that can add and create the value the customer is looking for and will entice him to buy this product). And thus, the VC ensures that a product has a competitive advantage, through which a company can beat its competitors along with fulfilling customer preferences. And VCM focuses on managing those activities that would eventually generate this value.

Let us take a couple of clarifying examples:

1. A certain production and assembly stage can be done manually, and the piece would indeed be ready for the next stage in the supply chain to take and add to it. However, if the same activity is done with a technologically innovative tool it could be done more efficiently, accurately, and faster, thus adding more value to the process. In both cases, the activity is completed, and the supply chain is moving, however, innovation added a new level of value to the process and the end consumer will be ready to pay for that perceived value. That is why technology is something that could support every stage in the chain and make it get done better and faster and thus adding value to the consumer.

2. A finished product can be put in a retail outlet waiting to be seen by a customer until it is finally purchased. This would have completed the supply chain activities successfully. However, the fact that products are produced doesn't automatically mean that there are people willing to purchase them.

This is where marketing and sales come into place. It is the job of marketers and sales agents to make sure that potential customers are aware of the product and are seriously considering purchasing them. Activities associated with marketing and sales are therefore considered primary activities within the value chain as well, since they add an element that would make the product more *valuable and meaningful* to the consumer.

3. Walmart is constantly performing value chain analysis in order to keep costs low for its customers. From regularly evaluating suppliers and integrating in-store and online shopping experiences to being innovative in order to differentiate itself. Walmart is driven by its commitment to creating value for its customers by helping people save money. And thus, cutting cost through every step of the supply chain is the focus of its VCM.

SCM vs. VCM

Based on our discussion we can summarize the difference between the two concepts as follows:

- They are parallel activities that look at the same process but from two different perspectives.

- *Supply chain* is the interconnection of all the functions that starts from the manufacturing of raw material into the finished product and ends when the product reaches the final customer. It encompasses the flow and storage of the raw material, semi-finished goods, and the finished goods from point of origin to their final destination, i.e. consumption. The process which plans and controls the supply chain operations is known as supply chain management. It is a cross-functional system that manages the movement of raw material within the organization and the movement of finished goods out of the firm along with full customer satisfaction side by side.

- *Value chain*, on the other hand, is a set of activities that focuses on creating or adding value to the product at every single step by designing, producing, and delivering a quality product to the customer. Accordingly, value chain is a way of getting a competitive advantage, through which a company can beat its competitors along with fulfilling customer requirements.

- The difference in perspective between SCM and VCM has another significant implication from a management perspective. As SCM monitors the steps the garment takes from conception to final product, by moving from one stage and supplier to another, it becomes interested in ensuring that this process and garment progression is done efficiently and in a cost-effective manner. This is why SCM is considered an *operation management* activity because there is a focus on steps, logistics, and cost of goods. On the other hand, for VCM the main focus is *value* in the consumer's mind and thus managing the creation of value is the key. Accordingly, VCM is more of a *business management* discipline than a production and operations one.

Porter's Value Chain Analysis Model

The idea of the value chain is based on the idea of seeing a manufacturing (or service) organization as a system, made up of subsystems each with inputs, transformation processes, and outputs. Inputs, transformation processes, and outputs involve the acquisition and consumption of resources, money, labor, materials, equipment, buildings, land, administration, and management. Thus, how value chain activities are carried out determines costs and affects profits. According to Porter's model, the activities involved can be classified generally as either *primary or support* activities (Figure 2.2).[4] The primary activities are:

1. *Inbound Logistics.* These involve relationships with suppliers and include all the activities required to receive, store, and disseminate inputs.

2. *Operations.* These are all the activities required to transform inputs into outputs (products and services).

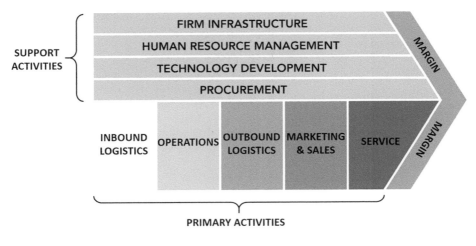

Figure 2.2 Porter's Value Chain.

Created by Author.

3. *Outbound Logistics.* These include all the activities required to collect, store, and distribute the output.

4. *Marketing and Sales.* These are activities that inform buyers about products and services, induce buyers to purchase them, and facilitate their purchase.

5. *Service.* This includes all the activities required to keep the product or service working effectively for the buyer after it is sold and delivered.

As you may have noticed, these activities roughly follow the logical sequence of events and steps in the supply chain: buying materials and components, assembling the product, distributing the product through retailers and wholesalers, marketing and promoting the product, servicing the product after sale, and accepting returns.

In order to help streamline these five primary activities, Porter suggests that the value chain also requires a series of *support activities* which are:

1. *Procurement.* Responsible for the acquisition of inputs, or resources, for the firm.

2. *Human Resource Management.* Consists of all activities involved in recruiting, hiring, training, developing, compensating, and (if necessary) dismissing or laying- off personnel.

3. *Technological Development.* Pertains to the equipment, hardware, software, procedures, and technical knowledge brought to bear in the firm's transformation of inputs into outputs.

4. *Infrastructure.* Serves the company's needs and ties its various parts together, it consists of functions or departments such as accounting, legal, finance, planning, public affairs, government relations, quality assurance, and general management.

Although value activities are the building blocks of competitive advantage, the value chain is not a collection of independent activities. Rather, it is a system of interdependent activities that are related by linkages within the value chain. Decisions made in one value activity (e.g. procurement) may affect another value activity (e.g. operations). Since procurement has the responsibility over the quality of the purchased inputs, it will probably affect the production costs (operations), inspection costs (operations) and eventually even the product quality. In addition, a good working automated phone menu for

Design ➝ Procurement ➝ Manufacturing ➝ Distribution and Logistics ➝ Sales

Figure 2.3 Fashion Value Chain.

Created by Author.

customers (technology development) will allow customers to reach the right support assistant faster (service). Clear communication between and coordination across value chain activities are therefore just as important as the activities itself. Consequently, a company also needs to optimize these linkages in order to achieve a competitive advantage.

Applying Porter's model to the fashion industry, we can envision the fashion industry's value chain to be expressed as follows (Figure 2.3):

- *Design (equivalent to Inbound Logistics)* specifies the look of the product

- *Procurement (another element of Inbound Logistics)* acquires the materials needed to make the product

- *Manufacturing (equivalent to Operations)* manufactures the product

- *Distribution and logistics (equivalent to Output Logistics)* distributes the manufactured goods to the appropriate warehouses or stores

- *Sales (equivalent to Marketing and Sales)* manages the sales process, including merchandising the product and managing the shopping environment; market the product

- *Service (equivalent to Service)* manages customer service, return policies and warranties, etc.

These activities are supported by effective HRM and IT departments, as support activities, to ensure better and effective results.

SIGNIFICANT FASHION MODELS IMPACTING THE SUPPLY AND VALUE CHAINS

The fashion industry is a fast-paced dynamic industry that is consistently evolving. As one of the leading industries in the world, it progresses into different and new mutations and formats in response to face fast- changing economic and social developments as well as the ever-evolving buying habits of its diverse customers. As a result, new business models continuously develop in order to meet these challenges and new realities. We will focus here on some of these models and business trends that have recently been impactful within the industry and had a clear imprint on the fashion supply and value chains.

The Fashion Conglomerates Model

Since the mid-1990s the luxury fashion segment has witnessed a number of acquisitions that led to the rise of multi-brand fashion conglomerates that currently dominate and define the luxury segment. The major conglomerates today are:

- *LVMH (Louis Vuitton Moët Hennessy)*. The French multinational luxury conglomerate was formed in 1987. It is the only group that is present in all five major sectors of the luxury market: wines and spirits, fashion and leather goods, perfumes and cosmetics, watches and jewelry, and selective retailing. LVMH fashion brands include Louis Vuitton, Christian Dior, Celine, Fendi, and Givenchy among others.

- *KERING*. The group was initially created in 1963, however, its first strategic move into diversification and specialized retail distribution came in 1990. Its focus then shifted to the luxury industry in the late 1990s acquiring the French luxury retail chain Le Printemps. Currently, Kering is a global luxury group composed of iconic brands such as: Saint Laurent, Balenciaga, Bottega Veneta, and Gucci among others.

- *RICHEMONT.* This Switzerland-based luxury goods holding company founded in 1988 owns several luxury brands such as: Chloe, Dunhill and Net-A-Porter e-commerce site.

- *PRADA.* The Italian luxury fashion house is a smaller conglomerate that owns fashion and shoe brands of Prada, Miu Miu, and Church's.

- *CAPRI.* The trend towards the creation of conglomerates seems to be going strong. In recent years, we have witnessed Capri holdings expand to include Michael Kors and other brands such as Jimmy Choo and Italian luxury brand Versace.

It is important to mention that conglomerates are not exclusive to the luxury segment. PVH Corp., formerly known as the Phillips-Van Heusen Corporation, is an American clothing company founded in 1881. It is one of the largest global apparel companies and owns mass-market mega brands such as Calvin Klein, Tommy Hilfiger, Van Heusen, IZOD, and Arrow among others. Also, VF Corporation formed in 1899 currently owns Timberland, The North Face, Lee, and Wrangler among other brands.

IMPACT OF FASHION CONGLOMERATES

- Conglomerates have proven to be a key factor for diversifying within the same segment (e.g. luxury) and thus taking advantage of economies of scale (*lowering cost by increasing production due to fixed cost being distributed across more produced pieces*), centralization of capabilities (e.g. purchasing power, technology, advertising), access to an exclusive network of suppliers, access to capital, and access to professional talent, among others. The bigger the corporation is, the more control of competitive advantages in a specific industry it will have. In return, conglomerates have proven to be effective in a volatile economy.

- A great aspect of these corporations is that they keep the fashion industry economically stable. If all of these companies within the conglomerate were to be totally financially independent, some would not be as successful. Being owned by a conglomerate leaves room for trial and error for these brands as they have money to support them when they become less successful. Moreover, since the conglomerates are so influential, brands that have started flatlining can easily be rebooted and brought back to life.

- Since the conglomerates fully own their brands, they have the final say over everything that relates to each brand including its creative direction as they decide on who becomes the creative director of each one. These luxury brand designers are usually the trendsetters whose ideas are copied by the rest of the industry. Thus, these conglomerates basically exert some control over the entire fashion industry as these brands are looked up to by other brands within and out of the luxury fashion industry.

The Fast Fashion Model

The fast fashion model relies on the ability to bring things to market fast and as responsive to fashion trends as possible. Their value proposition is to offer a flow delivery of new fashionable merchandise fast, regularly, and at affordable prices (e.g. Zara, H&M, Uniqlo, and Top Shop). Thus, it is based on reducing the time cycles from production to consumption such that consumers engage in more cycles in any time period. This can only be achieved by being vertically integrated (i.e. performing most or all activities within the supply chain by themselves and in their facilities and outlets). Traditionally, the mass-market is known for being low price and less trendy, but this model has changed this perception by being affordable but trendy. They are still not trendsetters but can be described as trend responsive.

The fast fashion model is a good example of benefits from innovations that support the apparel value chain because it was technology that enabled organizations to implement the principles of *quick response* (QR) and *just-in-time* (JIT). This, in return, allowed fashion companies to perfect the fast fashion model that created great value to the customer by allowing them to get trendy fashion fast and at an affordable price. The fast fashion model works best within a vertically integrated organization as decisions and changes need to be fast and totally managed. Thus, the core of features of this model are:

- Complete control over the whole supply and value chains (design, manufacturing, logistics, and distribution).

- Standardized store concepts and coherence between the retailer and the product.

- Brand collections are designed by their own design teams and sold under the company's brand. However, as trend followers and merchandise-oriented brands, they are not known for producing superstar designers.

- Quick responses to market fashion trends are strengthened by the fact that quantitative and qualitative information from the point of sales is quickly passed back to the design and procurement teams.

- While the fashion industry largely operates on a seasonal calendar, fast fashion retailers deliver new garments and accessories to their stores every four to six weeks or fewer.

- Sales risks associated with fashionable items are minimized by the acceleration of all processes within the value chain and controlled production quantities.

- Higher profitability is achieved by collecting margins normally shared between producers and retailers.

- The continuous release of new, trend-driven products essentially makes the inventory a highly cost-effective marketing tool that drives consumer visits, increases brand awareness, and results in higher rates of consumer purchases.

- The rapid speeds of delivery for which fast fashion retailers are known are largely based on the location of their manufacturers. While mostly manufacturing in local markets, such as Spain for Zara or Los Angeles for Forever 21, may be more costly than overseas locations, such as Bangladesh or China, these higher labor costs are offset by greater flexibility. Items are produced in lower quantities and so no extra inventory is left lying around and subsequently offered up at sale prices.

- However, as fast fashion companies expanded across the world, it was inevitable they would source garments and accessories from factories in countries where labor costs are extremely low.

- Disposability plays a key role in fast fashion. It's not uncommon for shoppers to wear items once or twice before discarding them due to the lower cost/lower quality associated with some brands.

- There has been a number of labor and environmental/sustainability concerns associated with fast fashion due to inferior working conditions in countries where cheap labor is located. On the other hand, the mass production of so much cheap clothing is also perceived as the cause of an enormous waste of resources such as fuel and water, thus raising environment and sustainability concerns as well.

Quick Response (QR) and Just-in-Time (JIT) in Fashion

As we just mentioned, QR and JIT play an instrumental role in the rise of the fast fashion model. QR is a management concept developed for the U.S. textile industry to cut lead times in order to survive the global competition with low-cost foreign companies and to increase consumer satisfaction. It is indeed at the core of the fast fashion business model as it aims to alter business practices by shortening the lead time from receiving an order to delivery of the products and thus increase the cash flow. Companies which reduce the time required across all business processes make decisions faster, develop new products earlier, and convert customer orders into deliveries sooner than competitors. As a result, they provide unique value in the markets they serve and they experience faster growth, higher quality products, lower costs, offer a broader variety of products and services, and enjoy the happiest customers. Hence, the basic idea of QR is to design infrastructure and a supply chain that performs without the bottlenecks, delays, errors, and inventories most companies live with. The faster information, decisions, and materials can flow through a large organization, the faster it can respond to customer orders or adjust to changes in market demands and competitive conditions. It is thus safe to say that developing a strategy of quick response requires both an evolutionary and revolutionary approach. The materials and information flows need a degree of horizontal integration in the supply chain. This requires:

- Management of data capture and flow across the functional boundaries without delay and distortion.

- Linking systems for purchasing, production and inventory control, distribution, customer order entry, and service.

- Shared ownership of information and a high degree of visibility across all functions.

It is important to remember that quick response is not mainly about technology; it is about enhancing logistical performance through the use of this technology in a manner meant to improve the supply chain management of the industry.

Another relevant concept is just-in-time (JIT) (*also known as lean manufacturing*) that became popular in the 1980s. This methodology is mainly designed to reduce the time of the production line starting from the production itself to the response time from suppliers and customers and improve profitability by ordering and receiving inventory of production material only when needed, as opposed to keeping a previously purchased stock of items (e.g. buy threads and buttons, etc. just before you start production and not months in advance). Thus, JIT complements and enables QR through:

- Reducing the need for raw material stocks

- Reducing the space required

- Reducing levels of finished goods waiting to be sold

- Cutting the costs of tying money up in stock

- Minimizing the need for large warehouses and related personnel, thus lowering costs

For both practices to work best there is a need for a reliable network of suppliers available and ready to deliver what is needed when it is needed, as well as good a communication system and an automated tracking and reordering system to track sales and inventory levels, so you can place orders for materials as needed without facing idle time or any holds.

See Now, Buy Now (SNBN)

The traditional fashion calendar is a bit peculiar. When fashion shows for spring and summer are walking down the runways in September and October, most consumers aren't really thinking about a season that doesn't happen for another 4–5 months. They're thinking about fall and what they need before winter hits. This reality led fashion brands to explore a new concept known as "see now, buy now" (SNBN). It is a movement meant to re-think the fashion business model. The promotion of brands' collections on social media during and directly after fashion shows has led to a fashion immediacy among millennials, catering to their need for instant gratification. The SNBN business model was thought to reduce the traditional time-to-market from six months to the day after the fashion show. This is meant to create an urgency to buy now. Accordingly, SNBN could be considered the ultimate application example for both the *just-in-time* and *quick response* models of the apparel supply chain.

Among the first brands to adopt the SNBN business model was Burberry during the Spring/Summer 2017 fashion show season held in September 2016. Ever since then, more brands have adopted the model with mixed results.

MAIN FEATURES OF THE SNBN MODEL

Under SNBN, the alignment, agility, and adaptability of all steps within the processes, as well as quicker product development and a more efficient, small-scale production-oriented, fast-paced supply chain seems necessary to stay competitive. This is how it works:

- Under SNBN, the collection samples seemingly need to be finalized three months before the fashion show for buyers and press to preview in private showrooms or through look-books where non-disclosure agreements are signed. It's a secret society. Therefore, the order process appears to be similar to the traditional business model, where a collection inspection and order placement once done by buyers after the fashion shows is now shifted ahead in time, well before the shows.

- The fashion show's main purpose has changed. It is not selling to retailers; it is showing to consumers (main designer fashion shows are nowadays broadcast live over the internet as they take place) and developing brand awareness of instant availability which may raise more arguments against their purpose in today's fashion scene.

- Goods are then produced, controlled, and shipped directly from the brand to the retailers, where they are received and presented within the store for customers to purchase. As the delivery of merchandise to warehouses for subsequent distribution would take too much time, this step is generally eliminated.

SNBN AND THE SUPPLY CHAIN

The elimination of warehousing activities for direct distribution highly impacts the analysis and reporting of stock as constant and close exchange of information between brands and retailers needs to take place. It is a customer-driven supply chain, based on the collection of customer information and the supplier's understanding of the retailer and its customers.

A lower hierarchy and shorter processes, similar to those of vertically integrated retailers that is created by the model, might imply the cutting-off of certain process steps particularly in collection, inspection, and order placement. Brands can then plan and start production quicker, which shortens lead-times. Hence, a prerequisite to integrate the SNBN model in retailers' supply chains is agility, process shortening, and close supplier relationships. Therefore, SNBN works best for vertically integrated companies that control the entire production process.

For big brands with deep pockets and a mostly vertically integrated supply chain they have both the financial and operational means to pull it off, like Ralph Lauren, Burberry, and Tommy Hilfiger. At the other end, there are designers who haven't yet tied up their businesses in large networks of wholesale partners. They're running small enough businesses that a shift in strategy isn't going to sink their businesses. For mid-sized brands that largely sell through wholesale channels, the SNBN model requires more work to be taken on internally, including distribution and marketing, and such new responsibilities can overwhelm ones that aren't equipped for it. When you take out the intermediary, you are holding all responsibility, so you have to have a big platform that you can market to.

ARGUMENTS FOR THE SNBN MODEL

- Consumers get what they want, when they want it, regardless of any fashion seasonality.
- Allows brands to market to international consumers in different climates and in different time zones.

- It should increase sales because it enhances consumers' choices.

- It fits in with today's e-commerce environment and can generate consumer demand.

- It completes the destruction of the traditional two seasons a year forward-selling model.

- It creates an opportunity to replace the traditional trade show industry.

- It potentially relocates production back to local or onshore regions due to the needed speed and lower volumes, which is supported by advocates of local production.

ARGUMENTS AGAINST THE SNBN MODEL

- The model is based on the suppliers being given the orders months ahead of the catwalk shows. They are sworn to secrecy. This creates huge forecasting risks, particularly for high- end fashion. Forecasting risks leads to substantial stock risks, unless the SNBN merchandise is done on a very limited scarcity-based basis.

- Consumer reaction is unpredictable. Historically, the brand, by selling to the retailer, avoided direct consumer decisions. But under SNBN, the brand is delivering to the retailer what it believes the consumer wants now.

- It effectively turns brands into retailers, with all the forecasting, stock control, and markdown loss risks that retailers have to take.

- Top couture houses such as Christian Dior or Gucci have so far resisted the instant runway-to-shop model out of fear that fashion would become less attractive and less appreciated by organizing it in a way that makes it easier to obtain.

- Real practice has indicated that for SNBN collections that adopted the model, there was very little that sold out immediately. It appears that SNBN only increases turnover for short-production and high sell-through items.

- Traditionally in fashion, brand new collections are a novelty and therefore are launched at full price. However, high inventory levels for these collections suggest that the fashion merchandise is not moving out of the stores, and their high price points still make them inaccessible to the average shopper.

- More interesting, the data shows that some of the SNBN merchandise did not sell out on partner sites until discounted, which hurts profits. This is definitely a valid reason to stop executing this trend. The data also shows the retailers' inability to pass on high costs (like special fashion shows) to its elite shoppers. Most major European designers understand that offering steep discounts could tarnish their brand image, and refuse to participate in the SNBN model that could lead them to do so down that road

- It is also possible that the SNBN model is hurting the demand progression. The model might satisfy the consumer's need for instant gratification, but a good fashionista also wants to know what is coming up next, thus what to anticipate. And in this instance, the traditional runway show is satisfying that desire, which also helps boost demand. The model, in a way, kills the elements of anticipation.

- Retailers' supply chain processes take longer than SNBN allows for. So, the whole system will have to be restructured towards vertical integration, with shorter ways of product and information flows similar to fast fashion. Therefore, parts of retailers' processes will need to be done upfront. This will generate process wastage due to changes in the market or customer demand that differs from the plan.

- Retailers and brands must still plan for customer demand, inventory levels, turnover and budget as well as collections such as capsule collections, limited items, or fashion week independent shows where they would have to adjust space and their budget accordingly.

- The reality is the supply chain just cannot always work that fast. Brands cannot react to either winners (we cannot get any more of) or losers (as we have the stock already) that easily.

- Constant monitoring and updating of sales and performance is necessary to foster quick decision-making, and plans need to be loose and flexible as they depend on the procurement possibility.

- Under SNBN brands are empowered while retailers have less control. This is a major change that most retail businesses have not yet grasped.

- As a new model, SNBN is disruptive in nature and it is very hard to make that mental switch. Fear is a big part of it.

- Keeping up the pace of sales after an initial rush when an "instant" collection goes live might be challenging.

- Many argue that designers need to be free to make last-minute changes before a show and run with their emotions. Otherwise they would be tempted to make more low-key clothing to ensure it will be sold, which would be detrimental to their creativity.

So, it is clear that the challenges of the model seem to outweigh the benefits, which explains why a few brands have either abandoned the model after adopting it or are in the process of doing so. A good number of fashion designers have criticized the SNBN model, mainly for the cost and time scheduling inefficiency.

Tom Ford was probably the first designer to abandon the model. In an interview with WWD (Women's Wear Daily) he mentioned that his 2017 fall collection was delivered in July and August, like most fall collections. However, with the SNBN model the collection was held under embargo (the term used to describe new samples being held in secrecy until the fashion show) until the show went live in September resulting in loss of a month of selling time with merchandise sitting in stockrooms. Examples of other designers who have adopted the model with different levels of success include:

> *Examples of brands that have adopted SNBN in their main collection either fully or partially include* Burberry, Ralph Lauren, Mulberry, Porenza Schouler, and Rebecca Minkoff.

> *Examples of brands that have adopted SNBN with limited or capsule collections include* Michael Kors (capsule collection and limited items), Prada (bags and limited items), Louis Vuitton (accessories), Banana Republic (limited items), and Calvin Klein (limited items).

> *Examples of brands that have adopted SNBN and then abandoned it include* Tom Ford, Thakoon, Kate Spade, and Burberry (potentially abandoning it).

It looks like the traditional runway fashion shows model is here to stay, for now.

Box 2.2 See Now, Buy Now (SNBN)
Successes and Failures

Rebecca Minkoff

Rebecca Minkoff (RM) is among the first brands that has adopted the SNBN model and seems to have benefited from it. According to the company, it has witnessed a 211% increase in sales in the first season it adopted the model and about 264% in the second. In each of SNBN shows it had it would prominently display a few products that the brand thinks will sell best in the fashion-show setting, including a certain handbag or an Instagram-worthy leather jacket, etc. and according to the company, those pieces are always the first to sell out.

In 2017, in order to adopt the model, the company, went into some restructuring, abolishing many positions related to wholesale operations while adding new positions to support making direct retail, both in physical stores and online, 60% of the business. Second, it had to find new manufacturers which could turn around small-batch product orders quickly to accommodate a faster production schedule. Thus, the brand, which was manufactured in Asia, diversified its supply chain and partnered with manufacturers in Europe and America that were both closer to home and equipped for smaller volume orders.

Then the company had to lay out a new plan with its wholesale partners, which accounted for about 85% of sales. This involved an understanding that buyers would see new collections in private showings months ahead from when the collection would then be seen on the runway and shown to consumers. Ken Downing, fashion director of Neiman Marcus had stated that, "The new model is simple and effective. We buy quietly in the showrooms from samples under embargo, and our choices then go into production without the extravaganza of the runway." Finally, the company made sure that all the social media and, marketing initiatives are aligned towards its in-season fashion shows allowing customers to go to its site and buy the items showcased in the show with no delay.

Thakoon

Initially, fashion designer Thakoon seemed to have had the whole system worked out, aligning his collections with an in-season schedule in order to get new items to customers faster. As soon as they saw his new designs on the runway, they could shop them at Thakoon stores and on the brand's website. The wholesale intermediary was cut out entirely. However, in spite of being dedicated to the model and the product prices seeming right, the brand was apparently not yet ready. For such a model to succeed it had to be coupled with strong brand recognition and awareness, and a buzz factor was needed for this to work, and that wasn't happening in a coordinated way. It was a big move for the company that they couldn't pull off. As a result, after only two collections in six months the company announced in 2017 that it would be going on hold. Two years later in 2019, the brand returned to the scene with a new direct-to-consumer business model, offering everyday essentials at easy-on-the-wallet prices. A statement by the designer stated that after spending time thinking about the state of fashion, he "realized that elevated design is not a luxury; it belongs in every modern woman's wardrobe. The result: a direct-to-consumer line of high-quality pieces at an accessible price point."

The new model adopted by Thakoon is built around three main factors:

1. Produce 15 styles instead of the previous 200 runway styles per season.
2. As customer expectations had changed, the designer price point no longer made sense, instead they would offer high -quality pieces at accessible prices (*prices range from $75 to $165*).
3. Focus more on practicality and functionality than on making an artistic statement through his clothes.

Sources

1. Milnes, Hilary. "Three Seasons in, See-Now-Buy-Now is Going Nowhere". *Digiday*. September 18, 2017. https://digiday.com/marketing/three-seasons-see-now-buy-now-going-nowhere/
2. Paton, Elizabeth. "Fashion Shows Adopted a See-Now, Buy-Now Model. Has It Worked?" *New York Times*. February 7, 2017. https://www.nytimes.com/2017/02/07/fashion/see-now-buy-now-business-fashion-week.html

3. Petro, Greg. "How See-Now-Buy-Now is Rewriting Retail". *Forbes*. January 31, 2018. https://www.forbes.com/sites/gregpetro/2018/01/31/how-see-now-buy-now-is-rewiring-retail/#1da33c472c0b
4. Phelps, Nicole. "Thakoon is Back with a Direct-to-Consumer Line of Everyday Essentials and a Bricks-and-Mortar Store". *Vogue*. October 19, 2019https://www.vogue.com/article/thakoon-direct-to-consumer-new-york-store
5. Ryan, Rosanna. "See Now, Buy Now and What It's All About". *Launchmetrics*. September 11, 2017. https://www.launchmetrics.com/resources/blog/see-now-buy-now
6. www.Thakoon.com

CHAPTER QUESTIONS

1. Pick a fashion item (e.g. T-shirt) and track its path from inception to sales doing the following:

   a. Identify the stages and functions within its supply chain.

   b. Identify the challenges and risks linked to each of the production stages and how – as a manager – you could face them.

2. Pick a fashion organization of your choice and see if you can identify its primary and secondary value functions based on Porter's Model.

3. From a manager's perspective why has the SNBN model worked for some organizations and not worked for others? Research at least two brands that have adopted or experimented with the model and reflect on their experiences.

Case Study
Uniqlo: Global LifeWear

Background

Uniqlo was founded in 1984 in Hiroshima, Japan by Tadashi Yanai as an affordable basic casualwear company under the name "Unique Clothing Warehouse" which changed in 1988 to Uniqlo. In 1991, the holding company changed its name to Fast Retailing, Co. and in 1996 it opened a flagship store in the popular district of Shibuya and later in 1998 in Harajuku both in Tokyo. By 1998, the brand became famous for its polar fleece jacket and for not relying entirely on fashion trends in developing and marketing its clothes but rather for focusing on price and quality. It quickly became one of the hottest clothing brands in Japan and the number one fashion retailer in the country. Over the next 20 years, Uniqlo grew to become the fourth largest fashion retailer in the world with over 1,550 stores.

A "LifeWear" Brand

Uniqlo aimed to position itself as the world's only LifeWear brand. LifeWear referred to everyday clothes for a better life, high-quality, fashionable, affordable, and comfortable. The tag line is "simpler made better". The concept is built on the idea that direct customer feedback, based on practical everyday needs, was as important as fashion trends in shaping product R&D and research on natural and synthetic textiles. As a result of its strategy, Uniqlo's clothes are seen as a "basic" style of fashion that is available in a great variety of colors and high-quality materials.

Uniqlo is often compared to big brands in the fast-fashion category, such as Zara and H&M. Yet, while these two brands aim to reproduce the latest couture trends for the masses through their fast fashion model, Uniqlo isn't really in the business of chasing trends. Its staple items are available month after month, year after year, making it more in the footsteps of Gap, the American brand that revolutionized American retailing by making basics cool in the 1980s and 90s. And just like Gap did many years ago, Uniqlo had pioneered the model of "specialty store retailer of private label apparel" (SPA) in Japan, a model that had been successfully used by Gap in the U.S., and adopted later by major "fast fashion" companies, including the Inditex family of brands and H&M.

The constant comparison to Gap had raised a lot of questions about the future of Uniqlo and whether it will face the same fate of Gap, which eventually became a victim of its own success by being in every single mall, in every single town in America, leading to the brand losing its edge and "coolness". And thus, the question remains whether Uniqlo will fall into the same trap or learn the lesson.

Fast Fashion Supply Chain Model: Zara vs. H&M

While the Inditex family of brands (e.g. Zara) and H&M adopt the fast fashion supply chain model, they are still different at various levels. For instance, Inditex is a vertically integrated organization while H&M relies on a supplier network monitored by production offices overseeing a rather dispersed global supply chain.

The fast fashion business model eliminated the tradition model of seasonal collections created by "star" designers well in advance of sale dates, manufactured by subcontractors months before reaching stores, and marketed to the public with heavy advertising support. By outsourcing all production processes to low-cost locations, traditional fashion houses maximized marginal-unit cost reductions, but at the same time increased time-to-market. In contrast, a company like Inditex considered fashion apparel to be a non-durable consumer good with four-week sales periods. That meant that a continuous stream of new products, inspired by the latest luxury fashion and media trends, had to hit stores continuously, on an almost weekly basis, to meet customer demand. And instead of having a single designer, Inditex worked with a large in-house design team that constantly monitored trends to anticipate what the public wanted. In addition, point of sales (POS) data from Zara shops around the world, indicating which styles and products were selling the most, reached headquarters twice a week. Inditex being vertically integrated, owned 14 automated factories, all located in Spain. Production processes related to fabric procurement, dyeing, printing and marking, fabric cutting, quality control, packaging, logistics, and retailing were all under direct control. Inditex outsourced lower value-added activities, like sewing, to a network of small cooperatives located around La Coruna, Spain and in the north of Portugal.

H&M, the world's second largest apparel retailer, operated without directly owning production facilities and with longer planning times than Inditex. The design and planning processes were centralized at its Stockholm headquarters, where over 100 designers worked under the supervision of H&M's head designer. In contrast to Zara, H&M sold basic items of clothing that had a longer shelf- life than Zara's more fashion-oriented items. And thus, while Zara was constantly exploiting fashion trends and rolling out a large number of new in-season designs, H&M sales were dominated by seasonal collections, which accounted for 80% of total sales. The design process at H&M was integrated with sourcing and merchandising, as the retailer outsourced its production to over 700 garment manufacturers and 60 pattern suppliers, 60% of which were based in China, and the rest in Europe. H&M had over 30 directly owned production centers that controlled supplier quality, and a sophisticated IT infrastructure connecting its design center with the entire supply chain.

Uniqlo Global Supply Chain

Uniqlo's supply chain emerged as a mix of elements from both Zara and H&M. Uniqlo was a younger company, and while it took inspiration from its competitors, new elements were introduced, creating a mix of Inditex and H&M operational strategies.

Uniqlo's implementation of the SPA model, mentioned earlier, was based on an agile supply chain, where tight partnerships with a select number of suppliers were arranged in a network-like structure. Uniqlo was initially unable to meet the minimum order quantity (MOQ) of major garment manufacturers and did not have the expertise and structure to source directly from China or monitor quality. Thus, for the first ten years, the company relied on major Japanese trading houses, such as Marubeni, Mitsubishi Shoji, and Sojitsu, to produce its garments at low cost, sourcing materials from Chinese manufacturers. However, in 1994, when sales started to reach approximately $500 million, the company began to revise its sourcing strategy, taking direct control of its supply chain and moving to retain and develop the capability to source garments in China at low cost, as price advantage was fundamental to the brand.

Accordingly, Uniqlo reformulated its overall strategy, focusing on three core objectives:

- Accelerating retail sales growth by opening over 50 stores per year in Japan

- Restructuring the supply chain by bypassing trading companies and thus lowering purchase costs

- Maintaining a high-quality product level

In 1998, Uniqlo established its first two overseas production offices, one in Shenzhen and one in Shanghai, China. The new offices' first task was to reduce the supplier base, bringing it from a total of 120 to 40 suppliers. The rationale was that by working with fewer suppliers and increasing order sizes the unit prices will be lowered as volume would give the brand bargaining leverage. They also deployed an advanced IT system to connect supplier factories, stores, and its head office online in order to improve inventory management and forecasting processes with POS data.

In 2000, the company created the so-called Takumi team to assist suppliers in developing production processes to reduce defects, increase efficiency, and better coordinate the entire supply chain. The Takumi team was composed of veteran technicians from the Japanese garment industry, who each had over 30 years of experience in various specific phases of garment production, such as fabric cutting, dyeing, and sewing, and who were all versed in operations management.

By 2000, Uniqlo sold over 35 million of its affordable fleece jackets. The item's success was unprecedented and highlighted Uniqlo's product strategy of functionalism. Rather than serving the purely hedonistic aspects of fashion, its products were to supply practical performance and function, keeping customers warm and fresh, regulating moisture and dryness. Innovation was key to consolidation of the, by then, new LifeWear philosophy.

In 2003, Uniqlo partnered with Japanese fiber manufacturer Toray to develop a new superior-performance synthetic textile, in an effort to repeat the success of the "Uniqlo fleece" and consolidate the LifeWear philosophy.

To accommodate its success and growth, inventory management became essential. The company utilized a responsive supply chain with a design-to-store lead time of six weeks, mimicking the "just-in-time" supply methods pioneered by Japanese car manufacturer Toyota. And thus, only the inventory of year-round items like jeans, long-sleeved shirts, t-shirts and sweatshirts was carried over. Inventory carry-over for seasonal items was minimized by utilizing inventory pooling techniques, moving slow sellers at one store to locations where demand for the same items was strong. Store, warehouse, and factory-level inventory positions were updated daily.

To better serve customers, Uniqlo, in collaboration with Casio and Microsoft, created a device that allowed each member of the 40,000-strong in-store sales staff to check inventory on hand, prices, and the availability of every item being sold, all in real time.

By 2015, Uniqlo had still more stores in Japan than in the rest of the world combined. Store numbers were flat in Japan, where the company was focusing instead on e-commerce. It opened its first store in the U.S. in 2006 in Soho, New York, and by 2014 operated another 26 stores across the U.S., mostly on the east and west coasts. By 2019 it had 52 stores in the U.S. but far below the initial objective of opening 200 stores by 2020.

Growth in America and Brand Culture

Uniqlo had profited greatly from changes in American society. Millennial shoppers entered a job market with fewer jobs, while carrying more student debt, which limited how much money many of them could spend on clothes. In addition, the new work environment had also changed and became more geared than ever towards casual attire; where a suit was once called for, chinos and a button-down – or jeans and a hoodie – now are acceptable. It was a cultural shift, in which conspicuously expensive clothing fell out of favor.

These shifting social habits created an opening for the brand in the American market, one that a company as rooted in Japan's aesthetic history as Uniqlo managed to fill. Hirotaka Takeuchi, a professor at Harvard Business School who has studied the brand, explained once that clothing in the West is associated with status and rank. On the other hand, in Japan, clothing has traditionally been more standardized. Until the end of the nineteenth century, when Western influence became more prevalent, kimonos were commonly worn by Japanese people of varying ages and classes. The garment would differ depending on the wearer's ability to afford fine fabric or embroidery, but compared with the West, where the wealthy showcased their status with elaborate styles of dress, such signaling was far more subtle. Takeuchi sees Uniqlo as bringing this old Japanese view of fashion to the U.S. market focusing on customers' finances, while responding to their aspirations as well.

But Uniqlo, still has a small percentage of stores in the U. S. compared to its dominance in Asia. It also has less brand awareness especially in non-coastal cities where many Americans may have never even heard of Uniqlo, or don't know how to pronounce it. Other problems it initially faced coming to the U.S. market included "fit", as the American consumer is very different in physique than their Japanese counterpart. Yet for a certain segment of American shoppers; young, urban, professional, and practical, Uniqlo basics have become a cornerstone of their contemporary wardrobe. Partly because of its low prices (e.g. jeans retail for around $40, a hoodie for $30) and good quality. Nevertheless, the brand still has a lot to do in order to overcome all these hurdles and manage growth without losing its focus as Gap did in recent years.

Uniqlo Moving Forward

Fast retailing (FR) is the parent company of Uniqlo, which also operates GU and Theory. The company is considered the third largest manufacturer and retailer of private label apparel in the world and it had an ambitious global growth plan for its Uniqlo brand. In China, the brand's Chinese network of stores had surpassed 1,000 while expanding its online business including a stronger social media presence. In Southeast Asia, it had collaborated with UK-born designer Hana Tajimi to produce modest designs targeting the large Muslim population in the region as it predicted its revenue to double there by 2020. In Europe, the company planned to open stores in more European capitals.

Uniqlo continues not to own any production facilities and outsources all its production activities. Its *Customer Insight Team* is vital to its efforts to improve its products by analyzing huge volumes of requests and comments from online customers. Already, this analysis had helped improve many products such as sweatshirts, pajamas, and body shaper shorts. Going forward, the company plans to produce more products that fulfill customer needs by strengthening cooperation with specialist IT firms to further enhance its customer information analysis capability.

Case Study Questions

1. The case study questioned if Uniqlo will share Gap's fate and eventually stop being cool. How similar and/or different are the two companies' business models? In your assessment will Uniqlo's growth strategies lead to the same fate of Gap? Explain.

2. The case study highlights the strong impact culture has on strategy and managerial decisions. Identify and discuss at least three examples that emphasize this point from the case study.

Case Study Sources

1. Bagaria, Amit. "Uniqlo vs. Zara vs. H&M vs. The World of Fashion Retailing". *Economic Times*. February 10, 2014. http://retail.economictimes.indiatimes.com/re-tales/Uniqlo-vs-Zara-vs-H-M-vs-the-world-of-fashion-retailing/91

2. http://www.uniqlo.com

3. While, Gillian B. "Why Urban Millenials Love Uniqlo". *The Atlantic*. April 2019. https://www.theatlantic.com/magazine/archive/2019/04/uniqlo-millennials-gap/583219/

4. Yen, Benjamin and Davide Lentini. "Uniqlo: A Supply Chain Going Global". The University of Hong Kong ACRC (Harvard Business Press, 2016)

NOTES

1. Burns, Leslie D., Kathy K. Mullet and Nancy O. Bryant. *The Business of Fashion*, 4th ed. (New York: Fairchild, 2011), 93.
2. Ibid.
3. Londrigan, Michael and Jacqueline M. Jenkins. *Fashion Supply Chain Management* (New York: Fairchild, 2018), 29.
4. "Porter's Value Chain". University of Cambridge. Accessed July 3, 2019. https://www.ifm.eng.cam.ac.uk/research/dstools/value-chain-/.

BIBLIOGRAPHY

Books

Ballard, Marcella, Stephanie Sheridan, Paolo Strino, Jonathan Goins, Roxanne Elings, Nathaniel St. Clair and Charles Klein. *Navigating Fashion Law, 2016 edition: Leading Lawyers on Exploring the Trends, Cases, and Strategies of Fashion Law* (Eagan: Aspatore, 2016).

Brooks, Andrew. *Clothing Poverty: The Hidden World of Fast Fashion and Second-Hand Clothes* (London: Zed Books, 2015).

Burns, Leslie D., Kathy K. Mullet and Nancy O. Bryant. *The Business of Fashion*, 4th ed. (New York: Fairchild, 2011).

Chevalier, Michel and Gerald Mazzalovo. *Luxury Brand Management: A World of Privilege* (Singapore: John Wiley and Sons (Asia), 2008).

Choi, Tsan-Ming. *Fashion Retail Supply Chain Management: A Systems Optimization Approach* (London: Taylor and Francis Group, 2014).

Choi, Tsan-Ming and Bin Shen. *Luxury Fashion Retail Management* (Singapore: Springer, 2017).

Corbellini, Erica and Stefania Saviolo. *Managing Fashion and Luxury Companies* (Firenze: Rizzoli ETAS, 2012).

Granger, Michelle M. *The Fashion Industry and Its Careers: An Introduction*, 3rd ed. (New York: Fairchild, 2015).

Hameide, Kaled. *Fashion Branding Unraveled* (New York: Fairchild, 2011).

Hill, Charles W. L. and G. Tomas M. Hult. *Global Business Today* (New York: McGraw-Hill, 2016).

Keller, Kevin L. *Strategic Brand Management*, 4th ed. (Upper Saddle River: Pearson, 2013).

Kunz, Grace I., Elena Karpova and Myrna B. Garner. *Going Global: The Textile and Apparel Industry*, 3rd ed. (New York: Fairchild, 2016).

Leong, Wisner T. *Principles of Supply Chain Management: A Balanced Approach*, 3rd ed. (Mason: South-Western, 2012).

Londrigan, Michael and Jacqueline M. Jenkins. *Fashion Supply Chain Management* (New York: Fairchild, 2018).

Merson, Rupert. *Growing a Business; Strategies for Leaders and Entrepreneurs* (New York: Economist, 2016).

Morden, Tony. *Principles of Strategic Management*, 3rd ed. (Hampshire: Ashgate Publishing Limited, 2007).

Robbins, Stephan P. and Mary Coulter. *Management*, 7th ed. (Upper Saddle River: Prentice Hall, 2001).

Schramme, Annick, Turi Moerkerke and Karinna Nobbs. *Fashion Management* (Leuven: Lannoo, 2013).

Sherman, Gerald J. and Sar S. Perlman. *The Real World Guide to Fashion Selling and Management*, 2nd ed. (New York: Fairchild, 2015).

Van Gelder, Sicco. *Global Brand Strategy: Unlocking Brand Potential Across Countries, Cultures and Markets* (London: Kogan-Page, 2003).

Varley, Rosemary, Ana Roncha, Natasha Radclyffe-Thomas and Liz Gee. *Fashion Management: A Strategic Approach* (London: Red Globe Press, 2019).

Weiss, Joseph W. *Business Ethics: A Stakeholder and Issues Management Approach*, 6th ed. (San Francisco: Berrett-Koehler, 2014).

White, Nicola and Ian Griffiths. *The Fashion Business: Theory, Practice, Image* (New York: Berg, 2000).

Wong, W.K. and Z.X. Guo. *Fashion Supply Chain Management Using Radio Frequency Identification (RFID) Technologies* (Kidlington: Woodhead Publishing, 2014).

Other Sources

"7 Fashion Supply Chain Lessons from Zara". Supply Chain Opz. Accessed July 14, 2017. https://www.supplychainopz.com/2013/09/7-rules-fashion-supply-chain-management.html

"Benefits of Responsible Supply Chain Management". CSR Compass. Accessed July 4, 2018. https://www.csrcompass.com/benefits-responsible-supply-chain-management-0

"Comprehensive Guide to Value Chain Analysis with Examples by Industry". Smartsheet. Accessed September 7, 2017. https://www.smartsheet.com/everything-you-need-to-know-about-value-chain-analysis

"Fashion Brands Slow to See Now, Buy Now". Business of Fashion. February 20, 2108. https://www.businessoffashion.com/articles/news-analysis/fashion-labels-dither-over-see-now-buy-now

"Labor Remains a Wrinkle in Fashion industry's Supply Chain". Rutgers Business School. February 7, 2017. https://www.business.rutgers.edu/business-insights/labor-remains-wrinkle-fashion-industrys-supply-chain

"Luxury Goods Conglomerates: What Are They and How Do They Affect the Fashion Industry?" W-CKD. May 1, 2019. https://www.w-ckd.com/home/2019/5/1/luxury-good-conglomerates-what-are-they-and-how-do-they-affect-the-fashion-industry

"QR (Quick Response?". Lean Manufacturing Japan. Accessed July 12, 2018. http://www.lean-manufacturing-japan.com/scm-terminology/qr-quick-response.html

"Quick Response Systems + Just in Time". Revision. Accessed April 23, 2018. http://alevel-textilesrevision.blogspot.com/2011/08/quick-response-systems-just-in-time.html

"The Benefits of Supply Chain Management". Opentext. February 10, 2017. https://blogs.opentext.com/benefits-supply-chain-management/

"Value Chain Analysis: An Internal Assessment of Competitive Advantage". Business to You. March 15, 2018. https://www.business-to-you.com/value-chain/

"What is the Difference Between OEM and OBM". Accessed February 23, 2018. http://blog.royaleinternational.com/2015/11/what-is-difference-between-oem-obm-and.html

"Zara's Fashion retail Supply Chain Strategies". Supply Chain News. December 7, 2014. https://www.supplychain247.com/article/zaras_fashion_retail_supply_chain_strategies

Adams, Erika. "Instantly-Shoppable Runaways Are Here, But Do They Work". Racked. February 26, 2016. hhttps://http://www.racked.com/2016/2/26/11120066/nyfw-runway-see-now-buy-now-banana-republic-michael-kors

Gronkvist, Fredrik. "What's the Difference Between OEM and ODM Products?" China Importal. May 8, 2017. https://www.chinaimportal.com/blog/difference-between-oem-odm-products/

Harrison, Kayla. "What is Value Chain Analysis?". Business News Daily. August 28, 2019. https://www.businessnewsdaily.com/5678-value-chain-analysis.html

Jackson, Dory. "New York Fashion Week 2019: Rebecca Minkoff Talks Spring/Summer Line and Rise to Success". Newsweek. February 13, 2019. https://www.newsweek.com/nyfw-rebecca-minkoff-spring-summer-2019-collection-interview-1329353

Milnes, Hilary. "Three Seasons in, See-Now-Buy-Now is Going Nowhere". Digiday. September 18, 2107. https://digiday.com/marketing/three-seasons-see-now-buy-now-going-nowhere/

Murray, Martin. "Quick Response Manufacturing (QRM). The Balance Small Business. March 25, 2019. https://www.thebalancesmb.com/quick-response-manufacturing-qrm-2221224

Newbery, Malcolm and Yvonne Haschka. "What See Now, Buy Now Means for the Fashion Supply Chain". Just-Style. October 10, 2018. https://www.just-style.com/analysis/what-see-now-buy-now-means-for-the-fashion-supply-chain_id134666.aspx

Paton, Elizabeth. "Fashion Shows Adopted a See Now-Buy Now Model. Has it Worked?". NY Times. February 7, 2017. https://www.nytimes.com/2017/02/07/fashion/see-now-buy-now-business-fashion-week.html

Petro, Greg. "How See-Now-Buy-Now is Rewriting Retail". Forbes. January 31, 2018. https://www.forbes.com/sites/gregpetro/2018/01/31/how-see-now-buy-now-is-rewiring-retail/#1ce2b0ef2c0b

Phelps, Nicole. "Thakoon is Back with a Direct-to-Consumer Line of Everyday Essentials, and a Bricks and mortar Store". Vogue. October 19, 2109. https://www.vogue.com/article/thakoon-direct-to-consumer-new-york-store

Reidy, Stefan. "Fashion Supply Chain: Supply Chain Visibility to Streamline it". Arviem. February 4, 2019. https://arviem.com/fashion-supply-chain-needs-supply-chain-visibility/

Ryan, Rosanna. "See Now, Buy Now and What it's All About". LaunchMetrics. September 11, 2017. https://www.launchmetrics.com/resources/blog/see-now-buy-now

Silvia K. "The 4 Levels of the Fashion Industry". Be Global Fashion Network. December 11, 2017. https://made-to-measure-suits.bgfashion.net/article/15048/64/The-4-levels-of-the-fashion-industry#popup2

Tarver, Evan. "Value Chain vs. Supply Chain; What's the Difference?". Investopedia. Updated March 24, 2020. https://www.investopedia.com/ask/answers/043015/what-difference-between-value-chain-and-supply-chain.asp

White, Gillian B. "Why Urban Millennials Love Uniqlo". The Atlantic. April 2019. https://www.theatlantic.com/magazine/archive/2019/04/uniqlo-millennials-gap/583219/

CHAPTER THREE
Managing the Fashion Brand

LEARNING OUTCOMES

- Explore the meaning and purpose of the brand.

- Examine the branding process and how to approach it as a manager.

- Understand the concept of *positioning*, its relevance, and its implication.

- Identify the differences between *equity* and *value* and how to address them.

WHAT IS A BRAND?

Apart from its employees, an organization's brand/s could arguably be seen as its most valuable asset/s. After all, the brand represents the purpose of the organization's existence as it embeds its products or services offering, which in return are the direct source of revenue. Thus, it is essential for fashion managers to have a deep understanding of what a brand really is, as well as master the tools to develop, manage, and grow this valuable asset.

A *brand* can be defined in different ways based on your business perspective. For example. it is an *intangible asset* for an accountant, a *trademark* for a lawyer, etc. However, it is safe to say that the most common perception of what a brand is, has to be the one adopted by many marketing professionals which is a brand is a name and a logo given to a product or a service. However, this perception suffers from serious simplification as it totally ignores the role brands play in our lives, as well as in the organization's life. Thus, we will begin our discussion by understanding why we need brands in our lives in order to understand what brands truly are.

Why We Need Brands: A Consumer Perspective

- Successful brands have strong identities which make them easier to identify amongst competitors and easier to remember, which again helps us make safer and quicker decisions.

- Brands minimize buying risks as they make it easier to choose between options. Successful brands develop positive mental associations that help us make safer buying decisions based on previous experiences.

- While brands usually come with a premium price compared to similar non-branded products, such a premium also reflects an inherent value that the consumer expects in return. Such a value could be a rational one as in the case with most mass-market brands, such as value for money, or an emotional one as with luxury brands in general, such as feeling special or accomplished.

- An element of security, as successful brands are consistent brands which manage to always deliver on their promise. After all, if anything, a brand is indeed a PROMISE.

- Successful brands are innovative brands and thus consumers expect top brands to reflect their current and changing needs in terms of both function and aspiration.

Why We Need Brands: An Organization Perspective

- Brands are built on differentiation and thus they hold or reflect the organization's competitive advantage.

- Brands are the drive for economic return and profitability for the organization, either by demanding premium price or generating large sale volumes, which reflects on the bottom line.

- Brands add to the market value of any organization, e.g. Nike's estimated market value of $32.4 billion in 2019[1] is highly attributable to its brand power and name recognition, not to its acquired assets.

- Successful brands have strong and memorable identities which makes it easier for them to stand out in saturated markets. It makes it easier for consumers to buy and easier for salespeople to sell.

- Brands, through their promised value and strong identity, pave the way for consumers' loyalty which is the ultimate reward for any organization.

The Definition

Based on the lists of impact a brand has on our lives it is clear that a brand has to be more than just a name and a logo attached to a product or service. They also indicate that brands are indeed dynamic entities that develop and grow with a significant economic as well as cultural impact on our lives.

Accordingly, we can define a brand as follows:

> A brand is an entity with a distinctive idea expressed in a set of functional and experiential features with a promise of a value reward relevant to its end user, and an economic return to its producers (through the creation of equity). A successful brand has a strong identity (mentally and physically), is innovative, consistent, competitively positioned, and holds a matching positive image in the consumer's mind.[2]

This definition demonstrates a number of essential attributes of what a brand is. And it is the role of the manager to address, develop, and assess each of these attributes:

1. Entity. A product and a brand are not the same, as we will discuss shortly, and in spite of the intangible component that brands add to physical products (or to a service), a brand is still a legal entity. It is an entity because it has potential market value and financial worth. It also can be registered and for the most part legally protected.

2. Value. Any product (or service) is meant to solve a problem or satisfy a need. It achieves this for the most part through the functionality generated by its mix of tangible features (for a product) or experiential offerings (for a service). These features and offerings deliver a set of benefits that are meaningful to the consumer and thus translate into important values. All this adds up to one big meaning for the brand, a core competency and a promise which represents its core value. It is these values that drive the consumer to make the purchase decision and it is this core value that keeps them coming back. Brands strive on their core value. And as they remain consistent in demonstrating this value and in delivering their promise, they gain the ultimate reward, our loyalty.

3. *Identity*. Successful brands have strong identities (visual, audio, graphic, etc.) which makes it easier to identify them both mentally and physically.

4. *Innovation*. Successful brands are innovative brands. Innovation makes the brand relevant, current, and competitive. Innovation also prolongs the brand's lifecycle. Innovation might seem like a contradictory notion to that of consistency which we have raised earlier, but it is not. It all depends on what to innovate and what to be consistent at. A brand must continue to innovate its offerings and product features to stay relevant but with every innovation, it needs to be consistent with its core value and what it stands for as a brand.

5. *Positioning*. Brands are built on the concept of differentiation. They use their competitive advantage to position themselves in the market (and in our minds) in reference to competitors. If they position themselves correctly and manage to deliver on their proposal, they end up holding a positive image and mental association in the consumer's mind.

6. *Economic Value and Equity*. Brands generate revenue and economic return to their creators as well as rational and emotional values to people who experience them (note: we consume products but experience brands). In doing so, brands achieve market share, increase in economic value, and accumulate equity.

Let's take a closer look at some of the concepts we have just covered.

The Concept of Brand Value

If we have two products (such as two dresses) that are identical in design, price, and material but each with a different brand label, would it matter which one you would pick? The answer will most likely be "yes". It will depend highly on your familiarity with the brands and your subsequent expectations. If you are familiar with both or either one, you will pick the one with which you had previous positive experiences or the one you expect would deliver some value for you such as, quality, status, piece of mind, or simply feeling good. If you are unfamiliar with either brand, you may get clues from their identity signals. For example, a French-sounding name may trigger an expectation of style while an Italian name signals workmanship, and so on. What all this means is that when having a chance to choose between branded products there is usually something more than just its features and functions that influence our decisions, some kind of "value" that we are getting in addition to the direct benefits from the product features (e.g. protection, warmth, etc.). That value is an intangible value that was brought to us as a result of brand creation and accumulation of experiences, interactions, and stories we have experience with or heard about the brand. It's this extra thing that we mentally associate with this brand in contrast to the other brands.

This notion that brands generate values that go beyond the direct benefits of their features would also help us conclude that a *product (or service)* and a *brand* are obviously not the same. As a matter of fact, it is very common to have a "one brand, many products" strategy as it is in the case of most fashion brands. And while a product is in the core of most brands, branding, as a process, adds extra layers of benefits, values, and identity symbols that generate the core value that defines the brand in the market and in our minds and trigger the buying decision. So, brands are more than just a product with a name and a logo. Indeed, brand values are harder to develop than product features (or service elements) yet longer to last. A brand usually has a longer lifecycle than its products. And thus, while products die or get cancelled a brand can linger on even if just in our minds and is capable of generating a sense of nostalgia (e.g. Claude Montana, Halston).

Values are emphasized by how the brand behaves and the decisions it (and its managers) makes throughout its life. And thus, competing on the basis of value rather than on just functions or physical features is usually a stronger and more effective strategy. It is easy for a competitor to mimic and copy your product features (and they will), but it is harder for them to copy your core value (and core competency) to a level where they could be associated with it like you are. It is harder because core values, as mentioned, are defined through an accumulation of decisions, experiences and fulfilled promises. Think of Walmart and how it is known for its low prices and value-for-money strategy. Many market competitors could attempt to lower their prices and compete with Walmart, but not many can endure this strategy and sustain it even if at a temporary loss as Walmart can. Yet, even Walmart, and in spite of its ability to compete based on prices, does not really want to be seen or just defined as the *cheap or affordable brand*, but, instead, as the brand that makes its customers' lives better, the brand that stands by its customers, and the ultimate customer advocate. Consider its tagline "Save money. **Live better**". This is its core value, its philosophy, and reason for existence as a brand, standing beside its customers and making their lives better. Every decision Walmart makes from choosing sources and partners, setting prices, and hiring people is to accomplish this value and fulfill this promise. For this reason, competing on core values (and core competencies) is more effective than competing on product values (and features).

Let us explore this point a bit further.

If we ask, *Why would a consumer be willing to pay a premium price for a Chanel dress?* The answer may well be because of an expectation of exclusivity, high quality, excellent customer service, etc. However, in reality, all these benefits should also be expected when buying a Gucci, Louis Vuitton, or any other luxury brand. And thus, none of these values explain why the customer decided to buy a Chanel dress, they just explain why she is willing to buy a luxury dress. There must be something else, very specific to Chanel that made her choose it over other brands. That one specific thing (e.g. its unique sense of French elegance that defines feminism) is this brand's core value (Chanel is indeed the ultimate feminine brand as defined by its aesthetic and history). This dress may be copied by a different brand, even if with the same level of quality and details, but it will never be a Chanel. This is why brands (especially luxury brands) manage to survive knock offs and counterfeiting (even well-made ones) because the brand is not about this product or that, it is about the philosophy, the lifestyle, and the meaning behind these products. It is about their *core values*. Chanel is expected to always show us what feminism is, collection after collection. Rolex is the ultimate business executive watch, Ralph Lauren is the ultimate American sportswear brand, Nordstrom is the reference in customer service and Amazon is the supply chain master and the ultimate buying solution site, (its mission statement states that it aims to be earth's most customer centric company) and so on. Thus, based on the above, we can also conclude that there are two levels of values:

Segment-specific values: Values that are shared and expected by all brands within the same segment such as quality, exclusivity, etc. within the luxury segment. Value for money, convenience within mass-market, etc.

Brand-specific values: Values that are specific to the brand and differentiate it from other competitors within the same segment, e.g. Gucci's Eclectic Romanticism – Armani's Effortless Subtle Elegance, etc.

It is thus essential for the fashion manager to be able to identify the brand's core value. It is a strategic decision because:

- Core values define what the brand is and guide all decisions including its marketing and promotional efforts.

- Core values define the brand's market position and outline its competitive strategy.

- Core values solidify the mental image and associations customers have about the brand.

If we know who we are as a brand and why we exist, then it should be easier for us to figure out what we need to do and where to go.

The Concept of Brand Relevance

Every brand is meant to appeal through its promise of value (rational or emotional) to a targeted customer and a specific segment. Whether the customer responds to the brand proposal and ends up buying the product or not comes down to a number of factors, most important of all is how relevant the proposal is to him/her. *Relevance* is a keyword for the success of any brand as it indicates that the promised value *clicks* and makes sense to the consumer. Some managers, as a result of the brand's successes and popularity, believe that they can sell anything under the brand name and extend it into any category, only to find that customers did not respond favorably. The reason for failure is commonly attributed to the new offering not making sense to the consumer. It is *irrelevant*. This expensive mistake is a symptom of what we may call *brand ego*, whereby a brand overestimates its power, and believes it can enter any market it desires. Or a symptom of *brand amnesia* whereby a brand forgets what it is all about and what it stands for. The case of the Harley Davidson Cologne which it introduced in the 1990s is probably an excellent example of a product that failed simply because it did not make sense nor was it relevant to a customer who associates the brand with a "road warrior" lifestyle – one of motorcycles, dusty road journeys, leather jackets, and boots.

The Concept of Brand Identity

A brand identity is another major component of the brand structure, it speaks on behalf of the brand. It is a visual and possibly audio representation that communicates to the outside world who the brand is and what it is all about. Identity is an integral component of the brand's positioning proposal.

There are two elements or components that form a brand's identity: *symbols* and *personality.* Both work hand in hand and complement each other to form the brand's identity.

IDENTITY SYMBOLS

Identity symbols give a name (and possibly a sound) and a look to the brand, creating a high level of brand awareness and recognition. They are also a reflection of the brand's character and a tool to make it stand out amongst competitors. These symbols tend to be tangible elements for the most part. For example:

- *Name*. A brand's name can come in different styles such as:

  - *Designer or founder name (e.g. Dior)*: More common with luxury brands. Rooted in older days of craftsmanship.

  - *Fake Names (e.g. Alfani)*: More common with mass-market brands to create a "designer" illusion.

  - *Descriptive Names (e.g. American Apparel)*: While more common with mass-market brands, it could also be seen in luxury (e.g. Comme des Garçons which literary means "like boys" suitable for this brand known to incorporate menswear elements into womenswear).

  - *Meaningless/Made-Up Names (e.g. XOXO)*: Usually catchy, fun, and unique. If not being literal, they would give the brand more flexibility to grow into non-complementing categories (e.g. Amazon.com vs. Style.com).

  - *Acronyms (e.g. DKNY)*: Acronyms have a strong graphic element that make them suited for various applications. They could also eventually transform into a name or could be associated with one (e.g. YSL and Saint Laurent).

  - *Metaphoric/Lifestyle (e.g. Polo)*: Seen in all segments. They help define a lifestyle.

  What makes a good brand name?

  - Easy to remember.

  - Easy to pronounce. Important in the case of global distribution.

  - Choosing a name with no negative reference.

  - Names that anticipate potential growth. Designer names (real or made up) as well as initials usually allow for easier brand extensions (e.g. American Apparel will find it harder to extend into houseware than Ralph Lauren).

  - Available to be trademarked and legally protected.

- *Color*. Whether it is Tiffany's "1837 blue" or Valentino's hot red, colors create strong brand associations. Colors have meanings and strong cultural references as well. For example:

Red is excitement and bold (e.g. Diesel m Guess), *Black* is sleek and edgy (e.g. Calvin Klein, DKNY), *Blue* is friendly and warm (e.g. almost all social media sites such as Twitter, Facebook etc.), and so on

- *Packing.* Packaging is a form of visual identity. It plays an important role in brand awareness. Think of shopping bags, for instance, as a mobile form of marketing. Tiffany's "blue box", or Bloomingdale's "big brown bag" have become an integral element of their brand identity.

- *Logo.* A logo is a graphic visual element of brand identity. Just like names, logos come in different forms and styles and can convey specific messages and mental associations. For example:

  - *Monograms (e.g. LV):* Monograms and acronyms are graphic, easy to incorporate in various ways and formats as well as being timeless.

  - *Names (e.g. Chanel):* Names are commonly combined with monograms or acronyms (LV and Louis Vuitton). They are obviously suited for designer brands and imply heritage and craftsmanship.

  - *Signatures (e.g. Salvatore Ferragamo signature-like logo):* This logo style signifies elegance, luxury, and gives a personal touch.

  - *Symbols (e.g. Lacoste's alligator):* Strong graphic element, strong ability to establish mental associations, and good manifests of lifestyles.

What makes a good logo?

- Needs to be memorable and easy to identify and recognize.

- Communicates the brand's personality and provides an appropriate and consistent image of the brand.

- Could be legally protected.

- Works well across media in terms of its scale, form, and color. It needs to be clear enough to work across color as well as black and white publications and formats.

- *Typography.* Typography and the choice of fonts are related to names and logos. Every font style accommodates a set of values and meanings. For example, round-edged fonts reflect a calm, romantic, and feminine message, while bold fonts are masculine (e.g. BOSS). Fonts can also be whimsical (e.g. Betsy Johnson logo) or timeless and classic (e.g. BVLGARI), etc.

- *An item or pattern.* This is a very unique form of identity, when an item or a product holds an iconic status that it defines a brand. Examples include Chanel suit, Hermès Kelly bag, or Burberry's trench coat as well as its famous tartan plaid pattern.

PERSONALITY

Brands are dynamic entities that resemble humans in many aspects. Brands (through their owners) have characters that define how they behave and what decisions they make. And just like humans, brands have personalities too. A personality humanizes the brand by giving it similar mental references such as being fun, sexy, exciting, conservative, etc. And just like with humans, personalities are developed over time through experiences and actions. They are manifested through interactions and decisions made. Just like you cannot truly know a person until you interact with him/her, the same applies to brands. The power of personalities as an identity element is that unlike identity symbols such as names or colors, they are not easy to mimic or copy. A brand cannot "fake" a personality and get away with it because personalities are manifested in an accumulation of actions, cultures, and experiences, as mentioned.

STORE EXPERIENCE

Shopping is an emotional experience that has evolved into a favorite pastime where customers experience the brand before making a purchase decision. The store experience is also sensual. This sensual element is shaped by the physical appearance and feel of the store as defined by its layout, interior design, music, smell, and lighting, all of which combine to create what we may call a store *atmosphere* which is the equivalent of identity symbols for the product brand. In addition, the store experience is strengthened by the brand's personality. The personality is how the store behaves as a brand. This is strongly manifested by its culture and how it is interpreted in policies as well as the way employees interact with the consumer.

So, we can conclude that the shopping experience is a manifestation of the store's *identity* as a whole, as shaped by a mix of store aesthetics or *atmosphere*, emphasized by its layout, fixtures, music, lightning, etc., as well as the store *personality*, which is demonstrated by its culture, its employees, and the set of rules and policies that are ultimately inspired by its mission and vision statements. It is important to remember that service brands, such as retail stores, are unique in having the human factor (e.g. salespeople and how they look and behave) as an integral part of its identity as a brand.

THE CONCEPT OF BRAND POSITIONING

Positioning is one of the fundamental and key concepts of *branding*. **Positioning** is generally defined as *how the brand proposes to be perceived in a market in reference to its competitors*. Think of positioning as the *case for the brand*. Accordingly, positioning is built on differentiation and comparative advantages in order to allow the brand to stand out in a populated market. However, it is very important to remember that positioning is indeed a "proposal" or a "strategy" and in some cases a brand may not be convincing enough (in action and offerings) to be seen as proposed. Thus, managers need to first fully understand what their brand is all about, its core value, potential, and competitive advantage, and who the target customer is, in order to identify its best market positioning and thus, make decisions accordingly. The brand needs to talk the talk and walk the walk. If it does not, then customers will develop a different mental *image* of the brand and see it in a totally different light. In short, while *positioning* is the proposal of how the brand aims to be seen, an *image* is the actual way the consumer sees the brand.

There may be discrepancies between the proposed position and the actual one. These discrepancies can be due to many factors both internal and external, such as:

- Misunderstanding of the true potential of the brand and what it can and cannot deliver

- Failure to live up to the "promise" and/or be consistent about it

- Misunderstanding of competitors

- Misunderstanding of consumers' needs and priorities

- Predetermined perceptions that the brand failed to address (e.g. consumers have a predetermined perception that a *Made in China* product would be of low quality and price which in reality is not always the case)

Box 3.1 Disruptive Positioning

As we have seen, with a product mix, a strong identity, and a meaningful value, the brand can create a positioning strategy that establishes its comparative advantage to differentiate itself among brands in its own segment or target market. However, there could be a second approach to positioning, one which is based on the idea that a brand can differentiate itself from the category *as a whole* rather than from specific competitors within the category. This approach is known as *disruptive positioning* whereby a brand redefines or creates its own category (e.g. Swatch introduced its own category by introducing watches as fashion items while Apple created a whole new segment with its Apple Watch). And in doing so, the brand creates a new playfield where no competitors yet exist.

As mentioned, one example that demonstrates this strategy is the Swatch watch brand. Swatch is referred to as a *breakaway* brand, which when launched did not compete with any traditional watch category or segment that existed at the time. Instead, it created a totally new category through borrowing elements from existing segments.

Prior to the introduction of Swatch in 1983, the watch industry was basically segmented into two major segments: "watches as jewelry" as in the case of most expensive Swiss-made brands (e.g. Rolex) being sold and repaired by jewelers, and watches as "functional tools" as in the case in other cheaper mass-produced brands, such as Timex, sold in department and drug stores. Then came Swatch, and instead of competing within one of these two segments, it introduced, in many ways, a new sub-segment of "watches as fashion accessories". In other words, Swatch did not directly compete with individual brands in any of the existing sub-categories but created its own sphere where no competitors yet existed. It stood solely (for a while) on its own map and by the time others followed, it had established itself as the category leader and benefited from early market penetration (also think of Victoria's Secret in Lingerie).

This model seems suitable for fashion brands because fashion brands are not only highly categorized but highly tiered as well, meaning that in addition to having mass-market brands and luxury brands within these levels or tiers, we can have sub-categories such as conservative luxury brands, trendy luxury brands, sexy luxury brands, and so on. What this does is make distinctions a bit clearer and better defined. It also allows for personalities to clearly and distinctively position brands.

Although this positioning strategy comes with high rewards (e.g. market leadership), it is not an easy task and obviously requires good timing, as well as total dedication of effort and resources, in addition to a good understanding of the market.

Sources

1. Hameide, Kaled. *Fashion Branding Unraveled* (New York: Fairchild, 2011).
2. Moon, Youngme. *Rethinking Positioning* (Boston: Harvard Business School Publishing, 2005).

POSITIONING AND BRAND ALIGNMENT

For a brand to succeed, it has to be supported and understood by everyone who is involved in its existence from top management or the entrepreneur who made the initial decision and financial investment, to the executive managers who will strategize the process, mobilize individuals, and coordinate resources, all the way to every employee who will execute the strategy and finally, the consumer who will embrace it financially and emotionally. Everyone needs to be a *brand advocate*.

Professors Rajendra K. Srivastava and Gregory Thomas have reinforced this notion by referring to what they call *brand alignment*. According to them, in order to deliver a strong brand experience for customers the organization needs to develop strong internal alignment with the brand and internal stakeholders and resources, as well as strong external alignment with external stakeholders, partners, customers, and consumers.[3]

It is an alignment between brand visionaries (managers), brand providers (employees), and brand believers (customers). Brand visionaries are managers who set the brand strategy in motion. They are concerned with making promises of value propositions to the customer which requires understanding customer needs, as well as company and partner capabilities. Brand visionaries are also in charge of specifying what will be done for the brand providers, which include employees, channel partners, and franchisees. The role of brand visionaries is to help facilitate the brand providers' role in enabling and facilitating promises about value propositions to customers. Brand providers are in charge of how the brand is delivered in a way that embodies the value propositions of the brand. In short, it is a matter of aligning strategy with execution. The brand believers are the ones who validate these efforts and support the brand emotionally and financially.

THE CONCEPTS OF BRAND EQUITY AND BRAND VALUATION

Brand equity and *brand valuation* (i.e. *market value*) are measures that estimate how much a brand is worth. The difference between the two is that *brand valuation* (or brand market value) refers to the financial or economic value that the company upholds either through the value of its assets or its market value, while *brand equity* refers to the importance of the brand to a customer and its market share in his mind. Thus, it describes the value added to a product because of the brand associated with that product (i.e. the value of the branded product less its value as an unbranded product). A brand with a positive brand equity has a good chance succeeding when expanding into new products and categories due to the level of recognition and the positive association the customer upholds.

According to consultant group Interbrand, Nike has a market value of over $32.4 billion and is ranked #16 among the world's top 100 global brands in 2019, Louis Vuitton comes at #17 with a value of $32.2 billion, both brands are the highest-ranking apparel-related brands in the top 100.[4] These values reflect more than the value of assets acquired by either company. A great portion of their value is driven by their brand power and the role the brand plays in generating sales and acquiring market share.

Thus, *branding* adds to the economic and market valuation of the organization in many ways:

1. Branded products are more capable of demanding a premium price for their products than similar unbranded ones.

2. Branded products have the potential of achieving a level of market recognition and customer loyalty that could never be achieved by non-branded products. Loyalty is the ultimate asset and marketing goal.

3. The potential of future gains is another important element. As a matter of fact, it is not uncommon for a brand to be losing money at its early stages while still recognizing a healthy market value. The reason is the market expectations for future gains as measured by its net present value (NPV) used to decide if the project is worthwhile (i.e. NPV is the value of all future cash flows over the entire life of an investment discounted to the present OR the value in the present of a sum of money, in contrast to the future value it will have when it has been invested).

MEASURING BRAND EQUITY

An example of a company with a positive brand equity is Louis Vuitton which provides consistent customer experiences; it is dependable, innovative, and delivers on its promises to customers. All of these boast the brand's positive reputation, or brand equity. An example of a brand with negative equity is Pierre Cardin as consumers lost trust in its ability to deliver on its luxury promises as a brand.

So, what generates brand equity? And how is it measured? According to David Aaker, brand equity has four dimensions: *brand loyalty, brand awareness, brand associations, and perceived quality,* each providing value to a firm in numerous ways.[5] Once a brand identifies the value of brand equity, it can follow this roadmap to build and manage that potential value.

BRAND LOYALTY

Brand equity is a function of consumers' loyalty and the strength of attachment they have to a brand. Therefore, it is important to understand the depth of consumers' loyalty to a brand. It is important because it is synonymous with *customer retention*. Market share data and sales figures alone do not provide a complete measure of the loyalty consumers have to the brand.

The following is a list of statements commonly used to determine the depth of a consumer's loyalty to a specific brand:

- I consider this brand to have the best quality of all brands in its category.

- I am very familiar with this brand.

- Compared to alternative brands, I highly respect this brand.

- I have a high regard for this brand.

- This brand is different from alternative brands in the same category.

- This is the brand for me.

Consultant Millward Brown believes customers go through the following stages of commitment:[6]

- *Switchers*: At the start of the path to loyalty are consumers with low levels of loyalty. These consumers switch brands often and shop based on price.

- *Habitual buyers*: Those who prefer a specific brand but can be tempted to try other brands through promotional activities such as a coupon or a temporary price reduction.

- *Committed buyers*: View themselves as normally loyal to a brand and settle for an alternative only if their preferred brand is not available at the moment.

- *Brand loyal*: When a consumer will not buy a product other than the brand he prefers; he is said to be brand loyal.

This progression in involvement by the consumer could also be reflected in what Brown called the Brand's Dynamic Pyramid (Figure 3.1):

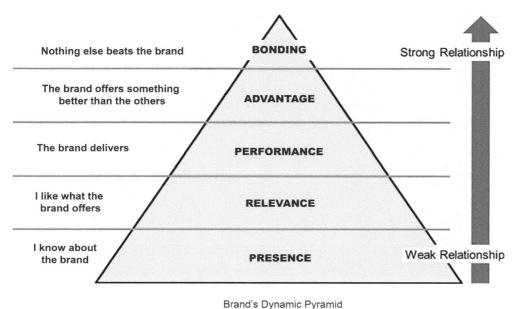

Brand's Dynamic Pyramid

Figure 3.1 Brand's Dynamic Pyramid.
Created by Author.

It is important to remember that there is a difference between *brand loyalty* and *brand preference*. Loyalty often requires some form of *testing*. Will customers pay more for it? Search for it? Resist competitive promotions? In addition, the stronger the degree of brand loyalty, the stronger a brand's power to command a price premium, control channels of distribution, and extend the brand into other categories.

THE LOYALTY MATRIX

The Loyalty Matrix, introduced by Walker Consulting, is a framework that segments customers into four groups based on their responses to a set of questions. The two axes in the matrix represent the two key aspects of loyalty – *behavior* (what a customer plans to do) and *attitude* (how they feel about buying or working with the brand). This forms the following four quadrants (Figure 3.2):[7]

THE LOYALTY MATRIX

Figure 3.2 The Loyalty Matrix.
Created by Author.

Truly Loyal. As indicated, these customers are high on attitude and behavior. They have every intention of continuing to do business with the brand and they have a positive attitude towards it. They are more likely to increase their spending and recommend the brand to others.

Accessible. These customers have a good attitude about the brand but do not plan to continue their relationship. It is a rather odd combination and thus, represents a very small percentage of customers. It typically means something has changed and they do not need your product or services any longer.

Trapped. These customers show every indication of continuing buying the brand, but they're not very happy about it. They feel trapped in the relationship. This is common among customers (people or organizations) that are locked into a long-term contract, lack a suitable substitute, or find it too hard to switch. Eventually, trapped customers will find a better option.

High Risk. As the name implies, these customers do not intend to return and don't really like the brand. Typically, they're halfway out the door and not only will they no longer be a customer but will also talk poorly about it in the marketplace.

This matrix is adopted by many organizations due to its flexibility and because it provides an ongoing snapshot of overall customer stability, and can be filtered by geographic region so performance comparisons can be made by branch, store, product, etc. Many also view the matrix as a multidimensional relationship that evolves over time.

PARETO'S 80/20 THEORY

This theory is very popular among marketing managers. It goes back to Italian economist Vilfredo Pareto who had discovered through statistical analysis of certain social patterns that there is a tendency for 80% of various outcomes to be traced to 20% of the causes. For example, 80% of wealth tends to be owned by 20% of the population. In terms of sales, 80% of sales are usually generated by 20% of customers. Thus, one task for managers is to identify this 20% in order to devise programs and measures to retain, nurture, and reward these customers. It is important to remember that loyal customers are more cost effective than new customers. It is less costly maintaining loyal customers who already know you as a brand than it is to convince new customers.

BRAND LOYALTY AND RELATIONSHIP MARKETING

Unlike in sales, from a marketing perspective the goal is not just making the sale nor is the relationship with the customer over by making one. For a marketing and brand manager the goal is to make a sale again and again. Customer retention, repeat purchase, and eventually, loyalty is the ultimate reward and goal. Hence, there is an important branch of marketing known as *Relationship Marketing* that focuses on the post-purchase stage of any transaction and the possible ways of maintaining a relationship with the customer in order to cultivate, gain, and sustain his loyalty. Examples of relationship marketing activities include rewards and loyalty programs, customer service and follow-ups, warranties, return policies, etc. The internet has created great opportunities for managers by expanding marketing communication channels, embracing consumer diversity, and increasing levels of involvement and engagement with the consumer through social media and live interactions.

BRAND AWARENESS AND RECOGNITION

Brand awareness is typically divided into *aided* and *unaided* awareness.[8]

- *Aided Awareness.* refers to simple recognition. It is when a consumer is familiar with a brand if he/she is given a list to choose from. If a target customer can associate Nike with athletic shoes when prompted with the brand, then the Nike brand has achieved recognition.

- *Unaided Awareness.* Once recognition has been achieved brands strive to become a member of the consumer's *consideration set.* Unaided awareness connotes a stronger relationship with the brand as it is defined by a consumer's ability to name the brand when asked about a product category (e.g., when prompted with "athletic footwear", someone's consideration set may include Nike, Adidas, and Reebok). This is a higher level of awareness.

Finally, value is highest when a brand is the first one that comes to mind (top-of-mind) within a product category. If Nike is the first brand consumers think of when they think of athletic shoes, then the brand has attained top-of-mind awareness. Awareness creates an anchor to which other associations can be attached, as well as a level of familiarity and visibility that helps signal a level of substance and gain commitment.

BRAND ASSOCIATIONS (INCLUDING PERCEIVED QUALITY)

Brands live in minds and hearts. We have mentioned earlier that brands are the collective perceptions of an organization's key constituents (customers, suppliers, investors, employees, etc.) and are defined more by actions and deeds than by words. A brand is how we experience the products and services and the communications around them. The goal of the marketer, then, is to build and maintain a brand through marketing activities that will move target customers along the continuum of commitment discussed earlier.

Brand associations are linked to the identity signals mentioned earlier such as name, logo, packaging, color, shape, product, spokesperson, etc. The ability of any of these signals or attributes to trigger mental associations with the brand once we see them is a sign of strong brand identity and solid associations. These associations play an important role in leveraging the brand power into new product categories as we will discuss later. Brand associations can thus achieve the following:

- Help communicate information
- Differentiate and position the brand
- Provide a reason to buy
- Create positive attitude and feelings
- Be used as basis for brand extensions

BRAND EQUITY CHECKPOINTS

McKinsey Consultant group has recommended five crucial checkpoints towards strong and sustainable brands:[9]

1. *Taking stock of corporate strategy.* What does the brand stand for? How do we aspire to set our company apart from its competitors? How can the brand help deliver our business strategy?

2. *Mapping primary stakeholders.* Who are the primary target groups and stakeholders of our brand? What drives their perceptions and decisions? How do they perceive our brand (or brands)?

3. *Determining value proposition and brand architecture.* Which strengths can we build on to differentiate our brand? How can we integrate the needs of different stakeholders, including talent? Which roles should we assign to corporate, divisional, and product brands?

4. *Clarifying the degrees of freedom.* How does the central brand positioning play out in divisions and business units? Which degrees of freedom apply at different levels of the organization? Which mechanisms do we need to ensure a consistent brand experience?

5. *Laying down the ground rules for activation.* Which touch points are suited to activate our (new) brand positioning? How can we use specific touch points to reach different stakeholders? Can we leverage digital media to create scale effects?

BRAND VALUATION

Brand value is commonly used to refer to the financial or economic value of the brand, However, since we have used the term *brand value* earlier in reference to both rational and emotional benefits (or values) generated by the brand, and in order to avoid any confusion, we will refer to its financial value as brand valuation, or brand market value instead.

Determining a brand's market value is not that easy, nor is there a standardized method due to the fact that what branding does to a product or a service is adding layers of intangible benefits and values that cannot be easily assessed. Accordingly, there are literally dozens of proposed methods to calculate the brand financial or market value. It is no wonder then, that one brand could be valued differently and with a large amount of deviation by two different market analysts or consultants. Another reason for the presence of so many methods is that each one usually approaches the valuation process from a different angle and with a different perspective. The table below initially put together by Tatiana Soto, gives an indication of the various methods available to evaluate the brand. As the table indicates these methods could roughly be grouped into three main categories: *financially oriented methods, behaviorally oriented methods,* and a *combination* of both (Table 3.1).[10]

FINANCIAL-ORIENTED METHODS

These methods focus solely on the monetary aspect of the brand and thus use accounting data as the main source of measure. They are among the most commonly used, especially in cases of acquisitions, licensing, investment, etc. to compute a monetary value for the brand. Each of the proposed financial models has a different focus. For example, *the cost-based methods* sum up all costs that have been incurred by a brand since its development. These costs are then discounted to their present value for the corresponding period. *Profit-based methods* determine financial value based on the brand's potential and thus use the future brand earnings over the valuation period which are also discounted in order to determine the present value of the expected cash-flow, while the *price-oriented methods* are based on the concept that a branded product can demand a premium price compared to a similar non-branded one. And thus, these methods determine the market value by determining the extra premium a brand can demand.

The main advantages of these methods are that they use available and accessible organization data compared to behavioral methods which require extensive and expensive market research to collect the needed data. In addition, financial methods, as they are numeric and formula-based, are usually easier to calculate.

On the other hand, the fact that financial methods take an accounting and finance perspective while ignoring the role consumer behavior plays in generating brand financial value, as well as do not give high consideration to the competitive environment in general, make managers always on the search for other options to get a better picture of how a business or a brand is actually doing.

Example of a Financially Oriented Model: **Licensing Valuation Method**

Brand Finance is a UK consultant company that focuses on valuation of firms' intangible assets. One of its methodologies is the *Royalty Relief Method*, which estimates the fees that a firm would have to pay a third party to license its brands if it did not own them itself. Brand financial value is calculated by

Table 3.1 Brand Valuation Methods

Financial-Oriented Methods	Behavioral-Oriented Methods	Combined Financial/Behavioral Methods
Cost-Based models	Brand Equity Ten	Interbrand Brand Valuation
Licensing models	Brand Asset Valuator	Brand Equity Evaluator
Profit-Based models	Brand Championship	Market-based Brand Valuation
Price-Based models	Brand Dynamics	Brand Valuation
Market-Based models	Brand Potential Analysis	Brand Performancer
Capital Market-Oriented models	Brand Stewardship	Brand Rating
	Brand Trek	Ansatz zur Finanziellen Bewertung von Marken
	EquiTrend	Markenwertmodell
	Equity Engine	Markenkraftmodel
	Konsumentenmodell	Indikatormodel
	Markenbarometer	Semion Brand
	Markenmonopole	
	Markensimulator	
	McKinsey	

estimating the brand's future sales, then, using the royalty rate (selected from a range of comparable royalty rates for brands that have similar brand ratings), calculate the net present value of after-tax royalties. Brand ratings, used to compare the brand to other brands, are derived from the brand strength index, which benchmarks the strength, risk, and future potential of a brand relative to its competitors according to Brand Finance's internal research.

BEHAVIORAL-ORIENTED METHODS

These models stem from the belief that consumers are the main source of brand market value, and they define value from a consumer evaluation perspective and not from a monetary one. For these models, brand knowledge is a key factor to build brand market value. Brand knowledge itself is defined in terms of *brand awareness* and *brand image* Thus, the data used to measure market value is not numeric but data collected from surveys or observations, etc. to measure brand awareness, loyalty, and market share all from the consumer perspectives. It is also common for specialists to refer to things like brand strength, brand status, or brand power when they approach valuation from a consumer perspective since these are terms relevant to the consumer and how they perceive the brand. These models set weights or score points to a list of indicators (e.g. repurchase rate) that measure the brand strength compared to other brands and decide which is more valuable from a consumer perspective. Add up the scores and the higher the score the higher the market value. A major challenge of these models is that they do not consider the organization's perspective. In addition, these strength measures are not easy to transform into monetary terms.

Example of a Behaviorally Oriented Model: The Brand/Asset Valuator (BAV) Model

Young & Rubicam (Y&R), a diversified marketing communication agency, has developed a brand diagnostic tool called the Brand/Asset Valuator (BAV) to track brand equity.[11] Based on this model, brands are rated using the following four criteria:

1. *Differentiation.* To what extent is the brand different and what distinguishes it from all others?

2. *Relevance.* The personal appropriateness of the brand to consumers. Does it respond to the consumer's personal need?

3. *Esteem.* The extent to which consumers like a brand and hold it in high regard.

4. *Knowledge.* The extent to which consumers are aware of the brand and understand what it is for.

Then a two-dimensional scale is used to plot the four pillars and determine the brand's position on the diagram by measuring *Brand Strength* on one axis and *Brand Stature* on the other as seen in Figure 3.3:

Brand Strength: Indicates the brand's strength and vitality which reflects on its growth potentials
According to the Y&R methodology, the degree to which a brand is both *differentiated* and *relevant* to consumers drives the brand's *strength* in the marketplace.

Brand Stature: Refers to the brand's prestige
According to the Y&R methodology, the brand's *stature* is determined by the relative performance of the brand in terms of the *esteem* and *knowledge* measures.

Finally, the brand's power with consumers is the culmination of the brand's *strength* and its *stature*. Thus, the model assumes that these patterns can reveal much about the brand's current and future status as well as strength and equity. Check Figure 3.3.

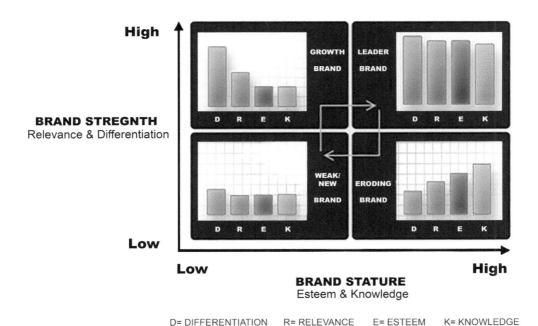

THE BAV MODEL

Figure 3.3 The Brand/Asset Valuator (BAV) Model.
Created by Author.

Thus, based on the model, a brand starts at the lower left box and then moves upward and clockwise:

1. *New Brand.* In this case, both the *Brand Strength* and *Brand Stature* are low. The new product or service may already be distinctive, but not yet known to consumers. Marketing is required to get the brand in the minds of consumers and to convince them to give the new product a try.

2. *Development Brand.* Here the *Brand Strength* is high, and the *Brand Stature* is low. The brand is distinctive enough with regard to competitors, but more awareness needs to be generated. This is done through promotional activities and information transfer.

3. *Brand Asset Valuator and Brand Leadership.* At this point, the *Brand Strength* and *Brand Stature* are both high, which means the highest goal has been achieved. It is recommended for companies to do all they can to maintain this status. A name change isn't a good idea here, and neither is a rigorous change of the product or service. After all, the customer relies on the brand.

4. *Brand Loss.* At this level, the *Brand Strength* is low and while *Brand Stature* is high it is primarily due to a high level of knowledge which means that the brand is better known than liked. This may be due to various factors such as changes in the environment, new developments and trends, and scandals and negative publicity; they can all bring a brand to the edge of the abyss. Competitors have taken over the market and the organization will have difficulty returning to their previous position.

IMPLICATIONS OF THE BAV MODEL:

Using the Brand/Asset Valuator (BAV) can give an indication of a brand's market position. Organizations can create their brand policy by analyzing the environment and implementing an appropriate strategy. For example, marketing campaigns can promote and expand the brand name while improving the market position even further. The stronger the brand, the more familiar it will be among potential customers and the more appreciation it will evoke. This ensures consumers become loyal to a specific brand, as a result of which they will make repeat purchases. They will have a positive impression of the brand and experience with it, and they will likely share these with others. Generally speaking, loyal consumers have gone through all stages and are now more or less fans of "their" brand. However, there is always the danger that consumers will get bored with a brand. In other words, organizations must work continuously on building their brand proposition.

COMBINED FINANCIAL/BEHAVIORAL METHODS

As the name implies these are models that try to take the integral approach of taking both the consumer's as well as the organization's perspective into consideration. These models attempt to overcome the shortcomings of the other two approaches. For instance, the way they perceive brand strength is that the higher the brand strength the more it can achieve financial and monetary benefits such as price premium, higher sales, lower cost, etc. which in return would increase profits. So, the brand's strength from a consumer perspective translates into quantifiable success and financial outcome. Accordingly, data used in these methods are consumer oriented as well as accounting and market oriented in an attempt to transform calculated brand strength (using models such as BAV discussed earlier) into monetary terms. To do that these methods use indicator models and formulas that are beyond the scope of this book, however we will take a closer look at one of the most popular of these models which is the Interbrand Valuation Method.

Example of a Financial/Behavioral-Oriented Model: Interbrand Valuation Method[12]

Interbrand is a global brand-strategy consulting agency. Each year, Interbrand ranks the top 100 global brands. It has developed a model for determining the market value of a brand that separates the tangible (product) value from the intangible (brand) value. The model is built on three pillars of value creations:

1. *Financial Forecast.* Forecasted profits generated by the brand's products and services.

2. *Brand's Role.* The brand's influence on customer choice, i.e. the portion of the decision to purchase that is attributed to the brand relative to other factors.

3. *Brand Strength.* Strength here refers to measuring brand performance in reference to competition to identify areas of highest business impact. A stronger brand generates more loyal customers, reduces risk, and increases brand market value.

The results from analysis of these financial and consumer behavioral measures are combined to reach a single measure that represents the brand's contribution to business results and profits.

Thus, the process begins by calculating the intangible cash flow. Then, the role of branding in the product or service category is measured to determine the percentage of intangible earnings attributable to the brand. For example, if branding is responsible for 78% of customer demand, then the earnings are multiplied by 78%.

The riskiness of the brand (discount rate) is determined through a brand-strength score. The higher the brand strength, the lower the discount rate (to represent the lower risk of a strong brand). The discount rate is then used to determine the net present value (NPV) or current financial value of the brand. In terms of the brand's strength, according to Interbrand, it is driven by both internal and external factors:[13]

Internal Factors

1. *Clarity.* Clarity about what the brand stands for in terms of its values, positioning, and proposition. As well as about target audiences, customer insights, and drivers.

2. *Commitment.* Internal commitment to the brand, and a belief internally in its importance. The extent to which the brand receives support in terms of time and influence (recall what we said about everyone being brand advocates).

3. *Governance.* The degree to which the organization has the required skills and an operating model for the brand that enables effective and efficient deployment of the brand strategy.

4. *Responsiveness.* The organization's ability to constantly evolve the brand and business in response to, or anticipation of, market changes, challenges, and opportunities.

External Factors

1. *Authenticity.* The brand is based on an internal truth and capability. It has a defined story and a well-grounded value set. It can deliver against the (high) expectations that customers have of it.

2. *Relevance.* The fit with customer/consumer needs, desires, and decision criteria across all relevant demographics and geographies.

3. *Differentiation.* The degree to which consumers perceive the brand to have a differentiated proposition and brand experience.

4. *Consistency.* The degree to which a brand is experienced without fail across all touchpoints or formats.

5. *Presence.* The degree to which a brand feels omnipresent and is talked about positively by consumers, customers, and opinion setters in both traditional and social media.

6. *Engagement.* The degree to which consumers show a deep understanding of, active participation in, and a strong sense of identification with, the brand.

The Branding Process

In short *branding is the process of value creation.* Value to the consumer is through the building of equity and economic value for the producer in the form of financial return. As a process, branding is a multi-functional one that transforms the product or service into this value proposal. Accordingly, one big management mistake or misconception is to view branding as solely a function of marketing. While any brand starts as a top management or an entrepreneurial decision, the transformation of the brand from an idea or a vision to a true asset is indeed the responsibility of every person within the organization. It is a strategic decision that involves every department and impacts every decision. Accordingly, the branding process is a roadmap that transforms a product (or a service) from an idea to a dynamic brand, which could be summarized in the following five major stages:

1. The Brand Decision

2. The Positioning Strategy

3. The Brand Communication

4. The Brand Audit and Evaluation

5. Growth or Brand Repositioning

Thus, the process aims for value creation through the developing of a product mix with clear benefits, the building of equity through effective positioning, a successful communication of the brands story and potential, and finally the monitoring and evaluation of the process.

The Brand Decision (i.e. The Vision)

The branding decision starts by recognizing that there are both external and internal needs for creating the brand. An internal need means that it is a potentially profitable endeavor for the organization and would promote its strategic goals and vision. A branding decision, therefore, cannot be made in isolation from the organization's financial and marketing goals. Answering questions like: *Who are we? What kind of business are we in? What are our strengths and what are we all about? What is our mission? What is our vision for the company?* are essential to making strategic decisions that work to achieve your goals. These goals are usually laid out in the organization's *mission* and *vision* statements (discussed in Chapter 1) or interpreted through the owner's vision for the business. Although the brand decision, being a strategic one, starts with top management (or an entrepreneur), we can say that there are actually three major parties that join forces to shape and define the brand. They are the: *Customer, Company,* and *Culture* (or the 3Cs).

The Company. Is the one which pulls the trigger and bears the financial risk for the new brand project.

The role of the manager is to:

- Conduct market and competitive analysis to understand the external environment.

- Mobilize resources to support the brand.

- Mobilize employees, galvanize them around the brand, and enlist them as true brand advocates. Managers therefore need to engage in what is known as *Internal Marketing,* meaning promoting and selling the brand concept and purpose to everyone inside the organization first before marketing it to the outside world. You need to believe in it and live it to sell it.

- Understand that while brand managers may be working under the umbrella of the marketing department, a brand is really a multi-functional activity.

- Understand that brands strive on innovations. Thus, managers need to encourage a culture of innovation and creativity.

- Consider available legal options to protect the brand (at the early stages a brand may just be a name and a concept which could still be protected).

The Consumer. The consumer signals the needs that the brand is created to address. We have also established that it is the customer who actually ends up determining the brand's true market positioning through the image he/she creates for the brand. And thus, the consumer's presence is evident throughout the brand's creation process.

He is the one who triggers the need for the brand to exist and eventually the one to embrace the brand and generate the revenue stream.

The role of the manager is to:

- Research and understand what the customer wants. Market research is essential.

- Identify the value proposals that respond, and are relevant, to those needs and to promote them.

- Engage the customer throughout the process; before, during, and after the purchase.

- Aim to develop consumer loyalty through innovation, relevance, consistency, and *Relationship Marketing*

- Solicit feedback. Consumer feedback is instrumental to the success of the brand (e.g. reviews, social media, emails, surveys, direct feedback, etc.).

The Culture: Culture is the society's personality. It is dynamic in nature and changes over time. Thus, it defines the current external environment that shapes our needs and what we see as acceptable, relevant, and cool. It also impacts laws and regulations (e.g. labor laws). Accordingly, culture has a big impact on the managerial decision-making process, leadership styles, and the management of human resources.

The role of the manager is to:

- Respond and test market trends, technological advances, and cultural sensitives. Customers are empowered by technological advances, and the brand's role is not to fight but embrace them.

- Be aware of current labor laws, educational, and vocational training practices, as well as industrial standards and regulations.

- Embrace cultural values that develop interpersonal trust and teamwork.

- Understand and address cultural differences to ensure a productive environment and healthy social life within the organization, as well as embracing cultural diversity as seen in society.

THE POSITIONING STRATEGY

Based on our previous discussion on positioning, we now understand that positioning is indeed a process and a strategy that is inclusive of all activities, with the aim of getting the consumer to see the brand (i.e. create an image for it) the way the brand proposes. Any positioning strategy must have a clear focus. No brand can be everything for everyone. And as positioning is built on differentiation, these differences need to be relevant and meaningful to the customer, or positioning will be ineffective.

Positioning is concerned with the value creation through the building of a cohesive product mix with a clear set of benefits and a clear identity. Hence, we have two major components for the positioning strategy:

1. For Product-Based Brands: *Product Mix and Identity*

   Product Mix = Product, Price, Service (e.g. customer service), Distribution
   Product Identity = Identity Symbols (e.g. name, logo, color, packaging, tune, font, etc.) + Personality

   Product branding is about choosing a product, defining its features and attributes (its mix), and creating an emotional and functional experience through a unique identity and personality.

2. For Service-Based Brands: *Service Mix and Identity*

   Service Mix = Merchandise, Price, Location, Service
   Service Identity = Identity Symbols + Experience (Atmosphere + Personality)

   Store branding is about choosing a retail model, defining its concept and service mix, and creating an emotional and functional experience through a unique atmosphere (look and feel) and personality. Store brands are intangible service brands.

THE POSITIONING STATEMENT

According to marketing scholar J. N. Kapferer, the positioning process can be summarized in the following four questions:[14]

a. *WHAT.* A brand for what benefit? The brand promise and value to the consumer needs to be clearly identified.

b. *WHOM.* Who is the target, the potential customer?

c. *REASON.* What are the differentiators that support and can create such a benefit?

d. *AGAINST WHOM.* Who is the competition?

This process is commonly expressed in what is known as the positioning statement. Managers should find it beneficial to start the process by putting together such a statement that encapsulates their brand positioning as they see it. A well-constructed positioning statement is a good way to bring focus and clarity to the marketing strategy, because every decision that is made regarding the brand will be judged by how well it supports the positioning statement. Accordingly, a positioning statement should at least cover the following four elements:

1. *Target audience (For Whom?).* The group of customers that mostly represent the brand's target market.

2. *Frame of reference (i.e. your market: What is it? and Who needs it?).* The category in which the brand competes.

3. *Benefit and point of difference (i.e. your brand promise: Why and How different?).* The most motivating benefit that the brand proposes relative to the competition.

4. *Legitimacy (i.e. your evidence: Why we can do it).* The most convincing reason to believe that the brand delivers what it promises.

Examples of a positioning statement:

Example 1: JCPenney
For modern spenders and starting-outs in mid-income levels who shop for apparel, accessories, and home furnishings, *we offer* private-label, supplier exclusive, and national brands, *that,* deliver value than that of our competitors, *because of* our unique combination of quality, selection, fashion, price, and shopping experience. (source: jcpenney.com)

Example 2: Pantene
For females 18–49 who possess dry damaged hair and believe they cannot achieve truly healthy/shiny hair, *Pantene is* a hair care system (shampoo/conditioner/styling aids) *that offers hair so healthy it shines because it penetrates from root to tip* through its patented Pro-Vitamin B5 formula (source: pantene.com)

THE POSITIONING MAP

The positioning map is another popular and effective tool for managers to analyze the market and allocate a vacant slot in it that is not occupied or populated by competitors. To use the positioning map, marketers need to identify two variables or criteria for comparison. These two variables placed on each axis need to be relevant to the brand and its segment which could be *price vs. quality, distribution vs. creativity, or price vs. image*, etc. Existing brands (representing both direct and indirect competitors) are then mapped out in relevance to these variables. Accordingly, the map offers a visual representation of saturated market spaces and potential market positioning gaps that can be occupied by the new brand. See Figure 3.4.

The effectiveness of the positioning map is based on the firm's ability to:

1. Identify a desirable position on the positioning map (the positioning strategy).

2. Develop a marketing plan to capture and dominate this desired position vis-à-vis other competitors in the category (execution of the positioning strategy).

In other words, companies need to allocate a vacant slot on the positioning map that is not occupied by competitors. Companies hope to achieve that by developing their market leadership (i.e. your weapon to beat the competition).

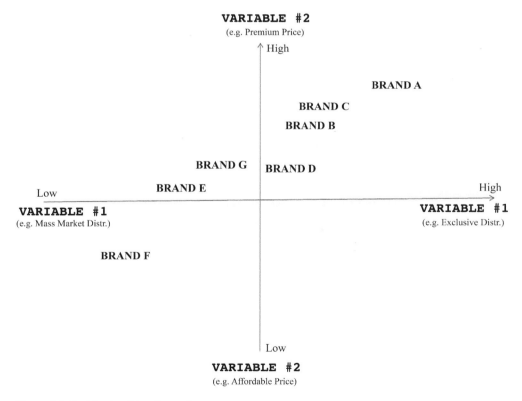

Figure 3.4 Positioning Map Example.
Created by Author.

THE BRAND COMMUNICATION

Brand communication refers to the promotional mix available for communicating the brand's presence, identity, and value through advertising and other channels. Communication is a two-way street. While it is a channel to communicate the brand, its attributes, and values to the world, it is also a channel for collecting feedback and input from the outside world to and about the brand.

In general. communication channels play one or more of the following roles in the life of any brand:

- *Inform.* Deliver information about the brand, such as announcing the launch of a new product

- *Remind.* Make people not forget the brand (common with older brands)

- *Convince.* Attempt to convince people that the brand and its products are better than the competition (i.e. emphasize the positioning strategy)

Communication does not only focus on functional values but emotional ones as well. For instance, most luxury brands' ads do not focus on products or their features, and they almost never highlight prices (in contrast to mass-market brands). Instead they mainly focus on the lifestyle and personality of the brand. The dream.

Thus, the goal of communication is to convey the positioning proposal, polish it, and persuade the consumer to purchase the brand's products. The choice of the right channels depends on many factors such as the brand's positioning strategy, core value, segment, cost, and available technology. Nowadays, the promotional mix options available are wide and variable and may include:

- Advertising (printed or online)

- Public relations (e.g. charity events, launch events, fashion shows, social activities)

- Publicity (promotion not paid for by the organization such as editorials, word of mouth)

- In-store promotions (signage, flyers, etc.)

- Online marketing such as: ads, influencers, emails, newsletters, etc.

Box 3.2 Branding and Influencer Marketing

The arrival of YouTube (2005) and later Instagram (2010) together with other social media platforms including blogs have paved the way for the emergence of a new impactful marketing and communication force known as the "influencers". Influencers are public figures who exert influence on the habits and commercial choices of their followers through their social media platforms. According to research conducted in 2019 by Mediakis, 85% of marketers find that *influencer marketing* is indeed effective (and stating YouTube and Instagram as the most strategically important channels by 89% and 70% respectively). According to Influencer Marketing Hub the influencer marketing industry was worth close to $10 billion in 2020 (up from $500 million in 2015). And while an influencer may cover a wide range of topics, many have become key opinion leaders who are experts on a specialized topic within a particular field such as beauty, yoga, etc. And today many consumers come to these social media mavens for advice, knowledge, and trend recognition rather than listening to companies. An influencer who is an ordinary person like their audience, saying a brand is high quality is more impactful than the brand saying the same about itself. In addition, they are more accessible than traditional stars are. They are a more democratic version of celebrities. Fans see them as their friends, not idols.

Types of Influencers

1. *Nano Influencer.* They are the smallest in terms of following, usually less than 1,000 followers. But they may have the best level of engagement, typically within a local or super niche community. Nano influencers are very selective about the products or brands they endorse.
2. *Micro Influencer.* Has 1,000–100,000 followers. Micro influencers also have more defined and specific audiences and are respected experts in their field. A smaller audience allows them to bond with the people who follow them more regularly (as compared to a celebrity with millions of fans). This makes them appealing to work with for businesses looking to develop personal relationships among their target audience. Their followers are also specifically interested in those niche sectors
3. *Macro Influencer.* Has 100,000–1 million followers. A macro influencer's reach usually spans a broad audience, like young women or teens, as opposed to a more niche segment.
4. *Celebrity Influencer.* Has followers in the millions. They are widely recognized and, therefore, have the potential to be very successful in influencing a brand's target audience.
5. *Key Opinion Leaders (KOLs).* These are influencers who become experts on a specialized topic within a particular field. For example, a KOL might specialize in makeup application, or Bikram yoga, etc. They are seen as an authority on the topic and usually have a large following as well.

It is interesting to note that because nano and micro influencers, have fewer followers than macro or celebrity influencers, and thus tend to have a less diverse audience with fewer diverging interests, they generally boast a higher engagement rate than their better-known peers. This makes them even more suited for *targeted marketing*. They can answer any questions the audience members may have about the products, communicate their personal experiences, and direct followers to the brand's website or customer support team if necessary. On the other hand, macro and celebrity influencers, due to their celebrity status and large following, are well-suited for personal appearances, sponsorships, events hosting, providing coupons, writing reviews, etc.

Forms of Collaboration with Influencers

Brands use influencers in many ways such as:

1. *Brand Ambassadorship.* A *brand ambassador* is a brand expert who has inside-out product knowledge and is a genuine representation of the brand, reflecting a high level of authenticity as opposed to merely wearing or selling items within their portfolio of brands. Thus, brand ambassadors are hired by an organization to increase awareness about their brand. According to Tapinfluence, 71% of marketers see ambassadorship as the most effective form of collaboration.
2. *Sponsorships.* Many influencers have indicated that in their view, sponsored content is the most effective and popular way to engage and interact with followers. Yet, about 50% of marketers share the same view. Example: Amazon sponsored Khloe Kardashian's baby shower.
3. *Brand Reviews.* According to influencers this is the second most popular company content to their followers (even more than ambassadorship).

4. *Affiliate Links*. Affiliate marketing is a branch of influencer marketing that allows affiliates to send referrals to a company over time. Affiliates have dashboards whereby they can track successful clicks, leads, or sales.
5. *Brand Mentions and Event Coverage*. While important and effective, they are the least engaging marketing options and the least popular among marketers and influencers.

Examples of successful collaborations:

1. Toward the end of 2016, the shoe brand, Sperry, began working with more than 100 micro influencers on Instagram to create engaging content for its followers. Sperry identified fans of the brand on Instagram who were already sharing high-quality photos of its products and started inviting these users to develop visual content for its official Instagram account.
2. Gap's successful *Styld.by campaign* featured a number of influential social media personalities from bloggers like *Refinery29* and *WhoWhatWhere*, showing how they incorporate Gap clothing into their personal wardrobes. Users viewing the influencers' posts on social media were given options to "Shop this Look" conveniently located in the caption of photos.

Sources

1. Cook, Karla. "13 Influencer Marketing Campaigns to Inspire and Get You Started". https://blog.hubspot.com/
2. "Effective Types of Influencer Marketing". https://www.tapinfluence.com/
3. "Influencer Marketing 2019 Industry Benchmarks". https://mediakix.com/
4. "Influencer Marketing Report 2020". https://influencermarketinghub.com/
5. "The Wired Guide to Influencers". https://www.wired.com/

CO-BRANDING

Co-branding is the practice of using multiple brand names together on a single product or service. This form of alliance should have potential economic and commercial rewards to both parties. Co-branding agreements should cover marketing strategies, confidentiality issues, licensing specifications, warranties, payments and royalties, indemnification, disclaimers, and termination terms. They also include a lot of restrictions and provisions that regulate rights and obligations on both sides.

Co-branding is not a new strategy but has been a popular one lately, showcasing and communicating the brand in collaboration with another different company thus benefiting from the strengths, reach. and recognition level of each brand. Co-branding can be regarded as both a communication and growth strategy. While it opens new venues to showcase the brand, it also creates opportunities to expand and extend the brand through these collaborations. Indeed, it presents new investment and innovation opportunities through these collaborations (e.g. Stella McCartney by Adidas). Typically, brand collaborations see a more exclusive company hooking up with a larger well-known brand, as Adidas has done in the past, and as H&M attempted when it created limited collections with Karl Lagerfeld and Versace, among many others.

CO-BRANDING VS. CO-MARKETING

Co-marketing occurs when two brands align their marketing efforts to promote each other's product or service. While a hybrid product is not created as with co-branding, a co-marketing undertaking allows brands to leverage their relationships with other brands. We commonly witness co-marketing in the "exclusively at" forms of advertising when both a brand and a retailer, for instance, join marketing efforts to promote an exclusive product showcased and sold by that retailer.

BENEFITS OF CO-BRANDING

Each collaborator hopes to gain something from the relationship without cannibalizing either audience; the bigger brand earns credits and publicity, and the smaller name is exposed to a wider market while both benefit from an increase in sales and promotion. Here are some of the possible benefits:

- The possibility of creating new products that benefit from the strong image of both brands and capitalizes on both brand's equities.
- A great channel for creating brand extensions (to be discussed in a later chapter).
- Benefits from resources and infrastructure of the partner brand in expanding into new markets and segments as well as appealing to new customer groups.
- Enforces positioning and image building through associations with a strong established brand.
- Can form the basis of loyalty programs. In fact, many loyalty programs are built on co-branding and collaborations between brands, such as retail stores' credit cards.
- Provides a new source of financing and income.
- Allows for sharing of risk and marketing costs.
- Increases customers' confidence and interest.

CHALLENGES OF CO-BRANDING

- Lack of total understanding or compatibility between both partners.
- Potential difficulty dismantling the co-branding association; each brand may find it hard to re-establish itself again in the market on its own.
- The possibility that one brand might overpower and overshadow the other.
- The fact that co-branding might work to the advantage of one partner and damage the other (for example, if it were handled badly, the association between luxury designers and the mass-market brand H&M or Target could have easily hurt the designers brands' image).
- Legal headaches if anything goes wrong.
- Difficulty predicting future economic and social changes as well as shifts in consumers' habits and their effect on the future of such partnership.

EVALUATION AND BRAND AUDIT

Evaluation of strategy is an essential stage in any planning process. In management, it is what we have referred to earlier as *Control*. It is the stage where the organization assesses the brand's performance and measures customers' reactions. Based on the evaluation outcome, many decisions can be made regarding whether the brand is on the right track or not. Has the positioning strategy been successful? Is the brand at a stage where it should consider introducing extensions? Or should it consider expanding to international markets?

Evaluation uses quantitative and qualitative data such as sales records, customer feedback, turnover, sales per square foot, complaints, returns rates, publicity, etc. The main goal is to measure the level of success of the branding policy and positioning strategy, as well as the customers' actual perceptions of the brand. Based on the analysis, a brand decides to either continue with or revisit its strategy and/or considers various growth options.

Brand evaluation is also necessary because brands are meant to live long, but sometimes as time passes, managers lose focus of the brand's core values and the main purpose for which the brand existed. Therefore, this form of brand audit is necessary to remind its owners of what the brand is all about, and where it currently stands.

GROWTH STRATEGIES

Fashion brands are an interesting breed of brands in that they are in a continuous state of innovation, transforming themselves at a constant rapid pace. Fashion products usually have a shorter life cycle than many other products, and it is this level of innovation and creativity that brings excitement and interest to the brand. Innovation is always a source for growth.

A few growth options relevant to fashion brands are:

- Operational expansion through new branches or acquisitions (horizontal and vertical integrations)

- Licensing and/or franchising

- Global expansion

- Brand extensions

We will examine most of these growth strategies in the next two chapters due to their importance and for being common decisions to face the fashion manager.

In terms of local operational growth, expansion happens either through the opening of more outlets and branches, through the starting of new business operations or through acquisitions of existing brands. This type of operational growth and business integration can be categorized as: vertical integration or horizontal integration

Vertical Integration. As discussed earlier, vertical integration refers to the organization running operations at various stages of the supply chain. For example, a manufacturer may decide to get involved in producing its own fabrics and thus runs a mill, which is a step commonly located earlier to its manufacturing stage on the chain, so the move is described as a *backward vertical integration*. On the other hand, a manufacturing company deciding to open its own chain of retail stores would represent a case of *forward vertical integration*. A company that does all activities is *fully vertically integrated* such as Zara and Benetton (even though they franchise many of their stores they still own and run some too).

Horizontal Integration. Refers to expanding at the same level and stage of the supply chain, for instance, a manufacturer or a department store acquiring another similar operation. A few years ago, Macy's Inc. (then known as Federated) acquired major department store chains around the United States, such as May Company, I. Magnin, and Broadway Stores Inc., among others. All were retailers at the same supply chain level.

Both vertical and horizontal integration have direct effects on the brand. We have seen in chapter two the strong co-relation between vertical integration and the fast fashion business model. On the other hand, horizontal integration gave Macy's a larger market share and reach, as well as a market large enough to sustain its private labels and thus remain competitive.

BRAND REPOSITIONING, RE-LAUNCHING, AND REVITALIZATION

A brand is a long-term investment with a relatively long lifecycle. And just like people, as time goes by, a brand may get tired, lose focus, or start to lose equity due to stagnation. As a result, the brand does not mature or develop any further. Of course, the same problem can happen at any stage of a brand's life as a result of bad management and loss of focus and understanding of what the brand is all about. Brands, being organic entities, need to develop and stay relevant through innovation and continuous awareness of their external environment.

Therefore, as brands get older, they may reach a stage where they need to revitalize themselves to stay relevant and in tune with their customer. They may need to consider addressing a totally new segment, appeal to a different generation of consumers and redefine their image in the process. Basically, brands have three options to consider: *reposition, revitalize, or re-launch*. Each of these concepts means something different and requires different strategies to be implemented.

- *Repositioning*. A plan by which the brand redefines its market position, target customer, and strategy.

- *Revitalization*. An approach whereby the brand is refurbished and modernized in order to stay relevant to its existing customers with the possibility of gaining new groups. For the strategy of revitalization, innovation is a major tool.

- *Re-launch*. A strategy by which the brand is reintroduced after a period of demise or lack of market interest.

Repositioning: Why would a brand need to reposition itself? Sometimes as the brand gets older, so do its customers, and as a result their needs change. In other instances, the brand may realize it is in the wrong market. The brand then faces being in a position whereby it is losing its market share, and its sales plummet. Thus, it needs to establish a new relationship and relevance with a new group of customers, but to do so, the brand needs to tailor its message and products to match these new customers. One solution is repositioning, which in many ways is a reinvention or redefining of the brand. A good example of repositioning is the case of Burberry (formerly Burberry's) under the leadership of Rose Mary and the creative direction of Philip Bailey. Repositioning is a major task which requires massive marketing and communication activities. It usually involves efforts to convince new customers of the brand's new status as well as erase a fading, most likely not pleasant, previous status (before the Mary/Bailey successful campaign Burberry was not regarded as a luxury brand due to brand dilution from excessive and badly managed licensing in Asian markets and a general lack of focus).

Revitalization: Revitalization differs from repositioning in the fact that it does not necessarily include a repositioning strategy and is not meant to appeal to a totally different customer; rather, it focuses on becoming more current and relevant to its own market with the possibility of attracting more and new customers. When examining the prospect of revitalizing a brand, it is important to first determine what had caused the brand to disappear from the consumers' radar. If it was due to a major failure on the part of the brand, it is unlikely that revitalization efforts will succeed. If the brand simply lost its focus, however, or became irrelevant to its target consumers, there may be an opportunity for the brand to make a comeback (e.g. Gucci).

There are several advantages to revitalizing a faded brand. It is often much easier to create a "buzz" about a brand that is being exciting again. Consumers are often nostalgic, and a brand they recognize often has preconceived positive associations with a simple, happy time in their past. Such positive associations increase interest in the revamping of the brand and therefore boost the effectiveness of marketing communication efforts. Gucci after Tom Ford is a great example of brand revitalization. What Tom Ford did was rejuvenate and revitalize the brand while maintaining its original vision and values. Alessandro Michele's genius with Gucci was building on previous successes by infusing his romantic creativity to keep the brand relevant, current, and innovative. On the other hand, Raf Simmons, in his attempt to revitalize Calvin Klein, during his short tenure took measures that attempted to reposition and redefine the brand which was not the intended goal of the collaboration in the first place, thus the efforts backfired and the collaboration was not successful.

Re-Launch: Many brands eventually die when they fail to remain relevant and updated (or due to the demise of its founder), thus losing market share and consumer interest. However, one advantage of branding is that even when they do not physically exist in the market, they may still remain in people's minds. There is always a level of awareness of the brand, even if not of its products. Thus, brands can outlive their products. Awareness and a sense of nostalgia remain major assets that brands can rely on for a second attempt into a market re-launch. A re-launch could be combined with a repositioning and/or revitalization strategy. A re-launch requires a lot of investment, similar to introducing a new brand. However, the brand's power and awareness may propel the process (or necessitate more effort if it was a negative one).

Balenciaga has been off the fashion radar since the death of Cristobal Balenciaga and the closedown of the house in 1968. The brand was later re-launched in 1986. Through subsequent creative designers and the final ownership by the Gucci Group, the brand has been revitalized into a modern, sophisticated, and profitable luxury brand.

Box 3.3 Raf Simons at Calvin Klein: A Failed Revitalization

Renowned Dutch designer Raf Simons and former creative director of luxury icon Christian Dior was hired by PVH owner of Calvin Klein, with great anticipation and media attention, as the new Creative Director of all lines in 2016. It was the first time since the departure of Mr. Klein himself that one person would be responsible for creative decisions to all its womenswear and menswear lines. However, in 2018, less than two years, the two sides decided to part ways and it was announced that Calvin Klein had decided on a new brand direction different from Simons' creative vision. Analysts and industry observers have worked hard to analyze the failure of the once hyped collaboration and to understand why shoppers did not flock to Simons' collections the way PVH had anticipated. According to Business of Fashion (BOA), the Signature collection labelled as "205w39nyc" sold so poorly in department stores and boutiques that hundreds dropped the line and PVH CEO Emanuel Chirico blamed the designs for being too fashion-forward for the brand's core consumer.

Other factors that lead to the failure according to analysts could be summarized in the following:

- The failure accentuates that Calvin Klein is a largely wholesale-driven company. The bulk of the Calvin Klein business is driven by better-price sportswear and accessories rather than designer apparel. On the other hand, directly controlled retail is the dominant business model for the most successful designer labels and luxury goods companies that Simons was accustomed to and what shaped his vision.
- And thus, from the very beginning of Simons' tenure, there was a disconnect between his personal aesthetic and the needs of a multi-billion-dollar, multi-tiered brand, driven less by high design and more by mass marketing, an area in which Simons had no experience.
- Creative directors are meant to be the face of the brand and hence recognition and acceptance is an essential element. However, in the case of Simons, while known and respected in the world of luxury and in Europe, he was not a household name in the United States.
- From the start, hiring a high-concept fashion designer for a brand best known to consumers for its denim, underwear, and provocative marketing was a risky move. But PVH leadership saw competing businesses like Ralph Lauren stagnating for lack of

creative innovation, while European stalwarts like Gucci soared after radical creative overhauls and clearly PVH had hoped that Simons would do for Calvin Klein what Alessandro Michele did for Gucci, a 360-degree change in creative direction that has led to stellar growth and successful brand recognition. But Calvin Klein is not Gucci , nor is it primarily luxury. The CK Jeans and underwear labels are so embedded in mass culture and distribution, it was always going to be risky to expect a creative like Raf Simons to play in the mass field, an area where he has little experience.

This experience highlights how a misplanned decision to revitalize the brand led to it being an unwarranted repositioning attempt. It also highlights the importance of cultural harmony within an organization, the inherent differences in structure and operational philosophy between mass-market and luxury organizations, as well as the different market forces that drive the American fashion market and how it compares to the European one.

Sources:

1. Adegeest, Don-Alvin. "Raf Simons Out at Calvin Klein: What Went Wrong?" *Fashion United*, December 22, 2018. https://fashionunited.uk/news/fashion/raf-simons-out-at-calvin-klein-what-went-wrong/2018122240701
2. Feernandez, Chantal. "Raf Simons and Calvin Klein: Behind the Breakup". *Business of Fashion*. December 21, 2018. https://www.businessoffashion.com/articles/news-analysis/raf-simons-exits-calvin-klein
3. Lockwood, Lisa. "What's Next for Calvin Kleing Following Raf Simons Split?". *WWD*. December 24, 2018. https://wwd.com/fashion-news/designer-luxury/whats-next-for-calvin-klein-following-raf-simons-split-1202941088/

CHAPTER QUESTIONS

1. "A brand is a promise."
   a. Explain what this statement means.
   b. How can a brand manage to keep up its promise given the rapidly changing nature of the fashion environment and products?

2. Brand Value, Brand Equity, and Brand Valuation.
   a. Identify the differences between the above listed terms.
   b. What is the role of each concept in the brand and branding process?
   c. As a manager how can you assess or measure each of these terms and their impact?

3. Pick a fashion brand and do the following:
   a. Create a positioning map, choosing two criteria of comparison.
   b. Identify and place at least three direct and three indirect competitors on the map.
   c. Create a table of comparisons between your brand of choice and two of its direct competitors highlighting the following: customer profile, product mix, and competitive advantage for each brand.

Case Study
Longchamp: The Subtle Brand

Background

In 1948, Jean Cassegrain took over his father's traditional tobacco business "Au Sultan" established in Paris. In the 1950s, he introduced the world's first luxury leather-covered pipes loved by celebrities such as Elvis Presley. He then started his company, where he began to create small leather goods and eventually expanded the collection to include women's handbags, luggage, ready to wear, shoes, and men's leather collections. In the outskirts of Paris was a horse racetrack called Longchamp, or "long field". Just next door to the track was an old flour mill that Cassegrain used to pass in front of every day. As the name "Cassegrain" literally means "crush grain" (or miller) in French, Jean Cassegrain decided to name his new brand after the racecourse and as a nod to the flour mill. He also used a jockey on a galloping racehorse as the new logo. What originally started as a smoke shop brand would eventually grow to be one the world's top luxury brands. Today, the house is in the hands of the third generation of Cassegrain: his eldest son, Jean is the CEO, his daughter, Sophie Delafontaine, the creative director, and his younger son, Olivier, leads the brand's development of American boutiques.

Le Pliage

The brand's first real breakthrough with women came with the launch of Le Pliage in 1993, the famous foldable, leather-trimmed nylon bags inspired by Japanese origami. Nylon bags were unusual, but the material had proved to be resilient and lightweight, allowing for the bag to be easily folded and unfolded. When collapsed, Le Pliage was no bigger than a paperback book; however, when fully expanded it was large enough to carry almost anything. Thus, it became especially popular among travelers. Longchamp carried six different sizes of Le Pliage. The product became a sales hit and remained Longchamp's best-selling iconic model decades later, gaining a cult following. Distributed alongside the luxury leather bag collections, Le Pliage was much more affordable. Prices ranged between € 55 and € 125 in France, depending on the size, while Longchamp's leather handbags were priced between € 160 and € 870. There was a firm no-discount policy: the classic Le Pliage models never went on sale.

   Another surge in popularity occurred in 2006, when Longchamp's first campaign with Kate Moss brought a sense of modernity to the brand that had a halo effect on the entire product line. So, Longchamp played with its best seller. Special seasonal colors and limited-edition prints were introduced twice a year. Delafontaine collaborated with artists such as Sarah Morris, Tracy Emin, and Jeremy Scott, who put their fresh perspectives on the product. By 2015, Le Pliage had been made in more than 150 colors, patterns, and fabrics, including velvet, flannel, linen, and canvas. Its constant reimagining provided consumers with ways to continuously renew their relationship with the product.

   No one at Longchamp could deny the universal appeal of Le Pliage but explaining how it happened and how it sustained itself for such a long time was complicated. It was a sociological anomaly: old and young, rich and modest wore it, and no one seemed offended that a lot of other people wore the same bag as they did, a paradox in the world of luxury fashion, where uniqueness and exclusivity reigned. Indeed, a word often used to describe Le Pliage was "democratic", as the product line did not exclude anybody, making it all the more difficult to pinpoint the typical Le Pliage customer or use occasion. And while Longchamp associates its successes with its quality, many analysts attribute it to its utilitarian value; its simplicity, practicality, sturdiness, and lightness, as well as for its non-utilitarian values; its stylishness, timelessness, luxury, discretion, whimsy, and elegance. It addressed existential values (needs for identity, differentiation, and travel), while at the same time delivering against non-existential values (its high quality-to-price ratio, accessibility, and innovation).

A Lifestyle Brand

While Longchamp had ready-to-wear collections for many years, the bags remained the input to the creation of their ready-to-wear collections. At Longchamp, the ready-to-wear was the accessory, not the bag. However, under the artistic direction of Delafontaine evolved into a true lifestyle brand expanding its ready-to-wear with a runway show at New York Fashion Week making it count among the big fashion brands in the world. And just like for the bags, they were driven by audacity and Parisian elegance, always having the strong and independent yet sensual Longchamp woman in mind.

Despite the success of Le Pliage, the company's long tradition of leatherworking kept the focus on leather handbags such as the Penelope, Effrontée, and Longchamp 3D, as well as Le Pliage Cuir (the leather version) which all became bestsellers. Longchamp manufactures most of its handbags in its workshops, six of which are located in France. The rest were located in China, Mauritius, Morocco, and Tunisia. The workshops produced 90 to 100 different models per season. The company considers this strategy to be a significant competitive advantage. While every fashion brand sells handbags, very few actually make them. The company sees this as a guarantee of authenticity and a manifestation of its heritage. And in 2007, Longchamp received the French "Living Heritage Company" label, in recognition of its craftsmanship expertise and industrial excellence.

Longchamp was also fielding many requests from licensing partners, such as fragrance, cosmetics, and eyewear companies, that wanted to create new Longchamp-branded product lines. Traditionally, the family had resisted licensing in order to maintain complete control of the brand. Delafontaine, claiming that "perfume is not our job", worried that straying too far from the company's leather expertise was dangerous. But others were convinced that diversifying the product offering while choosing the right licensing partners to ensure quality would help Longchamp evolve into a global fashion house and confirm its status as a lifestyle brand. Today, Longchamp offers its customers, in addition to its collection of women's bags, shoes, and ready to wear, a range of accessories that includes sunglasses, belts, scarves, and jewelry as well as accessories for men.

Longchamp prides itself on its roots and in not being cold and aloof like its rivals. It aims to show that European brands can offer something warm and joyful, yet practical, too. Chic and casual cross-generational and cross-purpose bags are a status symbol that anyone can get on board with, even if to some it appears a bit old fashioned. And although the brand had branched into higher-priced leather goods and ready-to-wear its core strategy of pricing predominantly based on manufacturing costs rather than marketing aspirations, has not changed. In addition, the fact that the vast majority of its goods are made in the company factory in the Loire Valley of France seems to be very meaningful to its foreign customers.

The Longchamp Woman

Creative Director Delafontaine acknowledges that the Longchamp woman is not easy to categorize.

She likes fashion, but she's not a fashion addict or victim. She is a real woman living a real life. She is active, dynamic, and takes her life into her own hands. She's several women at the same time; she can be a businesswoman, a mother, a party girl, multifaceted, and multitasking. She needs to feel self-confident. She pays attention to what she buys and likes to find a good balance between quality and fashion. The Longchamp bag is a part of her life. She can wear it a lot, as it becomes nicer with age, and she always comes back to it. She is emotionally attached to it. And while marketing people often classify customers by age or social class, Delafontaine preferred to classify her based on "mood" stressing that she is creating products for different moments of life and for the different moods a woman has, such as feeling sexy, glamorous, casual, or powerful.

Accessible Luxury and the Brand's Positioning

Brands such as Tory Burch, Kate Spade, Coach, and Michael Kors had created a new segment dubbed by many analysts as "accessible luxury" or premium brands, characterized by lower prices and widespread availability in multiple channels. Unlike traditional luxury brands such as Louis Vuitton whose leather bags, can go for over $3,000, accessible luxury or premium brands offered middle-class consumers a taste of luxury at prices that were not out of their reach. A Coach bag for instance could range from between $120 and $700. While the market for premium brands was expected to continue growing, few analysts believe that it is a volatile category where brands tend to gain popularity for a limited time before they expire. On the other hand, luxury brands usually have greater heritage, more brand equity, and are therefore more stable and resilient.

Questions have been raised whether Longchamp should be categorized as an accessible luxury/premium brand given that its prices tend to be more affordable than many other luxury brands, but the brand stresses it has nothing in common with these premium brands. First of all, Longchamp is still more expensive and has a higher cost structure. Second, most of these brands have no factories and thus, unlike Longchamp, their products are basically 100% made in China. And finally, they use licensing heavily to expand their brands quickly. Longchamp prefers to be compared to traditional Italian houses such as Ferragamo and Tod's, which had strong roots in leather goods and family involvement. Cassegrain explained that the main reason the brand was perceived as accessible luxury was only because of Le Pliage's lower price points which put the brand in an awkward middle-market position, more expensive than accessible luxury but less expensive than traditional luxury. Yet, while Le Pliage's popularity makes it likely to sustain a higher price point, the company feared that a higher price would lead to more counterfeit products and would give room to competitors to encroach on its customer base.

Thus, according to Longchamp, a lady who has a Chanel or Hermès bag will never buy anything from Michael Kors, but she is going to be a Longchamp customer. Interestingly, a survey among consumers, found American women dubbing Longchamp as "the little Hermès", which seems to confirm this view.

Cassegrain believes that being a specialist in leather craftsmanship differentiates the brand where its core value stems from its quality artisanship and fine leatherworking history. But he also acknowledges that these values may not be enough to bring customers back every season. Accordingly, he supported Delafontaine's vision for the brand to be a fashion-forward, lively, relevant, and contemporary one that is moving with time.

Nevertheless, its unique market position does make the brand susceptible to competition from the growing flow of cheaper premium brands, all of which are introducing leather bags, especially if consumers do not recognize the brand's superior quality and make decisions solely on price.

Distribution Strategy

Coming from an artisanal wholesale-driven background, the brand found it challenging to balance Longchamp's retail and wholesale businesses. While flagship stores were important for branding, the wholesale business was more profitable than the retail business. Wholesale profitability was higher because of lower fixed costs, but it was harder to manage the brand's image there than in Longchamp's own store network. As a result, the brand decided to be more of a retailer than a wholesaler.

Longchamp is available in 100 countries through over 1,500 points of sale, including fully owned or franchised flagship stores, online sales, and wholesale distribution through department stores and multi-brand leather goods stores. Longchamp's flagship stores are located on the world's most fashionable shopping boulevards, such as London's New Bond and Regent Streets and Paris's Champs-Élysées. Delafontaine brought artist Astrid Krogh, to work on the brand's Champs-Elysées store in Paris, and for the New Bond Street store in London, Delafontaine called on renowned American artist Maya Hayuk to transform the space. In 2014 and 2015, the company opened new stores in Barcelona, Rome, Munich, Vienna, as well as in cities in Paraguay, Peru, Macao, and Cambodia. By 2015, it directly managed 299 points of sale.

U.S. department stores bought Longchamp's products wholesale and sold them alongside other brands, earning a margin of about 50%. Longchamp used a concession model in Europe and Asia, where department stores, for roughly a 20% commission, allowed it to directly manage its own branded shop-in-shop. Revenues in concession outlets could be triple what they were in wholesale outlets. At the concession outlets, customers received better service from Longchamp salespeople and the need to discount was rare, as the company could control pricing. In addition, out-of-stocks were reduced through inventory planning. Longchamp also operated about ten outlet stores to sell off excess inventory at discounted prices. Finally, pressured by its retail partners, Longchamp developed its online e-commerce channel which proved to be yet another perfect channel for selling Le Pliage.

Marketing Strategy

Longchamp had used different marketing campaigns over the years to promote its brand. In the 1980s, the company's advertising focused on the well-bred elegance of the equestrian world, associating the company's products with jockeys and stable boys. This evoked an upscale, masculine world, so later, as it aspired to appeal to women, Longchamp pushed femininity and fashion to the foreground of its communications, with the help of fashion ambassadors such as model Kate Moss beginning in 2006. Longchamp's choice of Moss, while being under media fire for cocaine use at the time, came as a surprise to many especially given the brand's strategy to

Figure 3.5 Longchamp Le Pliage Bag.

be discreet and subtle, yet it believed that at times it needed to express itself loudly. Kate Moss brought a lot of attention to the brand and helped transform its image.

More recently, the brand brought in Alexa Chung as its spokesperson. a globally recognized *it girl*, and fashion ambassador. Journalists described the campaign as vibrant, alive, active, energetic, etc. and one that made Longchamp take on the allure of a true luxury brand. And in order to make certain that Americans were aware of what Longchamp represents in an overflowing, youth-obsessed marketplace, the company enlisted Kendall Jenner to be the face of its Fall 2018 advertising campaign (Figure 3.5).

Questions

1. Identify and explain the product mix for Longchamp.

2. Assess Longchamp's approach to growth and brand extensions. Compare its strategy to another luxury brand of your choice highlighting similarities and differences.

Case Study Sources

1. Avery, Jill, Tonia Junker and Daniela Beyersdorfer. *Longchamp* (Cambridge: Harvard Business School, 2017).

2. Darbal, Anupam. "Sophie Delafontaine is Making Longchamp a Brand of the Future". *Life Style Asia*. February 1, 2020. https://www.lifestyleasia.com/ind/style/fashion/sophie-delafontaine-longchamp-interview/

3. Paton, Elizabeth. "Furla and Longchamp: Quiet Success Stories". *The New York Times*. November 13, 2017. https://www.nytimes.com/2017/11/13/fashion/accessories-handbags-furla-longchamp.html

4. www.longchamp.com

Notes

1. Interbrand. "Best Global Brands 2019". Interbrand. February, 2020. http://www.interbrand.com
2. Hameide, Kaled. *Fashion Branding Unraveled* (New York: Fairchild, 2011), 5.
3. Srivastava, Rajendra and Gregory M. Thomas. "Managing Brand Performance: Aligning Positioning, Execution and Experience". Springer. July 26, 2010. https://link.springer.com/article/10.1057/bm.2010.11
4. Interbrand
5. "What is Brand Equity?" Prophet. September 4, 2013. https://www.prophet.com/2013/09/156-what-is-brand-equity-and-why-is-it-valuable/
6. Farris, Paul, Eric Gregg, Brandon Chinn and Mariela Razuri. *Brand Equity: An Overview* (Darden Business Publishing, 2016), 12.
7. Gibbons, Patrick. "Making Loyalty Actionable". *Customerthink*. January 30, 2012. http://customerthink.com/making_loyalty_actionable/
8. Farris, 11.
9. McKinsey and Company. *McKinsey Marketing and Sales Practice, Business Branding Bringing Strategy to Life* (McKinsey, 2013), 8.
10. Soto, Tatiana J. *Methods for Assessing Brand Value* (Hamburg: Dilpomica Verlag, 2008), 39.

11. "Brandasset Valuator". BAV Group. Accessed November 2, 2019. https://www.bavgroup.com/about-bav/brandassetr-valuator
12. Interbrand
13. Interbrand
14. Hameide, 72.

BIBLIOGRAPHY

Books

Aaker, David. *Managing Brand Equity: Capitalizing on the Value of a Brand Name* (New York: Free Press, 1991).

Aaker, David. *Aaker on Branding: 20 Principles that Drive Success* (New York: Morgan James Publishing, 2014).

Burns, Leslie D., Kathy K. Mullet and Nancy O. Bryant. *The Business of Fashion*, 4th ed. (New York: Fairchild, 2011).

Chevalier, Michel and Gerald Mazzalovo. *Luxury Brand Management: A World of Privilege* (Singapore: John Wiley and Sons (Asia), 2008).

Choi, Tsan-Ming and Bin Shen. *Luxury Fashion Retail Management* (Singapore: Springer, 2017).

Corbellini, Erica and Stefania Saviolo. *Managing Fashion and Luxury Companies* (Firenze: Rizzoli ETAS, 2012).

David, Fred R. *Strategic Management: Concepts and Cases*, 13th ed. (Upper Saddle River: Pearson, 2011).

Farris, Paul, Eric Gregg, Brandon Chinn and Mariela Razuri. *Brand Equity: An Overview* (Charlottesville: Darden Business Publishing, 2016).

Feldwicke, Paul. *What is Brand Equity Anyway?* (Henley-on-Tames: World Advertising Research Center, 2002).

Hameide, Kaled. *Fashion Branding Unraveled* (New York: Fairchild, 2011).

Jin, Byoungho and Elena Cedrola. *Fashion Branding and Communication: Core Strategies of European Luxury Brands* (New York: Palgrave, 2017).

Kapferer, J.N. *The New Strategic Brand Management: Creating and Sustaining Brand Equity Long Term*, 4th ed. (London: Kogan Page, 2008).

Keller, Kevin L. *Strategic Brand Management*, 4th ed. (Upper Saddle River: Pearson, 2013).

Morden, Tony. *Principles of Strategic Management*, 3rd ed. (Hampshire: Ashgate Publishing Limited, 2007).

Neal, William and Ron Strauss. *Value Creation: The Power of Brand Equity* (Mason: Cengage Learning, 2008).

Robbins, Stephan P. and Mary Coulter. *Management*, 7th ed. (Upper Saddle River: Prentice Hall, 2001).

Schramme, Annick, Turi Moerkerke and Karinna Nobbs. *Fashion Management* (Leuven: Lannoo, 2013).

Sherman, Gerald J. and Sar S. Perlman. *The Real World Guide to Fashion Selling and Management*, 2nd ed. (New York: Fairchild, 2015).

Soto, Tatiana J. *Methods for Assessing Brand Value: A Comparison Between the Interbrand Model and the BBDO's Brand Equity Evaluator Model* (Hamburg: Diplomica Verlag, 2008).

Van Gelder, Sicco. *Global Brand Strategy: Unlocking Brand Potential Across Countries, Cultures and Markets* (London: Kogan-Page, 2003).

Varley, Rosemary, Ana Roncha, Natasha Radclyffe-Thomas, Liz Gee. *Fashion Management: A Strategic Approach* (London: Red Globe Press, 2019).

White, Nicola and Ian Griffiths. *The Fashion Business: Theory, Practice, Image* (New York: Berg, 2000).

Wong, W.K. and Z.X. Guo. *Fashion Supply Chain Management Using Radio Frequency Identification (RFID) Technologies* (Kidlington: Woodhead Publishing, 2014).

Other Sources

"Brand Asset Valuator". BAV Group. Accessed October 3, 2018. https://www.bavgroup.com/about-bav/brandassetr-valuator

"Brand Positioning Statements (With 8 Examples)". Merlin One. Accessed September 3, 2019. https://merlinone.com/brand-positioning-statements-with-6-examples/

"Build Brand Equity". Hartford. Accessed, October 4, 2019. https://www.thehartford.com/business-playbook/in-depth/building-brand-equity

"Effective Types of Influencer Marketing". Accessed November 12, 2019. https://www.tapinfluence.com/thank-effective-types-influencer-marketing/?submissionGuid=71bcc9d6-1112-42cc-b7ef-e2a0dc539716

"Influencer Marketing 2019: Key Statistics from Our Influencer Marketing Survey". Mediamix. Accessed February 3, 2019. https://mediakix.com/influencer-marketing-resources/influencer-marketing-industry-statistics-survey-benchmarks/#gs.cwtjta

"Methodology". Interbrand. Accessed February 3, 2019. https://www.interbrand.com/best-brands/best-global-brands/methodology/

"The Style Guide to Missoni, Knitwear Revolutionaries". The Culture Trip. August 22, 2016. https://theculturetrip.com/europe/italy/articles/the-style-guide-to-missoni-knitwear-revolutionaries/

"The Wired Guide to Influencers". Wired. December 6, 2019. https://www.wired.com/story/what-is-an-influencer/

Aaker, David. "What is Brand Equity?". Prophet. September 4, 2013. https://www.prophet.com/2013/09/156-what-is-brand-equity-and-why-is-it-valuable/

Alindaho, Karla. "Object of Desire: Longchamp Le Pliage Nylon Tote Bag". Forbes. June 24, 2019. https://www.forbes.com/sites/karlaalindahao/2019/06/24/best-travel-tote-longchamp-le-pliage-nylon-bag/#7e9ea0ddcf0c

Bhasin, Hitesh. "Product Market Expansion Grid". Marketing91. February 3, 2018. https://www.marketing91.com/product-market-expansion-grid/

Carnrite, James, "What is Brand equity? Definition, Components and Measurement". Study. Accessed May 23, 2019. https://study.com/academy/lesson/what-is-brand-equity-definition-components-measurement.html

Cook, Karla. "13 Influencer Marketing Campaigns to Inspire and Get You Started with Your Own". Hubspot. Accessed October 23, 2019. https://blog.hubspot.com/marketing/examples-of-influencer-marketing-campaigns

Dabral, Anupam. "Sophie Delafontaine is Making Longchamps a Brand of the Future". Lifestyle Asia. February 1, 2019. https://lifestyleasia.com/ind/style/fashion/sophie-delafontaine-longchamp-interview/

Forsey, Caroline. "KOLs: What They Are and Why They're Key to Your Marketing Strategy". Hubspot. Accessed October 15, 2019. https://blog.hubspot.com/marketing/key-opinion-leaders?_ga=2.183704870.1897501079.1558381982-1493293515.1553017609

Guttmann, A. "Statistics and Facts on Luxury Advertising and Marketing". Statista. August 27, 2018. https://www.statista.com/topics/4149/luxury-advertising-and-marketing/

Hayes, Adam. "Brand Equity". Investopedia. May 3, 2019. https://www.investopedia.com/terms/b/brandequity.asp

https://us.longchamp.com

Khan, Maryam. "Growing Pains: The Evolution of Influencer Marketing". Berkley Political Review. June 22, 2019. https://bpr.berkeley.edu/2019/06/22/growing-pains-the-evolution-of-influencer-marketing/

Leonard, Katherine. "The Gap's Styld.by Campaign Uses Bloggers to Build Connections". Lonelybrand. March 6, 2017. https://lonelybrand.com/blog/the-gaps-styld-by-campaign-uses-bloggers-to-build-connections/

Morrison, Kimberlee. "Report: 75% of Marketers Are Using Influencer Marketing". Adweek. October 13, 2015. https://www.adweek.com/digital/report-75-of-marketers-are-using-influencer-marketing/

Novinson, Eric. "What is the Difference Between Brand Equity and Brand Value?". Biz Fluent. September 26, 2017. https://bizfluent.com/info-8535356-difference-brand-equity-brand-value.html

Paton, Elizabeth. 'Furla and Longchamp; Quiet Success Stories". NY Times. November 13, 2017. https://www.nytimes.com/2017/11/13/fashion/accessories-handbags-furla-longchamp.html

Prentice, Nancy K. "Inside the Influencer Evolution". Mr. Magazine. February 11, 2020. https://mr-mag.com/inside-the-influencer-evolution/

Rafferty, Tod. "The Rise and Fall of Harley-Davidson Perfume". Ride Apart. June 6, 2017. https://www.rideapart.com/articles/253742/the-rise-and-fall-of-harley-davidson-perfume/

Stec, Carly. "Co-marketing vs. Co-Branding: What's the Difference". Impact. November 27, 2013. https://www.impactbnd.com/co-marketing-vs-co-branding-whats-the-difference

CHAPTER FOUR

Managing Fashion Brand Extensions

LEARNING OUTCOMES

- Examine various brand growth strategies.

- Assess growth advantages and risks.

- Determine the potential and challenges of brand extensions.

- Understand the principles of managing risk.

WHY GROW?

In almost every organization the issue of growth and extension of operations, markets, and/or products, will be raised and considered at some point and for various possible reasons. Recognizing that brands are among their most valuable assets, organizations will usually think about leveraging the brand power by introducing a wide range of new products under some of their strongest brand names. They hope that such diversity will enable them to increase market share while appealing to multiple customer segments with their new offerings. This strategy is known as *brand extensions*.

In general, growth may be fueled by different reasons such as:

- Overcoming various internal and external pressures, such as changing economic conditions in existing or other markets.

- Competitive pressures.

- Responding to internal pressures for better utilization of resources, etc.

- Leveraging brand power by creating new sources of cash flow and following.

Any one or a combination of these factors would force management to rethink their existing *one brand – one product* policies and explore possible growth opportunities. In this and the following two chapters, we will examine possible growth channels for the fashion organization, including brand extensions, licensing, global growth, and exporting. In this chapter, we will start by examining the concept of growth in general, and focus on brand extension as a popular strategy in the fashion industry.

GROWTH STRATEGIES

When considering growth, the fashion manager has various options and decisions to consider and examine. One of the first decisions to make is whether to direct the focus of their growth strategy towards existing customers or attempt to branch out into new territories with the goal of growing through acquiring new markets and new customers. Let's start by examining both options:

Growth Through Existing Customers

Growth through your existing customer base could be achieved in different ways.[1] For example:

1. *Increasing sales volume per capita of present customers for existing products.* This could be achieved by changing factors that may dictate current purchasing patterns such as product seasonality or usage patterns. Every product is meant to solve a problem and fulfill a specific need; hence it is highly common for products to be consumed within a particular situation or occasion. However, finding new situations of usage could create new growth opportunities. For example, Victoria's Secret had transformed women's lingerie from being a utilitarian item purchased occasionally and when necessary, into a rather exciting multi-purpose sexy item.

2. *Increasing sales volume by addressing existing barriers of consumption.* Giving existing customers new purchase alternatives may remove existing barriers that deter higher sales. For example, the fragrance industry is known to offer fragrances in two main size packages: 50 ml (1.7 oz) or 100 ml (3 oz). However, in the niche and indie markets where fragrances are relatively more expensive, their high prices are a clear barrier for many customers. In return, many niche fragrance houses started adding more accessible and cheaper alternatives such as 30 ml (1 oz), sampling or travel set bottles (12 ml or less) as well as miniature sizes. Outside fashion the example of soda drinks makers realizing that caffeine and sugar in their soft drinks could be clear consumption barriers to a wide range of their customers, they offered them decaffeinated and diet alternatives of the same soda brands while claiming to maintain the same taste.

3. *New product development and line extensions.* We will be discussing line extensions in more detail later in this chapter, however we can indicate here that brands can introduce new products (or lines) or variations in price ranges that cater to different needs. For example, a men's dress shirt maker can introduce a new line of dress shirts at a lower, more accessible, price range say in a cotton blend instead of their traditional 100% Egyptian cotton. It is important to realize that these new offerings could still be under the same brand name and umbrella and thus they form an example of line extensions as they are primarily meant to diversify their offerings to their current customers rather than enter new market segments (although they can still attract a new group of customers).

4. *Growth through innovation.* Innovation can help modify a competitive situation and give the brand a comparative advantage (as well as create new markets). For example, when Nike and other apparel manufacturers introduced online product customization options, the new platform excited existing customers (as well as attracted new ones) who found the new option not only fun to use but a welcome opportunity to create a product that suited their exact needs with an acceptable surcharge.

Growth Through New Users and Situations

Most of the options listed above (such as creating new products and line extensions or repurposing the product for new situations) could entice current customers to purchase more and in return fulfill new needs in their lives. They could also appeal to new customer groups and introduce the brand and its products to a new market segment, thus creating new sales opportunities. We can also add to these options more possibilities that are meant to focus primarily on acquiring new users, such as:

1. *Global expansion.* Going global, which will be discussed in more detail in a separate chapter, is a great opportunity for an apparel brand to cater to a new group of customers in new markets in which it had no earlier presence.

2. *Extending the brand into new products and categories that are different from its current core offerings.* This is primarily what the concept of brand extension is all about. It is a strategic move that utilizes the brand power into introducing new products and categories that may or may not complement existing brands. Thus, this

strategy is considered brand extension rather than line extension as we will be discussing later in more detail. For example, a fashion brand introducing a new line of sunglasses or cosmetics, etc. This type of growth through brand extension is very common in the fashion luxury segment because luxury brands are meant to be lifestyle brands. A lifestyle brand is a brand that relates to and defines a specific lifestyle and translates that in products that you can and are willing to see in different aspects of your life such as your home, bathroom, vacation, kitchen, etc. Brand extensions allow luxury brands to fulfill this mission and confirm their status as aspiring lifestyle brands.

3. *Extension through brand creation.* In this option the aim is not to appeal to existing customers as much as to attract and approach new ones. Management can decide to explore trading up, by introducing more expensive offerings or a brand appealing to a higher market segment, e.g. COS from H&M, or trade down by offering a cheaper extension appealing to the lower market segment with their new offerings such as DKNY from Donna Karan. Private labels created and owned by retailers rather than manufacturers could also be seen as a form of extension through brand creation (e.g. Alfani and INC by Macy's).

THE GROWTH MATRIX: ANSOFF'S PRODUCT/MARKET EXPANSION GRID[2]

The Asnoff expansion grid is a known management tool that addresses growth options like the ones we have discussed so far. The model sums up the options into four major growth strategies as indicated in the growth matrix seen in Figure 4.1.

The grid suggests four strategies with different possible levels of risk:

A. Market Penetration

B. Market Development

C. Product Development

D. Diversification

MARKET PENETRATION STRATEGY: EXISTING PRODUCTS + EXISTING MARKETS

Risk Level: Low Risk

The Market Penetration Strategy refers to a situation where customers are already aware of the product, yet for some reasons are not using it. The goal here would be to sell more of the same things to the same markets. Possible strategies to achieve this would be:

- Increase or grow the market share of current products with pricing strategies, promotions, and advertising.

- Increase your sales force's activities, restructure sales incentives, or better training.

- Identify which markets offer the best prospects for existing products and focusing on them to secure market dominance.

- Utilize aggressive pricing and promotional campaigns not just to increase sales but to drive competitors out of an already saturated market.

- Some organizations may consider buying a competitor company (particularly in mature markets), also known as Horizontal Extension or Integration.

- Introduce loyalty programs and rewards incentives.

- Revise your current, or develop a new, marketing strategy to encourage more people to choose your product, or to use more of it.

- Utilize common management tools such as the Boston Matrix to help determine which products are worth further investment and which should even be totally disregarded.

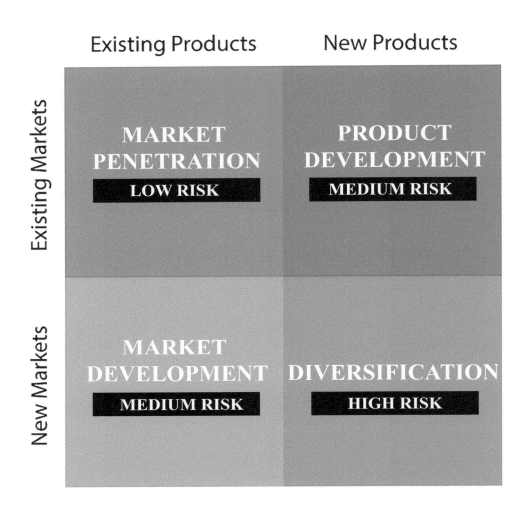

Figure 4.1 Ansoff Matrix.
Created by Author.

THE BOSTON MATRIX (BCG MATRIX)

The Boston Matrix is a well-known tool for the marketing manager that fashion managers could easily utilize. The tool was developed by the Boston Consulting Group (BCG). It is meant to be used as part of the product portfolio and long-term strategic planning by helping a business review its portfolio. In return, it can determine growth opportunities for its products and decide which products to invest in further, to discontinue, or to develop. Figure 4.2 demonstrates how the matrix is constructed. As seen, the matrix is divided into four quadrants based on an analysis of market growth and relative market share (relative to the competition).[3]

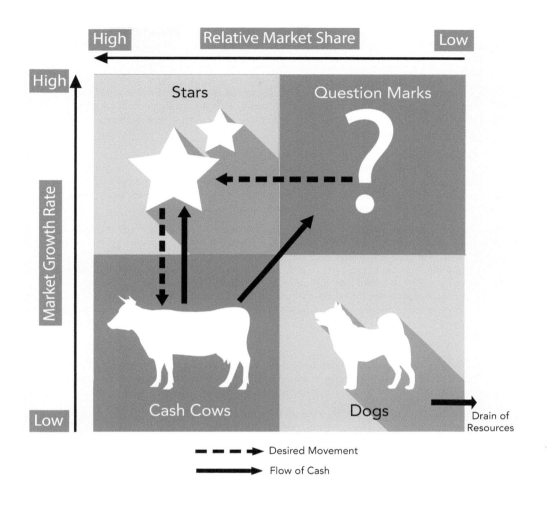

The BCG Matrix

Figure 4.2 The BCG Matrix.
Purchased with License from shutterstock.com.

The four product categories or quadrants are:

1. *Dogs.* These are products with low growth or small market share in slow growth markets which may all translate into low growth potential. While they may have experienced earlier successes, they could have currently lost consumer interest. In many cases such products enjoy a misguided level of loyalty from management that keeps them alive in the firm's portfolio. Some dogs could be revitalized. However, in most cases, the general recommendation is to remove any dogs from your product portfolio as they are a drain on resources. This could be done either though liquidation or selling them if another firm would be interested

2. *Question Marks (Problem Child).* These are products that compete in high-growth markets, yet their market share is low. This situation is common when a new product is launched into a high-growth

market but with an existing clear market leader. As a result, the new product's fate would be questionable and reflects a question mark situation as it may not be clear if it will become a star or drop into the dog category. These products often require significant investment to transform them into stars.

3. *Stars*. These products are the market leaders. They are products in high-growth markets with high market share. Stars generate more return on investment (ROI) than other product categories, yet it is important to remember that stars still require ongoing investment to sustain their growth and defend their leadership position.

4. *Cash Cows*. These are products in low growth markets but with high market share. They are often mature, well-established products and the goal here is to "*milk these products as much as possible*". Since their markets are generally mature markets with low growth potential, the need for investment is also reduced. Thus, these products are usually the most profitable in the company's product portfolio. Levi's iconic 501 jeans have been its cash cow for a long time.

The manager needs to closely examine the organization's portfolio of products and think strategically when devising an action plan that ensures some level of balance and product editing. For example, they would need to get rid of any dogs at the same time as utilizing funds generated by cash cows to turn question mark products into stars, which may eventually become cash cows. On the other hand, some of the question marks may end up being dogs, and this means that the manager will need a larger contribution from the successful products to compensate for these failures. The diagram (Figure 4.2) also indicates the possible desired paths of such scenarios as illustrated by the directional arrows.

Observations on the BCG Matrix tool:

1. The model seems to assume that higher rates of profit are directly related to high rates of market share. This may not always be the case. A new novel product can quickly gain market share yet still suffer from high development and maintenance costs associated with many new products.

2. The model also seems to oversimplify a complex set of decisions. For instance, it assumes that market share can be achieved by spending more on marketing which is a simplistic view.

3. In addition, it can be difficult to classify products in smaller businesses into these four categories as its relative market share is too small to quantify. Thus, the model seems more suited to relatively larger firms with a diverse portfolio of products or services.

MARKET DEVELOPMENT STRATEGY: EXISTING PRODUCTS + NEW MARKETS

Risk Level: Some or Average Risk

The Market Development Strategy creates growth through the introduction of current products to new markets. This strategy is used when a company has identified markets that were previously unidentified or ignored. So, the firm is trying to sell more of the same things to different people. Possible strategies in this scenario would be:

• Target new and untapped geographical areas and markets at home or abroad. Conducting a PEST Analysis may be beneficial to identify opportunities and threats in this different and new market.

• New distribution and sales channels can be created to offer products in new ways and to new customers. Online or direct sales could be alternatives or complements to existing agents' or intermediaries' channels.

• New pricing procedures can be used to attract new target audiences.

• Conduct market segmentation to identify and in return target different groups of people with different age, gender, or demographic profiles from existing customers.

- Identify the marketing mix (a.k.a. the 4Ps: product, price, place, promotion) to understand how to position your product in the new markets.

THE PEST ANALYSIS

The PEST Analysis is a simple tool that helps managers understand the big picture forces of change their organization is exposed to by examining and analyzing the changes in four areas in the business environment which are the: political, economic, socio-cultural, and technological changes, see Table 4.1.

This type of analysis allows managers to take advantage of the opportunities that these areas represent in the market. Opportunities can come from new technologies that help you reach new customers, from stable economies, stable political environment, government regulations that welcome and protect foreign investment, possible new funding channels, sizeable market potential, etc. On the other hand, threats can include deregulation that exposes you to intensified competition, a shrinking market, or increases to interest rates, which can cause problems if your company is burdened by debt or restriction on money transfer which would trap your earnings in local markets.

PEST analysis is often used in conjunction with the SWOT analysis we have discussed in Chapter 1. Both tools have clear different areas of focus that in a way would complement each other. While the SWOT analysis examines the threats and opportunities from a specific business, organization, and product levels, the PEST analysis looks at *big picture* factors that might influence a decision, a market, or a potential new business.

PRODUCT DEVELOPMENT STRATEGY: NEW PRODUCTS + EXISTING MARKETS

Risk Level: Some or Average Risk

The Product Development Strategy is a growth option used when a company introduces new products into existing markets where the company has identified new segments that it may have had missed before. A company would typically use this approach when current products are no longer selling. This strategy is likely to be more expensive and requires more time compared to other options as new competencies and skills may be required by the company to successfully develop the new products. Emphasis needs to also be placed on a detailed analysis of customer needs, research, and development, and early introduction to ensure products are first to market. Possible strategies would be:

- Extend existing products by producing different variations or repackage them.

- Add new features to existing products which might also redefine them.

Table 4.1 PEST Analysis Example

P	E	S	T
Political	Economic	Social	Technological
Examples:	Examples:	Examples:	Examples:
■ Stability of government	■ Economic growth	■ Income distribution	■ New technologies
■ Potential changes to legislation	■ Employment rate	■ Demographics	■ Communication infrastructure
■ Labor laws	■ Inflation rates	■ Lifestyle factors	■ Potential copyright infringement
■ Tax policy	■ Monetary policy	■ Population growth	■ Level of training
■ Trade policy	■ Consumer confidence	■ Cultural trends	■ Technology access
■ Environmental laws	■ Disposable income	■ Buying trends	
		■ Media views	

Created by Author.

- Develop related products or services that would be relevant to existing customers.

- Adopt innovation and invest in research and development.

DIVERSIFICATION STRATEGY: NEW PRODUCTS + NEW MARKETS

Risk Level: High Risk

The Diversification Strategy is used when new products are introduced to new markets. In such a scenario, the demands of the new market might be different from the current markets where the company operates. Diversification is the riskiest of all the approaches because you are not totally relying on existing expertise. In addition, by producing totally new products you are not gaining from the economies of scale achieved by producing more of the same (i.e. lower cost as production increases). This strategy requires the highest amount of investment of both time and resources as it may require the company to gain new skills, techniques, and possibly new facilities. However, while it is likely to be the costliest strategy, it can also offer a company security and an advantage should it suffer in one sector of the business, because it can then rely on another. Accordingly, good feasibility studies and research are key to ensure a winning approach. There are three diversification strategies that an organization can consider:

- *Concentric Diversification.* Leveraging a company's core technical knowhow to diversify its current products into new markets.

- *Horizontal Diversification.* The introduction to existing markets of products that are unrelated to a company's core products.

- *Conglomerate Diversification.* Purchasing another company in order to diversify.

Determining the best strategy depends on weighing the different factors, costs, and opportunities generated by each of the listed options or strategies. Conducting a risk analysis may be necessary to gain a better understanding of the options and opportunities associated with each.

SMART GROWTH

It is clear that growth can create new business risks due to the required dedicated resources (financial, human, logistic, etc.) which imposes a challenging strain on resources and operations. Moving the organization into a different business level where it will compete with bigger and more established organizations to which the organization will be the newcomer would surely result in different types of risk.

Thus, Edward Hess introduced a concept that he called *Smart Growth* which aims to account for the complexity of growth. Smart Growth recognizes that authentic growth is a process characterized by complex change, entrepreneurial action, experimental learning, and the management of risk. It is a strategy that requires companies of all sizes to follow what he calls the *4Ps of Growth: Plan, Prioritize, Process, Pace.* [4]

1. *Plan* for growth before kicking the strategy into gear. Think about how growth will change what you need to do. What new processes, controls, and people will be needed and at what cost?

2. *Prioritize* what changes or additions to the business have to be made to accommodate the growth. This is a way to make the essential investments first, so as not to deplete cash reserves before new income starts rolling in.

3. *Processes* must be put in place to ensure there are adequate financial, operational, personnel, and quality controls for a bigger business. These are like dams on a river: if the water starts flowing faster and with more volume, those dams need to be reengineered to handle it.

4. *Pace* growth so as not to overwhelm yourself, your people, and your processes. Growth can be exciting, but it is also almost always stressful. If you underestimate the need for effective change management, and for a phased approach to implementation, you increase your chances for failure,

GROWTH THROUGH BRAND EXTENSIONS

The product development and diversification strategies discussed above, were mostly examples of growth options through the creation of new products under the umbrella of an existing brand rather than creating a totally new brand. Many of these strategies can, in return, be seen as forms of *brand extensions*. Brand extensions could be defined as *a marketing strategy in which a firm that markets a product with a well-developed image uses the same brand name but in a different product category.*[5] Such a tactic helps increase and leverage brand equity linked to a brand's name and identity. And as the definition implies, an important component for the success of a brand extension strategy is the customer perception of the strategy. Consumers' evaluations of brand extensions depend on the perceived quality of the parent brand, the fit between the brand and the extensions' category (i.e. relevance), the characteristics of the product category in which the brand is extended and lastly the sequence of extensions.

Brand extensions give the brand owner the opportunity to complete the product range by supporting cross-selling and making both the core and non-core business increase. This strategy is also a way to reach a target market that cannot afford the core product, as in the example of luxury brands extending into cosmetics or accessories which are generally more affordable items compared to the core fashion pieces, thus allowing a new group of customers to get a taste of the brand. It is also a tool to strengthen the brand image and define a lifestyle positioning, and a way to get additional communication spending thereby increasing brand awareness. Yet, success in a crowded and difficult marketplace lies in a mix of elements such as existence of a market opportunity, the brand heritage, the original core business, the values and stylistic codes associated with the brand, the quality and innovativeness of the new product, and the right business model for the specific category as examined below.

Finally, it is important to remember that brand extensions are possible for both mass-market and luxury brands. Yet, luxury brands are the most suited to create extensions because they are meant to be aspirational lifestyle brands. However, the strategy needs to be handled with great care as we will discuss, because over-extending the brands into categories that are irrelevant to the brand's value proposition and philosophy may either dilute the brand value or hurt its image and status as a luxury brand.

Brand Extensions Categories

Brand extensions fall into three general categories:

1. *Line Extensions.* This strategy refers to launching a new line of products with the same brand and in the same product category but targeting and/or adding a different customer group or a new market segment (thus, it is not usually what comes to mind when the term brand extensions is mentioned). A line extension often adds a different flavor or ingredient variety, a different form or size, or a different application for the brand. For example, introducing a line of cotton blend shirts to a current line of silk shirts or adding a menswear line to the existing womenswear line. A product line is considered *too short* if the manager can increase long-term profits by adding items; and the line is *too long* if the manager can increase profits by dropping items. Increasing the length of the product line by adding new variants or items typically expands market coverage and therefore market share,

but it also increases costs. From a branding perspective, longer product lines may decrease the consistency of the associated brand image if all items use the same brand name.

Managers must determine the optimal product line strategy for their brand. To do so, they need a clear understanding of the market and the cost interdependencies between products. This in turn means examining the percentage of sales and profits contributed by each item in the product line and its ability to withstand competition and address consumer needs. For line extensions, consumers must also understand how the new product relates to existing products in order to minimize possible cannibalization or confusion.

2. *Vertical Brand Extensions.* Vertical brand extensions refers to extending the brand up into more premium market segments (e.g. COS by H&M). An upward extension can improve the brand image, because a premium version of a brand often brings positive associations with it. It can also be downward into more value-conscious segments (e.g. DKNY by Donna Karan) as a means of attracting new groups of consumers. However, this type of extension is commonly described as brand creation as mentioned earlier, since the products are commonly created under a new name. The central logic here is that the equity of the parent brand can be transferred in either direction to appeal to consumers who otherwise would not consider it. In fashion, many companies have succeeded in extending their brands to enter new markets across a range of price points. For example, the Armani brand has extended from the high-end Armani Privé, to mid-range luxury with Armani Collezioni, to affordable premium with Emporio Armani and Armani Exchange.

Extensions in either direction can offer consumers variety, revitalize the parent brand, and permit further extensions in a given direction. Higher-quality extensions are likely to improve evaluations of the parent brand. On the other hand, it's a strategy that also comes with some challenges:

- Its new price point, whether higher or lower, can confuse or frustrate consumers who have learned to expect a certain price range from a brand.

- Consumers may reject the extension and the parent brand's image will suffer.

- For prestige brands in particular, firms must often maintain a balance between availability and scarcity such that people always aspire to be a customer and do not feel excluded.

- Introducing associations common to lower-priced brands, such as inferior quality or reduced service.

- A downward brand extension may result in cannibalizing sales of a parent brand if it succeeds. While it may bring new consumers to the brand franchise, it may also bring over a greater number of existing customers and away from the parent brand.

- Upward brand extensions pose a unique challenge as it may be difficult to change people's impressions of the brand enough to justify a significant upward extension (Table 4.2).

3. *Category Extensions.* This type of extension is what usually comes to mind when someone mentions the term *brand extensions*. It is a strategy of leveraging on an existing brand to enter a totally new product category (e.g. from apparel to footwear, fragrances, or eyewear). This strategy will be the focus of our interest as we examine it a little further. The strategy could also be divided into two categories: *strategic* category extensions and *complementary* category extensions.

   A. *Strategic Category Extensions.* Diversifying the brand portfolio through category extensions is a strategic decision in nature as it is essential in transforming the brand into a true and legitimate lifestyle brand which, as we mentioned earlier, is within the expectation of most luxury brands given their aspirational and creative nature. Brands thus aim to become real players within the new business, for example, Dior extending into eyewear, fragrances, or cosmetics. Dior and Chanel cosmetics lines are considered among the top global beauty lines.

Table 4.2 Calvin Klein Brands

Brand	Segment	Image	Lines
Calvin Klein Collection	Designer	Sophisticated Luxury High Quality	Sportswear, outerwear, dress shirts, neckwear, eyewear, handbags, socks, footwear
ck Calvin Klein	Bridge	Sexy Urban Youthful	Sportswear, outerwear, suits, dress shirts, neckwear, socks, hosiery, footwear, handbags, eyewear, watches, jewelry, fragrance, cosmetics
Calvin Klein	Better	Timeless Modern Fashionable	Sportswear, outerwear, suits, dresses, dress shirts, neckwear, formalwear, jeanswear, underwear, performance, golf, swimwear, kids, socks, hosiery, footwear, handbags, eyewear, fragrance, watches, home

Created by Author.

This type of extension requires heavy investment and the risks are usually much higher than in complementary brand extensions if mismanaged or badly planned by extending into the wrong categories or introducing the wrong products. The result could be dilution of the brand equity, damaging its image, hurting customer loyalty while alienating core customers and causing fragmentation of the overall marketing efforts. Thus, managers need to start by clearly identifying the unique feature that the brand is bringing to the new category that will inspire a repeat purchase.

B. *Complementary Category Extensions.* When the new extensions are not core to the brand's long-term strategy but are meant to complement the lifestyle image, bolstering the existing brand values and emotional associations, and thus creating a stronger affiliation with customers. An example would be Giorgio Armani opening his chain of boutique Armani Hotels in Milan and Dubai with the objective of nourishing the core brand image as a lifestyle brand reflecting elegance, simplicity, and sophistication which are his signature aesthetics carried across from fashion to a new service operation.

Brand Adjacency and Relevance

Brand adjacency is defined as *the extent to which a particular brand extension is consistent with the brand's core value*.[6] The concept asserts that the more symbolically consistent it is, the greater the degree of adjacency and the more successful the extension. Strategic category extensions tend to be more adjacent than complementary ones. For example, when luxury jewelry maker Cartier extended into watches or when various fashion houses extend into fragrances, these extensions usually make sense to the consumer as they complement the core product and reinforce the core value of the parent brand. On the other hand, Pierre Cardin extending a luxury fashion brand into baby potty seats (with little regard to quality or price point) is clearly a non-adjacent extension. As a result, this once iconic brand suffered from serious brand dilution and an unrecoverable decline in status.

Relevance is another key factor to successful extensions, especially complementary category extensions, that might not be perceived as adjacent as strategic category extensions may be. In the example of Armani Hotels, while not as adjacent as extending into fragrances, it may still make sense to the affluent world-traveling Armani customer.

Box 4.1 Pierre Cardin: The Fall of the Licensing King

After apprenticing at a tailor at 17, Cardin worked at some of the top fashion houses such as Paquin, Schiaparelli, and Dior where he helped create the iconic *New Look* collection of 1947. Cardin was also considered to lead the Dior house after the founder's death. In 1950, Cardin started his business and his styles were often described as modern, geometric, experimental, futuristic, and mostly sculpturally-shaped albeit impractical at times. His iconic designs included the bubble skirt, the egg-carton dress, and space-age dresses. His fascination for experimentation and new materials was evident when he introduced his own fabric, called *Cardine* in 1968, which he used to produce a line of mini-dresses that were embossed with geometric and abstract shapes and cutouts. In 1971, Cardin visited NASA and became the first civilian to put on the spacesuit worn by astronaut Buzz Aldrin confirming his fascination with space which seemed to have inspired many of his designs.

In addition to his iconic designs, Pierre Cardin became famous for being one of the first designers to introduce a ready-to-wear line and add his name to hundreds of products through international licensing. The multi-award-winning designer even opened a fruit shop, and took ownership of the reputable French restaurant Maxim in 1981, which he expanded into other cities as well. Cardin was making a lot of money. While no one seemed to know how much exactly, due to the volume and diversity of the business, it has been speculated to reach over $1 billion in total sales, making him one of the wealthiest designers in Europe by the 1980s.

Dubbed as the "The Licensing King" in a 2002 interview with the New York Times, Cardin said about his licensing business: "I've done it all! I even have my own water! I'll do perfumes, sardines. Why not? During the war, I would have rather smelled the scent of sardines than of perfume. If someone asked me to do toilet paper, I'd do it. Why not?". Pierre Cardin had always claimed, though, that he personally met with license prospects and that every license deal was done under his direction and supervision. However, he had also signaled a lack of control in many incidents. For example, he had confessed his inability to convince licensees to avoid the excess use of the brand name and logo on their product, a practice that he described as being "vulgar". The reality is, that these licensing mishaps and brand overreach had led to the devaluation of the Pierre Cardin brand which eventually fell from being one of the most esteemed labels in fashion to a bargain-bin cast-off and became a case study in brand dilution due to over-extension and uncontrolled licensing. As a result, the once coveted luxury brand, never recovered from the loss of credibility. Cardin attempted to sell the business in 2011 but was unsuccessful due to his over-exaggeration of its value. When asked why did he favor money over the integrity of his brand, Cardin replied, "I don't want to end up like Balenciaga and die without a nickel, then, 20 years after I'm dead, see others make a fortune from my name."

Sources

1. "A History of Pierre Cardin". Pens. Accessed September 1, 2019. https://www.pens.co.uk/news/blog/history-of-pierre-cardin.php

2. Borrelli-Person, Laird. "There's a Pierre Cardin Exhibit at the Brooklyn Museum, Here Are 5 Things You Didn't Know about the French Design Legend". *Vogue*. July 19, 2019. https://www.vogue.com/article/pierre-cardin-exhibition-brooklyn-museum-of-art
3. Dike, Jason. "Digging Deeper: Pierre Cardin's Demise to "Licensing King"". *Highsnobiety*. November 23, 2015. https://www.highsnobiety.com/2015/11/23/digging-deeper-pierre-cardin/
4. Farago, Jason. "Pierre Cardin's Space-Age Fashion Takes Us Back to the Future". *New York Times*. August 22, 2019. https://www.nytimes.com/2019/08/22/arts/design/pierre-cardin-brooklyn-museum-review.html
5. www.Pierrecardin.com

Guidelines for Implementing a Brand Extension Strategy

Our discussion so far indicates that there is no one simple formula to guarantee success in extensions. However, businesses that get it right are usually the ones which follow the following paths:[7]

1. Embracing a consumer perspective

2. Innovating the extended category

3. Continuing to nurture the core business

4. Defining the right business model

1. *Embracing a Consumer Perspective.* It is important as a manager and decision-maker to think from the consumer perspective in order to avoid confusing them. Keep the customers' needs in mind in terms of relevance and credibility, by asking: Does the core brand have qualities that are credible and acceptable to sell the brand extension? And is the brand extension relevant to the brand's value proposition and thus to its customer? A few guidelines to keep in mind are:

   A. The more intangible the brand extension the more distant the product category open to extensions. Brands that are already perceived as lifestyle brands and associated with specific (emotional and aspirational) values are more likely to succeed in introducing new and distant categories compared to brands associated with technical attributes or product features. For example, while Armani, a fashion brand, has succeeded in extending into the hotel business, McDonalds in 2001, had launched the Golden Arch four-star hotel in Zurich, Switzerland, which closed two and a half years later. The failure was highly attributed to low brand associations between the parent brand and a four-star type of hotel even though both were service activities.

   B. The closer the association at a product level the more distant the product categories open to brand extensions. A brand may not have intangible association but still be able to succeed when there is a strong link between the brand's core product and the extended product, e.g. Swiss Army known for its tools, etc. extending into outerwear. Also, equally importantly, is the core category from which the brand starts its extension process. For instance, there are closer associations between clothing and fragrances than shoes and fragrances, consequently it may be more difficult for a brand starting from shoes to extend into distant categories such as fragrances and cosmetics than a fashion one.

2. *Innovating the Extended Category.* A second aspect of successful extensions is the capability of bringing a new and unique vision and innovating the category with respect to what already exists. Undertaking a "me too" strategy is simply not enough to make a brand extension investment profitable. The intangible

equity as an asset of the fashion brand is not enough to simply transpose the brand's codes to new product categories. Brands should propose a definite vision in terms of clients, channels, product features, and technologies, a vision that's new, relevant, and different from existing alternatives and that refers to the unique capabilities of the company. If it's a clear vision, it is easily recognizable regardless of the product to which it is attached. This is perhaps why some successful fashion brands are associated with people who have strong competencies and personalities and are not trying to please everyone on the market. Innovation gives the brand the capabilities it needs to extend within a reasonable scope and reinforce the overall brand image. This is not just a special feature of luxury or fashion but applies to any industry. In 2007, Prada launched its first phone. It did not just place its logo on a phone. It did work with the licensing partner, Korean LC, to study a totally new concept in phones. As a result, Prada was able to launch an innovative touch screen phone even before Apple launched the iPhone. The phone also displayed unique features that reflected the sophisticated brand in terms of icons, music, and functionalities.[8]

3. *Continuing to Nurture the Core Business.* Neglecting the core business is one of the most obvious dangers related to brand extensions, but one that may be hard to avoid. While extending the brand, the company has to spend time to keep developing and nurturing its original core business. This is a fundamental step in order to secure the firm's strength to then penetrate into a new product category. French fashion house Cacharel's successful perfume line (e.g. best seller Anaiis Anaiis) overshadowed its fashion line which it eventually totally dropped and later brought back solely online as secondary to the perfume line.

4. *Defining the Right Business Model.* The way the extension is managed is another important element. The designer's feeling and passion for the new category is fundamental to innovate and implement a long-term strategy for it. It reflects on his/her ability to transfer to it the stylistic codes of the iconic products. Equally essential is the company's ability to transfer its skills and experience to the brand extension in terms of a business model for managing the new category. Choosing the right business model to create extensions is very important and here we have different options:

   A. Developing internal capabilities by setting up a new organization for the new category or entering into an equity agreement with a specialized company (e.g. joint venture).

   B. Entering into a licensing agreement. In fashion this has been the most popular business model for distant categories such as eyewear and fragrances in order to leverage competencies and market coverage of big license partners. The assumption is that extensions through licensing are easier and do not require any dedicated resources. However, in reality, while the production cost in licensing is carried by the licensee there are still time, cost, and a level of dedication to ensure the licensed products are of acceptable quality and creativity levels.

Advantages of Brand Extensions

- There are many reasons why it is a better strategy to have brand extensions rather than creating a new brand. The first is cost. While not necessarily cheap, developing a brand extension is still expected to be much cheaper than developing new brand elements which would require a larger investment in research, packaging, personnel, logo design, etc.

- It may be increasingly difficult to support multiple brands through advertising and other resources. Brand extensions increase efficiency of promotional expenditures by allowing you to spend less on advertising than comparable new brands due to name recognition and brand association.

- Brand extensions may have a much better chance of succeeding in the marketplace than new brands, as retailers may be more willing to allocate shelf or store space to a well-known brand than to a new one.

- Reduce risk perceived by customers. Thus, consumers generally show a higher rate of trial conversion and repeat purchase for a brand extension than for a new brand.

- A faster move to defend the brand against competition which is particularly relevant where products or services are easily imitated.

- Allow for packaging and labeling efficiencies in situations where similar or identical packages and labels for extensions are used. This can result in lower production costs.

- Being attached to one product, a brand carries the risk of becoming too dependent upon the product lifecycle. By transcending the actual product, the brand can stay young and alive even if some products disappear.

- By offering new experiences to your existing customers, you demonstrate the brand's will to respond to changes in consumer taste, habits, and expectations through continuous innovation and improvements.

- Defend the brand against competition, which is particularly relevant where products or services are easily imitated. It also allows the brand to be up to date with category-threatening innovations which may occur in categories where the technology is superseded by developments that often come from outside the category.

- Improve brand image as a true lifestyle brand with a strong proposition by using and reinforcing the accumulated image capital of the brand. Consumers tend to form similar inferences and expectations about the extensions as they do for the brand. The extension does not only provide the brand with added revenue and profit but added credibility.

- Creating "news" and bringing attention and positive feedback to the parent brand.

- Permit consumer variety-seeking. A complement of line extensions can also encourage consumers to use the brand to a greater extent or in different ways as extensions allow the brand to offer a more complete solution to its consumer. A brand that offers menswear products can complement its lines with related accessories such as socks, belts, etc.

- Clarify brand meaning. Extensions can help clarify the meaning of a brand to consumers and define the kinds of markets in which it competes.

- Bring new customers and increase market coverage.

- Revitalize the brand. Sometimes brand extensions can be a means to renew interest in, and liking for, the brand.

- Finally, an unsuccessful extension does not prevent a firm from backtracking and introducing a more relevant extension. On the other hand, successful extensions, especially a category extension, would serve as the basis for subsequent extensions.

Challenges of Brand Extensions

- Extra cost of production if these extensions are produced by the organization.

- A major question raised is whether these extensions are truly necessary. Many of the world's top global brands are ones that focus on a particular product category (e.g. Nike) and have become leading experts of their category in terms of credibility and innovation.

- Misconception that extensions through licensing is easy and does not require any dedicated resources. In the case of licensing while the production cost is carried by the licensee there are still time, cost and a level of dedication to ensure the licensed products are of acceptable quality and creativity levels.

- Different varieties of line extensions may confuse and perhaps even frustrate consumers about which version of the product is the "right one" for them, which may induce shoppers to buy less.

- Can succeed but cannibalize sales of parent brand (e.g. Cacharel). Even if sales of a brand extension are high and meet targets, success may result merely from consumers switching from existing offerings of the parent brand. This is more common with line extensions designed to establish some parity with current offerings in the parent brand category.

- One risk of linking multiple products to a single brand, even if the extension succeeds, is that the brand may not be strongly identified with any one product. Thus, brand extensions may obscure the brand's identification with its original categories, reducing brand awareness.

- Can cause the company to forgo the chance to develop a new brand with its own unique image and equity. For example, the boost Levi's earned from Dockers pants, which attracted a whole new segment of consumers looking for casual pants.

- Can fail and hurt parent brand image (e.g. Halston's extension for JCPenney). And while the extension may succeed, it may still hurt the image of the parent brand. If customers see the brand extension's attribute or benefit associations as inconsistent or even conflicting with the corresponding associations for the parent brand, they may change their perceptions of the parent brand as a result.

- Dilute brand meaning. The potential drawbacks of a brand extension's lack of identification with any one category and a weakened image may be especially evident with high-quality or prestige brands. To protect their brands from dilution, many new fashion brands seeking to establish their brand through a brand extension, are now forging exclusive licensing partnerships with a single retailer. Target had exclusive deals with designer Isaac Mizrahi and later developed similar deals with Todd Oldham and others. These exclusive licenses enable the brand to better control the inventory, avoid discounts, and, most importantly, protect itself from dilution.

- Can increase retailer resistance as many retailers do not have enough shelf or display space to stock the large number of new products and brands continually being introduced even if they wanted to. So, some consumers may be disappointed when they're unable to find an advertised brand extension.

- Bad timing. Timing is key with any strategic decision and extending the brand is indeed one of those. A young fashion brand can rush into introducing a new perfume too soon before it has established itself and gained market recognition. The failure of French house Christian LaCroix's perfume in many countries outside of France (before the brand's demise) was highly attributed to being introduced too soon into the market, way before it had any name recognition.

- A brand that is seen as prototypical of a product category can be difficult to extend outside the category (e.g. Levi's Jeans).

- Tangible and concrete attribute associations tend to be more difficult to extend than abstract benefit associations. This is why luxury brands known primarily for their abstract, aspirational, and emotional benefits are among the best suited for creating brand extensions.

- Consumers may transfer associations that are positive in the original product class but become negative in the extension.

- It can be difficult to extend into a product class that is seen as easy to make (i.e. easy-to-make products tend to be similar in quality with little differentiation, hence new extensions into them may not be convincing to consumers, e.g. consumers do not see or expect major differences in quality across shaving creams).

- Cultural differences across markets can influence extension name success.

Brand Extensions and Equity

- New products and brand extensions may take from the brand equity if they are irrelevant, badly timed, or badly executed. In this case they could diminish the strength, favorability, or uniqueness of any existing associations the parent brand may have. On the other hand, extensions that are consistent with the parent brand's values and associations may strengthen the brand and contribute to its equity.

- Extensions must have a sufficiently high level of awareness, which will depend primarily on the marketing program and resources devoted to spreading the word about the extension. it will also obviously depend on the type of branding strategy adopted. The more prominently we use an existing brand that has already achieved a certain level of awareness and image to brand an extension, the easier it should be to create awareness of, and an image for, the extension in memory.

- For brand extensions to be successful and contribute to the brand's equity, managers need to start by assessing what Kevin Keller has described as the points of party (i.e. matching points) and desired points-of-difference[9] (i.e. competitive points). Without powerful points-of-difference, the brand risks becoming an undistinguished "me too" entry, vulnerable to well-positioned competitors. For example, Diesel became a leader in the jeans category by creating strong points-of-difference on the benefits of styling, innovative finishes, and creativity which young consumers valued in a fashion brand. Thus, when it leveraged its brand equity into categories such as sportswear and fragrances, Diesel was able to establish category points-of-parity and compete as a premium fashion brand before it managed to find and promote new points-of-difference in these categories.

Box 4.2 Diesel: The Rebel Brand

The Italian brand Diesel created by Renzo Rosso is considered one of Europe's top manufacturers of designer jeans and apparel. Diesel is distributed through a network of company-owned and franchised Diesel retail stores and it is available in more than 10,000 chain and department stores in more than 80 countries worldwide.

The Diesel story began in 1978 when Renzo Rosso joined Moltex, an Italian manufacturing company. He later borrowed money from his father to buy a 40% holding in the company and changed its name to Diesel. In 1985 he bought out his partner to have full ownership of the brand. Rosso had chosen the Diesel name for the brand due to its international appeal being pronounced more or less the same all over the world. By 1979, he had created his first full menswear collection and by 1982 expanded sales internationally. In 1984, he debuted Diesel Kids and extended the company's jeans-based fashions to cover the entire range of youth markets. The Diesel Female collection was introduced in 1989 which expanded the company's target markets.

With full control of his brand, Rosso had hired a new generation of design staff, giving them the mandate to ignore what the rest of the world's fashion community was doing and instead create clothing to reflect their own, and Rosso's, personalities. Designers were also required to travel at least two times a year, were given complete freedom and an unlimited budget to choose their destinations, and in turn were given the mission to return to the company's headquarters with the inspiration to create the next season's line of Diesel clothing. The strategy helped the company develop a reputation for offbeat and avant-garde designs and proved immensely appealing to the company's core European youth market. In 1991 Diesel hired Swedish advertising firm DDB Paradiset which introduced a number of very successful global campaigns for the brand such as the "For Successful Living" advertising campaign. In 1995, Diesel became the first fashion company to launch a website. And in 1996, it opened its first U.S. store in New York City deliberately opposite Levi's on Lexington Avenue to "show how beautiful our product was, in front of them," explained Rosso.

Declines in the jeans market toward the end of the 1990s led Diesel to begin looking for ways to expand its range of clothing. The company debuted a new line of upscale, more fashion-conscious clothing under the label "Diesel StyleLab". By 2003, Diesel had three distinct fashion lines; "Diesel StyleLab", the priciest fashion-forward designer label; "Diesel", a fashion brand that focused heavily on denim, and "55DSL", the sport-inspired streetwear line that blended fashion and function. In 2005 StyleLab was cancelled and 55DSL incorporated into the main collection in an attempt to upgrade the core brand. In 2008, the brand introduced Diesel Black Gold as its new luxury ready-to-wear line and in the same year the company partnered with Adidas to co-produce a sport denim line. In 2013 Diesel underwent another rebranding effort, including hiring Nicola Formichetti as its first artistic director. Formichetti had worked earlier for Thierry Mugler and was Lady Gaga's stylist. The collaboration later ended amicably in 2017.

In spite of these changes, Diesel remained in financial trouble. Its mass-produced jeans and other apparel were heavily discounted. Its average customer age was above 40 and young consumers were looking to athleisure and streetwear brands such as Supreme, or new labels like Vetements and Off-White instead. Diesel needed to regenerate the engine. In March 2019, Diesel filed for U.S. bankruptcy protection and began an executive and strategic overhaul that has involved cutting off the brand's cash-generating mass-fashion lines, killing Diesel's lower-priced and lower-quality apparel in 2018, which they said were diluting the brand in the eyes of fashion-interested consumers. The move cut Diesel's U.S. business in half. However, it also allowed the brand to get out of expensive store leases in places like New York and Hawaii. In 2018, Rosso launched a "Red Tag" sub-label of Diesel to serve as a forum for a stream of collaborations enlisting a series of designers including Shayne Oliver and Gosha Rubchinskiy to create higher-priced capsule collections. Diesel claimed that unlike past diffusion lines, this is aimed at "fashion people". Rosso hoped the collaborations would place Diesel in the collectable category of fashion. "The young people want exclusives," he said, "and they want to re-sell it and make money."

Sources

1. Binkley, Christina. "How Renzo Rosso Returned Diesel to Growth". *Vogue*. October 28, 2019. https://www.voguebusiness.com/companies/renzo-rosso-diesel-founder-denim-growth-samuel-ross
2. Grigorian, Vadim. *Diesel for Successful Living: Branding Strategies for an Up-Market Line Extension in the Fashion Industry* (Fontainebleau, France: INSEAD, 2004).
3. Luisa, Zargani and Rosemary Feitelberg. "Exclusive: Diesel, Nicola Formichetti Part Ways". *WWD*. December 18, 2017. https://wwd.com/fashion-news/denim/exclusive-diesel-nicola-formichetti-end-collaboration-contract-11076973/
4. Picchi, Aimee. "Diesel, Jeans Company Known for Pricey Denim, Goes Bankrupt". *CBS News*. March 6, 2019. https://www.cbsnews.com/news/diesel-bankruptcy-jeans-company-denim-chapter-11/www.diesel.com
5. "The History of Diesel Jeans". The Jeans Blog. June 2, 2014. https://thejeansblog.com/denim-brand-history/the-history-of-diesel-jeans/

Licensing and Brand Extensions

Brand extensions in the fashion industry are commonly done by subcontracting the process to a third party/manufacturer through licensing. Accordingly, licensing has become a major arm of the industry with estimated total revenues of nearly $32.2 billion in 2018.[10] Given the importance of this segment to the fashion industry we will be dedicating the next chapter to the topic.

Naming Strategies for Brand Extensions

Brand and product names are an important component of their identity and a trigger of mental associations that the consumer creates based on his/her experiences with the brand and the perception of value he/she has developed. For instance, when brands are old there is a tendency to introduce extensions under a new name which in return makes the old brand look even older. Thus, choosing the right and relevant name is an important branding decision and a strategic one from a management perspective.

- Extensions naming decisions must satisfy the following goals:

  - Help the extension succeed as it underlines a specific trait, benefit, or image.

  - Do not dilute the parent brand equity.

  For example, Chanel's use of the name *Precision* for its cosmetics line was intended to overcome the general conception of cosmetics as being not very scientific products and more of a fashion item.[11] Tom Ford's line of higher-priced fragrances named *Private Blend*, evokes exclusivity, quality, and craftsmanship.

- In general, the more remote the brand extension is from the brand core purpose the more likely it is to have its own name. Another option is in the form of sub-branding whereby an extension to the name is included. On the other hand, the closer it is to the core the more it should adopt an umbrella architecture and receive a generic or descriptive name. For example, when a fashion brand such as Donna Karan extends into accessories, the new products carry the same name. However, when the brand decided to extend into a different and lower market the move had to be done through brand creation (i.e. vertical extension) and by using a totally different name DKNY (CK by Calvin Klein, Y-3 by Yohji Yamamoto, etc.).

- By developing unique brand names, companies pursuing vertical expansion can avoid a negative transfer of equity from a "lower" brand to a "higher" brand, but they also sacrifice some ability to transfer positive associations. Yet, when the parent brand makes no secret of its ownership of the vertical brands (e.g. Armani Exchange), some associations may be transferred because the parent acts as a "shadow endorser" of the new brand.

Managers and Brand Extension Opportunities

Based on our discussion, it is clear that getting into brand extensions is a strategic management decision that has a long-term impact on the brand's equity and image. Thus, if the fashion manager decides to proceed with this strategy, he/she should consider their strategies carefully by conducting thorough market research and following some steps that could help with the making of such a decision. Some of the steps to consider are:[12]

1. To identify possible extension candidates, managers should clearly understand their main or parent brand and must know what is/are the basis of positioning and core benefits satisfied by the brand as well as identifying the actual and desired levels of consumer knowledge of these proposals. Thus, consumer and market research are essential for this task.

2. In evaluating an extension, managers must understand where it would like to take the brand in the long run, because the introduction of an extension can change brand meaning and can affect consumer response to all subsequent marketing activity as well.

3. Evaluate the potential of the extension candidate. In forecasting the success of a proposed brand extension, marketers should assess, through judgment and research, the likelihood that the extension will realize the advantages and avoid the disadvantages of brand extensions discussed earlier. At this point managers need to assess the extension's ability to achieve its own brand equity, as well as the likelihood that it can affect the parent brand's existing brand equity.

4. Marketers must take not only a consumer perspective in evaluating a proposed brand extension, but also a broader corporate and competitive perspective. For example, how effectively are the corporate assets leveraged in the extension setting? How relevant are existing marketing programs, perceived benefits, and target customers to the extension? What are the competitive advantages to the extension as consumers perceive them, and possible reactions initiated by competitors as a result? One of the biggest mistakes marketers make in launching extensions is failing to properly account for competitors' actions and reactions. Brand counterextensions, whereby a competing brand in the extension category chooses to launch its own extension into the parent brand's category, can pose a significant threat.

5. Design marketing programs to launch the extension. Too often companies use extensions as a shortcut means of introducing a new product and pay insufficient attention to developing a branding and marketing strategy that will maximize the equity of the brand extension as well as enhance the equity of the parent brand.

6. Choosing brand elements. By definition, brand extensions retain one or more elements from an existing brand. They do not have to leverage only the brand name but can use other brand elements too, such as package designs that distinguish different line extensions or brand types but reveal their common origin at the same time. A brand extension can retain or modify one or more brand elements from the parent brand as well as adopt its own brand elements. In creating new brand elements for an extension, marketers should follow the same guidelines of memorability, meaningfulness, likeability, protectability, adaptability, and transferability that we need for the development of any brand.

7. Leveraging secondary brand associations. A brand extension differs in that there is always some leveraging of another brand or company (e.g. as in the case of licensing). The extent to which these other associations become linked to the extension, however, depends on the branding strategy the firm adopts and how it brands the extension.

Box 4.3 Tom Ford: An Unorthodox Approach to Licensing

In April 2005, after his departure from Gucci, Tom Ford, with the help of the former CEO of the Gucci Group, Domenico de Sole, launched the Tom Ford label based solely on two licensing deals: one with Estée Lauder for perfume and cosmetics and another with Marcolin Group for eyewear. These licensing partners have allowed Ford to build a bigger business, more quickly, with a smaller investment than if he had tried to do everything on his own. Thus, the Tom Ford brand had launched these products at more accessible price points and run by trusted partners requiring little to no cash investment from Ford himself before he expanded his fashion operation. In April 2007, he opened his first directly owned flagship store in New York on Madison Avenue which also coincided with the debut of the Tom Ford Menswear and Accessory collections. In September 2010, he presented his much-anticipated womenswear collection. This approach taken by the brand was highly unorthodox as most luxury fashion businesses start off with very expensive in-house ready-to-wear collections, which require significant upfront investment to gain market presence before they consider their licensing options. Of course, Tom Ford had the advantage of name recognition from his successful tenure at Gucci (and briefly at Yves Saint Laurent) which allowed him to secure such an arrangement. Deals like these usually come with multi-million-dollar budgetary commitments by the licensee to advertise the product lines. These global campaigns, which Ford directed and oversaw himself, would give further visibility to the Tom Ford brand and help him reach a vast consumer base from day one. "I realized that [the licensing deals] would keep my name very public, (so) that if I chose to go back into fashion it would even make my name bigger," Ford has said of the move. Now that the brand has been established as a significant fashion brand, especially in menswear, further growth by licensed extensions was inevitable. For example, in 2017, Tom Ford International announced the creation of Tom Ford Underwear in partnership with Albisetti International, a global leader in the design, manufacturing, and distribution of the highest quality men's and women's undergarments.

Sources

1. Amed, Imran. "The Business of Being Tom Ford". *The Business of Fashion*. September 26, 2013. https://www.businessoffashion.com/articles/people/the-business-of-being-tom-ford-part-iwww.tomford.com
2. "Tom Ford International Announces the Creation of Tom Ford Underwear for Men". PR Newswire. February 6, 2017. https://www.prnewswire.com/news-releases/tom-ford-international-announces-the-creation-of-tom-ford-underwear-for-men-300402878.html

GROWTH AND RISK MANAGEMENT

While the term "risk management" is commonly used in relevance to financial risk or project management, it remains a very relevant topic from a general management perspective as well. And when strategic decisions are made, which by definition impact the whole organization and have long term implications, the topic of risk becomes more relevant and essential.

The simplest definition of risk is *an unplanned event with unexpected consequences*.[13] Thus, risk management starts with *risk analysis* which is a process that helps managers identify and manage potential problems that could undermine key business initiatives. From a risk management perspective there are many ways to classify risk faced by an organization. Risk can be classified by categories, by type (*a category is a larger spectrum that may cover more than one "type", i.e. types fall under categories*) or by time frame:

- Risk could be approached based on *CATEGORIES*:

  Strategic risks. These are risks associated with operating in a particular industry, which may also include going into a joint venture or a competitor coming into the market, etc. Strategic risks are not always undesirable since they are expected (and accepted) as apart of actions that the organization take to make high financial or market gains. Managers need to develop a system that would allow them to manage those risks but not stop taking them. As a matter of fact, a manager may be willing to take bigger strategic risks if he/she expects even bigger financial returns.

  Operational (or Internal) risks. These are risks associated with the business' operational and administrative procedures, which include supply chain, or computer system breakdown. These types of risks are generally *preventable* and controllable, and managers need to eliminate or avoid them if possible.

Environmental (or External) risks. These are risks associated with external factors, which include economic downturns, natural disasters, or political unrest in a foreign market. These risks are generally beyond the control or influence of the organization. Thus, they are *unpreventable* and management will be concerned with being able to identify them and mitigate their impact.

Financial risks: These are risks associated with the financial structure of the business, or its external financial transactions, which may include non-payment by a customer (e.g. an importer) or increased export fees. Financial risks could actually fall under any of the other three categories.

- Risk could be approached based on TYPES:

Hazard risk. Which tends to be operational (e.g. health and safety problems from operations).

Compliance risks. Which are risks from failing to comply with legal or regulatory measures.

Control risks. Which are risks arising from uncertainty and issues that are hard to predict.

Opportunity risks. Which are risks/dangers associated with taking on an opportunity, i.e. what you are giving up as a possible alternative for the new venture. But there are also risks associated with not taking on the opportunity.

Introducing a new brand or line of products may involve adapting new machinery or computer systems, building or acquiring new facilities, restructuring, etc. which could incur *hazard risks.* The new operations or global outreach through export, for instance, may require abiding by foreign market regulations and guidelines which may involve regulatory and legal measures incurring *compliance risks.* Any new endeavor or project implementation comes with a series of unknowns and uncertainties which represent *control risks* and, in return, any new investment incurs a level of *opportunity risk* by giving up other alternatives in order to direct focus and finances to this one of choice.

It is important to remember that some risks could indeed fall under more than one category and type. A computer breakdown could be seen as a financial risk and an operational risk that carry hazard and compliance risks. Also, extending into a new category of brand extension may prompt a strategic risk which would include activities that trigger all stated *types* of risk (e.g. compliance, hazard, opportunity, and control) and so on.

- Risk could also be approached based on the TIMEFRAME of their impact:

Long term. Long-term risks will have an impact for several years, perhaps up to five years, after the event occurs or the decision is taken, as in the case of launching a new product. Long-term risks therefore relate to strategic decisions.

Medium term. Medium-term risks have their impact sometimes after the event occurs or the decision is taken, and typically this will be about a year later. Medium-term risks are often associated with projects or programs of work. For example, while installing a new computer software system is a long-term or strategic decision, decisions regarding the projects that would implement the new software will be medium-term decisions with medium-term risks attached.

Short term. Short-term risks have their impact immediately after the event occurs. Accidents at work, traffic (and shipping) accidents, fire, and theft are all short-term risks that have an immediate impact and immediate consequences as soon as the event has occurred and are probably the easiest types of risks to identify and manage.

How to Manage Risk?

Risk is inevitable and every new endeavor or project is subject to different types of risk, as mentioned. A manager may identify more than one risk at the same time. In such a case it might be advisable to:

A. Start by *ranking* these risks once they are identified. This can be done by considering the consequence and probability of each risk.

B. Creating a list of risks is a good starting point, but it isn't enough. The manager needs to put an action plan per risk in order to be able to manage them effectively.

A risk management action plan may include the following three steps: *Identify, Assess and Plan, Control.*

IDENTIFY

Any risk management initiative begins with scope and risk identification. These activities answer the question: What risks are we managing? This includes identifying its scope (e.g. is it project, department, or strategy related, etc.) and initial goals that were associated with this activity. For example, if the scope is to manage sales risk associated with introducing a new product, then identify what was the initially planned sales process, what were its related objectives, and what are the list of risks.

ASSESS AND PLAN

Once risks are identified, it is time to assess them and plan to control them. Risks are assessed according to their probability. This involves prioritizing risks based on their impact. Low probability and low impact risks have low priority. Plan and identify the types of control measures possible that are relevant to each risk as described in the next step.

CONTROL

Execute the risk management plan to control and manage risks based on the five possible options listed below. The plan must also include monitoring, measuring, and communicating risk and control results.

There five main ways to manage and control risk are: acceptance, avoidance, transference, mitigation, or exploitation. Let us examine each one.

1. *Accept the Risk.* Accepting the risk means that you recognize it but decide to take no action to deal with it. This happens if the cost of eliminating it is too high. This is more common with very small risks that will not have much of an impact on your operation and thus may be better to use resources for something else.

2. *Avoid the Risk.* Change the plans completely to avoid the risk. This is a good strategy when a risk has a potentially large impact on the company.

3. *Transfer the Risk.* Transferring a risk is a strategy that is more common in projects or endeavors where there are several parties involved. Essentially, you transfer the impact and management of the risk to someone else. For example, if you have a third party contracted to write your software code, you could transfer the risk that there will be errors in the code over to them. They will then be responsible for managing this risk. Using insurance is another good example. If you are transporting goods as part of your project (e.g. exporting goods) then using insurance to cover transportation accidents is an example of transfer of risk.

4. *Mitigate the Risk.* Mitigating against a risk is probably the most common risk management technique and the easiest to implement. What mitigation means is that you limit the impact of a risk, so that if it does occur, the problem it creates is smaller and easier to fix. For example, if you are launching a new product and the sales team then has to demonstrate it to customers, there is a risk that the sales team doesn't understand the product and can't give good demonstrations. As a result, they will make fewer sales and there will be less revenue for the company. A mitigation strategy for this situation would be to provide good training to the sales team. There could still be a chance that some team members don't understand the product, or they miss the training session, etc., but the impact of the risk will be far reduced as the majority of the team will be able to demonstrate the new product effectively.

5. *Exploit the Risk.* Acceptance, avoidance, transference, and mitigation are great to use when the risk has a negative impact on the project. But what if the risk has a positive impact? For example, the risk that the new product is so popular that you don't have enough sales staff to do the demonstrations. That's a positive risk, something that would have a benefit to the company if it happened. In those cases, you want to maximize the chance that the risk happens, not stop it from happening or transfer the benefit to someone else. Exploitation is the risk management strategy to use in these situations. Look for ways to make the risk happen or for ways to increase the impact if it does. You could train a few junior sales administration people or hire independent sales people, etc., so that the chance that there is lots of interest in the new product is increased, and there are people to do the demonstrations if needed.

It is very common to use a combination of techniques and strategies that best suit the risks and the skills of the available team. It is also important to remember that risk management is a continual process of identifying, accessing, and controlling that is repeated over and over again.

Chapter Questions

1. In Chapter 1 you have created a SWOT analysis for a brand of your choice. Now create a PEST analysis for the same brand and highlight how both models complement and reinforce each other.

2. In reference to the BCG matrix:

    a. Identify a real fashion product that could be categorized as a Cash Cow.

    b. As a manager what measures can you take to transition a brand from Question Mark to a Star instead of to a Dog?

3. A manager for a fashion retail operation is considering expanding business and opening a new branch overseas. Discuss the type/s of risk he/she needs to consider and could encounter with this move. Examine how he/she can address these risks.

Case Study
Halston: A Tragic Fashion Epic

Background

Halston started off his career as a hatmaker in 1953 with his own millinery salon at the Ambassador Hotel in Chicago. In 1958, he moved to New York to work under milliner Lilly Daché before going over to Bergdorf Goodman's hat salon. As a milliner, Halston had Kim Novak, Gloria Swanson, and Fran Allison as clients. His career skyrocketed when Halston designed the iconic pillbox hat worn by First Lady Jacqueline Kennedy in 1961 at President John F. Kennedy's inauguration. In 1966, Halston expanded his business to include apparel, both couture and ready-to-wear, under the business Halston, Ltd. The line also included hats, scarves, furs, leather apparel, shoes, and jewelry. He later set up Halston International to offer a more accessible line with knitwear and accessories. In a first-of-its-kind deal for a fashion designer, Halston and his partners sold both the Halston businesses and the Halston trademark to Norton Simon Industries (NSI), a large multi-brand corporation, in 1973. With the financial backing, the Halston brand grew and his fame soared. In 1975, he then established a separate menswear collection. By now, he was known for revolutionizing clothing, offering products like fur coats, argyle sweaters, and leather jackets as part of his collection. Halston was a fixture in New York City's party scene. He was also a regular at Studio 54 and was inspired by the scene to make designs that defined the seventies disco style. He became a friend to some of the biggest artists and socialites of the time such as Liza Minnelli and Bianca Jagger. Halston's affinity for New York's nightlife led to one of his most iconic designs, the halter dress, becoming a staple among disco-going women. He also pioneered the Ultrasuede material, using the fabric in his famous shirtdress and other types of apparel and in luggage. Ultrasuede was used as the title for a documentary released about him in 2012.

Design Impact

Halston is perhaps the single most influential figure in the history of American fashion and the first true American superstar designer. He won four Coty Awards including two awards for his millinery designs in 1962 and 1969 and two for his fashion designs in 1971 and 1972. In 1973, Halston joined four other American fashion designers, Oscar de la Renta, Bill Blass, Anne Klein, and Stephen Burrows, to show their designs against five French fashion designers, Yves Saint Laurent, Hubert de Givenchy, Pierre Cardin, Emanuel Ungaro, and Marc Bohan, in a fashion showdown in 1973 referred to by WWD as "The Battle of Versailles", which was meant to raise funds for the restoration of the palace. In 1974, Halston was inducted into the Coty Hall of Fame. At the height of his career in the mid-seventies, Halston was designing four ready-to-wear, four sportswear, and two made-to-order collections per year, as well as furs, shoes, swimwear, robes, intimate apparel, menswear, luggage, uniforms for both Avis Rent A Car System and Braniff Airline employees and costume designs for the Martha Graham Dance company and his celebrity friends such as Liza Minnelli.

Halston III for JCPenney

In 1983, Halston decided to extend his brand into new territory by signing a deal with JCPenney to create a line of lower-priced apparel. The "Halston III" line was forecast to generate $1 billion in its first six years. Halston said that after dressing the rich and famous, he wanted to dress the rest of America. Prices ranged from $24 for a casual shirt to $200 for a coat and included splashy items such as an ostrich-trimmed velvet jacket. In keeping with the venture's populist spirit, Halston made appearances on "Phil Donahue" and "Good Morning America". White- and chrome-fixtured Halston departments were built in the individual stores to house the line. "The idea is to display the merchandise to its best advantage, without things like Dynel wigs taking away from them," Halston joked. However, the designer's association with a mid-tier retailer such as JCPenney shocked the fashion and retail industry at the time and resulted in a major backlash as the label had grown to encompass everything from fragrance to luggage to carpets, and the name Halston itself became a joke on *Saturday Night Live*. In fact, the impact was disastrous. Bergdorf Goodman dropped Halston's main line immediately, along with other higher-end department stores which stopped selling the higher-priced Halston lines. While the Halston brand became more accessible and a household name, it lost its prestige.

The Decline

The Halston III was later dropped by JCPenney before the first six-year period was over. Moreover, Halston had already sold the rights to his name to Norton Simon, which was eventually sold to Esmark Inc., a huge consumer-goods conglomerate. And thus, Halston Enterprises was suddenly relegated to being a subsidiary of International Playtex, a company best known as the manufacturer of bras and girdles. Less than a year later, the ownership of the parent company changed hands again, and Halston became even more estranged and angry with his new owners as they limited his creative freedom. In the summer of 1984, Halston stormed out of his Olympic Tower office in a tantrum and stopped working altogether. On October 12 of that year, he was removed from his position as president of his own company. Halston spent the rest of his life trying to buy back his brand from its owner at the time, Revlon, but was ultimately unsuccessful. He was later diagnosed with AIDS and died in San Francisco in 1990 at the age of 57 from lung cancer complicated by HIV.

Fashion Changing Times

The fallout from the Halston III at JCPenney line had a negative impact on licensing decisions by designers for a long time. At a New York Times talk in 2009, designer Marc Jacobs discussed the impact that the Halston III line with JCPenney had had on his licensing decisions by saying: "When I got into this business, licensing was a big thing. I don't think that it's about that anymore. One doesn't have to sign themselves up for this lifestyle their mugs in their kitchen will reflect. I remember when Halston did that thing with JCPenney, it was very bad for his couture business."

At the time of Halston there were no internet stores like Bluefly or outlet malls, both of which made designer brands more accessible to the masses. It was ironic that almost 30 years to the day that Halston launched his line for JCPenney, Isaac Mizrahi launched his successful line with Target which became more successful than Mizrahi's higher-priced lines at stores like Barneys and brought him nationwide fame and praise. And while Jacobs resisted the urge to create a masstige line, other designer houses, most notably Karl Lagerfeld and Versace, have embraced the concept, successfully creating collections for H&M. Design houses like Missoni, Proenza Schouler, and Zac Posen, had collections with Target as well. These masstige lines were seen as a way to expand their brand awareness among a wider customer group, while also creating an entry point for their higher priced brands – an ironic sign of how times have changed.

Halston Today

Since his death, many have tried to revive the brand, including Sarah Jessica Parker, who was enlisted as the creative director for the more affordable Halston Heritage line after she wore two of its dresses in *Sex and the City* in 2009. However, the attempts were plagued with unstable management and halfhearted investors, who did not want to invest the necessary energy and resources to see the project through, and thus, they could not recapture the magic. Sarah had since left the brand. Halston Heritage still exists under a new management based in Los Angeles, but unfortunately, the Halston name seems to have lost its place on the high fashion radar, at least for now.

Case Study Questions

1. While Halston's collaboration with JCPenney was not well received by the industry and ended up hurting his brand, similar collaborations today are usually well received and celebrated. Give examples of recent similar collaborations that had succeeded and examine the cultural and economic changes that may have resulted in this shift in perception and attitude.

2. Based on our extended discussions in Chapters 3 and 4:

   a. How would you best describe the attempts to revive the Halston brand (e.g. repositioning, revitalization, etc.)?

   b. What other factors could have contributed to the failed attempts to revive the brand? In your assessment, what could have been done to make it work?

Case Study Sources

1. Brady, Tara. "Halston: The Story of the Most Famous Fashion Designer in America". *The Irish Times*. June 7, 2019. https://www.irishtimes.com/culture/film/halston-the-story-of-the-most-famous-fashion-designer-in-america-1.3915480

2. Cochrane, Lauren. "The Enduring Legacy of 70's Disco Designer Halston". *The Guardian*. June 5, 2019. https://www.theguardian.com/fashion/2019/jun/05/halston-70s-disco-designer-rise-fall-bianca-jagger-iman-studio-54

3. Gaines, Steven. "The Man Who Sold His Name". *Vanity Fair*. June 24, 2014. https://www.vanityfair.com/news/1991/09/halston-life-story

4. Hayland, Veronique. "Halston's Penney's Serenade". *WWD*. May 12, 2010. https://wwd.com/fashion-news/fashion-features/halston-j-c-penney-3068848/

5. Ilchi, Layla. "How Halston Became One of America's Most Iconic Fashion Designers". *WWD*. July 25, 2019. https://wwd.com/fashion-news/fashion-scoops/halston-fashion-designer-facts-cnn-documentary-trailer-1203226534/

6. Ponsford, Matthew. "The Rise and Fall of Halston, The Man Who Redefined American Fashion". *CNN*. August 6, 2019. https://www.cnn.com/style/article/halston-american-fashion/index.html

7. Rottman, Fred. "Halston". *Love to Know*. Accessed October 7, 2019. https://fashion-history.lovetoknow.com/fashion-clothing-industry/fashion-designers/halston

8. www.halston.com

NOTES

1. Kapferer, J. N. *The New Strategic Brand Management*, 4th ed. (London: Kogan-Page, 2008), 219.
2. Keller, Kevin L. *Strategic Brand Management*, 4th ed. (Upper Saddle River: Pearson, 2013), 404.
3. "Growth Share Matrix". Boston Consulting Group. Accessed September 10, 2017. https://www.bcg.com/.
4. Hess, Edward. *Smart Growth: Building an Enduring Business by Managing the Risks of Growth* (New York: Columbia University Press, 2010).
5. Corbellini, Erica and Stefania Saviolo. *Managing Fashion and Luxury Companies* (Milan: Rizzoli ETAS, 2012), 240.
6. Reddy, Mergen, et al. *How Far Can Luxury Brands Travel? Avoiding the Pitfalls of Luxury Brand Extension* (Indiana: Kelley School of Business, 2009), 191.
7. Extension paths (page 244).
8. Prada phone.
9. Keller, 421.
10. "Global Sales of Licensed Goods and Services Reach US$280.3 Billion, Fifth Straight Year of Growth for the Licensing Industry". Licensing International. June 04, 2019. https://licensinginternational.org/news/global-sales-of-licensed-products-and-services-reach-us-280-3-billion-fifth-straight-year-of-growth-for-the-licensing-industry/
11. Chanel precision.
12. Keller, 424.
13. Hopkin, Paul. *Fundamentals of Risk Management*, 4th ed. (London: Kogan Page, 2017), 17.

BIBLIOGRAPHY

Books

Aaker, David. *Aaker on Branding: 20 Principles that Drive Success* (New York: Morgan James Publishing, 2014).

Battersby, Gregory J. and Danny Simon. *Basics of Licensing: How to Extend Brand and Entertainment Properties for Profit* (Norwalk: Kent Press, 2012).

Birnbaum, David. *Birnbaum's Global Guide to Winning the Great garment War* (New York: The Fashiondex, Inc., 2000).

Bruce, Margaret, Christopher Moore and Grete Birtwistle. *International Retail Marketing: A Case Study Approach* (Burlington: Elsevier, 2005).

Burns, Leslie D., Kathy K. Mullet and Nancy O. Bryant. *The Business of Fashion*, 4th ed. (New York: Fairchild, 2011).

Chevalier, Michel and Gerald Mazzalovo. *Luxury Brand Management: A World of Privilege* (Singapore: John Wiley and Sons (Asia), 2008).

Choi, Tsan-Ming and Bin Shen. *Luxury Fashion Retail Management* (Singapore: Springer, 2017).

Corbellini, Erica and Stefania Saviolo. *Managing Fashion and Luxury Companies* (Firenze: Rizzoli ETAS, 2012).

David, Fred R. *Strategic Management: Concepts and Cases*, 13th ed. (Upper Saddle River: Pearson, 2011).

Hameide, Kaled. *Fashion Branding Unraveled* (New York: Fairchild, 2011).

Hess, Edward D. *Smart Growth: Building and Enduring Business by Managing the Risks of Growth* (New York: Columbia University Press, 2010).

Hill, Charles W. L. and G. Tomas M. Hult. *Global Business Today* (New York: McGraw-Hill, 2016).

Hopkin, Paul. *Fundamentals of Risk Management: Understanding, Evaluating, and Implementing Effective Risk Management*, 4th ed. (London: Kogan Page, 2017).

Kapferer, J. N. *The New Strategic Brand Management: Creating and Sustaining Brand Equity Long Term*, 4th ed. (London: Kogan Page, 2008).

Keller, Kevin L. *Strategic Brand Management*, 4th ed. (Upper Saddle River: Pearson, 2013).

Kunz, Grace I. and Myrna B. Garner. *Going Global* (New York: Fairchild, 2011).

Kunz, Grace I., Elena Karpova and Myrna B. Garner. *Going Global: The Textile and Apparel Industry*, 3rd ed. (New York: Fairchild, 2016).

Morden, Tony. *Principles of Strategic Management*, 3rd ed. (Hampshire: Ashgate Publishing Limited, 2007).

Reddy, Mergen, Nic Terblanche, Leyland Pitt and Michael Parent. *How Far Can Luxury Brands Travel? Avoiding the Pitfalls of Luxury Brand Extension* (Indiana: Kelley School of Business, 2009).

Robbins, Stephan P. and Mary Coulter. *Management*, 7th ed. (Upper Saddle River: Prentice Hall, 2001).

Schramme, Annick, Turi Moerkerke and Karinna Nobbs. *Fashion Management* (Leuven: Lannoo, 2013).

Sherman, Gerald J. and Sar S. Perlman. *The Real World Guide to Fashion Selling and Management*, 2nd ed. (New York: Fairchild, 2015).

Van Gelder, Sicco. *Global Brand Strategy: Unlocking Brand Potential Across Countries, Cultures and Markets* (London: Kogan-Page, 2003).

Varley, Rosemary, Ana Roncha, Natasha Radclyffe-Thomas, Liz Gee. *Fashion Management: A Strategic Approach* (London: Red Globe Press, 2019).

Wheelen, Thomas L. and J. David Hunger. *Strategic Management and Business Policy: Toward Global Sustainability*, 3rd ed (Upper Saddle River: Pearson, 2012).

White, Nicola and Ian Griffiths. *The Fashion Business: Theory, Practice, Image* (New York: Berg, 2000).

Other Sources

"Diesel SpA History". Funding Universe. Accessed July 4, 2019. http://www.fundinguniverse.com/company-histories/diesel-spa-history/

"The Diesel Story". First to Know. August 4, 2017. https://www.ftkclothing.com/blogs/news/the-diesel-story-ireland

"The History of Diesel Jeans". The Jeans Blog. June 2, 2014. https://thejeansblog.com/denim-brand-history/the-history-of-diesel-jeans/

"The History of Diesel, The Rebel Brand". Accessed Bang and Strike. Accessed September 10, 2019. https://www.bangandstrike.com/pages/the-history-of-diesel-the-rebel-brand

"The History of Diesel, The Rebel Brand". Bang and Strike. Accessed May 9, 2018. https://us.bangandstrike.com/pages/the-history-of-diesel-the-rebel-brand

"PEST Analysis". Expert Program Management. Accessed. July 14, 2018. https://expertprogrammanagement.com/2018/05/pest-analysis/

"PEST Analysis". Group Map. Accessed May 4, 2018. https://www.groupmap.com/map-templates/pest-analysis/

"The Product Market Expansion Grid Explained". Product 2 Market. Accessed April 20, 2018. https://product2market.walkme.com/product-market-expansion-grid-explained/

"What is Influencer Marketing: An in Depth Look at Marketing's Next Big Thing". Influencer Marketing Hub. Updated March 16, 2020. https://influencermarketinghub.com/what-is-influencer-marketing/

Administrator. "BCG Matrix: Portfolio Analysis in Corporate Strategy". *Business to You*. Novemeber 30, 2017. https://www.business-to-you.com/bcg-matrix/

Bae, Koun. "Introducing the New Diesel Gold by Andreas Melbostad". *Flaunt*. February 16, 2017. https://www.flaunt.com/content/people/introducing-new-diesel-black-gold-andreas-melbostad

Barmash, Isadore. "Penney's $1 Billion Gamble on Chic". *NY Times*. July 10, 1983. https://www.nytimes.com/1983/07/10/business/penney-s-1-billion-gamble-on-chic.html

Binkley, Christina. "How Renzo Rosso Returned Diesel to Growth". *Vogue*. October 28, 2019. https://www.voguebusiness.com/companies/renzo-rosso-diesel-founder-denim-growth-samuel-ross

Borrell-Person, Laird. "There's a Pierre Cardin Exhibit at the Brooklyn Museum. Here are 5 Things You Didn't Know About the French Design Legend". *Vogue*. July 19, 2019. https://www.vogue.com/article/pierre-cardin-exhibition-brooklyn-museum-of-art

Brady, Tara. "Halston: The Story of the Most Famous Fashion Designer in America". *The Irish Times*. June 7, 2019. https://www.irishtimes.com/culture/film/halston-the-story-of-the-most-famous-fashion-designer-in-america-1.3915480

Carvell, Nick. "Meet Andreas Melbostad, the Man Behind Diesel Black Gold". *GQ*. May 26, 2016. https://www.gq-magazine.co.uk/article/andreas-melbostad-diesel-black-gold-interview

Gaines, Steven. "The Man Who Sold His Name". *Vanity Fair*. June 26, 2014. https://www.vanityfair.com/news/1991/09/halston-life-story

Hanlon, Anmarie. "How to Use the BCG Matrix Model". *Smart Insights*. July 16, 2019. https://www.smartinsights.com/marketing-planning/marketing-models/use-bcg-matrix/

http://fashiongear.fibre2fashion.com/brand-story/diesel/productline.asp

Hyland, Veronique. "Halston's Penney's Serenade". *WWD*. May 12, 2010. https://wwd.com/fashion-news/fashion-features/halston-j-c-penney-3068848/

IIchi, Layla. "How Halston Became One of America's Most Iconic Designers". *WWD*. July 25, 2019. https://wwd.com/fashion-news/fashion-scoops/halston-fashion-designer-facts-cnn-documentary-trailer-1203226534/

Jurevicius, Ovidijus. 'PEST and PESTEL Analysis". *Strategic Management Insight*. February 13, 2013. https://strategicmanagementinsight.com/tools/pest-pestel-analysis.html

Morris, Wesley. "Halston Review: The Designer as Unsolved Mystery". *NY Times*. May 23, 2019. https://www.nytimes.com/2019/05/23/movies/halston-review.html

O'Connor, Clare. "Blue Jean Billionaire: Inside Diesel, Renzo Rosso's $3 Billion Fashion Empire". *Forbes*. March 25, 2013. https://www.forbes.com/sites/clareoconnor/2013/03/06/blue-jean-billionaire-inside-diesel-renzo-rossos-3-billion-denim-empire/#4f9cfdcb58a5

Odell, Amy. 'From Disco to JCPenney: The Enduring Tragedy of Halston". *The CUT*. December 19, 2011. https://www.thecut.com/2011/12/halston-from-the-disco-to-jcpenney.html

Pavitt, Jane. "A Brief History of Brands; Diesel". *The Guardian*. July 9, 2001. https://www.theguardian.com/media/2001/jul/09/marketingandpr.g28

Picchi, Aimee. "Diesel, Jeans Company Known for Pricey Denim, Goes Bankrupt". *CBS News*. March 6, 2019. https://www.cbsnews.com/news/diesel-bankruptcy-jeans-company-denim-chapter-11/

Ponsford, Matthew. "The Rise and Fall of Halston, The Man Who Redefined American Fashion". *CNN*. Updated August 6, 2019. https://www.cnn.com/style/article/halston-american-fashion/index.html

Rappold, Laurianne. "Diesel History". *Behind Jeans*. October 10, 2014. https://behindjeans.wordpress.com/2014/10/10/diesel-history/

Rottman, Fred. "Halston". *Love to Know*. Accessed May 16, 2019. https://fashion-history.lovetoknow.com/fashion-clothing-industry/fashion-designers/halston

Sutton, Dave. "6 Vital Steps for Brand Extension Success". *Top Right*. November 21, 2016. https://www.toprightpartners.com/insights/6-vital-steps-brand-extension-success/

Warren, Liz. "Diesel's Renaissance Makes the Brand Cool, and Profitable, Again". *Sourcing Journal*. October 29, 2019. https://sourcingjournal.com/denim/denim-brands/diesel-denim-renaissance-renzo-rosso-177003/

Zargani, Luisa and Rosemary Feitelberg. "Diesel, Nicola Formichetti Part Ways". *WWD*. December 18, 2017. https://wwd.com/fashion-news/denim/exclusive-diesel-nicola-formichetti-end-collaboration-contract-11076973/

CHAPTER FIVE
Managing Fashion Licensing

LEARNING OUTCOMES

- Understanding how the licensing and franchising models work

- Appreciate the challenges and potentials of both licensing and franchising

- Familiarize with the licensing and franchising contracts

- Identify the differences and similarities between both models

THE STATE OF LICENSING

In the previous chapter we have examined brand extensions as one of the most common options for brand growth, especially for lifestyle and luxury brands. We have also mentioned that brand extensions in the fashion industry are commonly achieved through licensing. A licensing agreement can be defined as *an agreement in which one party grants to another the right to exploit certain intellectual property, subject to guidance oversight and other specific constraints in return for royalties.*[1] Thus, there are two parties in a licensing agreement: The Licensor and the Licensee:

The Licensor: Is the owner of the brand and the intellectual property which grants the license.

The Licensee: Is the manufacturer which will lease the rights to incorporate the brand's name into its merchandise. The licensee does not share ownership of the brand name but just obtains the rights to use it.

According to the annual Global Licensing Survey the global licensing industry reached $280.3 billion in sales in 2018 with an increase of 3.2% from the previous year maintaining a trend of growth for five consecutive years with royalty revenue that reached $15 billion, an increase of 4%.[2] Licensing is common in many industries, not just in fashion. For instance, the largest segment in licensing sales comes from character and entertainment (43.8%) while fashion and related industries (accessories and beauty) came in third position with about $32.2 billion in revenue accounting for 11.5% of total global licensed retail sales. Other industries include corporate brands (second position around 21%) and sports (fourth position with 9.9%).

In addition, the U.S. and Canada remain the largest global regions for licensed merchandise with total sales reaching $162.68 billion (in all licensed categories) which represents a 58% market share.[3] These numbers signify the size and scope of licensing and the integral role it plays in global retail sales. Hence, it is necessary that we dedicate a whole chapter on the topic, especially that while many may be aware of the concept itself, they may not be aware of some of the details that go into such an arrangement which in return is very essential for managers to understand. We will also cover as part of our discussion in this chapter the concept of franchising as it represents the licensing equivalent in retailing which is equally relevant and important to the fashion industry.

ROLE OF THE LICENSING AGENT

A licensor who does not want to spend time identifying and soliciting potential licensees and administering a licensing program may want to engage a licensing agent. The licensing agent definition is *a person who identifies possible licensees for the licensor's property, represents the property in trade shows, and presents the property and proposals to licensees while negotiating contracts terms.*[4] For a licensor which doesn't want to do these tasks, hiring a licensing agent is a good idea. This service may be available at an additional fixed or hourly charge. But typically, agents receive a portion of the royalties or profits generated through the licensing agreement that has been facilitated by them. Choosing the right agent is important. It is essential that he is someone whose strategy is aligned with that of the licensor, especially as agents have an incentive to sign as many licensing agreements as possible given that they do not get paid until the agreement is signed and revenues start to flow.

Agents may help the licensor in many ways such as:

- The agent will review the license by obtaining and reviewing samples of the licensed product or help in developing it, and negotiate license agreements, as well as collecting royalties and other payments. Some licensors prefer to receive the samples and payments and pay a commission to the agent.

- Develop a strategic licensing plan, including identifying promising retail channels and identifying licensees capable of assisting in the execution of the licensing objectives.

- Provide guidelines on realistic financial goals.

- Monitor performance and assist in quality control.

Agents obviously could be very helpful to new and small brands but they could also offer hard unconventional opportunities to well-established brands. For example, a watch company could be advised to target automotive companies for prestige product placement through branded interior clocks, or a fragrance company can introduce perfumes for cars brands, etc.

Scope of the Agency Agreement

The agent agreement should list or define the products that the agent will be authorized to represent, as well as the product lines and territories covered by the agreement. Some products may have potential for publishing, software, film, or other uses beyond the typical merchandise categories. The licensor may want to exempt those uses from the agent relationship, particularly if the agent does not have any experience or track record in securing licenses in those areas.

Things to consider in an agency agreement are:

- *Exclusivity.* Most agent appointments will be exclusive. This means that the agent is the only agent that can represent the licensor.

- *Ownership and Control.* The licensor retains ownership of the property and should have final approval over all license terms.

- *Commissions and Expenses.* Commissions for licensing agents generally average between 30% to 40% of gross licensing revenue and may run as high as 50%. In addition, some agents require the licensor to pay part or all of certain expenses incurred by the agent in representing the licensor. These expenses may include trade show costs, the costs of creating promotional packages and display and solicitation materials, travel costs, and legal fees. The licensor should ensure that the agreement specifically identifies all costs to be paid by the licensor. In addition, the licensor may want the right to approve all expenses in advance and may want to impose a cap on the total amount of expenses for which it will be responsible.

- *Term.* Most agents require a minimum initial term of two or three years, since it often takes that long to develop a product, find licensees, and begin to receive royalties. The licensor may be able to get the right to terminate the agreement earlier if certain performance benchmarks, such as a minimum amount of royalty income or a minimum number of new licenses, are not reached by a specified point in the term.

- *Renewal.* The agent will usually want an option to renew the relationship for one or more additional terms to have the opportunity to stay around and reap the rewards from that investment. In many cases, renewal could be automatic unless either party gives notice by a certain date before the end of a term. It can also be conditioned on a certain level of royalty income having been reached during the first term.

- *Termination of Authority.* It is common that the licensor can terminate the agent's authority to act on behalf of the licensor at any time. However, the licensor cannot terminate the agent's right to receive commissions from licensing deals achieved during the term of the agreement.

- *Termination of Agreement.* The licensor should always have the right to terminate the agreement if the agent fails to pay net royalties to the licensor within the time required under the agreement, or enters into any license agreement without the licensor's approval.

WHAT TO LICENSE?

Licensing may cover many different types of intellectual property rights (IPR) such as: Trademarks, Copyrights, Registered or Unregistered Design Rights

Licensing Trademarks

Registered or unregistered trademarks are very commonly licensed. For a fashion business this is likely to be the designer's name, label name, brand name, or the name of a particular product range. For more established fashion brands, it may also be a design or image that has become synonymous with the brand and registered as a trademark, such as the Paul Smith striped pony. The licensing options for trademarks include:

- Allowing a licensee to use the trademark on a range of products that it designs and produces (for example, Denim Jeans for Calvin Klein).

- Allowing a licensee to use the trademark on a range of products that are designed and produced by the licensee (such as Italian sunglasses manufacturer Luxottica, which has produced sunglasses for designers such as Chanel and Ray-Ban under licensing).

- Allowing a licensee to use the trademark alongside its own brand on a range of products designed in collaboration with the designer (for example, womenswear designer Peter Pilotto's collaboration with Kipling Bags).

- Allowing a licensee to use the trademark in a new geographic territory or to meet a new target group, either with or without design collaboration (such as Italian brand Stefanel has initially done in some Middle East markets).

- Working with a licensee to develop a new trademark to feature on a diffusion range of products, such as H! by Henry Holland and Debenhams or D&G by Dolce & Gabbana.

INVESTMENT VS. CONSUMPTION CATEGORIES

Not all licensed products are the same or impact the parent brand the same way. For a fashion luxury brand licensing into products such as: perfumes, watches, and ready-to-wear do improve its status as an aspirational brand and thus these categories are considered *investment* categories. On the other hand, products such as underwear, belts, or handkerchiefs, while still rewarding, tend to benefit more from the brand image than add value or status to it and thus should be regarded as *consumption* categories. A successful portfolio of licenses is one that has a balance of both categories.

LICENSING COPYRIGHT

This is especially relevant to designers who may produce print or textile designs, since these are likely to be of interest or potential commercial value in a range of product areas beyond that of the licensor. For example, a print design could be licensed for use on soft furnishings, luggage, or stationery. The licensing options for copyright include:

- Allowing a licensee to reproduce and market the copyright design on a range of its products (for instance, Takashi Muramaki's designs used on Louis Vuitton handbags).

- Allowing a licensee to reproduce the copyright design on a range of its products designed in collaboration, such as Tracey Emin's design of a range of luggage also carrying reproductions of her artwork in collaboration with Longchamp.

LICENSING REGISTERED AND UNREGISTERED DESIGNS

This covers specific designs, three dimensional products, or parts of products. Options for licensing designs include:

- Allowing a licensee to reproduce the design in a new geographic territory.

- Allowing a licensee to reproduce the design in a way that makes them appeal to a new target market, perhaps through use of lower-priced materials or production methods.

It is possible for a license arrangement to include the right to use more than one type of IPR, for example the trademark or brand name/logo, together with signature design features, or original prints which are associated with the designer.

ADVANTAGES AND CHALLENGES OF LICENSING

Advantages to the Licensor

- Licensing allows the brand to be engaged in controlled expansion without having the financial risk of investing in costly infrastructure.

- Expansion into new product categories through licensing increases market penetration. Licensing can open up new market segments that a designer may not be able to exploit. For example, luxury brands often grant licenses for sunglasses and fragrances, making their brands accessible to a new, broader market, i.e. a customer who purchases Prada frames or Gucci perfumes may never have been able to afford a designer outfit from either company but many aspire to and thus enjoys a small part of the brand through the purchase of the sunglasses or perfume.

- Expansions enhance brand awareness as they are supported by new points of sale in prime locations such as the first floor of department stores (commonly occupied by beauty products and fragrances) or in different categories of stores, e.g. home goods stores.

- Allows the licensor to enter international markets. Licensors may benefit from access to foreign distributors and retailers which have established local commercial relationships and expertise. Local retailers will of course benefit from introducing a foreign brand and products to their home locations as well.

- Increasing revenue as the licensor receives injections of working capital through fees and royalty payments.

- Well-constructed licensing deals with higher profile partners can raise brand awareness of emerging designers. Licensing deals that provide increased high street presence, additional PR coverage, and positive brand associations can aid the growth and profile of an emerging fashion business.

- Accessing expertise as the designer can seek out a licensee with all the required knowledge, experience, and expertise to access these new markets and product lines.

- One of the key benefits to the licensor is that the licensee is taking on the administrative burden of running the business, leaving the designer free to focus on creative output. Additionally, such arrangements can be attractive to potential retail buyers who may have concerns about the ability of small designers to meet order requirements.

- Successful collaborations. Businesses may want to work together in order to expand into new product areas, or appeal to new customers. In 1987 Donna Karan had already established a high-end womenswear brand when she determined that the hosiery market was not meeting the needs of consumers willing to pay more for better quality. Lacking experience in this sector, she designed a range in partnership with Hanes, which produced them under license.

Disadvantages to the Licensor

- *Loss of maximum revenue.* A designer could make greater returns if his/her business is capable of fully commercializing its own IP. As a licensor, a designer will typically receive only a percentage, for example, 10% of gross profits, from licensed sales.

- *Over extending.* Some licenses may reduce the value of the IPR by extending the brand too far or reducing the exclusivity of the product. Pierre Cardin, as mentioned earlier, has licensed intellectual property rights in his business to hundreds of licensees over the years, some of those products are quite removed from the fashion industry.

- *Loss of control as it increases opportunities for IP theft.* Once a licensor begins to license its intellectual property and products, it is exposing itself to higher levels of exposure. There will be more opportunities for theft, piracy, and misuse because it doesn't have full control over how the licensee conducts operations.

- *It creates added competition in the marketplace.* Although licensing prohibits making products that are directly competitive to the licensor's brands and products, many licensors have found that their licensees eventually become competitors in their own marketplace.

- *It could damage the reputation of both parties.* When one element of the relationship is mismanaged with licensing, then both parties can see a reduction in the brand reputation of the IP involved.

- *It is not a guarantee of revenues.* There is no guarantee that a licensing agreement will generate cash. The licensor could agree to a specific royalty rate with a licensee, then never see anything because the licensee is unable to generate any sales.

- *It takes time for royalty payments to arrive.* For many licensing agreements, the royalty payments are offered just once per quarter. That means it could be 5–6 months before a licensor sees its first meaningful royalty payment, even when the product is doing well in other markets.

- *One of the biggest issues that licensors face with licensing agreements is a refusal by the licensee to validate royalty statements.* They may not let licensors audit their statements for accuracy. This does allow the licensor to take legal action which tends to be a very expensive process. For that reason, arbitration clauses are becoming a common component of licensing agreements. Some are even requiring ongoing royalty statement audits as a condition of the license continuing.

Box 5.1 Calvin Klein: The Ups and Downs of Licensing

Licensing has been an important arm of the Calvin Klein business for many years. However, its history with licensing sheds light on both the potential and downsides of this strategy. Before being purchased by PVH, the brand had a highly publicized bitter lawsuit with the brand's largest licensee at the time, the Warnaco Group. The lawsuit, which Klein filed in May 2000, accused the Warnaco Group and its CEO, Linda Wachner, of diluting the Calvin Klein brand name by producing merchandise that was not authorized or approved by Calvin Klein, and distributing Calvin Klein Jeanswear through unapproved discount outlets and warehouse clubs, such as Costco and BJ's. The suit was settled in 2001, and Warnaco was able to retain its Calvin Klein licenses, but Calvin Klein was able to regain some of the creative control he had lost in the original license.

Calvin Klein was eventually purchased by PVH in 2013. PVH is a leading fashion conglomerate in the U.S. and operating in over 40 countries. It had generated $9.7 billion in revenues in 2018, through a portfolio of famous global fashion brands it operates with a strategic combination of wholesale, retail, digital commerce, and licensing operations. PVH currently operates three business groups; Calvin Klein, Tommy Hilfiger, and Heritage Brands which include Van Heusen, IZOD, ARROW, and Geoffrey Beene among others. It is also considered the world's largest dress shirt and neckwear company. After acquiring Calvin Klein, PVH worked on transforming the brand's business model from being licensing-driven to a more directly operated business with a better structured and managed licensing operation. As a result, Calvin Klein direct operations expanded to Europe, Asia, and Latin America with revenues growing to over $7.8 billion in global retail sales in 2013. On the other hand, licensing continued to be a significant component of Calvin Klein's business, as 53% of global retail sales under the brand in 2018 were generated from licensed businesses. Among Calvin Klein's largest licensees in terms of global retail sales was G-III Apparel Group, Ltd. (G-III), which generated approximately $1.9 billion in global retail sales in 2018 (primarily in North America) selling men's and women's coats, swimwear and luggage, women's suits, dresses, sportswear (casual apparel) and performance apparel, handbags, and small leather goods. Additionally, in 2019, the brand entered into a license agreement with G-III for the CALVIN KLEIN JEANS women's jeans wear collections in the U. S. and Canada, with the first collection launched in Spring 2020. The second large licensee is Coty, Inc., (fragrance licensee), which generated approximately $1.3 billion in global retail sales in 2018. Currently, Calvin Klein has over 50 licensing arrangements. Table 5.1 demonstrates examples of some of its licensing partners:

Sources

1. *Phillips-Van Heusen Corporations Annual Report, 2018.* Accessed October 11, 2019. https://www.pvh.com/investor-relations/reports
2. *Phillips-Van Heusen Corporations Annual Report, 2009* Accessed October 11, 2019. https://sec.report/Document/0000078239-09-000013/

Table 5.1 Examples of Calvin Klein Licensing Partners

Licensing Partner	Product Category
CK21 Holdings Pte, Ltd.	Men's and women's bridge apparel, shoes and accessories (Asia, excluding Japan)
Coty, Inc.	Men's and women's fragrance and bath products (worldwide)
DWI Holdings, Inc.	Soft home bed and bath furnishings (U.S., Canada, Mexico, Central America, and South America)
G-III Apparel Group, Ltd.	Men's and women's coats, women's better suits, dresses and sportswear, women's active performance wear (U.S., Canada, Mexico)
Marchon Eyewear, Inc.	Men's and women's optical frames and sunglasses (worldwide)
Markwins Holding Co., Ltd. (Markwins International Corp.)	Colo cosmetics and skin care products (worldwide)
Onward Kashiyama Co. Ltd.	Men's and women's bridge apparel and women's accessories (Japan)

Created by Author.

Advantages to the Licensee

- Marketing and producing a famous brand enhance the licensee's access to retailers.

- It creates new business opportunities. A licensee can benefit from this type of arrangement because it requires less money to start a business opportunity. It can purchase a license instead of outright ownership, then begin to make profits right away. It takes less upfront cash to pay for a license. So, licensing represents a way for a manufacturer to take advantage of all the brand building and image building that has been done. When a licensee can improve upon a product, it can make even more money from its venture. Even if the item wanted is a trademark or brand name, the new business benefits from the reputation and consumer awareness of the information.

- As mentioned earlier it reduces risks for both parties. Licensing is designed to reduce the risks involved in doing business for everyone involved. From a licensee standpoint, there are fewer risks in product development, market testing, manufacturing, and distribution.

- It creates an easier entry into foreign markets.

- It offers the freedom to develop a unique marketing approach. A licensee knows its market much better than the average licensor. That knowledge allows an intellectual property to be marketed in a way that is more attractive to the average consumer. It is a chance to expand the reach of a message, product, or concept without actually needing to invest into them fully. Even when certain elements of the arrangement are pre-planned, there is still a certain level of freedom and control given to the licensee in the management of its business.

Disadvantages to the Licensee

- In taking on a license, a licensee takes on a financial obligation, and also an obligation to adhere to agreements in such areas as submitting products for all necessary approvals, creating a product to agreed-upon standards, and marketing the product.

- The risks that the licensee faces in a licensing program are fewer in number than those of the licensor, but potentially greater in magnitude. The major risk is financial such as royalties, guarantees, and advances. Even if the products do make it to the market, there is no certainty at all that they will do well, no matter what property a manufacturer chooses.

- It creates a dependency upon the licensor. The licensee is dependent upon the quality of the IP being used to make its own profits. There is also no guarantee of exclusivity with many licenses, which means multiple businesses could be competing in the same marketplace, using the same tools and products, to generate revenues.

- Most licenses are only offered for a limited time with no guarantee of renewal. Although that time period may be 5–10 years, there is an expiration date which must be considered by the licensee. So a licensee needs to determine if it is worthwhile to invest time, effort, and cash into the promotion of goods or services that may not be available to them at the end of the licensing period.

- It could damage the reputation of both parties. When one element of the relationship is mismanaged with licensing, then both parties can see a reduction in the brand reputation of the IP involved. This is why many license agreements include a series of best practices to follow, creating consistency within the brand across all licenses.

THE LICENSING AGREEMENT

Before entering into a license transaction, the licensor and licensee should agree on the terms of the license, and should sign a written license agreement to serve as the road map for their relationship. The license agreement is at the heart of every merchandise licensing transaction. While there are some generally accepted rules in the industry, the licensor and the licensee are usually free to put together the best deal that each can negotiate. It is important to keep in mind that as companies seek to tap new markets in other countries, the question arises as to whether licensing strategies which are effective in one country will also be effective in other countries. Therefore, it is particularly important for a licensor to realize that each country differs in its specifics and must be looked at as a separate territory. Differences may exist, not only in language and the relative effectiveness of different licensing strategies, but also in areas such as market structures, retail patterns, legal systems and limitations, and tax implications. In addition, the agreement should require the licensee to abide by all international, national, and local laws as well as meeting human rights law and operational safety requirements. Some of the key issues to be addressed in a merchandise license agreement are discussed below (Figure 5.1):[5]

The Licensed Property

The license agreement should clearly identify the property or properties to be licensed (e.g. character, design, trademark, etc.), and if applicable, copies of the licensed property should be attached as exhibits to the agreement. The licensee should determine that the property is protectible under copyright, trademark, or other applicable laws, and may want registration numbers to be listed in the agreement. If the licensed property is a trademark, the licensee may also want to require that the mark be registered for use on the types of merchandise to be produced under the license agreement.

The Licensed Products

The agreement should contain a complete description of the licensed merchandise, including dimensions, colors, and materials. In most cases, the licensor will want to limit the licensee's rights to the specified merchandise only and will want the right to approve any changes in that merchandise. The licensee may want an option or a right of first refusal in the event the licensor decides to license the property for certain other product lines (i.e. the licensee is to be asked if it is interested in taking on (or refusing) the new license before it is offered to another licensee).

Licensing Agreement - Michael Kors (HK) Limited

EX-10.6 13 d232021dex106.htm LICENSING AGREEMENT - MICHAEL KORS (HK) LIMITED

Exhibit 10.6

CERTAIN PORTIONS OF THIS EXHIBIT HAVE BEEN OMITTED PURSUANT TO A CONFIDENTIAL TREATMENT REQUEST. OMITTED INFORMATION IS INDICATED BY AN ASTERIK (*) AND HAS BEEN FILED SEPARATELY WITH THE SECURITIES AND EXCHANGE COMMISSION

LICENSE AND DISTRIBUTION AGREEMENT made as of this 1st day of April 2011, by and between MICHAEL KORS, L.L.C., a limited liability company existing under and by virtue of the laws of the State of Delaware, with offices at ██████████ New York, NY, 10036, USA ("Licensor") and Michael Kors (HK) Limited, a Hong Kong limited company with offices at ██████████, 850-870 Lai Chi Kok Road, Cheung Sha Wan, Kowloon, Hong Kong ("Licensee").

RECITALS

A. Michael Kors is a world-famous designer of women's and men's apparel and accessories;

B. Licensor has the sole and exclusive rights in the trademark MICHAEL KORS, MICHAEL MICHAEL KORS, and variations thereof; and

C. Licensee wishes to obtain, and Licensor wishes to grant, an exclusive license for the importation, sale, distribution and promotion of "Licensed Products" (hereinafter defined) upon the terms and conditions set forth herein.

NOW, THEREFORE, for good and valuable consideration including the mutual agreements contained in this Agreement, the parties agree as follows:

2. LICENSE GRANTED

2.1 License Grant. In accordance with the terms and conditions of this Agreement, Licensor hereby grants to Licensee, and Licensee hereby accepts, the License.

5.5 Seconds, Returns and Excess Inventory. Licensee may sell its inventory of Discounted Goods to Off-Priced Stores and to approved off-price accounts as provided in Section 5.4. Licensee shall clearly and permanently "red line" the labels of any Seconds, and shall require any off-price accounts not to advertise or promote the Licensed Products. Unless otherwise agreed in writing, Discounted Goods sold by Licensee in each Contract Year shall not exceed * percent (*%) of the total units of Licensed Products sold by Licensee in such Contract Year.

6.2 Marketing. Licensee shall spend such amounts as are reasonable and customary for the business contemplated herein on other marketing and promotional activities with respect to Licensed Products not specifically delineated hereunder including, but not limited to, cooperative advertising, trade advertising, point-of-sale materials (including fixtures and signage), fashion shows, seasonal product presentations and events with fashion editors. Licensee shall not undertake any marketing or promotional activities, or produce or distribute any marketing or promotional materials of any kind in connection with Licensed Products, without Licensor's prior written approval. Any Collateral Materials to be used by Licensee in connection with its activities pursuant to this Section 6.2 (including, without limitation, look books, catalogs and pictures) shall be produced either (i) by Licensor, with Licensee to pay Licensor the cost of such materials plus a * percent (*%) commission, or (ii) by an agency approved by Licensor, with all costs thereof to be paid by Licensee.

7. ROYALTIES AND REQUIRED MINIMUM NET SALES

7.1 Royalty Rate. In consideration of the license granted herein, Licensee shall pay to Licensor a percentage royalty (the "Percentage Royalty") in each Contract Year of * percent (*%) of Net Wholesale Sales, plus (i) * (*%) of Licensee's Net Retail Sales during the first ten Contract Years of the Term, and (ii) * (*%) of Licensee's Net Retail Sales thereafter.

8.4 Use of Trademarks and IP Rights. Licensee shall use the Trademarks and IP Rights solely in connection with the Licensed Products. Licensee shall use and display the Trademarks only in such form and manner as are specifically provided or approved by Licensor. Licensor may promulgate, from time to time, reasonable rules and amendments thereto, relating to use of the Trademarks, and Licensee shall comply with all such rules and amendments.

9.3 Licensor's Right of Termination. Licensor shall have the right to terminate the Term by delivering written notice to Licensee pursuant to Section 3.2(a) and 3.2(b) and Licensee shall have no right to cure. In addition, Licensor shall have the right to terminate the Term, subject to Licensee's right to cure set forth herein:

(a) If Licensee fails to pay royalties or any other amount due Licensor hereunder on the date due;

(b) If Licensee materially breaches any of its representations and warranties herein;

(c) If Licensee attacks the title or any rights of Licensor in and to the Trademarks; or

(d) If Licensee shall otherwise fail to perform any term of this Agreement to be performed, not covered by the preceding sections.

Figure 5.1 Excerpts from a License Agreement Sample.
SEC.GOV public records

The Grant of Rights

The agreement should grant the licensee the right to manufacture, import, market, distribute, and sell licensed products, and should specify whether the grant will be exclusive or non-exclusive. If the grant is exclusive, the licensor will not be able to grant the same rights to any other licensee in the territory. If the grant is non-exclusive, the licensor will be able to grant the same rights to others, provided it does not try to do so on an exclusive basis. In addition to manufacturing, importation and distribution rights, the licensee should acquire the right to use the licensed property in advertising for the merchandise to be produced.

Exclusivity

As mentioned, rights granted under a license may be exclusive or non-exclusive. Under an *exclusive* license, the licensee is the only entity authorized to exploit the licensed intellectual property in the designated territory. Since fashion is manufactured in Asia and other places where the licensee may not be authorized to sell, exclusivity is commonly limited to distribution and sale and not manufacturing in a discrete territory. Exclusive rights will command higher rates of compensation by the licensor.

On the other hand, when a brand is well known and product lines and brand extensions require multiple manufacturers, it is common for a fashion licensor to have separate licenses for different categories, for example one for swimwear and one for shoes, etc. It is very rare that one licensee is granted exclusivity in all categories. Thus, the category should be clearly defined. Licensors do not want to grant an overly broad territory which limits the licensor's chances to expand through other licensees, nor offer an overly narrow territory that may stifle brand expansion as the licensor may fail to fully exploit an opportunity to expand brand recognition. Thus, both parties must ensure that an adequate consumer market exists in the territory for the licensed products.

A licensor will typically prefer to grant a *non-exclusive* license, while a licensee will want to be the exclusive seller of the product covered by the license. If the licensor is only willing to grant a non-exclusive license, then before signing the agreement, the licensee should determine if there is a likelihood of others entering the market. In some cases, even though the license is non-exclusive, the licensor may have difficulty finding other licensees willing to take on a license for the same products, given that there will already be one licensee with those products in the marketplace. If this is the case, the licensee can probably accept a non-exclusive license, and may even be able to use that fact to its advantage to negotiate for a lower advance, guaranty or royalty than would be the case for an exclusive license. However, if there is a risk of others taking on the same license and flooding the market with the same types of licensed products, the licensee may want to pass on the non-exclusive license.

Duration

Another important component of a licensing agreement is that it must specify the duration and what happens upon termination or expiration of the agreement. Licensors usually prefer an initial short term to give the licensee as an introductory period of performance. On the other hand, the licensee may want a very long term if it is making a substantial investment in infrastructure or personnel. Terms may be renewed upon written notices or be automatic which is usually not advised for new and first-term agreements. The licensor should always retain the ability to terminate the agreement upon a material breach such as failure to pay royalties, meet quality obligations, meet sales minimum, or an unauthorized sale of products.

It is important to note that the agreement may also include post-termination rights which covers things like ways to dispose of product, the use of licensed intellectual property, obligations to pay royalty beyond termination, maintaining confidentiality and refraining from challenging the trademark registration, disposition of inventory, buy-back options, or such details as in the case of termination in advance of natural expiration where the payment of minimum royalties for the balance of the licensed item is accelerated and is due immediately.

In most cases, it is to the licensor's advantage to have a shorter rather than a longer term. If the licensing arrangement is successful, a shorter term will give the licensor an opportunity to negotiate a higher royalty rate before renewing the license agreement. As a compromise, the licensor and the licensee may agree to a short initial term with an automatic renewal if certain sales or royalty targets are met, or, alternatively, to a longer term with an automatic termination if specific sales or royalty targets are not met.

Design

License agreements must explicitly provide how licensed products will be designed, the approved process, the creation of prototypes and schedules relating to production, delivery, promotion, and market delivery of the goods. It should also state whether third party contractors are permitted, and the extent to which such parties are governed by the terms of the agreement as well as indemnities and ethical compliance guidelines.

Quality Control

Quality control (QC) of the licensed product is imperative as lack of control may weaken or destroy a brand's reputation. Thus, the licensor should retain the right to control the design of the licensed product, including materials used, overall quality, and manufacturing processes. These QCs should include the right to inspect manufacturing plants and review and comment on samples and prototypes throughout the manufacturing process.

The licensor may accept an active role in supervising quality. The licensor should have the right to approve all licensed merchandise and all related packaging and advertising materials before any merchandise or advertisement is released to the public. Depending on the property and the type of merchandise covered by the agreement, the licensor may want approval rights at various stages, including initial plans and specifications, production mock-ups and final production runs. Licensors can maintain control over manufacturing by requiring the licensee to identify its manufacturer by name and address, and by reserving the right to inspect the manufacturer premises for human rights compliance and QC. The licensor should also have the right to obtain random samples of merchandise and advertising materials during the term of the agreement to confirm that there has been no deviation from the previously approved samples. If the licensed property is a trademark, the license agreement must include adequate QC provisions or the licensor will risk losing its rights in the mark.

Distribution

The licensor should specify the appropriate channels of distribution for sale of the products. License agreements often restrict the channels of distribution into which the licensee can sell the licensed products. For example, if the license is for luxury brands the licensor may prohibit inappropriate distribution of articles baring the licensed marks to discount outlets, mass market discounters, and warehouse stores, etc. Or an agreement may limit distribution to a few classes of retail stores, but the licensee may typically sell its products to gift stores or other stores not included in the channels of distribution. A licensee should ensure that the channels of distribution identified in the agreement include all types of stores into which the licensee normally sells its products.

Product distribution guidelines may also be set including standards for marketing and retailing, cost of products, whether approval is required for changes in cost, and how and where the product will be distributed. If the products will be sold in retail outlets the agreement may specify requirements for the location of the product within the store, the type of display and the number of sales staff or expertise of the sales staff on location. Product placement in the showroom and at trade shows may also be specified

The license agreement should specify the geographic areas and channels of trade in which the licensed merchandise can be sold. The licensor will want to limit the territory to countries in which the licensee has a presence, and may want to limit the channels of trade (e.g. upscale department stores, mid-tier department stores, or mass market stores) in which the licensee can sell merchandise. The licensor will also want to prohibit the licensee from selling to any of the licensee's affiliates at below market prices.

In the 1980s and 1990s a number of French luxury brands such as Rochas, Paco Rabanne, and Revillon, had a full range of licensed products in Japan that did not exist in their hometown of Paris. Such a practice could be very profitable to some brands which can use the royalty revenues to develop and grow their brand's presence back home or in Europe through free-standing stores, etc. However, in today's world as people travel more, especially the luxury customer, they expect to find similar products of the brand's offering in Paris, Milan, New York, Tokyo, and other major cities.

If the products are to be sold over the internet, the agreement may specify the website format or placement of the products on the website, the pictures used, the placement of promotional pictures, unique brand subpages or sites within a larger retail website, use of social media and mobile platforms, and the geographical territory in which the products may be sold and delivered to customers.

Sales Efforts

The licensor will want to ensure that the licensee makes a good faith effort to manufacture and sell licensed products, particularly if the license is exclusive. The parties should agree upon sales guidelines such as the size and nature of the sales staff that the licensee must employ (e.g. the agreement may require the assignment of a global brand manager). The license may also specify a schedule for regular licensing meetings and stipulate who will pay for travel expenses to these meetings. Some of the other provisions that can be used to ensure licensed product sales:

- A licensor may require a guaranteed minimum amount of royalty to be paid, as will be mentioned later. However, while a guarantee will ensure that the licensor receives some compensation for the license, it may not ensure that the licensee will actively sell licensed products. For example, a licensee may decide that it is more cost effective to pay the guarantee than to manufacture and sell licensed products, especially if the licensee enters into a license for other potentially competitive products that offer a greater profit potential. In order to prevent this from occurring, a licensor can also include annual minimum sales requirements.

- Product introduction and sale dates. For some categories of products, failure to exhibit prototypes at an annual industry trade show will effectively keep the licensed products out of the marketplace for another year. In these situations, the licensor will want to require that the licensee introduces a certain number of styles of the licensed products at the appropriate trade show. The licensor will also want to require that shipments of products begin no later than whatever date is determined to be the deadline for the appropriate peak marketing period (e.g. back to school, Halloween, Christmas holiday season, etc.). Failure to meet any of these dates will be grounds for termination of the license.

- Finally, If the license agreement grants the licensee responsibility for sales and customer interactions, the licensor should have the ability to review customer service complaints and responses.

Advertising

The licensor will often want the licensee to commit to spend a certain amount, usually calculated annually, on advertising for the licensed products. The agreement should list the types of expenditures that will be included or excluded in satisfying the advertising commitment. Some licensees may offer a large advertising commitment in lieu of, or as a partial credit against, a guarantee mentioned under sales.

The license should specify where and when the licensee may advertise and promote the licensed product and should require the licensee to submit advertisements or promotions to the licensor for prior review and approval. Such controls help maintain brand integrity and can prevent an association with a person or campaign contrary to the goals of the brand, and it also gives the licensor an opportunity to supervise the licensee's marketing efforts.

Spending expectations on advertising differ by product category. For instance, the perfume market is quite large and competitive. Strong advertisement in this segment can increase brand awareness and help boost the fashion brand image, as was the case with Calvin Klein which was virtually unknown in Europe before its licensed perfume advertisements changed that. Accordingly, the perfume category commonly works on an advertising-to-sales ratio that can be as high as 15%, while it is generally around a 2–4% ratio in ready-to-wear.

Delivery

Delivery of designs, prototypes, and/or product samples may be specified on a production schedule. Delivery of product samples may also be required on a continuing basis to ensure quality control. Structured deadlines will help keep production on schedule and avoid delays. A complete agreement will also include a structure or calendar for product development that includes product launch dates.

Sublicensing

The agreement should indicate whether the licensee may grant sublicenses which may be necessary for manufacturing certain products or to allow affiliates of the licensee to use the marks or sell the licensed products. In general, licensor should restrict the right to sublicense and require prior written approval to maintain the quality and integrity of the brand as the sublicensee may not be acceptable or of poor track.

Sublicensing is very common in some markets such as Japan, where it is common for a luxury fashion brand to sign a *master-licensing* agreement with a licensee who would in turn sign sublicense agreements with different local companies. However, this approach has become less common as many brands look to China to handle these tasks.

Restrictions on Consumers

The licensor may limit the types of customers to whom a licensee may sell licensed products. It could be to minimize parallel importing (i.e. grey markets) which happens when goods bearing valid trademarks are manufactured abroad but are then imported to the U.S. (or any other market) without the trademark owner's authorization and thus end up competing with the licensor's goods intended for domestic sale.

Audit Rights

The licensor should have the right to audit the licensee's books and records to verify sales and royalty reports. The licensee may want to impose a time limit within which the books and records for any particular accounting period can be audited, and may want to bar the licensor from conducting more than one audit with respect to any particular accounting period. A licensor should be wary of any lengthy advance notice requirement for conducting an audit, since a substantial advance notice period may give the licensee time to cover up any shortages.

Notices and Credits

The agreement should require the licensee to include proper copyright and trademark notices on the merchandise or on labels or hang tags attached to the merchandise. The licensor may also want to be credited as the owner of the licensed property. This is especially true for licenses where the licensor's primary motivation for entering into the license is often to gain enhanced publicity and name or brand recognition rather than royalties.

Indemnification and Insurance

The licensee will want indemnification (i.e. compensation) against copyright, trademark, and other infringement claims arising from use of the licensed property. The licensor will want indemnification from the licensee against any claims of product liability arising out of the sale or use of the licensed products, and will also want to be indemnified against fines imposed by any government agency for unsafe products and against any claims for unfair trade practices, deceptive advertising, or other actions by the licensee in the advertising and distribution of the licensed products.

The licensor may try to limit its exposure to indemnification by agreeing to indemnify only for actual infringements as determined by a final court judgment, or to cap the amount of indemnification at the total amount of royalties received under the license. In addition, the licensor will want the licensee to carry adequate product liability insurance and will usually want to be named as an additional insured under the licensee's policy.

Termination

The licensor will want the right to terminate the license prior to the end of the term if the licensee fails to perform certain obligations under the agreement or engages in certain activities outside the scope of the agreement. The agreement will often provide for three categories for events of termination:

- Events that are grounds for immediate termination without any cure period.

- Events that will become grounds for termination if not cured within a reasonable time after notice.

- Events that are confined to only a portion of the license, and that will become grounds for the termination of that portion unless cured within a reasonable time after notice.

Sales After Termination

The licensee will usually want the right to distribute any licensed products remaining in its inventory after termination, provided termination is not due to a breach of the agreement by the licensee. If the licensed property is likely to have continuing value after the agreement terminates, the licensor will want to keep the licensee's sell-off period as short as possible, and will want to require that all sales during that period be made in the ordinary course of business at regular prices. The licensor should condition any sales after termination on the licensee having provided a sworn statement showing the total quantity of licensed merchandise in its inventory as of the termination date. The licensor may want to include additional safeguards in the agreement to prevent the licensee from over manufacturing in anticipation of termination.

Compensation and Royalty

In negotiating the compensation for a licensing deal, it is important to look at both the royalty percentage and the base against which that percentage will be applied. Royalties are usually based on net sales of licensed products (in general net sales equal gross sales minus specified discounts and returns) rather than on profits because profits are reduced by many costs that don't concern the licensor and thus should not impact its cut. In addition, accounting figures can easily be manipulated to show minimal profit that's subject to royalties. A licensee would prefer to have royalties be based on profits rather than sales, and if the licensee is dealing from a position of strength may get the licensor to agree. Thus, the most common practice is for royalties to be based on net sales.

However, the definition of net sales can still vary considerably from one agreement to another. The problem comes in identifying items that will be permitted to be deducted from the wholesale price to arrive at net sales. Items that may or may not be deductible include credits for returns, quantity discounts, cash or early payment discounts, advertising allowances/coop advertising, new store allowances, freight charges, sales commissions, and uncollectible accounts. The agreement should also state the exclusions or deductions that are not allowed. For example, foreign withholding taxes on royalty income in certain countries can be as high as 30% and can be excluded from the net sales calculations. Obviously, the licensor will want to limit deductions as much as possible, and may want to put a cap on the total amount that can be deducted. Any deductions that are allowed should be reflected on sales invoices or other records that can be easily audited by the licensor.

Thus, the license agreement should address all of the following issues with respect to the calculation of royalties:

- In general royalty rates can range from 2 to 20% of the licensee's net sales. Rates will vary depending on the type of licensed rights, the types of licensed products to be manufactured, the current or anticipated demand for the licensed products, and the track record of the licensor. While the common standard for royalty is 10% on the wholesale volume, the rate can differ by industry and segment. For example, in fashion the range is commonly 5–15% of revenue (which could be defined as *wholesale sales, gross sales,* or more commonly *net sales as mentioned*). In perfumes which could be a very large business with sales in large volumes, royalty rates are commonly 3–5% of wholesale and export. On the other hand, products that are relatively more difficult to develop and sell, such as men's ready-to-wear, royalties could be 6–8%. Products that are not very close to the licensor's core business tend to have a lower direct impact on the brand's image and thus the licensor can request a 12% royalty to justify the move.

  Royalties may also be set on an escalating or descending basis. A licensor may want to include a royalty rate that escalates based on the number of units sold or the amount of net sales proceeds received.

  In general royalties calculated on wholesale generate the greatest income to the licensor because there are fewer returns, costs, and discounts, etc. to account for.

- For established mature brands, it could request both a guaranteed minimum annual royalty generally paid in advance and prorated in quarterly basis, as well as a minimum annual net sales obligation. This minimum guarantee avoids the warehousing of the brand. It also allows the licensor to terminate the agreement if such objectives are not being met and the licensor can thus seek another licensee.

- The licensor can require the licensee to guarantee that royalties will reach a certain amount. If total royalties do not reach that amount, the licensee will be obligated to pay the difference to the licensor. A portion of the guarantee may be payable as an advance, and the guarantee may be allocated on an annual basis over the term of the agreement. The amount of the guarantee is usually equal to 50 to 75% of the estimated royalties expected to be earned from sales of the licensed products, and as much as 25% of the guarantee may be payable as an advance.

- The licensor may also have to consider other issues in the calculation of royalties. For example, will there be a minimum royalty for free goods given to purchasers as a bonus for buying a specified quantity of products? How will royalties be determined on sales to affiliates of the licensee? and since taxes on royalty income in some countries can be very high, how will it affect royalty calculations?

Statements and Payments

Royalties are usually accounted for and paid on a quarterly basis for all sales deemed to have occurred during the quarter. The license agreement should specify when a sale is deemed to have occurred and be accompanied by a detailed statement of sales, credits, discounts, etc. Statements and payments are typically due thirty days after the end of each quarter. The licensor including a provision for *penalty* for late payments is also common, as well as provisions for permitting termination for nonpayment or chronic late payments.

The license should also specify the mode and currency of payment and provide for a right to audit the licensee's records for up to three years following the expiration or termination of a license. The licensee will usually apply the same accounting and payment practices to all of its licenses, and will not change those practices for any individual licensor.

Other Issues to Consider

Finally, in addition to the above, license contracts should include references to representations, warrantees, and risk controls, as well as bankruptcy and its impact on the trademark, etc.

Box 5.2 Ralph Lauren Licensing Business Overview

The following excerpt is taken from Ralph Lauren Corporation annual report, published 2019, outlining an overview of its licensing business:

Our Licensing Segment

Through licensing alliances, we combine our consumer insight, design, and marketing skills with the specific product or geographic competencies of our licensing partners to create and build new businesses. We generally seek out licensing partners who are leaders in their respective markets, contribute the majority of the product development costs, provide the operational infrastructure required to support the business, and own the inventory. Our licensing business has been aggregated with other non-reportable segments.

Product Licensing

We grant our product licensees the right to access our various trademarks in connection with the licensees' manufacture and sale of designated products, such as certain apparel, eyewear, fragrances, and home furnishings. Each product licensing partner pays us royalties based upon its sales of our products, generally subject to a minimum royalty requirement for the right to use our trademarks and design services. In addition, our licensing partners may be required to allocate a portion of their revenues to advertising our products and sharing in the creative costs associated with these products. Larger allocations typically are required in connection with launches of new products or in new territories. Our license agreements generally have two to five-year terms and may grant the licensees conditional renewal options. We work closely with all of our licensing partners to ensure that their products are developed, marketed, and distributed to reach the intended consumer and are presented consistently across product categories to convey the distinctive identity and lifestyle associated with our brands. Virtually all aspects of the design, production quality, packaging, merchandising, distribution, advertising, and promotion of Ralph Lauren products are subject to our prior approval and continuing oversight. We perform a broader range of services for most of our Ralph Lauren Home licensing partners than we do for our other licensing partners, including design, operating showrooms, marketing, and advertising.

Table 5.2 lists the largest licensing agreements as of March 30, 2019 for the product categories presented.

Except as noted, these product licenses cover North America only.

Table 5.2 Examples of Ralph Lauren Licensing Partners

Licensing Partner	Product Category
Hanesbrands, Inc. (includes Japan)	Menswear: underwear and sleepwear
Peerless Clothing International, Inc.	Menswear: Chaps, Lauren, and Ralph Lauren Tailored Clothing
S. Rothschild & Co., Inc.	Womenswear: outerwear
Manhattan Beachwear, Inc. (includes Europe)	Womenswear: swimwear
L'Oréal S.A. (global)	Beauty Products: fragrances, cosmetics, color, and skin care
Luxottica Group S.p.A (global)	Eyewear
Ichida Co., Ltd. (Japan)	Bedding and bath

Created by Author.

International Licensing

Our international licensing partners acquire the right to sell, promote, market, and/or distribute various categories of our products in a given geographic area and source products from us, our product licensing partners, and independent sources. International licensees' rights may include the right to own and operate retail stores. As of March 30, 2019, our international licensing partners operated 108 Ralph Lauren stores, 39 Ralph Lauren concession shops, and 138 Club Monaco stores and shops.

Source

Ralph Lauren Corporations Annual Report, 2019 Accessed June 11, 2019. http://investor.ralphlauren.com/static-files/68fc21c4-168b-44eb-b23d-16e551109737

FRANCHISING (RETAIL LICENSING)

Franchising is best defined as *one party (the franchisor) grants to another party (the franchisee) the right to operate a business that sells products and/or services produced or developed by the franchisor, under the franchisor's business format and management system in return for an initial franchise fee and a royalty fee.*[6] The franchisee is allowed to use the franchisor trademark and system and the franchisor in turn, will provide ongoing consulting and support and teach them how to operate the business. The franchisee will usually work for the franchisor for a month or two learning the business at its own expense and pay all the costs of establishing a replica of the business. That may include buying the land, building the building, buying the equipment, making the leasehold improvements, buying the inventory, furnishings, fixtures and signage, and providing all of the working capital needed to establish this business and operate it on an ongoing basis.

The franchisee may, in addition, buy equipment and supplies from the franchisor. The franchisor may contribute to the initial capital investment, development efforts, knowhow and experience and the franchisee would contribute the (usually far greater) supplemental capital investment, plus its motivated effort and operating experience in a variety of markets. The franchisee will pay a continuing royalty as well. The term *royalty* as we already know, refers mostly to the license concept of paying a fee for the continued use of the name or system. Royalties are usually paid weekly as a percentage of gross sales.

According to an IFA report, franchise businesses produced goods and services worth $868.1 billion in the U. S. in 2016 and supplied an annual payroll of $351.1 billion, accounting for 3.4% of the private sector gross domestic product. Franchise businesses contributed indirectly to the U.S. economy in other ways. According to the same report, franchises were the cause of more than 16 million jobs, $723.2 billion of annual payroll and $2.1 trillion of annual output, which ultimately accounted for 7.4% of the GDP.[7]

Mixed System

Once the firm is successful in its initial franchising efforts, it can sell its company-owned outlets to the franchisees and become fully franchised. On the other hand, a firm may find it advantageous to have a mix of franchised and company-owned stores.

A mixed system can be established in two ways:

- First, a firm can start by franchising all locations, then take over some of the stores later. Going this route allows a firm to gain the initial benefits of franchising while discovering which stores are worth bringing under company ownership in terms of monitoring costs, profitability, and risk.

- Initially opening only company-owned stores, then franchising some new locations at a later stage. Many companies find themselves in this situation by default, having existed for some time before deciding to franchise. It allows for gradual growth. In addition, establishing company-owned stores first gives the organization direct knowledge of operational issues and allows it to test and implement marketing strategies franchisees may not be willing or able to do at their stores.

Many fashion brands have expanded their retail footprint locally and internationally, primarily through the franchising model, such as Benetton, others have adopted a more balanced strategy of self-owned and franchised stores, e.g. Zara, while others relied totally on self-owned outlets, e.g. Forever 21.

FRANCHISING VS. LICENSING

Though the structure of franchise relationships may vary, in general franchising could easily be described as licensing in retail. However, while there are indeed many similarities in both models there are also a few differences between licensing and franchising. The most obvious difference is that a franchise involves sharing your business model which is not necessarily the case in licensing where the biggest risk involved is the intellectual property. Table 5.3 compares both models:[8]

Table 5.3 Franchise vs. License

Franchise	License
Franchisees use the franchisor's intellectual property (e.g. trademarks) and duplicate its business model	Licensees use the trademark and intellectual property of the licensor
Franchisor determines a unified method and system for all franchisees to adopt	Licensees are free to determine their own system for operating the business
Franchisor monitors the franchise performance based on specified criteria/quota	No requirement to comply with performance criteria determined by licensor
Franchisee pays certain fees, which could include payments to a marketing fund	Licensees pay certain fees. The licensor does not operate a marketing fund
Common marketing plan for all franchisees	Each licensee determines its own marketing

Created by Author.

Franchise Categories

There are two broad categories of franchises: *Start-up* and *Conversion*. The vast majority of franchises are *start-up*, which is a new version of the franchisor's existing business at a new location. Most are sold to individuals who know nothing about the business. A few know nothing about any business. *Conversion* franchises are sold to an individual or group already in the same business, operating under their own name which is more common in the real estate type of franchise than in fashion. Whether it is a start-up or a conversion category, there are generally three types of franchises:[9]

1. *Individual Franchise.* Most franchises are sold to one individual for one physical location or one territory where demographics will support the business.

2. *Multiple Unit Franchises (also called master, area, or territorial franchises).* The multi-unit franchisee, unlike the individual franchisee, is given a specific territory in which it is required to open a specific number of units on a scheduled basis. Typically, the initial franchise fee is discounted and the multi-unit franchisee is required to pay half of the aggregate amount due for all of the franchises at the execution of the contract. As each unit is opened, it pays the balance of the franchise fee due on that unit. For example, if the individual franchise fees were $35,000, a franchisor might discount it to $30,000 for a multiple buyer. Thus, if the multiple buyer buys a ten-unit territory for $300,000, the franchisor would collect $150,000 when the contract is executed and $15,000 as each unit is opened. The franchisee might be required to open one unit in the first year, two units in the second year, and three in the third year and so on. If at any time it did not open a unit on schedule, it would forfeit the money paid in advance but could continue to operate units already opened, so long as those units remained in conformance with operating standards.

3. *Sub-franchising.* Some franchisors over the years have sold large territories to sales-oriented individuals or groups who, in turn, sell individual franchises in their market and service them. This is called sub-franchising. It has been used primarily by conversion franchises or franchises with low-volume businesses. Sub-franchising may entail more risk and loss of control but could be a strategy which achieves faster penetration of a market.

Whatever franchise strategy or type is chosen, the goal of the franchisor is to create value for everyone involved. Thus, the franchisor must create a network of franchises that produces enough revenue to return a profit on the licensing of its name, technology, system, and ongoing assistance. The franchisees must also benefit through profits and through the achievement of business ownership. Though franchisees use the franchisor's name and business system they are nonetheless independent owners. Ultimately, consumers must also benefit by gaining access to a well-managed business that provides desirable, fairly-priced goods or services (Table 5.4).

Advantages and Challenges of Franchising

Advantages of Franchising to the Franchisor

- Reduce market risk and the ability to expand operations with reduced investment. Firms often franchise because they cannot readily raise the capital required to open their own stores. On the other hand, a firm seeking growth may be able to raise capital, but it may lack the managerial resources required to set up a network of company-owned stores.

- Increase capital reserves and working capital. Franchise deals usually have some form of up-front payment plus continuing payment in the form of royalty.

- Expand in a timely fashion. The ability to not just grow but grow quickly within an area is key in gaining footholds in markets which is otherwise not possible without outside investment.

Table 5.4 Franchise Categories Pros and Cons

Individual Franchise	
Pros	**Cons**
■ Furnishes own capital	■ Owners tend to be less sophisticated or experienced
■ Owner operator	■ Limited capital
■ Builds a strong company foundation	■ More training and support required
■ Faster saturation in market	■ Slower growth

Multiple Unit Franchise (*Area Development*)	
Pros	**Cons**
■ Faster growth	■ Need to be big to get the more sophisticated owners
■ Locks out competition	■ Higher up-front expenses
■ Gets there first	■ Can be too big to handle
■ More sophisticated owners	■ Requires large and complex infrastructure
■ Capitalizes on window of opportunity	■ Rapid growth tends to expose weaknesses in the system
	■ Slower saturation in a given market

Sub-franchising	
Pros	**Cons**
■ Faster growth	■ Harder to control quality which may impact quality sensitive businesses
■ Might be the only way available to expand with low volume businesses	■ Relegating screening of prospective franchisees to a third party which may have negative long-term impact
■ May solve field support costs	■ Relegating field support to a third party
■ In a way salespeople are paying you to sell your product	

Created by Author.

- Company-owned retail stores are run by employee managers who may often perform poorly if they are not supervised. A company, therefore, has to supervise its store managers. As a result, it will incur monitoring costs. But because franchisees have invested capital in their own stores, and because their earnings come from the profits of those stores, they are motivated to work harder than company managers who do not have as much stake in the profits and success of the outlet.

- Franchising also provides an effective way to trade off certain functions and thereby minimize production costs. In general, franchisors are more cost efficient than franchisees in performing functions that decrease in cost with a substantial level of output such as product development and national promotion.

Challenges of Franchising to the Franchisor

- Desire to better protect intellectual property, techniques, and contacts. It is very common that franchisees eventually start their own business based on what they have learned and the contacts they have established while being part of the franchise agreement.

- Franchisors only pull a percentage of revenue as a fee from their franchisees, while if a company owns all its franchised entities will pull 100% of revenue; of course, there is no guarantee that these auxiliary entities will be profitable

- A company may not have enough margins to attract franchisees. A franchisee requires significant net margins on top of any fees it owes to a franchisor. If the business itself does not produce these kinds of margins, potential franchisees will walk away. Ensuring that the expansion will create these margins is crucial.

- Inadequate staffing. It requires resources and talent to be able to teach others to run an operation. Thus, physical (such as cash) and intellectual resources are needed.

- Too specialized a niche. A business may be too specialized and specific that there is not enough demand to justify franchising it.

- Franchising will test the franchisor's organizational skills, including its ability to create and manage a complex infrastructure.

Advantages of Franchising to the Franchisee

- Buying into a business that has already grown and produced wealth for the parent company and other business units. And while not risk free, many mistakes and common risks that new businesses make can be avoided since there is a history of work as their guide.

- Selling a product that already has name recognition and possible loyal customers.

- Most successful franchises offer effective training programs that range from weekend retreats to online seminars.

- Franchisors either offer tools for marketing or run national marketing campaigns themselves. Tools and assistance could be in the form of negotiating advertisements on local television and in newspapers or ideas and techniques to make flyers, etc.

- All franchises have some rules and regulations on how the franchise must operate. Examples include assistance in obtaining leases and provide help negotiating with real estate brokers to get a good deal on the facility in which to build the business.

- Franchisors tend to have built-out models and contactor guidelines that can provide substantial efficiencies when constructing properties. They also provide assistance in determining layout, amount of furniture, etc.

- One of the most crucial advantages to franchising is when franchises buy in bulk from their suppliers, which substantially lowers pricing per unit.

Challenges of Franchising to the Franchisee

- Franchise owners must disclose earnings possibilities to their investors and provide a picture of the financial outlook. Of course, performance can differ due to tax codes, different costs in different areas, etc.

- Franchises have some sort of start-up cost fee or cost structure. This is a cost that must be accepted as a condition to wining a franchise and must be properly accounted for.

- Cannibalization. Unless the franchisee owns territorial exclusivity, another franchise can open in a close area and eat out of the franchise profits.

- A franchisee can also be hurt, in spite of its efforts, by the misconducts of another unit in the franchise network.

- Limited independence and limited opportunity to express creativity. No creative decisions can be made that are not approved by the parent company.

- There will always be limited legal rights for the franchisee. In case of legal disputes, the contracts are generally written in favor of the franchisor giving them the upper hand.

- Royalty payments must be made to the franchisor and a fee structure must be set up.

- Almost all franchise agreements have non-compete clauses that stop the franchisee from creating a similar business for a fixed amount of time once the relationship with the franchisor is terminated.

- Franchisee will encounter advertising fee and mandatory upgrades which are usually fees beyond royalties.

- Franchisors have the ability to change their models if business conditions warrant it.

- Franchisors have the right to terminate the agreement and partnership under conditions that are spelled out in the franchise disclosure document.

What Makes a Business Franchise-able?

Any new fashion franchise concept has probably been done before. The main source of success from one franchise to the other is heavily dependent on the execution and the operating system. A successful franchise operation will thus, rely on the following factors:

THE MODEL PROTOTYPES

To franchise you must have a profitable operating model. The prototype may be your principal business or it may be a version of it designed for franchising. You may decide, for example, that your business will be easier to operate and be more profitable if you eliminate some of the marginal products or services you offer now, maybe even reduce its size and place it in a different location. The prototype needs to be lean and mean, which means that before franchising you must examine it for weak spots.

FINANCIAL CONTROLS

Good financial controls to allow for monitoring accounting and performance are essential to any operating system.

PROFITABILITY

Prototypes should have positive cash flow and be profitable to entice franchisees.

THE MARKETABILITY OF THE BUSINESS

It is essential to demonstrate a point of difference between your business and that of your competitors. For many of the large franchise operations, finding locations for new units could be quite challenging. However, as most businesses that start selling franchises have only one operating unit, the fact that the franchisee could be working directly with the founder who has a vested interest in its success could be an attractive proposal. It is also important when going global to avoid the mistake of thinking the country is all one market.

FACILITIES AND PERSONNEL

One of the keys to successful franchising is your ability to assist franchisees in finding locations for their franchises. In fact, some franchisors do not sell franchises unless the physical location has been identified beforehand.

TEACHABILITY

As mentioned, your business must be marketable not only to consumers but to franchisees, and one of the most critical qualifications is your readiness to teach a franchise owner how to run the business within four to eight weeks. Some franchises require longer training periods.

CREDIBILITY

Another aid to marketability is reputation. Prospective franchisees respond to success stories. Any favorable publicity, letters, or even customer comments about your business will enhance the marketability of your franchise.

COST

The perception that the more expensive the business the smaller the pool of prospective franchisees may not be necessarily true. Other factors tend to be more important such as the amount of up-front cash required of the franchisee investor. And more important yet is the ratio of that investment to the total cost of the business. For example, a franchise that requires the franchisee to pay the total cost of a $100,000 business up-front will be, other things being equal, far less attractive than the franchise that requires a franchisee to pay $100,000 down on a business worth $1,000,000.

What to Look for in a Franchisee

In the case of multi-unit franchise, you need a contender who is affluent and highly experienced in business due to the volume and scope of operations. In the case of sub-franchisors, they must be excellent salespeople, among other attributes, in order to be able to market and sell the concept to other contenders.

Individual franchisees on the other hand, are likely to have less money and less business experience which is totally fine. The main approach and a good benchmark for an individual franchisee is that he/she should be the same type of person you would hire if you were opening another branch and seeking a manager. *Like managers*, individual franchise owners should have leadership, sales, and people skills, as well as physical stamina and job experience. *Unlike managers*, they will put up the capital as well. When the time comes to select franchise applicants, it is advisable for the franchisor to request detailed personal information such as school transcripts, work experiences if any, etc.

The Franchising Agreement

Similar to the licensing agreement, the franchising agreement should stipulate a number of fundamental provisions such as those mentioned here (Figure 5.2).[10]

Location/Territory

This describes the franchisee's territory (be it exclusive or not) and sets up a time schedule by which the franchisee must find a bricks-and-mortar location, must have the plans for the unit approved and must be built-out and opened. This section may also disclose other matters such as the computer equipment needed to operate the business, and the like.

Exclusive territorial rights can be considered in territories that can sustain three or more within a few years. However, many factors needed to be considered such as population changes, business patterns, new product offerings, shopping patterns, and surrounding environments.

During the sales process, some franchisors offer the *right of first refusal* or an *option* on an adjacent territory. Franchisees tend to exercise their *option* only after you have spent months of hard work getting a prospect to agree to buy the adjacent area. Thus, a franchisor can require the franchisee which wants the rights to an adjacent territory to deposit half the franchise fee for that additional market with the stipulation that the franchisee opens that unit within a specified period of time, usually one year, or lose the deposit.

Exhibit 10.30

FRANCHISE AGREEMENT

THIS FRANCHISE AGREEMENT is made as of the 15 day of October, 2004.

BETWEEN:

LULULEMON ATHLETICA INC., a corporation incorporated under the laws of Canada, having its registered office at ▮▮▮▮▮▮▮▮▮▮▮▮

(the "Franchisor" or "Lululemon")

AND:

LULULEMON ATHLETICA (AUSTRALIA) PTY. LTD.
ACN 110 186 233, a corporation incorporated under the laws of Australia, having its registered office at ▮▮▮▮▮▮▮▮▮

(the "Franchisee")

RECITALS

WHEREAS:

A.   Franchisor has developed a format, system and plan for the operation of retail stores featuring and offering for sale Lululemon Athletica trade-marked clothing and accessories, and related products and services, all of controlled quality, in accordance with Franchisor's prescribed standards, specifications, policies and procedures, under the name, trade mark and style of "Lululemon Athletica" (the "system");

B.   Franchisor owns and controls the trade name and trade mark Lululemon Athletica and related trade marks and designs used in connection with the franchised business and system (the "Marks" or the "Trade Marks"); and

C.   Franchisee has applied for a franchise to operate a Lululemon Athletica retail store utilizing and in conformity with Franchisor's Winning Formula, business method (including the 80/20 Store Operations Guide), format and system and the Trade Marks, at one or more approved retail locations, and to distribute Lululemon Athletica trade-marked clothing and accessories at such approved retail locations within the Franchised Territory set out below, and Franchisor has agreed to supply Lululemon Athletica trade-marked clothing and accessories and to grant such a franchise to Franchisee upon the terms and conditions of this Agreement.

2.   Term, Renewal and License Fee

(a)   Subject to any right of earlier termination as provided for herein, the initial term of this Agreement shall be for a period of five *(5)* years (the "Initial Term"). The Initial Term shall commence on the Commencement Date.

6.   Training of Franchisee

(a)   Franchisor shall furnish Franchisee and the management personnel, if any, proposed to be employed by Franchisee in the franchised business with initial training of at least seven (7) days in duration in respect of the management, administration and operation of a Lululemon Athletica franchised business. The training shall be given at a location designated by Franchisor. Franchisor will pay no compensation for any services performed by trainees during such training and all expenses incurred by Franchisee or the trainees in connection with such training shall be for the account of Franchisee. Such initial training is intended to enable Franchisee or its management personnel thereafter to hire and train its assistant manager and other employees. Franchisee shall also furnish Franchisee with retail store opening assistance of seven (7) days in duration but only upon the opening of the first Approved Retail Location of Franchisee. The cost of such initial training for up to three (3) persons at the same time and of such retail store opening assistance shall be charged back to the Franchisee as outlined in Schedule "C". Additional persons will be accommodated for such initial training or for

18.   Pricing

Franchisor may recommend or suggest MSRP prices for products or services to Franchisee based upon its experience, however such recommended or suggested MSRP prices are not binding upon Franchisee, who is at all times free to charge prices of its own choosing for any product or service, and failure to accept or follow any such recommendation or suggestion

20.   Advertising Fund

(a)   When in Franchisor's opinion there are sufficient franchised Lululemon Athletica locations in operation, Franchisor shall have the right upon six (6) months' written notice to institute an advertising fund, Franchisor agrees that all Franchisees entering into Franchise Agreements after this one and all of Franchisor's corporate owned and affiliate owned retail locations shall make contributions to the advertising fund of at least the same percentage of Gross Sales and at the same times as are applicable to Franchisee under this Agreement.

Figure 5.2 Excerpts from a Franchise Agreement Sample.
SEC.GOV public records

Duration

The document will detail the length of the duration of the franchise agreement. Two factors are in play here. One is the size of the franchisee's investment. It is unreasonable to expect someone to make a large investment and get a short, one- to five-year, agreement. The second factor is your self-interest. So long as a franchise is performing well, you will want the franchise to be part of your program indefinitely. For these reasons most individual franchises are issued for a period of twenty years. However, to protect you in the event that changes in your franchise structure are needed, you will want to divide your twenty-year agreement into five-year increments. Franchisees have the option of renewing the agreement every five years, provided that they sign the then-current franchise agreement with its then-current terms.

Remember that you can terminate a franchise if at any time it is not operating in compliance with your quality and operating standards.

Protection of Proprietary Information, Marks, and Other Intellectual Property

The franchisor is granting only a temporary license to the franchisee which could be enforced by adding specific language that identifies each item that makes up its proprietary, confidential, and trade-secret information and by then stating the limitations that are placed on the franchisee's right to use such information. It is important protection for the franchisor.

Operations

This section details how franchisees are expected to run their units.

Training and Ongoing Support Services

Franchisors offer training for franchisees and their staff. Training may take place at corporate offices or out in the field. All ongoing administrative and technical support will also be outlined in the agreement.

You should determine as much as you can in advance what services you will offer franchisees and what the cost will be. The best training you can provide is to have the franchisee work for you for a month or two and become intimately involved in all aspects of your business.

Quality Control

As the name suggests, franchisors will address the franchisee's specific quality control requirements. This is sound franchising and is necessary to ensure that the goods and services offered throughout the system meet the franchisor's minimum requirements.

Defaults, Damages, and Complaint Limitations

All franchise agreements will contain some recitation of the violations of the franchise agreement that will be treated as a breach. These violations may be divided into those breaches that result in the immediate termination of the franchise agreement, for which no cure is given, and those violations for which cure is provided.

Obligations Upon Expiration or Termination

Once the franchise relationship has ended, either because the term has naturally concluded and no renewal has occurred, or because the franchise agreement was terminated, it is usual for the contract to list a series of steps that the franchisee must take to de-identify the business and the franchisee's association with the franchise system.

Franchisor's Right of First Refusal

Most franchise agreements give the franchisor the option, but not the obligation, to exercise a first right refusal to purchase the franchisee's business, in the case where the franchisee seeks to transfer the business, or the first right to purchase the franchisee's assets at the time that the franchise agreement expires or is terminated.

Transfers

Virtually all franchise agreements control the franchisee's right to transfer its interest in the franchise relationship. This section will list the prerequisites to a transfer as listed in the previous point.

Relationship Between the Parties

Franchisees are always treated as independent contractors of the franchisor. This has several important implications. An independent contractor is not an employee or agent of the franchisor. Instead, the independent contractors are in business for themselves. The parties to this relationship pay their own taxes, hire on their own, are responsible for their own employees, and generally operate independently of the other in carrying out the contract between them.

Indemnification

All franchisee agreements will contain an indemnification article, so that the franchisee will reimburse the franchisor for any losses it suffers as a result of some negligent act or wrongdoing of the franchisee. This article is almost always in favor of the franchisor, given that the franchisee and not the franchisor is responsible for the day-to-day operation and maintenance of the business.

Non-Competition Covenant and Similar Restrictions

A non-competition covenant (i.e. agreement) is one that seeks to prevent the franchisee from opening a business that would compete with the franchised business. Virtually all franchise agreements will have non-competition covenants. The covenant is often broken into two parts: the *in-term* covenant and the *post-term* covenant.

As the name suggests, the *in-term* covenant prevents the franchisee from competing against the franchisor and any other franchisees while the franchise agreement is in force. Typically, this covenant covers a geographic area around each franchised, company-owned, and affiliate-owned business. The *post-term* covenant covers the former franchisee after the franchise agreement expires or is terminated earlier because of an uncured breach.

Dispute Resolution

This article spells out the methods the franchisor uses to resolve disputes with franchisees.

Most often one will see at least a nonbinding mediation requirement followed by a binding arbitration requirement. In other cases, these two methods of resolution will be preceded by the requirement that the parties first meet face-to-face.

Insurance

All franchise agreements will require the franchisee to obtain insurance to cover its business operations. In all cases, each of the franchisee's insurance policies will require that the franchisor be named as an *additional insured*, meaning that the franchisor enjoys the same coverage as does the franchisee, even though the franchisor is not paying for the coverage.

Additional or "Miscellaneous" Provisions

This section includes commonly used language seen in any contract. In virtually all franchise agreements, this includes covenants that cover mergers, modifications or amendments, non-waiver provisions, state-specific addenda, etc.

Trademark/Patent/Signage

This section will outline how a franchisee can use the franchisor's trademark, patent, logo, and signage.

Advertising/Marketing

The franchisor will reveal its advertising commitment and what fees franchisees are required to pay towards those costs.

Usually the franchisor helps the franchisee advertise in two ways:

- Provide in-store ads, print ads, mailers, and commercials that have worked for the company in the past. As time goes on, the franchisor will create new advertising as well.

- In addition, when the franchise reaches a certain size the franchisor will place regional or national advertising designed to benefit all franchisees.

For all of these activities, franchisors generally charge an advertising fee to franchisees of 1–1.5% percent of gross sales.

Franchises also often require participation in a common advertising or marketing fund. This fund is frequently a national program, but it can also have a regional or local market focus. As with royalty fees, this can be a fixed contribution, but is more often a percentage of revenue in the 1–4 % range.

A typical new business starts with a *soft opening* for a month or two while the business trains employees, gets used to traffic patterns, makes adjustments on equipment, product offerings, pricing, and attains a comfort level. This is followed by a grand opening event. Many franchisors require that a franchisee set aside between $5,000 and $10,000 for such an event.

The franchisee may also be required to spend a minimal amount against a percentage of sales for ongoing local advertising. One thousand dollars per month or 4% of sales, whichever is greater, is frequently stipulated. This must be spent on company-approved advertising programs. Some franchisors prescribe *guerilla advertising* programs for franchises that open an isolated unit in a new market.

"Guerrilla marketing" is an advertisement strategy in which a company uses low-cost surprise and/or unconventional interactions in order to promote a product or service.

Renewal Rights/Termination/Cancellation Policies

The franchise agreement will describe how the franchisee can be renewed or terminated. Some franchisors include an arbitration clause. This requires, in the event of any legal action, that an arbitrator review the case before it goes to court.

Exit Strategies

Every franchise has its own resale policy. Some allow franchisees to sell their franchises at their discretion. Other agreements include buy back or right of first refusal clauses. These allow the franchisor to buy back the franchise at a rate determined by them or to match any potential buyer's offer.

Some franchises hire outside brokers to handle franchise sales which is generally not recommended, especially at the beginning. All the evidence suggests that franchise sales should be made directly by the franchisor.

Franchise Fee/Investment

There will generally be an upfront initial franchise fee that grants the franchisee the right to use the franchisor's trademark and operating system. Those costs will be clearly outlined. Most franchise companies require a new franchisee to pay a one-time initial fee to become a franchisee. This fee can be as low as $10,000 to $15,000 or as in some cases well over $100,000. The average or typical initial franchise fee for a single unit is about $20,000 or $35,000.

Royalties/Ongoing Fees

This section details the franchisor's royalty structure. Most franchisors require franchisees to pay an ongoing royalty.

This fee is normally expressed as a percentage of the gross revenue of the franchised business but can also be a fixed periodic amount such as $500 per month, regardless of revenue. Royalties could be collected weekly. The average or typical royalty percentage in a franchise is 5 to 6% of volume, but these fees can range from a small fraction of 1 to 50% or more of revenue, depending on the franchise.

Three factors will weigh heavily upon the royalty rate.

* *Competition.* Considering what similar businesses in the franchise marketplace are charging.

* *Affordability.* A good measure to keep in mind is that a franchisee needs to make a manager's salary plus a minimum of 15% return on invested capital. A service business can afford to pay higher percentages because its expenses are lower, but so are its gross sales. Businesses selling products with narrow margins will have higher sales levels but will pay smaller percentages.

* *Expense.* How often must you visit each franchise? Who will you send? What will the salaries, car expenses, airfares, and hotel costs be? You may want to consult professionals with franchise experience to assist with these estimates.

Box 5.3 Plato's Closet Franchise Model

Winmark Corporation has been in the franchising business since 1988 managing a portfolio of franchised brands that focus on the purchase of gently used products and reselling them at below retail prices. One of its brands is Plato's Closet which started in 1999. The chain of franchised stores focus on fashion products that appeal to females and males between 12–24 years old. Accordingly, its most popular brands are Abercrombie & Fitch, Aeropostale, Guess, Forever 21, True Religion, and Hollister among many others that appeal to this age group. They focus on the latest styles that are no more than 12 to 18 months old, to accommodate its customers whom they say expect "ultra-high value".

The Franchisee Profile

According to Plato's Closet most of its franchisees are individuals or couples, typically between the ages of 30 and 55, who first experienced these brands as the parents of their core customers. They come from a wide variety of personal and professional backgrounds, including many from corporate America, the military, and people who may be re-entering the working world after caring for their children. And as common with franchising, the majority of its franchisees do not come from a retail background.

For an interested candidates to be considered as a new franchisee they need to:

* Be prepared to invest between $251,700 and $390,700 (i.e. have a net worth of around $400,000).

- Have at least $90,000–105,000 cash or liquid assets.
- Have equity to be used as collateral for the loan needed to cover the financed balance.
- Find alternatives to provide the capital needed (e.g. partner with someone, etc.).

Franchise Steps

Candidates who meet the above criteria would complete a qualification form and upon confirmation the company coordinates meetings for them with current franchisees. Candidates would visit these stores, see how they operate and speak with the franchisees about their experience running the business. After the visits are complete, candidates receive an invitation to attend the "Discovery Day" at the company's headquarters in Minneapolis. In this event, they meet with Plato's Closet franchise team and learn how the company supports its franchisees and the types of training they offer, etc. The event also gives the company a chance to interview the candidates and learn more about them and their backgrounds. If all goes well, both parties get the franchise agreement ready and the future franchisee is enrolled in its training program. Franchisees attend additional training sessions after the new store lease is signed followed by a 12-week period for buying merchandise, store buildout, and more training before the new store is opened.

Franchisee Support

Winmark offers its franchisees a set of training and support measures such as:

- Site selection. Since most franchisees have never owned a franchise before, and thus have not been through the process of finding and negotiating a retail lease, Winmark and its network of brokers assist with this process from site review to lease signing.
- Business plan development (which could be essential for getting the financing needed).
- Sore layout and design.
- Store retail operations.
- Inventory management assistance.
- Franchise-specific product and trend training.
- Merchandising and marketing materials, including signage and digital tools.
- Proprietary computer-systems and online reporting and business intelligence.

Plato's Closet claims that its model results in a high rate of franchise agreement renewals.

Source

1. "Plato's Closet Franchise Report". https://www.winmarkfranchises.com. Accessed March 4, 2020. https://www.winmarkfranchises.com/platos-closet/become-an-owner/#~x5P5r42

CHAPTER QUESTIONS

1. What are the fundamental differences between the franchising and licensing models?

2. Research any two fashion franchised operations and compare both models based on the following:

   a. Product and customer profile.

   b. Fee structure and financial requirements.

   c. Assess the challenges and opportunities related to both operations.

3. Luxury vs. mass-market. How is each of these categories suited for expansion and growth through licensing and franchising? Explain your answers highlighting the challenges that each category may face adopting either model.

Case Study
Benetton: Franchising 2.0

Background

Luciano and Giuliana Benetton, the founders of the Benetton Group, came from humble origins. Giuliana Benetton at age five, fell in love with knitting. In her early teens, Giuliana worked during the day in a tiny knitting business, producing scratchy, somber-colored woolen sweaters. At night, she used a borrowed knitting machine to make her own brightly colored designs. The siblings eventually sold their bicycle and accordion and scraped together enough cash to buy their first secondhand knitting machine in 1955. Then Luciano sold a small collection of Giuliana's knitted creations to local Veneto area stores. The enthusiastic reception of her designs gave the company a solid start.

In 1965, the Benetton company was formed as a partnership, called *Maglificio di Ponzano Veneto dei Fratelli Benetton*, to compete in the casual clothing market, which is marked by its competitive and volatile nature. To attract attention to their sweaters, Luciano decided to sell directly to the consumer through specialized knitwear shops rather than to retail outlets that sold competing products. This decision formed the basis for the Benetton retail outlets, which sell the Benetton line exclusively; the first such store was opened in 1968. The following year, the company opened its first shop in Paris. Production at the company was also unique. In 1972 it introduced dyeing assembled garments made of unbleached wool rather than batches of yarn before knitting. By doing so, manufacturing time was trimmed and Benetton could produce garments upon demand, which minimized the need to maintain an extensive inventory. To produce many sweaters at reduced cost and financial risk, about 80% of production was farmed out to 450 subcontractors in the Veneto region. The remaining 20% of value-added, capital-intensive production, quality control, and cutting and dyeing, was performed in house. In 1979 the first store was opened in North America. By 1981, Benetton had become the world leader in the field of knitwear, generating three times the sales volume of the next largest manufacturer. Benetton was opening stores at the rate of one each working day. In 1984, 55% of

Benetton's $303 million in sales was generated from foreign turnover. The U. S. became Benetton's fastest growing market by early 1985. As Benetton shifted to global manufacturing, it started looking for local partners able to penetrate difficult or emerging markets in the developing world primarily through a franchise and licensing business model. Benetton also adopted a strategy to eventually convert these license operations into production and marketing joint ventures with producers in noncompeting industries such as a new joint venture called United Optical formed to produce spectacles, etc.

By 1989, the trademark United Colors of Benetton was adopted. To beat the worldwide recession and increase market share, Benetton developed, in 1992, strategies to achieve the following goals: improve operating margins, reduce prices by about 15%, increase production volume, improve the product mix, improve operating efficiency, and reduce number of styles of its collection from 4,000 to 2,600, among other measures. Benetton also gained much attention through its global advertising campaign which succeeded in generating a mix of praise and criticism and, ultimately, a fair amount of free publicity since 1989.

Benetton's Harsh Ride in the U.S.

In 1988, after years of double-digit profit growth, Sales stalled in Italy and in the U.S., revenue fell by 20%. The slowdown was due to a weak dollar, rising apparel prices, saturated markets, the rising cost of Italian labor, and shifting tastes, especially in the U.S. The American consumer, known for bargain hunting, was also turned off by high prices and the inability to exchange or refund products across franchised stores. In addition, the group's practice of clustering stores, which was intended to promote competition among store owners, resulted in brand cannibalization amongst franchisees. Signs and claims of disorganization were evident, and by late 1988 several U.S. Benetton store owners filed lawsuits against Benetton's agents, alleging unfair trade practices.

Market Challenges

The 1990s saw the rise of a new breed of trendy designer-retailers who soon were beating Benetton at its own game. Such names as H&M and Zara, which mastered the fast fashion model, began drawing consumers from Benetton stores. In a desperate attempt, the brand launched a massive licensing scheme, placing its brand name on items ranging from condoms to mineral water to wallpaper. As one consultant told *Forbes:* "That is not a good sign. It's usually an indication that a brand is over the hill." Benetton's desperation to recapture its former glory was highlighted by a distribution agreement with Sears, Roebuck and Co. in 1998. The anticipated sales never materialized. American shoppers turned away from the brand and its too-controversial advertising campaigns. Benetton continued to struggle into the 2000s and by 2014 all U.S. stores were closed.

The Come Back: Franchise 2.0

In 2017, the company devised a new strategy to make a major global comeback. It planned to increase its self-owned and managed stores while maintaining and updating its franchising business which remains the backbone of its business model. And thus, the company introduced its *Franchising 2.0*. A new franchising model that encourages increased integration between all its stores, both owned and franchised, through developing closer ties to headquarters, direct exchange of best practices, and a shared commitment and greater support and resources from the company to its franchisees.

The new model included many features such as:

- *Getting Closer to Consumer.* The focus of the model is to move closer to the consumer, to quickly satisfy demands and needs both in the store as well as through e-commerce. In the shop, through mobile devices, employees will know what products clients have viewed online and what they have already purchased and be able to suggest appropriate combinations or accessories.

- *New Store Concept.* The Benetton new store is to become an urban and contemporary showroom where a 360° story of the United Colors of Benetton brand is staged and where the shopping experience is increasingly omnichannel. Inspired by the use of natural textures, typical of the Italian style, a welcoming atmosphere is recreated inside the stores where the vibrant and luminous furnishing system, simple and easy to install, ensures that the product is always in the spotlight. Some of these new store features include:

    - *The "On Canvas" store model:* The new format uses a series of flexible movable canvas walls, based on the Lego concept, by making it possible to create separate rooms, alternating the clothes that are shown on the racks, adjusting them according to demand, and to the season. Stores are to be updated with new stock as fresh ranges come in and with the flexible structure the retailer can rearrange the store to highlight different collections. This flexibility also ensures a level of sustainable practice that Benetton has embraced.

    - *Light colors:* A special lighting system including both direct and indirect light sources meant to bring out the happiness of the colors of the displayed products as described by architect Tobia Scarpa

    - *Digital LED displays:* The displays feature models promoting the collections in an attempt to bring the retailer's entire online range to its stores. The screens are like live posters. In addition, each member of shop staff uses a tablet, enabling them to show shoppers other colors, sizes and related items on the digital display in real time, as well as further information on the product on the tablet. It also allows the company to schedule content relevant to each store based on shared data.

- *Pop-up stores.* The first pop-up Benetton store was introduced in Santa Monica, California in 2019. It was the first physical U.S. store since the close down of all Benetton stores. However, these pop-up stores do not carry inventory, but only size runs for shoppers to try on and then place orders online to be shipped direct to them for free as a reward for stopping at the store. The concept also added to Benetton's effort to eliminate waste and contributes to their sustainability efforts.

- *New app and new site.* The company introduced a new app as well as new site for the U.S. market. The strong online sales promoted the company to consider getting into permanent retail outlets again in the U.S.

- *New design philosophy.* The company embarked on a number of collaborations, and in 2019 veteran French designer Jean-Charles de Castelbajac, known for his colorful designs that were once worn by Madonna, joined Benetton as artistic director. The company also brought in Ugo Giorcelli, the former Salvatore Ferragamo CFO, as its General Staff Manager. Earlier in 2018, Benetton had joined forces again with Oliviero Toscani the photographer responsible for its earlier extremely successful, yet controversial, advertising campaigns. However, he got fired in 2020 due to some public remarks he made.

- *Embrace sustainability.* Benetton pledged that by 2025, 100% of the cotton used will be sustainable, whether organic, recycled or sourced from Better Cotton Initiative (BCI) farmers.

Figure 5.3 Benetton New Redesigned Store.

It is clear that Benneton has taken some bold and strategic decisions, but only time will tell their impact on the Benetton brand and its franchise partners (Figure 5.3).

Case Study Questions

1. How different (or similar) is the new franchising model adopted by Benetton from the competing fast fashion model?

2. Why has Benetton initially failed in the U.S. market? And in your opinion, will the new measures taken by the brand make it succeed the second time around? Finally, as a manager what would be some of your recommendations for Benetton to succeed in the U.S. market?

Case Study Sources

1. "Benetton Focuses Brand Marketing on Italian Essence as it Unveils New Store Concept". Marketing Week. Accessed October 6, 2019. https://www.marketingweek.com/benetton-focuses-brand-marketing-on-italian-essence-as-it-unveils-new-store-concept/

2. "Benetton Group S.p.A, Company Profile, Information, Business Description, History, Background Information on Benetton Group S.p.A". Reference for Business. Accessed October 2, 2019. https://www.referenceforbusiness.com/history2/92/Benetton-Group-S-p-A.html

3. "Benetton Unveils Enhanced Worldwide Franchising Strategy". World Franchise Associates. March 16, 2017. https://www.worldfranchiseassociates.com/franchise-news-article.php?nid=3788

4. "Press Releases and Statements". The Benetton Group. Accessed May 8, 2018. http://www.benettongroup.com/media-press/press-releases-and-statements/benetton-group-hits-the-retail-accelerator-launching-a-programme-of-new-store-openings/

5. "The United Colors of Benetton Campaign History". Innovation Design Strategy. Accessed October 18, 2019. https://innovativedesignhistory.wordpress.com/2014/04/08/the-united-colors-of-benetton-campaign-history/

6. Ganz, Barbara. "Benetton Unveils Enhanced Worldwide Franchising Strategy". *Italy 24.* March 7, 2017. http://www.italy24.ilsole24ore.com/art/business-and-economy/2017-03-06/benetton-131441.php?uuid=AErOCdi

7. Hays, Kali. "Benetton Ready to Test Retail Again in U.S.". *WWD.* October 17, 2019. https://wwd.com/fashion-news/fashion-scoops/benetton-ready-to-test-retail-again-in-u-s-1203346152/

8. Meliado, Edoardo. "Benetton Appoints Former Ferragamo CFO Ugo Giorcelli to Management". *Fashion Network.* December 17, 2018. https://uk.fashionnetwork.com/news/Benetton-appoints-former-ferragamo-cfo-ugo-giorcelli-to-management,1046204.html

9. Riera, S. and L. Molina. "Benetton: The Eighties Star Rearms Itself to Rescue Its Former Glory". *The Global Fashion Business Journal.* June 29, 2018. https://www.themds.com/back-stage/benetton-the-eighties-star-rearms-itself-to-rescue-its-former-glory.html

10. "The Benetton Story". Pentagram. Accessed September 14, 2019. https://www.pentagram.com/work/benetton/story

11. Van Elven, Marjorie. "Benetton to Open "Numerous" New Stores Around the World in 2019". *Fashion United.* April 29, 2019. https://fashionunited.com/news/retail/benetton-to-open-numerous-new-stores-around-the-world-in-2019/2019042927498

12. Wilson, Mairianne. "Benetton to 'Pop-Up' in Return to US Retail". *Chain Store Age.* October 21, 2019. https://chainstoreage.com/benetton-pop-return-us-retail

13. www.benetton.com

NOTES

1. Jimenez, Guillermo C. and Barbara Kolsun. *Fashion Law* (New York: Fairchild, 2016), 115.
2. "Global Sales of Licensed Goods and Services Reach US$280.3 Billion, Fifth Straight Year of Growth for the Licensing Industry". Licensing International. June 04, 2019. https://licensinginternational.org/news/global-sales-of-licensed-products-and-services-reach-us-280-3-billion-fifth-straight-year-of-growth-for-the-licensing-industry/
3. Ibid.
4. "Licensing Agent Definition: Everything You Need to Know". Upcounsel. Accessed March 20, 2018. https://www.upcounsel.com/licensing-agent-definition
5. Battersby, Gregory J. and Danny Simon. *Basics of Licensing* (Norwalk: Kent Press, 2011), 103.
6. "Expanding Business by Franchising". Course Hero. Accessed September 15, 2019. https://www.coursehero.com/file/p6u13ip/Through-franchising-the-restaurant-owners-obtained-the-benefit-of-the/
7. Franchise Industry 2018 Report. USA Department of Commerce.

8. 'What is the Difference Between a License and a Franchise Agreement". Lexology. Accessed November 16, 2018. https://www.lexology.com/library/detail.aspx?g=81ec6bb9-381e-40d9-9a4a-9be17b15069d

9. Boroian, Donald D. and L. Patrick Callaway. *Franchising Your Business* (Olympia Fields: Francorp, 2008), 86.

10. Pipes, Kerry. "The Franchise Agreement". Franchisng.com. Accessed November 16, 2018. https://www.franchising.com/guides/he_franchise_agreement.html

BIBLIOGRAPHY

Books

Aaker, David. *Aaker on Branding: 20 Principles that Drive Success* (New York: Morgan James Publishing, 2014).

Battersby, Gregory J. and Danny Simon. *Basics of Licensing: How to Extend Brand and Entertainment Properties for Profit* (Norwalk: Kent Press, 2012).

Boroian, Donald D. and L. Patrick Callaway. *Franchising Your Business* (Olympia Fields: Francorp, 2008).

Bruce, Margaret, Christopher Moore and Grete Birtwistle. *International Retail Marketing: A Case Study Approach* (Burlington: Elsevier, 2005).

Burns, Leslie D., Kathy K. Mullet and Nancy O. Bryant. *The Business of Fashion*, 4th ed. (New York: Fairchild, 2011).

Chevalier, Michel and Gerald Mazzalovo. *Luxury Brand Management: A World of Privilege* (Singapore: John Wiley and Sons (Asia), 2008).

Choi, Tsan-Ming and Bin Shen. *Luxury Fashion Retail Management* (Singapore: Springer, 2017).

Corbellini, Erica and Stefania Saviolo. *Managing Fashion and Luxury Companies.* (Firenze: Rizzoli ETAS, 2012).

David, Fred R. *Strategic Management: Concepts and Cases*, 13th ed. (Upper Saddle River: Pearson, 2011).

Hameide, Kaled. *Fashion Branding Unraveled* (New York: Fairchild, 2011).

Hill, Charles W. L. and G. Tomas M. Hult. *Global Business Today* (New York: McGraw-Hill, 2016).

Jimenez, Guillermo C. and Barbara Kolsun. *Fashion Law*, 2nd ed. (New York: Fairchild, 2014).

Jin, Byoungho and Elena Cedrola. *Fashion Branding and Communication: Core Strategies of European Luxury Brands* (New York: Palgrave, 2017).

Keller, Kevin L. *Strategic Brand Management*, 4th ed. (Upper Saddle River: Pearson, 2013).

Kunz, Grace I. and Myrna B. Garner. *Going Global* (New York: Fairchild, 2011).

Kunz, Grace I., Elena Karpova and Myrna B. Garner. *Going Global: The Textile and Apparel Industry*, 3rd ed. (New York: Fairchild, 2016).

Leong, Wisner T. *Principles of Supply Chain Management: A Balanced Approach*, 3rd ed. (Mason: South-Western, 2012).

Londrigan, Michael and Jacqueline M. Jenkins. *Fashion Supply Chain Management* (New York: Fairchild, 2018).

Morden, Tony. *Principles of Strategic Management*, 3rd ed. (Hampshire: Ashgate Publishing Limited, 2007).

Murray, Iain. *The Franchising Handbook: A Complete Guide to Choosing a Franchise* (London: Kogan Page, 2006).

Neonakis, Nick, Sagar Rambhia and Aditya Rengaswamy. *The Franchise MBA: Mastering the Four Essential Steps to Owning a Franchise* (Middleton: CreateSpace Independent Publishing Platform, 2016).

Reddy, Mergen, Nic Terblanche, Leyland Pitt and Michael Parent. *How Far Can Luxury Brands Travel? Avoiding the Pitfalls of Luxury Brand Extension* (Indiana: Kelley School of Business, 2009).

Schramme, Annick, Turi Moerkerke and Karinna Nobbs. *Fashion Management* (Leuven: Lannoo, 2013)

Sherman, Gerald J. and Sar S. Perlman. *The Real World Guide to Fashion Selling and Management* 2nd ed. (New York: Fairchild, 2015).

Van Gelder, Sicco. *Global Brand Strategy: Unlocking Brand Potential Across Countries, Cultures and Markets* (London: Kogan-Page, 2003).

Varley, Rosemary, Ana Roncha, Natasha Radclyffe-Thomas and Liz Gee. *Fashion Management: A Strategic Approach* (London: Red Globe Press, 2019).

Wheelen, Thomas L. and J. David Hunger. *Strategic Management and Business Policy: Toward Global Sustainability*, 3rd ed. (Upper Saddle River: Pearson, 2012).

Other Sources

"A History of Pierre Cardin". Pens. Accessed September 7, 2019. https://www.pens.co.uk/news/blog/history-of-pierre-cardin.php

"An In-Depth Look at Licensing and Retail in North America". License Global. Accessed February 3, 2018. https://www.licenseglobal.com/magazine-article/depth-look-licensing-and-retail-north-america

"Benetton Focuses Brand Marketing on Italian Essence as it Unveils New Store Concept". Marketing Week. Accessed October 6, 2019. https://www.marketingweek.com/benetton-focuses-brand-marketing-on-italian-essence-as-it-unveils-new-store-concept/

"Benetton Group S.p.A, Company Profile, Information, Business Description, History, Background Information on Benetton Group S.p.A". Reference for Business. Accessed October 2, 2019. https://www.referenceforbusiness.com/history2/92/Benetton-Group-S-p-A.html

"Benetton Unveils Enhanced Worldwide Franchising Strategy". World FranchiseAssociates. March 16, 2017. https://www.worldfranchiseassociates.com/franchise-news-article.php?nid=3788

"Franchise Agreement". Law Insider. Accessed November 3, 2017. https://www.lawinsider.com/contracts/7w7OGj10iuuQgl7Z8dIuqY/lululemon-corp/franchise-agreement/2007-06-11

"Global Revenue from Licensed Goods and Services Grows to US\$272.6 Billion". Licensing International. May 22, 2018. https://licensinginternational.org/news/global-revenue-from-licensed-goods-and-services-grows-to-us271-6-billion/

"Licensing in the Fashion Industry". The Fashion Network. Accessed November 12, 2017. https://thefashionetwork.com/licensing-in-the-fashion-industry/

"Licensing is One Fashion Trend that Isn't Going Away". The Fashion Law. Accessed June 4, 2018. https://www.thefashionlaw.com/home/licensing-is-one-fashion-trend-that-isnt-going-away

"Lululemon Athletica Inc. Form 10-K". SEC. Accessed February 5, 2019. https://www.sec.gov/Archives/edgar/data/1397187/000095012310028033/o60149e10vk.htm

"Own a Plato's Close". Plato's Closet. Accessed October 3, 2019. thttp://www.platoscloset.com/own-a-platos-closet

"Phillips-Van Heusen Corporation Form 10-K". SEC. Accessed February 12, 2019. https://www.sec.gov/Archives/edgar/data/78239/000007823909000013/tenk020109.htm

"Press Releases and Statements". The Benetton Group. Accessed May 8, 2018. http://www.benettongroup.com/media-press/press-releases-and-statements/benetton-group-hits-the-retail-accelerator-launching-a-programme-of-new-store-openings/

"The 6 Major Types of Licensing Royalty Rates". Flowhaven. July 4, 2017. https://blog.flowhaven.com/major-types-of-royalty-rates-in-brand-licensing

"The Plato's Closet Process". Accessed October 5, 2019. https://www.winmarkfranchises.com/platos-closet/steps-to-ownership/#~R0N4B42

"The United Colors of Benetton Campaign History". Innovation Design Strategy. Accessed October 18, 2019. https://innovativedesignhistory.wordpress.com/2014/04/08/the-united-colors-of-benetton-campaign-history/

"Tom Ford International Announces the Creation of Tom Ford Underwear for Men". PR Newswire. February 6, 2017. https://www.prnewswire.com/news-releases/tom-ford-international-announces-the-creation-of-tom-ford-underwear-for-men-300402878.html

Achim, Adina-Laura. "The Art of Luxury Brand Licensing". Jing Daily. September 19, 2019. https://jingdaily.com/the-art-of-luxury-brand-licensing/

Adegeest, Don-Alvin. "Raf Simons Out at Calvin Klein: What Went Wrong?". Fashion United. December 22, 2018. https://fashionunited.uk/news/fashion/raf-simons-out-at-calvin-klein-what-went-wrong/2018122240701

Canalichio, Pete. "10 Benefits of Brand Licensing". Brand Strategy Insider. October 3, 2010. https://www.brandingstrategyinsider.com/2010/10/10-benefits-of-brand-licensing.html#.XY_BMpNKjzI

Cochrane, Lauren. "The Enduring Legacy of 70s Disco Designer Halston". The Guardian. June 5, 2019. https://www.theguardian.com/fashion/2019/jun/05/halston-70s-disco-designer-rise-fall-bianca-jagger-iman-studio-54

Dike, Jason, "Diggin' Deeper, Pierre Cardin's Demise to "Licensing King". Highsnobiety. November 23, 2015. https://www.highsnobiety.com/2015/11/23/digging-deeper-pierre-cardin/

Farago, Jason. "Pierre Cardin's Space-Age Fashion Takes Us Back to the Future". *NY Times*. August 22, 2019. https://www.nytimes.com/2019/08/22/arts/design/pierre-cardin-brooklyn-museum-review.html

Fernandez, Chantal. "Raf Simons and Calvin Klein: Behind the Breakup". *Business of Fashion*. December 21, 2018. https://www.businessoffashion.com/articles/news-analysis/raf-simons-exits-calvin-klein

Fury, Alexander. "Pierre Cardin's Bizarre Back-Catalogue of Licensing". *Another*. January 11, 2018. https://www.anothermag.com/fashion-beauty/10489/pierre-cardins-bizarre-back-catalogue-of-licensing

Gaille, Brandon. "14 Licensing Advantages and Disadvantages". *Brandon Gaille*. October 12, 2018. https://brandongaille.com/14-licensing-advantages-and-disadvantages/

Ganz, Barbara. "Benetton Unveils Enhanced Worldwide Franchising Strategy". *Italy 24*. March 7, 2017. http://www.italy24.ilsole24ore.com/art/business-and-economy/2017-03-06/benetton-131441.php?uuid=AEr0Cdi

Hays, Kali. "Benetton Ready to Test Retail Again in U.S.". *WWD*. October 17, 2019. https://wwd.com/fashion-news/fashion-scoops/benetton-ready-to-test-retail-again-in-u-s-1203346152/

Irwin, Terry. "Licensing Arrangements, The Pros and Cons". *TCII*. October 26, 2017. https://www.tcii.co.uk/2012/10/26/licensing-arrangements-the-pros-and-cons/

Koehser, David. "The Role of Licensing Agents". *Attorney at Law*. Accessed February 22, 2018. http://www.dklex.com/the-role-of-licensing-agents.html

Lockwood, Lisa. "What's Next for Calvin Klein Following Raf Simons Split? *WWD*. December 24, 2018. https://wwd.com/fashion-news/designer-luxury/whats-next-for-calvin-klein-following-raf-simons-split-1202941088/

Meliado, Edoardo. "Benetton Appoints Former Ferragamo CFO Ugo Giorcelli to Management". *Fashion Network*. December 17, 2018. https://uk.fashionnetwork.com/news/Benetton-appoints-former-ferragamo-cfo-ugo-giorcelli-to-management,1046204.html

Pipes, Kerry. "The Franchise Agreement". *Franchising*. Accessed April 4, 2018. https://www.franchising.com/guides/the_franchise_agreement.html

Riera, S. and L. Molina. "Benetton: The Eighties Star Rearms Itself to Rescue Its Former Glory". *The Global Fashion Business Journal*. June 29, 2018. https://www.themds.com/back-stage/benetton-the-eighties-star-rearms-itself-to-rescue-its-former-glory.html

Sander, Elizabeth. "Brooklyn Museum's Pierre Cardin Show Salutes Future-Forward Thinking, in Fashion and Beyond". *Observer*. July 20, 2019. https://observer.com/2019/07/pierre-cardin-retrospective-brooklyn-museum-future-fashion/

Tharp, Bruce M. "Product Licensing 101: So Let's Tal Money". *Core77*. September 11, 2012. https://www.core77.com/posts/23366/Product-Licensing-101-So-Lets-Talk-Money

"The Benetton Story". Pentagram. Accessed September 14, 2019. https://www.pentagram.com/work/benetton/story

Van Elven, Marjorie. "Benetton to Open "Numerous" New Stores Around the World in 2019". *Fashion United*. April 29, 2019. https://fashionunited.com/news/retail/benetton-to-open-numerous-new-stores-around-the-world-in-2019/2019042927498

Wilson, Mairianne. "Benetton to 'Pop-Up' in Return to US Retail". *Chain Store Age*. October 21, 2019. https://chainstoreage.com/benetton-pop-return-us-retail

CHAPTER SIX
Managing Fashion Global Growth

LEARNING OUTCOMES

- Identify the opportunities and challenges of global expansion
- Assess the organization's potential for entering foreign markets
- Explore various global growth options
- Familiarize with the exporting process and the parties involved

THE GLOBAL MARKET

The global apparel market is valued at $3 trillion, and accounts for 2% of the world's Gross Domestic Product (GDP).[1] To have a better perspective:

- The womenswear global industry is valued at $621 billion.
- The menswear global industry is valued at $402 billion.
- The retail value of the luxury goods global market is $339.4 billion.
- Children's wear has a global retail value of $186 billion.
- Sports footwear is valued at $90.4 billion.
- The bridalwear industry is valued at $57 billion.

INTERNATIONAL VS. GLOBAL

It is important to understand that there is a difference between being a global brand and an international one.

International presence. Going international, or internationalization as it is sometimes known, refers to any foreign presence by the organization. For instance, if the organization opens any branches, offices, offers different products in different international markets, or any other form of geographic extension of its economic activities beyond national boundaries, that would be considered going international.

Global presence. Globalization implies not only international presence, but also functional integration between its internationally dispersed activities and most importantly consistency in the brand offering and core value with acceptable minimal adaptation in markets where it is present. In other words, it is expected to offer a one *global* brand with the same value proposition in all markets (with minimal acceptable modifications as will be discussed later).

Accordingly, all global brands are international brands (*because they exist overseas*) but not all international brands are global brands (*unless they offer a global brand with the same brand proposal in all markets*).

WHY GO GLOBAL?

Before we address how can a brand transform into being a global brand and successfully expand in foreign markets, we need to understand first why does it need to consider this as a growth option. Global expansion requires a lot of money, resources, and planning. Moreover, the brand may not yet be set for global expansion. Here are some reasons why a brand would consider this expansion strategy:

- Saturation of the brand's target segment or a slowing growth rate for the entire category in the domestic market.

- Price erosion because of intensified competition.

- Price pressures from retailers and suppliers.

- An end to the brand's product lifestyle.

- Reduced margins because additional marketing and sales efforts are required.

- Overcapacity as a result of optimistic market predictions.

- Various market barriers such as legal barriers, the total size of the market, sunk costs, network externalities that may affect the uptake of a product or service. And advantages that accrue to incumbents in the marketplace.

- Economic necessity, production is usually the first business function to be delocalized. Economies of scale provide a strategic factor as they contribute to competitive pricing since for a brand to be competitive, its innovation must be offered immediately to all at the lowest possible price.

- The emergence of global segments and lifestyles. A single global brand would be necessary if the clients themselves are operating worldwide as with luxury brands.

- It is a way to overcome grey/parallel markets which is a very relevant concern with fashion, cosmetics, and perfume, etc. (Other strategies may include changing products and creating regional ones or creating a price corridor for a region.)

- Globalization tends to enhance a brand's image in many forms:

  - It is an indicator of quality and status due to perceived global reach.

  - Global brands are often associated with a country of origin with a stereotype of competence such as France (creativity), Italy (quality), or the U.S. (American way of life).

Many of the market pressures mentioned, such as price pressures, segment size, etc. may be experienced early in the brand's life which it would only survive by expanding its geographic markets. This is very common with luxury and niche brands which by definition serve small and exclusive local markets and thus cannot survive economically locally. In addition, the nature of their consumer who is traditionally very homogenous across borders and is generally an affluent traveler, make luxury brands born to be global.

INTERNAL AND EXTERNAL ANALYSIS

Based on the above, it is clear that managers need to conduct a thorough internal and external analysis to determine the necessity and potential of global expansion for their organization. Sicco van Gelder summarized the type of analysis needed as follows:[2]

Internal Analysis

There are three areas to address to conduct a successful internal analysis of the organization and they are: The organization as a whole – The brand and its proposal – The marketing mix and strategy.

THE ORGANIZATION

As mentioned, brands always start small and locally and thus their initial plan, mission, and vision statements as well as strategy are always tailored to address local realities. Thus, managers will need to determine the elements that reflect the organizational path and strategy and may still apply when going overseas. To answer this question, managers need to examine and determine the following:

1. Whether the organization possess a valuable intangible asset such as technology, patent, or brand proposition that would justify the move and allow it to compete in a foreign market.

2. Whether there is sufficient and steady demand in the new markets for the kind of services or products offered and for that asset it possesses.

3. Whether the organization will be able to replicate the consumer experience it offers locally abroad.

Accordingly, managers need to consider whether the elements of their business strategy (the vision, mission, and ambition) still apply when going overseas and ask themselves the following questions:

- Are the anticipated social, political, economic, and regulatory developments the same and as relevant outside the original country or region?

- How do players in the foreign market differ from those in the home market?

- Are there different stakeholder groups to consider in these foreign markets, such as local distributors, local partners, local communities, governments, and environmental pressure groups?

- What are the marketing factors that are driving the business strategy into foreign markets?

- What are the expectations of and objectives for such a move?

- How does the business model differ in the foreign market?

- What are the skills, technologies, and talents that are needed to make this move a success and how do they differ from the home market?

- What are the resources needed to make it a success and how do they differ from the home market?

- Are management and staff motivated to make this move a success?

THE BRAND PROPOSAL

Under the chapter on branding we have discussed that a brand is built on symbols, actions, and routines, etc. and thus management needs to think how to transplant these relevant conventions to foreign markets. And whether they need to be transferred with or without adaptations. Another important question is whether these will be transferred and implemented through management hired locally or expatriate management be brought in to prepare local management. And will this approach be adopted to all countries?

Management also needs to assess whether the competencies and resources available to the organization in the host country are compatible with transferring the home country brand proposal.

In the home country the brand may be faced with a saturated market and the focus of the business strategy is geared towards attaining customer loyalty while in the foreign market it could be a new brand and the strategy is geared towards market penetration. Thus, another thing to consider is the role of the brand. The brand may be the lead brand to the organization in a new country while it is one in a portfolio in the home country.

Managers may ask themselves:

- What is the required brand experience that the brand is supposed to achieve in the host country?

- Does management in the host country understand the brand the same way management does in the home country?

- What is the role of the brand for the organization in the host country?

- Does it matter whether the brand proposal and positioning differ between the host and home?

- Do the stages of brand development in the host country warrant a different brand proposal or positioning?

MARKETING MIX

Can the home country marketing mix be transferred to the host country? A marketing mix, also known as the 4Ps, consists of: price, product, place (i.e. distribution), and promotion (i.e. marketing and communication activities).

Price. Price is the component of the marketing mix that is most likely to vary between countries. Price would match market lines if the brand is facing competition and can go beyond if the brand is superior or different. However, price changes need to be addressed with care as they impact the brand perception and positioning.

People. People supporting the brand (e.g. staff) will differ by country. They will differ in terms of culture, education, and experience, etc. But the main issue is whether the service they provide to support the brand differs by design.

Products and Services. Products and services offered can differ even while the brand expression does not. Sometimes products and services are designed differently because they better convey the brand expression that way. We will examine this point in more detail later.

Place. Brand distribution varies because of the need to adapt to local distribution structures which could differ from country to the other. However, brand distribution may also differ in order to better express the brand. Luxury brand Louis Vuitton is sold through exclusive distribution in most parts of the world to emphasize exclusivity. However, in Hong Kong its bags are sold from stands in shopping centers such as Times Square Shopping Center.

Promotion. Brands try to standardize their marketing and advertising strategies across their markets because they consider communication as a cost burden. However, choosing different channels and messages are inevitable to accommodate cultural differences and the brand positioning in the new market.

Marketing managers need to ask themselves the following questions:

- How does the brand expression translate into the actual marketing mix in the host market?

- Does the local implementation of the brand expression require an adaptation of the marketing mix?

- Does standardization of the brand expression lead to a standardization of the marketing mix or is an adaptation of the marketing mix sufficient?

- Should the marketing implementation be transplanted to the host country, or should the organization adapt its operations and customer interface to ensure that it functions according to the brand expression?

EXTERNAL ANALYSIS

When entering a new market, it is necessary to understand what moves and motivates consumers and what will influence their brand perception. These factors can be learned through the following:

- *Cultural conventions.* These are a set of agreed, or generally accepted cultural standards, norms that often take the form of a custom.

- *Needs conventions.* Refers to motives.

- *Category conventions.* Refers to structural factors.

And thus, the real question when entering a new market is whether to abide by or to challenge prevalent conventions as a way of creating value for consumers and their local communities.

A convention is considered solid when consumers are not accepting an alternative. It is considered flexible when the convention is undergoing development or erosion in consumers' minds. Then there is an opportunity to challenge such a convention and to obtain differentiation from competitors and offer distinct value to consumers.

ENTERING A FOREIGN MARKET

Assuming both internal and external analyses have indicated that the organization is ready for global expansion, a series of other important questions will be raised such as:

- Whether to standardize or customize the brand's offering and the marketing strategies?

- How to enter the foreign market (i.e. best mode of entry)?

- The political stability and level of development in the foreign market. You would consider a place that has a free market system with no dramatic rise in inflation rates or private sector debt.

- The value an international business can create in a foreign market which depends on the suitability of its product offering to that market and the nature of local competition.

- Time of entry once attractive markets are identified. Being a *first mover* entering the market early has advantages such as the ability to preempt rivals and capture demand by establishing a strong brand name. On the other hand, the disadvantages include costs that an early entrant has especially when the business system in the foreign country is so different from that in a firm's home market that the enterprise has to devote considerable effort, time, and expense to learning the rules of the game. Also, the costs of promoting a product offering and educating customers. *Late entrants* benefit form observing and learning from the mistakes of early entrants, but suffer from competition and a crowded market.

- Scale of entry is another business decision to consider as it involves the commitment of many resources.

Foreign Market Modes of Entry Options

There are many options to consider when deciding to enter a new foreign market. Each mode has its advantages and challenges. In many cases the decision is governed by local regulations and market realities. It is important to note that one organization can end up adopting different formats in the different countries they have presence in. Here are examples of the most common modes of entry:

LOCAL DISTRIBUTORS

Local distributors purchase the products with their own money. They build local inventories and sell in their own country. Local distributors are usually granted an exclusive right to distribute a product or a brand in a given country.

Distributors generally represent several brands in order to spread their cost such as the cost of their salesforce across them. This also gives them better bargaining power with local department stores and other outlets. For example, F J Benjamin in Singapore is the exclusive distributor of brands such as Banana Republic, Céline, Gap, Givenchy, Guess, Marc Jacobs, and Tom Ford among others, and across various territories such as Singapore, Malaysia, and Indonesia.

Advantages

- From the company's perceptive this is a very low investment option for expansion as local distributors assume all financial risk.

- The company knows how to negotiate for the best location with local department stores and get discounts for advertising.

- More affective in handling daily activities and dealing with local authorities and regulations.

Challenges

- Local distributors may not be very easy to control.

- They may conduct their own marketing locally without following the brand's guidelines.

- May give more attention to other brands they handle.

- If the brand is very successful, paying a percentage of wholesale sales to a local distributor may actually be more expensive than opening your own subsidiary. Thus, local distributors are usually ideal for starting and developing a brand but once the brand reaches a certain level of sales (e.g. 15 million) it may be better to start its own subsidiary.

- The shift from this mode to other modes may not be that easy.

JOINT VENTURE

A joint venture (JV) is a subsidiary that belongs in part to the brand headquarters and in part to a partner such as a local distributor, thus it is middle of the road between owning a subsidiary or dealing with a local distributor. A JV could eventually lead to 100% ownership and formation of a subsidiary if allowed. It is a popular way to enter new markets especially where it is difficult to go alone. Such an option would work best if:

- Exporting barriers exist.

- There is a large cultural gap.

- Assets cannot be fairly priced.

- High sales potential.

- Some level of political risk.

- Government restriction on foreign ownership.

- Local partner can provide skills, resources, distribution network, etc.

Advantages

- Overcome ownership restrictions and cultural distance.
- Combine resources and experiences of two companies.
- Potential of learning from new partner.
- Business will be perceived as an insider rather than totally a foreign entity.
- Shared investment.
- A firm benefits from a local partner's knowledge of the host country's competitive conditions, culture, language, political system, and business.
- In many countries political or market considerations (e.g. Japan) make JVs the only feasible entry mode due to how the market works or because it minimizes the risk of being subject to nationalization or other forms of government interference.

Challenges

- Could prove to be difficult to manage.
- Decreases level of control.
- It does represent a higher risk than exporting or licensing due to potential conflicts.
- Share of your knowledge and knowhow spill over.
- Partner may eventually become a competitor who knows a lot about you.
- As with licensing the firm risks giving control of its technology or knowhow to its partners. But agreements can be constructed to cover this aspect.
- JV does not give the firm the tight control over subsidiaries that it might need to realize experience curve or location economies.
- This shared ownership agreement can lead to conflicts and battles for control between the investing firms if their goals and objectives change or if they take different views as to what the strategy should be.

FULLY OWNED SUBSIDIARY

In this option the firm opens a new operation overseas and owns 100% of the stock. This option should be considered in the following situations:

- There are export barriers to the new market.
- Small cultural difference between your home market and the foreign one.
- Assets could be fairly priced.
- High sales potential that would justify the high investment.
- Low political risk.
- No legal or regulation restrictions.

Advantages

- Highest level of control, and in the case of a fashion brand that also opens and controls its own stores overseas, it has the best opportunity to showcase the brand the way it desires which is necessary in the case of luxury brands for instance

- Subsidiaries are in themselves a good marketing tool as companies appear bigger and more impressive.

- Allow for best knowledge of local market.

- Best environment to apply specialized skills.

- Protecting your knowledge and knowhow with minimum risk. Thus, reduces the risk of losing control over your competency, especially if it is a technological competency.

- Will be seen as an insider rather than an outside foreigner.

- Sales being consolidated at full value rather than export price.

- Gives the firm a tight control over operations in different countries thus engaging in global strategic coordination (i.e. using profits from one country to support competitive attacks in another).

- Achieve location and experience curve economies (i.e. cumulative experience increases efficiency in use of resources such as labor, etc.).

- Gives the firm 100% share in the profits generated in a foreign market.

Challenges

- Some countries (like Indonesia) do not allow 100% ownership for subsidiaries dealing with products manufactured and imported from overseas while others impose some form of restrictions. For instance, in Japan or New Zealand, a local resident manager must be employed. In other countries the majority of shares must be held by a local partner which may be sometimes helpful when dealing with local authorities.

- Higher risk than all other options due to higher investment and level of involvement.

- May be difficult to manage and deal with local resources and channels.

- It is the costliest method from a capital investment standpoint as the firm bears the full capital cost and risk. It requires much more resources, time, and effort commitment.

- Because subsidiaries are expensive, they do not make sense unless a certain minimum level of sales is expected, otherwise gross margin resulting from sales will not be sufficient to cover overheads and salaries. As a result, local inventory of products and accounts receivable may have to be financed by headquarters.

- It also includes the risk of learning to do business in a new culture and business environment.

- Subsidiaries could actually lead to the creation of grey markets in cases where subsidiary managers fall behind their yearly budgets and thus agree to use any channel of unloading their products.

Wholly owned subsidiaries can take two forms, either by setting up a new operation in that country, which is often referred to as a *greenfield venture*, or through acquiring an established firm in that host country and using that firm to promote its products.

Advantages of building a subsidiary from the ground up (i.e. Greenfield):

- Greater ability to build the kind of subsidiary you want.

- It is easier to establish a set of operating routines in a new subsidiary than to convert the operating routine of another.

- Could be less risky than acquisitions in the sense that there is a less potential for unpleasant surprises.

Challenges of building a subsidiary from the ground up:

- Slower to establish.

- They are risky as with any new venture.

- The possibility of being preempted by more aggressive global competitors which enter via acquisitions and build a bigger market presence that limits market potential for the new venture. Thus, this model may be more viable in a market where the company does not face such risk or when it is riskier to transfer their competencies and skills, etc.

Advantages of acquiring an enterprise in the target market:

- Faster to build presence in the target market.

- Firms make acquisitions to preempt their competitors.

- Less risky, as you buy a set of assets that are producing a known revenue and profit stream which may be uncertain for a greenfield company.

Challenges of acquiring an enterprise in the target market:

- The acquiring firm often overpays for the assets of the acquired firm.

- A clash between the cultures of the two firms. This is why there is usually a high management turnover after acquisitions.

- Attempts to realize gains by integrating the operations of both entities often face roadblocks and take much longer than forecasted.

- Inadequate screening and not thoroughly analyzing the potential benefits and costs.

DUTY FREE OUTLETS

A lot of products, especially in the luxury segment, as well as cosmetics and fragrances, are purchased by international travelers. It is estimated that 30% of all fragrances are sold in duty free.[3] In the past few years fashion and accessories have seen strong growth due to an enlargement of airport space dedicated to these categories, and upgrades in shops' merchandising and concept while offering customers discounted prices and real savings.

Products sold in these stores are not subject to import duties nor are they subject to local distributors' margins as they are not sold within the country. However, they still pay airport commissions which in some cases could be higher than local taxes and duties by two to three times. It is for this reason that in countries/cities where there are no import duties such as Singapore or Hong Kong, duty free stores are better off opening a store in the city as they can avoid paying the high airport commissions especially when not having to pay import duty. The problem with this model though, is that brands could already have local distributors in the same city and as such special arrangements and agreements need to be made. These complications and variations may result in having the price of one product vary from one airport to the other. An example of duty free operations is the DFS group owned by LVMH. Stores are commonly seen at airports as well as many downtown areas in many cities under the name *Galleria* such as in San Francisco where they have their headquarters. They operate over 150 stores in many countries which gives them a strong negotiating power when dealing with suppliers.

The general success of airport retail operations in past years has led to some airports bypassing operators and operating shops themselves. However, it is not yet a common trend and tends to be implemented in airports with critical mass and established retail operations (staff, logistics, etc.), such as Dubai, Amsterdam Schiphol and Rome Fiumicino, airports. Direct operation gives airports complete control over the offer and the concepts and because there are no turnover fees squeezing margins, it allows the airports to maintain competitive prices.

LICENSING AND FRANCHISING

We have discussed both options in detail in the previous chapter. A foreign market license agreement follows basically the same principles discussed earlier whereas a licensor grants the rights to intangible property to another foreign entity (the licensee) for a specified period and in return receives a royalty fee. Thus, the same rules discussed earlier apply, except in this case you are dealing with a foreign partner which could add a new level of risks, such as:

- Brands may have to deal with a foreign justice system.
- Transfer of funds and taxation. Some countries may not allow transfer of foreign currency outside their market.
- Fluctuations in exchange rates.
- Other cultural and social restrictions that may require product or marketing adaptations.
- Taxes on licensing royalty income in some foreign countries could be as high as 30%.

International licensing would work best if:

- It is not possible to have a fully owned presence due to import and investment barriers.
- Legal protection and effective legal systems exist in the foreign market.
- Low sales potential to justify full ownership presence.
- Some or large cultural differences that would be best addressed and understood by a local partner.
- Low risk for licensee to eventually become a competitor.

EXPORTING

Exporting *is the distribution and selling of product, service, technology, or idea that originates in one country to be sent and sold in another country to distributors or end users.* Exporting, is likely to be the first channel to explore when considering entering a foreign market for the first time, especially for a small and young organization. Accordingly, we will need to explore it in more detail and understand the steps involved in the process.

THE EXPORT DECISION

One of the key questions a manager faces is whether the company's product is exportable or not and whether as an organization they have the required resources of personnel, time, and money as well as top management commitment to pursue this move and make it succeed. Thus, for a product to be exportable it must meet the following criteria:

- Be legally exportable from the U.S. according to the Export Administration regulations (EAR).

- Be easily imported in the targeted foreign country without unreasonable taxes or administrative expenses.

- Be exempted from any market-related restrictions such as size of unit, nature of the product, or modifications cost.

- Possess unique qualities that provide competitive edge over foreign or international products (design, quality, or technology because a low price is no longer a guarantee of success overseas).

- Satisfy an existing and growing demand for the product's category and specific characteristics.

- Enjoy no existing prejudices against imports from the U.S. (or home country).

If the company determines that the product is exportable then it needs to direct its attention to address the following issues:

- What are the firm's export marketing goals? And are they realistic?

- Are the exporting goals consistent with overall corporate strategic planning?

- Can current company resources of personnel, production capacity, and finances support increased demands?

- Does the corporate business plan include an export marketing strategy that also provides a roadmap to foreign marketing success?

- Are adequate essential personnel resources available?

- Does the need the product attempts to fulfill exist overseas? And is a profitable market share attainable?

- Does the product require any modifications or supplemental products? If yes, will the cost be a barrier for export?

- Are there any legal, governmental, or other regulation restrictions?

Having an exportable product (from legal and marketing perspectives) as well as the capacity in terms of resources and management commitment would indicate that the firm is ready to export.

Advantages of Exporting

- More sales could lead to more profits over a reasonable period of time especially if the local market is mature and saturated.

- Counter economic cycles and seasonal purchases. If the product is subject to seasonal purchases then exports can overcome the downturn during out-of-season periods (e.g. if you sell summer products that will not sell locally in winter you can consider exporting to countries with hot weather all year or south of the equator where seasons are opposite). Thus, extend the product lifecycle. In addition, in cases of economic downturn the economy in another market may not yet have been affected and thus could be a lucrative market for exporting.

- If domestic products become technologically obsolete and out of fashion, the chances are they must still have a market in a different developing market. Thus, diversification from selling to foreign markets enables firms to balance market changes.

- Exports may enhance company image, presenting itself as a global operation

- Increased sales through exports can lower the per unit cost due to the benefits of economies of scale. By utilizing excess manufacturing capacity or reducing existing inventories exporters can realize economic benefits.

Challenges of Exporting

- Exporting requires a substantial amount of investment in travel, research, possibly hiring new staff, and perhaps modifying products or packaging.

- Exporting requires the commitment of top management not just early on but for the long haul. It requires sustained effort, resources, and time to establish relationships and maintain them in foreign markets including learning cultural differences, etc.

- Some brands may have no need to expand overseas as their local market is still large enough for growth.

- Difficulties in learning foreign languages, etiquette and business customs, and regulations in foreign markets.

- Exporting is complex and could be costly particularly in coping with payment and financing procedures.

Box 6.1 Leading International Fashion Trade Fairs

There are a large number of fashion and textile trade shows and fairs taking place in major cities across the globe. Trade fairs tend to have thematic focus on a certain segment or category of the industry and they are usually timed strategically to fit within the production cycle of their target market. Trade shows and fairs are good channels to explore export opportunities. Among the world's most popular shows:

U.S.

- *MAGIC (February, August), Las Vegas*. Showcases women's and men's apparel, footwear, accessories, and sourcing resources from around the world, facilitating connections between buyers and brands. During the event *PROJECT* takes place which is one of the most influential and comprehensive menswear market events (www.magicfashionevents. com).
- *CAPSULE SHOW (September), New York*. Show presents a unique combination of independent, often founder-run, labels alongside established industry favorites (libertyfairs.com).
- *TEXWORLD USA (January, July), New York*. Texworld USA is an international textile trade show that is both a business platform and order show that brings together suppliers, buyers, and designers (texworld-usa.us.messefrankfurt.com).
- *The COTERIE (February, September), New York*. The COTERIE Marketplace brings together four shows under one roof (COTERIE, FAME, SOLE COMMERCE, and MODA) presenting established and new brands of all categories of women's fashion (www. coteriefashionevents.com).

France

- *PREMIÈRE VISION DESIGNS (February, September), Paris*. Brings together a selection of specialized international studios to present their latest collections of textile patterns and designs. Covering six major industries including: yarns, fabrics, leather, designs, and accessories (www.premierevision.com).

- *TEXWORLD Paris (February, September), Paris:* An international trade fair for the clothing and textile industry. It reflects prêt-à-porter fashion with exhibitors from around the world (texworld-paris.fr.messefrankfurt.com).
- *APPAREL SOURCING (February, September), Paris.* The procurement of clothing and fashion accessories (apparel-sourcing-paris.fr.messefrankfurt.com).

Italy

- *MILANO MODA DONNA (February, September), Milan.* This Milan fashion week event has close to 80 shows and 30 events where manufacturers and producers show the current trends and fashions for the upcoming season. Attended by international buyers and wholesalers to compare offers and to establish contacts. *Milano Moda Uomo* for menswear takes place in January, June (www.cameramoda.it).
- *PITTI IMMAGINE UOMO (January, June), Florence.* An international fashion fair for men's clothing. *Pitti Immagine Bimbo* for children and youth fashion takes place in in January, June (www.pittimmagine.com).

UK

- *THE LONDON TEXTILE FAIR (January, July), London.* An exhibition for suppliers, buyers, distributors, manufacturers, and for fabric and textile manufacturers. A platform to introduce new products and establish business contacts (www.thelondontextilefair.co.uk).
- *MODA (February, August), Birmingham.* A men's apparel trade fair offering the latest trends in men's clothing with an outlook on the upcoming fashion seasons. The fair takes place along with the fairs *Moda Woman, Moda Footwear, Moda Accessories,* and *Moda Lingerie & Swimwear* (https://www.moda-uk.co.uk).

Spain

- *THE MOMAD METROPOLIS (February, September), Madrid.* An international fashion exhibition aimed at buyers and shop owners from around the world showcasing the latest trends and fashion styles of the coming season (www.ifema.es).

The Export Process

The export process could be summed up in the following steps:[4]

1. The first step based on the above discussion is to make the decision and determine the export potential of the organization and its brand. The firm does not need to be a large one to succeed in exporting. But it is important to determine if the brand and product has a worthwhile market outside the U.S. (or home country) based on the criteria listed above. This stage will entail a lot of market research.

2. Market research will allow the organization to understand foreign markets and their infrastructure, availability of resources, etc. and thus determine the level or existence of barriers. Research should help reveal the largest potential market for the product, market trends, market conditions and practices, competitive firms and products, overview, etc.

3. Develop an export marketing plan. The plan will act as a road map and a test for how an organization can deal with the business and legal environment in the foreign market. A marketing plan can include the following sections:

- Company profile

- Market research data

- Sales/marketing objectives

- Marketing strategy and timetable (what, where, who, and how)

- Inventory of resources in terms of people, money, and time

- Marketing components. Identify and evaluate your target market

- The product selection

- Pricing

- Distribution and delivery

- Promotions

- Terms and conditions

- Internal organization and procedures

- Sales goals profit and loss forecasts

- Primary target countries

- Secondary target countries

- Implementation schedule

- Follow-up steps

- Competitive environment

4. Once the plan is out and analyzed, the next decision is how to present the company and product information to interested parties overseas as well as how to obtain information from them. Apart from the internet and company websites, trade shows are an effective method for exposing the company and products to international buyers as well as collecting information and contacting distributor prospects. While it might be costly to attend international fairs for a small business, local shows could be as informative as they are attended by many foreign representatives as well.

5. Among the first positive feedbacks a company will receive is a request by interested parties for a quotation. This requires managers to be prepared to respond by offering them with what is known as *a pro forma invoice* which is a form describing the merchandise including its specifications, packaging, per unit price, and payment terms. Hopefully this will lead to an order by the interested party.

There are many types of export price quotes such as the following (Figure 6.1):

EX Works (Ex-Factory or Ex name of port), e.g. EXW Miami
Exporter: Is considered to have delivered the goods and fulfilled its obligation by placing goods in its premises (i.e. *it's the minimum level of obligation as transportation from factory to port is also paid by importer*).
Importer: Pays for ALL freight (land and sea) + insurance.

FOB (Free on Board + name of port of shipment), e.g. FOB Miami
Exporter: Is considered to have delivered the goods and fulfilled its obligation when the shipment passes the ship's rail and is cleared to ship (in the exporter's port)
Importer: Pays for ship freight + insurance.

FOB is the most common price quote type.

EX WORK

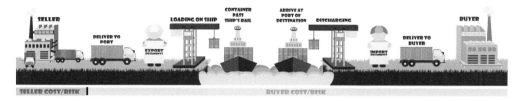

FOB - FREE ON BOARD

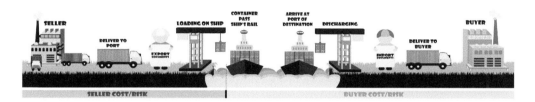

CFR-COST AND FREIGHT

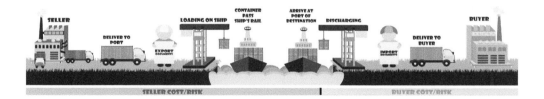

EXAMPLES OF COMMON EXPORT PRICE QUOTES

Figure 6.1 Examples of Common Export Price Quotes. Purchased with License from shutterstock.com.

CIF (cost, insurance and freight + name of port of destination), e.g. CIF Shanghai
Exporter: CIF differs from FOB in that the exporter is responsible for the goods until it reaches the buyer's destination port. Thus cost of freight + insurance (minimum coverage) are assumed by seller/exporter.
Importer: Pays any extra cost including risk of loss or damage.

6. After receiving the order, the exporter and importer will be engaged in a financial transaction process through their banks which involves sharing a number of documents. The importer's bank will prepare the necessary documents and informs the exporter's bank that the financial resources of the importer are satisfactory. The exporter's bank, in return, advises the exporter that the export payment is in place and thus the exporter would prepare the order for exporting and shipping.

Common Export Documents

- *Pro Forma Invoice.* As discussed, it is an invoice prepared by the exporter before shipping the goods, informing the buyer of the goods to be sent, their value, and any other key specifications. It also can be used as an offering of sale, or a first step sale price quotation.

- *Commercial Invoice.* This is a bill from the seller to the buyer. It includes details of the order. It is also used by the government to determine the true value of goods when assessing duties, etc.

- *Export Packing List.* A detailed list that indicate the seller, buyer, shipper, invoice number, date of shipment, mode of transportation, and the carrier. The list also itemizes quantity, description, the type of package (e.g. a box, crate, carton, etc.) package marks, and dimensions if needed. While the packing list can serve as a confirming document it is not a replacement for a commercial invoice. It could be used by U.S. and foreign customs to check the shipment.

Documents Related to Transportation

- *Airway Bill.* Shipping bill used for air freight shipments.

- *Bill of Lading (BL).* Shipping bill used for shipping by sea or domestic transportation. It is a contract between the owner of goods and the carrier. In case of shipping by sea there are two types of BL:

  - *Straight bill of lading* which is non-negotiable (i.e. cannot be transferred by endorsement, meaning no one else but the named person can use it to collect the goods when they arrive at the port).

  - *Negotiable (or shipper's) order bill of lading* instructs the carrier to deliver goods to anyone in possession of the original endorsed negotiable bill, which itself represents title to and control of the goods. Because it is negotiable and transferable, it could be bought, sold, or traded while the goods are in transit (so someone else will collect the goods). The buyer (or holder) will usually need an original form as proof of ownership to take possession of the goods.

- *Electronic Export Information Filing (EEI).* A very common export control document. It is used for compiling official U.S. export statistics and for enforcement of U.S. export laws. The EEI is required for shipments above $2,500 and for shipment of any value that requires an export license. An EEI is electronically filed online through AESDirect.

Other Documents

- *Export License.* Most goods exported from the U.S. don't require an export license; they're permitted to be exported under the designation NLR (no license required). However, there are some select classes of merchandise that *do* require an export license. (e.g. military products or goods exported to certain countries such as Cuba or Syria, etc.).

- *Consular Invoice.* Some countries may require exporters to submit this document to their embassy in the exporter's country specifying which goods are to be exported before the goods are sent abroad.

Terms of Payment by Importers

For export sales and import purchases there are various payment options. A few are more common than others due to the risk factor. Options include the following.

Cash in Advance

Obviously, this option would be highly preferred by exporters as it eliminates risk of future money collection. It also gives exporters immediate cash that could be used to fulfill the order as well as protect exporters from other economic or political uncertainties in the importer's country. However, this option is the least attractive to buyers/importers. It may be more acceptable with local buyers rather than foreign ones. And unless your product is very unique, has strong demand, or the buyer is attempting to support you as a new business, importers may be intimidated by the request and look for alternative sellers thus lowering your competitiveness or the chance to build a long-term relationship with the importer. A small business new in the export game may indicate to buyers that a down payment would allow them to offer the buyer their best price and thus, buyers who are willing to support new businesses may consider a down payment. But it is important to remember that for a buyer located in a foreign country there is a high risk of paying in advance and never receiving the shipment or it may create some cash flow problems for them.

FORMS OF CASH PAYMENT

- Electronic transfer of funds (ETF) (a.k.a. wire transfer) is where money is transferred from one bank to another. This works for both domestic and international transactions. It is relatively fast, being bank to bank.

- Credits cards are sometimes used in trade for generally low value transactions especially if the transaction has been done through the internet, etc. While a very convenient form of transaction, they come with some risks such as possible fees, fraud, or disputes.

- Advanced payment by check may result for some delay as it takes a few weeks for the check to be cleared which may defy the purpose of having an advance in the first place, especially if the check received and deposited in the bank for collection is in a foreign currency other than U.S. dollars. The process will be even slower if the check is drawn on a foreign bank. Payment could be partial or in full. However, if in full it gives the exporter the maximum protection possible. This method may be used for exclusive, made-to-order products or large capital goods orders.

Letter of Credit (LC)

This is the most common form of payment in international trade. It is sort of a compromise to *cash in advance* as it offers a level of security for both parties involved. An LC is basically a contractual agreement whereby the importer's bank which acts on behalf of its client (the importer) corresponds with the exporter's bank giving it the OK to pay the exporter once the importer's bank receives documentation confirming that the exporter has shipped the goods as agreed upon (as stipulated in the letter of credit).

Thus, it is important to remember that issuing the LC by itself is not a guarantee that as an exporter you will be paid no matter what. You, the exporter, have to fulfill all the terms and conditions agreed upon in the LC first before the funds are transferred to your bank and released for your collection. The fact that *reputable* banks represent both sides would give the exporter, as well as the importer, some level of comfort especially if both parties have not dealt with each other before and their credit history is not well known.

There are two banks involved in the LC transaction:

- The issuing bank (the bank of the buyer, i.e. the importer)

- The advising bank (the bank of the exporter)

CONFIRMING BANK AND CONFIRMED LC

The exporter's *advising bank* can also act as a *confirming bank* or any other local U.S. bank could play that role of a confirming bank and in this case the LC would be called a *confirmed LC*. So, what does that mean?

A *confirming bank* means that regardless of any consideration it must pay you – the exporter – as long as all documents are in order and the credit requirements are met. So, for instance if everything was done as agreed upon but for some reason the importer's bank did not transfer the funds as agreed, either due to unexpected political turmoil in the buyer's country or because for some reason the importer defaulted which means no cash is available to transfer. In this case if the LC is confirmed by a local (in the exporter's country) bank then it is still obliged to pay the exporter even if the issuing bank did not transfer the funds. Without this level of confirmation, the LC could be just called an *advised LC*. So, why would any bank agree to take this risk and act as a confirmed bank? Simply because every service a bank does and for every role it plays, it receives a fee. And usually a bank does this service when it has trust in the issuing bank.

Obviously, exporters should try to get confirmed LCs especially if they are not familiar with the foreign issuing bank or if they have any concerns about political or economic risks in the buyer's country.

TYPES OF LC

In general, there are two types of LCs:

A. Revocable

B. Irrevocable

Revocable LC

A revocable LC can be withdrawn and modified by the buyer/importer at any time without a notice or the consent of the seller/exporter. Obviously from an exporter point of view this type of LC is not recommended as it is much riskier.

Irrevocable LC

This is a legally binding LC and cannot be changed by any of the parties involved (buyer, seller, or banks) unless all parties agree to the changes and sign off an amendment (such as extending the payment due date, etc.) to the LC. Banks would usually take a fee for this service as well.

Accordingly, a *confirmed irrevocable* LC is the best LC for the exporter as it ensures payment on time once it meets its obligations and ships the goods as stipulated with no delay and with no changes.

The above two are the most common types of LCs. However, there is one more type to address known as a *revolving LC*

Revolving LC

It is an irrevocable LC issued for a specific amount of money and renews itself for the same amount over a given period (i.e. it revolves). So, it is a single letter of credit that covers multiple transactions over a long period of time. It is very specific and usually used for regular shipments of the same commodity between the same buyer (importer) and the seller (exporter). It avoids the need for repetitive arrangements to open a new letter of credit for every transaction. An LC revolves either in value (a fixed amount is available which is replenished when exhausted) or in time (an amount is available in fixed installments over a period such as every week, month, or year). For example: A letter of credit may stipulate that $100,000 can be drawn on monthly basis for a 12 month validity period.

HOW DOES THE PROCESS WORK?

Figure 6.2 explains how the trade and payment process works:

1. Once an order is agreed upon between you/the exporter and the foreign importer, the importer/ buyer will go to its bank, in its home country and request to issue an LC. The importer is thus called the *applicant* of the LC while the exporter is known as the *beneficiary*. Of course, the buyer must first have an account or a line of credit with the issuing bank to cover the amount that will eventually be transferred to the exporter once the goods are shipped.

2. The buyer arranges for its bank to open, say, a *confirmed irrevocable LC* in favor of the exporter/seller It would specify the documents needed for the transaction to be completed and payment made, including the commercial invoice, freight invoice, and LC, etc. The exporter can request that a particular U.S. bank be the confirming bank, or the foreign bank may select a U.S. correspondent bank to act as the confirming bank.

3. The buyer's bank electronically transmits the LC to the exporter's bank which forwards it to the exporter. It includes the details related to the purchase and payment with the LC.

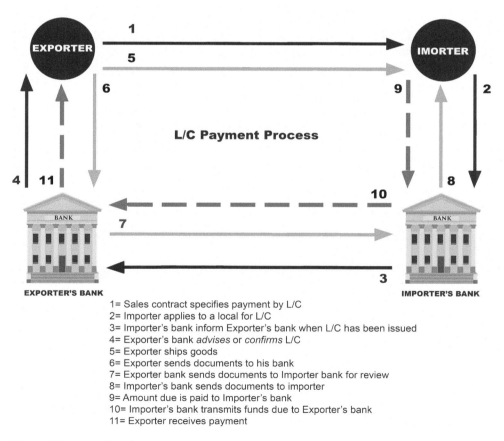

1= Sales contract specifies payment by L/C
2= Importer applies to a local for L/C
3= Importer's bank inform Exporter's bank when L/C has been issued
4= Exporter's bank *advises* or *confirms* L/C
5= Exporter ships goods
6= Exporter sends documents to his bank
7= Exporter bank sends documents to Importer bank for review
8= Importer's bank sends documents to importer
9= Amount due is paid to Importer's bank
10= Importer's bank transmits funds due to Exporter's bank
11= Exporter receives payment

Figure 6.2 Letter of Credit Payment Process.
Created by author.

At this point, the exporter feels assured that the money is set aside by the bank ready to complete the order and ship it. Accordingly:

4. The exporter completes the order and forwards the goods and documents to a freight forwarder (FF), a service provider which gets the shipment ready and prepares it for shipment on the exporter's behalf. The FF prepares all the shipping paperwork needed for the goods to exit the U.S. as well as the ones needed to enter the foreign country.

5. Once the FF receives the goods from the exporter, and arranges for them to be shipped on the boat or plane, it will provide the exporter with a receipt from the shipping company known as the *bill of lading* (BL) if the shipping is done by sea or an *air waybill* if shipping is by air. This BL or air waybill is basically a contract between the exporter and the shipping company to ship the goods to the importer's country. The importer is not a part of this agreement.

6. The exporter's FF will ship the goods and submit, say, the BL and other required documents as listed in the LC (e.g. insurance) to the exporter's bank. The exporter's bank checks the documents for compliance with the LC agreement and then forwards them to the buyer's bank for payment.

7. The importer's bank reviews the documents which indicate that the exporter shipped the goods as agreed upon. The LC usually stipulates that the buyer's bank will pay and transfer the money to the exporter's bank once the exporter and its bank submit a number of documents that confirm the exporter has fulfilled its part of the order and shipped the goods. Thus, if the documents are in order, the bank pays the exporter's bank, debiting the buyer's account for the amount. The exporter gets paid.

8. The importer's bank will then release the documents to the buyer so they can be used to collect and claim the goods once they arrive at port and are cleared from customs.

It is important to remember that both banks involved only deal with documents and not goods throughout the process. And as long as the documents they receive seem to be in order they will go ahead and complete the money transfer process. So, for example, if the order is about shipping 1,000 wool sweaters and the exporter made the mistake of shipping 1,000 cotton sweaters instead, but the documents still show that they are 1,000 wool sweaters, then to the bank there is no error because the documents match what is requested in the issued LC. Banks do not check goods; they only check documents. Such an error whether it is intentional or accidental is not the bank's responsibility and has to be resolved between the two parties (exporter and importer) by other means.

Other Forms of Payment

Although, as mentioned, an LC is the most common form of payment in international trade, there are other possible forms of payment that may work at certain situations:

DRAFT AT SIGHT OR TIME (I.E. DOCUMENTARY COLLECTION)

This is sometimes called a *bill of exchange*. It is like a foreign buyer's check which means it has the same risk of not being honored like any other check. However, in international trade transactions the title and ownership of the goods will not be transferred to the buyer until it pays the draft. There are basically two types of drafts: *sight drafts and time drafts*.

1. *Sight Drafts*. In a sight draft the exporter retains title and ownership of the shipped goods until they reach their destination and payment is made (*i.e. once the buyer receives and "sees" the goods, he/she should pay*).

   In this case the original shipping BL is to be endorsed by the exporter and sent through its bank to the buyer's bank together with the sight draft, invoice, and other supporting documents requested by the buyer or buyer's country (consular invoice, etc.). The buyer's foreign bank notifies the buyer. The buyer pays the draft and in return collects the BL, endorses it and then submits it to the carrier to collect the goods (*in case of shipping by air, airway bills do not need to be presented which makes it a riskier process*).

One risk in the process is if due to some unexpected circumstances the buyer/importer is not able to make the payment after the goods were shipped. In this situation and unlike in the case of LCs the bank is under no obligation to pay the exporter on behalf of the buyer. Also remember that under a sight draft the exporter maintains ownership of the goods until they are claimed by the buyer. So, if the buyer cannot collect the goods or pay for them, the goods remain under the ownership of the exporter. The downside of this is that it would be the exporter's responsibility to either return the goods back home or dispose of them in the foreign market, which could be a problem.

2. *Time Drafts.* In this type of draft the exporter is granting the buyer some time to pay for the goods. It is like extending credit to the buyer. For instance, the draft may state that payment by the buyer is due by a specific time after the buyer accepts the draft and receives the goods, e.g. 30 days after acceptance. Once the buyer signs the draft as accepted (also known as trade acceptance) then it is obliged to pay the exporter within the time frame stipulated. The exporter will hold on to this draft until maturity date to collect its money.

In some cases, if the exporter/seller happens to need immediate cash it can sell the draft to a bank (like an I.O.U.) at a discount for immediate cash and the bank will be the one to collect the full amount from the buyer at maturity.

DATE DRAFT VS. TIME DRAFT

A date draft is slightly different from a time draft in that it specifies a date on which payment is due rather than a time period (i.e. instead of saying within 30 days, it gives a specific date).

One major advantage of date drafts is that with either sight or time drafts the buyer can deliberately delay payment by not collecting the goods promptly if it is a sight draft or wait till the last days of the allowed period to pay under the time draft. But with date drafts both sides know in advance when payment is to be expected. Date drafts like all other types, need to be accepted (and signed) by buyers (or a bank) as well. If it is accepted by a bank it becomes the bank's obligation to pay as agreed. Such a document known as banker's acceptance could also be sold by the exporter for a discount to a bank for immediate payment.

OPEN ACCOUNTS

Under an open account, a buyer and a seller agree that payment be made at some specified future date when the seller/exporter ships the goods but without any negotiable instrument to secure payment and no bank to guarantee payment. Documents of title to goods are sent direct to overseas buyers, for example truck driver delivering documents with goods who then collects the signed document (it is similar to receiving a package from FedEx and signing for it to the driver who then gives you the package and the related documents).

It is a simple form of transaction with no charges incurred as in the case of an LC. It also can be used to provide credit to buyers which could enhance the exporter's competitiveness. However, this is obviously a risky option that should only be used when the buyer is well established and highly reputable or has a long-standing and favorable relationship with the exporter. If the buyer does not pay, then it becomes quite costly and hectic for the exporter to collect its money or pursue legal actions.

CONSIGNMENT

Consignment is not recommended or commonly used for international trade as it represents some transfer of possession to a buyer without any formal commitment to pay for the goods if they are not

MANAGING FASHION GLOBAL GROWTH

sold. Moreover, there is an added cost of bringing back unsold goods. Indeed, a buyer in this instance is not really a *buyer* but mainly a place for showcasing the exporter's goods until they get sold. Once sold the buyer is expected to pay the seller the agreed price.

How Can Organizations Finance Their Exports?

An exporter may need financing to fulfill production obligations (buy material, machines, other expenses, etc.) especially if the exporter had granted the importer credit terms and is faced with a gap between the time of delivery and the time of payment. Thus, in order to produce the goods and fulfill the export order an exporter may seek financing options from various sources such as the following.

Commercial Banks

A logical first step if you're seeking to finance short-term export sales is to approach the local commercial bank your company already uses. The bank will be familiar with your financial standing, credit need, repayment record, and ability to perform. It may also have a section dedicated to international business. Alternatively, you may wish to approach a commercial bank with an international department.

The responsibility for repaying a working capital loan with the bank ordinarily rests with you, the seller, even if the foreign buyer fails to pay. In some cases, especially when you ship capital goods, you may want the commercial bank to make medium-term loans directly to the foreign buyer to finance the sale.

In any case, you can work with your bank to deal with the risks of exporting in several ways, including by seeking loan backing and/or guarantees by the U.S. Export-Import (EXIM) Bank and Small Business Administration or by using various arrangements or instruments such as discounting and banker's acceptances (more on this later). Bank financing comes in different forms:

A. *Secured Financing.* Banks are not high-risk takers. To reduce their exposure to loss, they often ask for collateral. Financing against collateral is called secured financing and is the most common. A common method is funds against documentary title. In this case the exporter pledges the goods as collateral for a loan to finance them.

   You could also obtain a *banker's acceptance* (BA), which is a time draft presented to a bank by an exporter, obtained from the importer (the importer's bank literally *stamps* "accepted for payment" by (name of bank) on (date)) to show your bank that you will be paid by a reputable foreign bank once you deliver the goods). You can also sell the BA in the money market with a discount rate (there are specific criteria).

B. *Unsecured Financing.* Unsecured financing with no collateral is usually only for those who have a sound credit standing with their bank or have had long-term trading experience. For a small import/export business, unsecured financing will probably be limited to a personal line of credit.

Export Intermediaries

In addition to acting as export representatives, many export intermediaries, such as *export trading companies* and *export management companies*, can help finance export sales. They may provide short-term financing, or they may simply purchase the goods to be exported directly from the manufacturer, thus eliminating both the risks to the manufacturer that are associated with the export transaction and the need for financing.

- Export Trading Company (ETC): An independent company that provides support services for firms engaged in exporting such as warehousing, shipping, insuring, and billing on behalf of the client.

- Export Management Company (EMC): An independent company that acts like an export department for several non-competing manufacturers and suppliers, representing the product of its clients. They can offer many services ranging from consultation to taking possession of the goods and acting as a distributor.

Factoring

A *factor* is an agent which will, at a charge (*usually 5 to 6% of the gross*) buy receivables (*documents that show you will be receiving money in the future such as an I.O.U. or drafts*). Banks do 95% of factoring, the rest is by private specialists. The factor makes a profit on the collection because it buys it from the seller at a discount and then collects the full amount on the due date/time. Thus, it provides a source of cash flow for the seller, yet less than if they had waited to make the collection themself.

Example: Suppose you are an exporter and have a receivable for $1,000. A factor might offer you a $750 advance on the invoice. It will charge you 5% (i.e. $50) on the gross of $1,000 per month until collection. Remember the remainder is $250, If the collection is made within the first month, the factor will keep 5% of the $1,000 = $50 and give you the remaining $200. If the collection is in two months, it will keep $100 and give you $150 and so on. As an exporter you are getting less money but you are getting it sooner than the due date and thus you can use the cash to start or continue manufacturing without waiting.

Factors can actually offer you other services:

- A factor could be working with another factor overseas which could perform a credit check on the other partner. Both factors can work together on chasing overdue accounts or take legal actions on your behalf.

- Factors can also provide credit protection (insurance) cheaper than insurance companies.

- Factors can manage the whole export accounting process for a fee (just like you would go for a freight forwarder to handle the transport function for you, factors can handle all the financial aspects for you).

- In spite of their wide range of services many exporters would not wish importers to know they are using a factor because of the negative assumption that they did so due to a bad financial status, thus they would request an *undisclosed* factoring agreement.

Forfaiting

Forfaiting is similar to factoring but deals with high-value, long-term invoices (*over $50,000 and up, to and above 180 days*). Forfaiting does not include other services such as the credit protection or accounting services offered by factoring. Also, the cost and fee structure works differently (e.g. it is on non-recourse basis which means the forfeiter assumes all the risk if the buyer does not eventually make the payment).

Leasing

An exporter can lease the new machines or other capital equipment it needs to fulfill the new order instead of buying them. The leasing company owns the equipment which are leased to the lessee (the borrower).

Box 6.2 Sources of Assistance to Exporters

Exporting is encouraged by all countries as it promotes local products, creates jobs, and for most countries it is a good source for foreign currency. Accordingly, in the U.S., there are many local organizations that aim to support exporters with advice, credit options, and wide range of services. Government programs also aim to improve exporters' access to credit. Examples of such sources are:

Export-Import Bank (EXIM) provides export credit insurance, as well as loan guarantees to lenders, direct loans to exporters on market-related credit terms, and loans to foreign buyers. It can help with both pre-export and post-export financing (source: www.exim.gov).

U.S. Small Business Administration (SBA) provides, in partnership with national, regional, and community lenders, loan guarantees for export working capital and acquisition of plant and equipment, as well as capital for enabling small businesses to commence or expand export activity. Its Export Working Capital Program (EWCP), International Trade Loan Program, and Export Express Program guarantee and/or expedite loans for export working capital or other uses (source: www.sba.gov).

U.S. International Development Finance Corporation (DFC), formerly known as Overseas Private Investment Corporation (OPIC), provides financing for small businesses and women entrepreneurs in order to create jobs in emerging markets (source: www.dfc.gov).

Multilateral Development Banks (MDBs) owned by member governments, aim to promote economic and social progress in their developing member countries. Increasingly, MDBs are providing funding to private-sector entities for private projects. These projects present many opportunities to U.S. companies (source: home.treasury.gov).

Bureau of Industry and Security (BIS) is a U.S. government agency responsible for implementing and enforcing Export Administration Regulations (EARs) which regulates the export of most commercial items. BIS also issues the export licenses referred to earlier. Export licenses may be needed depending on an item's technical characteristics, destination, and end user. The proper classification of export items is essential to determine if any licensing requirements are needed under EAR. BIS can assist in identifying this, if needed (source: bis.doc.gov).

The United States Commercial Service (USCS) is the trade promotion arm of the International Trade Administration (ITA) within the U.S. Department of Commerce. The mission of the USCS is to promote the export of goods and services from the U.S., particularly by small- and medium-sized businesses; to represent U.S. business interests internationally and to help U.S. businesses find qualified international partners, conduct research, select trade shows, as well as offer training programs on various issues related to exporting (source: www.trade.gov).

IMPORTANT ISSUES TO CONSIDER AS AN EXPORTER

Developing vs. Developed Markets

Perhaps the most basic distinction we make between countries is whether they are developing or have developed markets. Differences in consumer behavior, marketing infrastructure, competitive frame of reference, etc. are so profoundly different among developing markets so that distinct marketing programs are often needed for each. For instance, while your product category may be well-developed in your local market it may not be well developed in the foreign market, so the marketing program must operate at a very fundamental level. This could happen with developing countries witnessing an economic boom and are about to open their markets for a whole new range of products and categories (e.g. luxury) for the first time or at a wider scope as happened with China in recent decades.

Standardization vs. Customization

The most fundamental issue in entering a new market and developing a global marketing program is the extent to which the product and/or the marketing initiatives should be standardized across countries. This decision has such a deep impact on production and marketing structure and processes. A product (being one of the 4Ps) is a component of any marketing program. Thus, it makes sense to address this issue of standardization vs. customization in reference to the organization's global marketing program as a whole.[5]

Global Marketing Programs

Marketers are increasingly blending global objectives with local or regional concerns. From these perspectives, transferring products across borders may mean consistent positioning for the brand, but not necessarily the same brand name and marketing program in each market. Similarly, packaging may have the same overall look but be tailored as required to fit the local customers and market needs, etc. Thus, the 4Ps of the marketing program need to be considered carefully from a global perspective.

PRODUCT STRATEGY

One major mistake by many companies going overseas is overlooking differences in consumer behavior by forgoing basic consumer research and simply preferring to put products in the market and see what would happen. As a result, products fail. Thus, it is necessary for managers and marketers to conduct research into local foreign markets. Market research should indicate whether product customization is necessary and to what degree. In many cases, marketing research may reveal that product differences are not justified for certain countries as in the case of luxury products whose customer is very homogenous, except for minor changes; such as sizes (e.g. a size L in the U.S. may be equivalent to XL in Japan). On the other hand, research may indicate that either dramatic adjustments be made or that the product is not suitable as a whole.

COMMUNICATION STRATEGY

Advertising is one area of marketing communications in which many firms face challenges internationally. Although the brand positioning may be the same in different countries, creative strategies in advertising may have to differ to some degree. Reasons for differences could be cultural. There are many examples of companies using an advertising campaign that was successful in the U.S. or their local markets to be used in a foreign market with failed results due to cultural differences or linguistic references. For example, Benetton was known for its evocative advertising meant to shock viewers and grab their attention. While these advertisements did succeed in creating a buzz around the brand, they were met with deep criticism in some markets like the U.S. and China which led to their banning for cultural insensitivity, or embedded messages (political or social). Thus, customization and editing may be necessary even in the area of advertising. On the other hand, advertisements showing bare parts of the body are usually edited or masked when published advertisements are shown in some conservative societies, as in the Middle East or Japan.

DISTRIBUTION STRATEGY

Distribution channels may present challenges to many firms because there are few global retailers, which necessitates searching for local alternatives relatively unknown to exporters. In addition, the distribution infrastructure differs greatly amongst countries, whereby in a country like Japan for example, it is historically very difficult for foreign brands to penetrate the market without working with a local distributor or partner due to the closely knit and tight local distribution system.

PRICING STRATEGY

When it comes to designing a global pricing strategy, Marketers need to understand consumers' perception of the value of the brand, their willingness to pay, and their elasticities with respect to price changes. Sometimes differences in these considerations permit differences in pricing strategies. Brands such as Levi's and Zara have been able to command a much higher price outside their domestic markets, because in other countries they have a distinctly different brand image. Differences in distribution structures, competitive positions, taxes, and exchange rates also may justify price differences. (e.g. Zara historically used to pass most of these costs on to the consumer hence their product prices differed drastically from one market to the other). In addition, retailers and suppliers in foreign markets can exploit price difference through other channels such as grey markets.

While price differences may change the brand's market positioning, they may still be inevitable, and acceptable sometimes, due to shipping costs and taxes imposed by different countries, etc. However, great attempts should be made not to move the product to a totally different positioning segment which could confuse and eventually alienate consumers. A consumer will not be happy to see a garment they paid top dollar for back home is selling for a fraction of the price in a different country and regarded as a lower segment brand. To address this issue, Hermann Simon, a German expert on pricing, recommended creating an international *price corridor*[6] (i.e. price range) that takes into account both the inherent differences between countries and alignment pressures. Specifically, the corridor is calculated by company headquarters and its country subsidiaries by considering market data for the individual countries, price elasticities, parallel imports resulting from price differentials, currency exchange rates, costs in countries and arbitrage costs between them, and data on competition and distribution. No country is then allowed to set its price outside the corridor: countries with lower prices have to raise them, and countries with higher prices have to lower them. Another possible strategy suggested by Simon is to introduce different brands in high-price, high-income countries than in low-price, low-income countries, depending on the relative cost trade-offs of standardization versus customization.

It is important to note that internet e-commerce is playing a strong role in bringing prices to more standardized levels as customers from all over the world can now purchase the same item from the same site. This has helped bring prices within a reasonable range for all markets. Still, some brands may not offer a global e-commerce site and prefer to offer different versions of their site for different regions. These sites are meant to better address local market needs as they are in the local language, showing prices in local currencies, etc. they could also facilitate differences in pricing based on location.

Advantages of a Global Marketing Program

A number of potential advantages could be attributed to a global marketing program such as: -

- *Economies of Scale in Production and Distribution.* From a supply-side there are manufacturing efficiencies and lower costs that derive from higher volumes in production and distribution.

- *Lower Marketing Costs.* Uniformity in packaging, advertising, promotion, and other marketing communication activities, may generate potential savings.

- *Power and Scope.* A global brand profile can communicate credibility. An admired global brand can also signal social status and prestige.

- *Consistency in Brand Image.* Maintaining a common marketing platform overseas helps maintain the consistency of brand and company image; this is particularly important where customers move often and expect to see the brand the same way across markets, as in the case of luxury. A Rolex customer expects to get the same experience and service whether they go to a Rolex store in New York or Tokyo. Media exposure also transmits images across national boundaries; hence consumers expect a level of consistency.

- *Ability to Leverage Good Ideas Quickly and Efficiently.* Globalization can increase and enhance the organization's impact on issues like sustainability, R&D, and in return enhances its ability to compete.

- *Uniformity of Marketing Practices.* Finally, a standardized global marketing program may simplify coordination and provide greater control of communications in different countries. By keeping the core of the marketing program constant, marketers can pay greater attention to making refinements across markets and over time to improve its effectiveness.

Challenges of a Global Marketing Program

- *Ignoring Differences in Consumer Needs, Wants, and Usage Patterns for Products.* Differences in cultural values, economic development, and other factors across nationalities lead customers to behave very differently. Ignoring these differences, may alienate customers

- *Differences in Consumer Response to Branding Elements.* Linguistic differences across countries can twist or change the meaning of a brand name (e.g. Barbour, the name of a premium outerwear brand, means *mucus* in some Middle Eastern slangs). Sound systems that differ across dialects can make a word problematic in one country but not in another (e.g. Japanese pronounce the letter R closer to L). Thus, cultural context is key.

- *Differences in Consumer Responses to Marketing Mix Elements.* Consumers in different parts of the world feel differently about marketing activity. U.S. consumers tend to be fairly cynical toward advertising, whereas the Japanese view is much more positive.

- *Differences in Brand and Product Development and The Competitive Environment.* Products may be at different stages of their lifecycle in different countries. Moreover, the perceptions and positions of particular brands may also differ considerably across countries. The nature of competition may also differ. Europeans tend to see more competitors because shipping products across borders is easy.

- *Differences in Administrative Procedures.* In practice, it may be difficult to achieve the control necessary to implement a standardized global marketing program. Local offices may resist having their autonomy threatened. Local managers who feel their autonomy has been reduced may lose motivation. Local managers may suffer from the *its not invented here* syndrome and raise objections that the global marketing program misses some key dimension of the local market.

- *Differences in the Legal Environment.* One of the challenges in developing a global advertising campaign is the maze of constantly changing legal restrictions from country to country. Advertising restrictions have been placed on the use of children in commercials in Austria, comparative advertisements in Singapore, and product placement on public television channels in Germany. Although some of these laws have been challenged or are being relaxed, numerous legal differences still exist.

- *Differences Also Exist in Advertising Style.* Japanese advertisements tend to be softer and more abstract in tone, whereas in the U.S. they are often richer in product information. On the other hand, European advertisements could be considered more risqué than would be accepted in the U.S.

- *Differences in Marketing Channels.* Channels of distribution, retail practices, media availability, and media costs all may vary significantly from country to country, making implementation of the same marketing strategy difficult.

Global Environment and Culture

The globalization of business has contributed to a huge increase in interactions between managers from different cultural backgrounds. These interactions may occur during brief business trips or in lengthy overseas assignments that last for years. Recent research has demonstrated that the expatriate manager's adjustment impacts satisfaction, willingness to stay in the assignment, and job performance. If an individual operating in a foreign culture doesn't understand its particular patterns of believing and behaving, the individual will interpret experience purely in terms of their own culture and will thus inevitably misinterpret and misunderstand actions and decisions.

Cultural Dimensions

According to Geert Hofstede's theory of Cultural Dimensions, there are six dimensions to consider:[7]

1. *Individualism vs. Collectivism.* Individualism (e.g. U.S. and Western cultures) represents the extent to which people in society think of themselves as autonomous individuals who are responsible primarily to themselves and their immediate families. This contrasts with collectivism (e.g. Asia and Latin America), which emphasizes collective purposes over personal goals and group harmony over individual achievement.

2. *Power Distance.* Power distance represents the extent to which people in the society accept a hierarchical or unequal distribution of power in their organizations and in society. High power distance in a culture reflects respect for social status or class boundaries (e.g. Eastern and Asian cultures). In these cultures, employees are more likely to accept the idea that the boss has power simply because she or he is the boss, and bypassing the boss is considered insubordination. Titles, status, and formality are important in these societies, and those with high status are given much leeway in their behavior.

3. *Masculinity vs. Femininity.* This refers to the distribution of roles between men and women. In masculine societies (e.g. Japan), the roles of men and women overlap less, and men are expected to behave assertively. Demonstrating success, and being strong and fast, are seen as positive characteristics. In feminine societies (e.g. Sweden), however, there is a great deal of overlap between male and female roles, and modesty is perceived as a virtue. Greater importance is placed on good relationships with your direct supervisors, or working with people who cooperate well with one another.

4. *Uncertainty Avoidance.* This dimension describes how well people can cope with anxiety and unpredictability. In societies that score highly for uncertainty avoidance, people attempt to make life as predictable and controllable as possible. If they find that they can't control their own lives, they may be tempted to stop trying (e.g. Middle Eastern cultures).

5. *Long-Term Orientation vs. Short-Term.* Every society has to maintain some links with its own past while dealing with the challenges of the present and the future. Societies which score low on this dimension prefer to maintain time-honored traditions and norms while viewing societal change with suspicion. It is also reflected in the country's strong sense of nationalism and social standard. The U.S. has a short-term orientation. This is reflected in the importance of short-term gains and quick results (profit and loss statements are quarterly, for example).

6. *Indulgence vs. Restraint.* Indulgence stands for a society that allows relatively free gratification of basic and natural human drives related to enjoying life and having fun. Restraint stands for a society that suppresses gratification of needs and regulates it by means of strict social norms.

Table 6.1 Examples of Tariffs

Tariff Type	Tariff Amount	Imported Item Value	Total
Ad valorem (% of value)	16%	$25	$29
Specific (set amount)	$10	$25	$35
Compound (% + set amount)	16% + $10	$25	$39

Global Trade Barriers and Opportunities

Most countries manage trade in an attempt to encourage exports while regulating imports to protect local industries and the flow of foreign currency. Hence, countries have signed a number of agreements to regulate trade to manage barriers as well as preferential treatments.

Among the trade barriers a fashion manager needs to be aware of:

1. *Tariff Barriers*: A tariff is basically a tax collected as a duty on imported and exported goods. Imposing tariffs obviously increase the cost of goods and thus the final selling price to the consumer. An example is the *nominal tariff*. This a tax rate published by each country usually in what is known as country's *tariff schedule* to determine the tax imposed on each type and category of product. Nominal tariffs come in three forms (Table 6.1):

   - *Specific Tariff.* (fixed sum for a physical unit) Easier to apply and varies inversely, i.e. as the import value goes up the tariff is a smaller proportion of the revenue gained from sale of the product and vice versa.

   - *Ad Valorem.* These are a fixed percentage of the value of the product which offers a constant degree of protection even when prices vary.

   - *Combined Tariff.* This is a mix of both types.

2. *Non-Tariff Barriers*: Barriers other than tariffs and taxes may include:

   - Import licenses

   - Documentation requirements

   - Health, safety, and quality requirements

   - Packaging and labeling

   - Product testing

   - Quotas (a restriction on the quantity of a certain good brought to the country)

   - Trade preference programs given to a number of other countries

TRADE AGREEMENTS AND PREFERENTIAL PROGRAMS

The apparel global trade is subject to many kinds of trade agreements that offer layers of protection and preferential treatments amongst signed-up members. Examples of such agreements include: Mercosur in Latin America, EU in Europe, ASEAN in Asia, CBTPA, ATPDEA, CAFTA-DR, NAFTA and other bilateral free trade agreements (FTAs), etc. The U.S. has FTAs with many countries such as Jordan, Israel, Morocco, Singapore, and others. According to these agreements, duties and commercial barriers to bilateral trade in goods and services originating in the U.S. and these trade partners are usually eliminated as well as a variety of non-tariff barriers which allow U.S. textile, apparel, footwear, and other goods exporters to be more price-competitive in the these foreign markets when competing with domestic suppliers and with third country suppliers that do not have the same duty benefits. The FTAs also oblige the other country to adopt stronger protection and enforcement provisions for copyrights, trademarks, patents, and trade secrets. These provisions, among others, provide U.S. and foreign businesses with a market base that is more accessible and easier to navigate.

Box 6.3 NAFTA 2.0

In December 2019 the U.S. Congress approved the new trade agreement between the U.S., Canada, and Mexico known as the *U.S.–Mexico–Canada Agreement (USMCA)* or *NAFTA 2.0* as it was based on the original NAFTA agreement signed by the three countries back in 1994. The goal was to govern over $1.2 trillion worth of trade by offering preferential treatments to products from the three nations as well as addressing various forms of protection. While the new agreement primarily addresses issues concerning the auto industry, intellectual property, and environmental protections, it also included provisions related to textile and apparel trade, making it of direct relevance to the industry. The new provisions intend to incentivize greater North American production in the textiles and apparel trade, strengthen customs enforcement, and facilitate broader consultation and cooperation among all parties. Among the provisions included:

- *Yarn-Forward Rules of Origin (RoO):* A criterion used to determine the *nationality* of a product in international trade. Only apparel products that meet the USMCA RoO are eligible for the preferential tariff treatment under the agreement. USMCA adopts the rule that was in the original NAFTA known as the *yarn-forward RoO* which means that fibers may be produced anywhere, but each component starting with the yarn used to make the apparel garments must be formed within the free trade area, i.e. by USMCA members. The *yarn-forward* rule sometimes is called *triple transformation* as it requires that spinning of the yarn or thread, weaving or knitting of the fabric, and assembly of the final apparel garments all occur within the free trade area so that the apparel item can be eligible for the import duty-free treatment under USMCA.
- According to USMCA, apparel garments might still be qualified for the duty-free treatment under the agreement, should all non-originating fibers and yarns make up less than 10% (up from 7% in the original NAFTA) of the weight of the *major part* of a garment.
- Other than the source of yarns and fabrics, USMCA also newly requires that some specific parts of an apparel item need to use inputs made in the USMCA region so that the finished apparel item can be qualified for the import duty-free treatment giving a transition period ranging from 12 to 30 months for the implementation of these new requirements.
- USMCA will continue to offer the duty-free treatment for apparel assembled in Mexico but using fabrics that are wholly formed and cut in the U.S. (commonly known as the 807A provision). However, when applying the rule, USMCA will allow visible lining fabrics to be sourced from anywhere in the world, which is more liberal than the original NAFTA.
- Tariff preference level (TPL), allows for a certain quantity of textile and apparel goods (usually yarns, fabrics, and cut pieces) from a country which is not part USMCA to qualify for the benefits. Compared with NAFTA, USMCA will cut the TPL, to those product categories with a low TPL (e.g. cotton or manmade fiber apparel exported from Canada to the U.S. already had small utilization of this benefit so its TPL will be cut further under USMCA), and expand it for a few product categories with a high TPL utilization rate (e.g. cotton or manmade fiber apparel exported from the U.S. to Canada).

- Similar to NAFTA, USMCA allows textile inputs (fibers, yarns, and fabrics) that are determined not available in commercial quantity in the NAFTA region to be sourced from anywhere in the world and the finished apparel garments can still enjoy the duty-free treatment provided by the agreement.

Finally, it remains to be seen whether USMCA will boost the *Made-in-the-USA* fibers, yarns, and fabrics by limiting the use of non-USMCA textile inputs. In the past, to produce and source apparel products in the least expensive way possible, sometimes companies would use non-NAFTA textile inputs for the apparel products despite being hit with higher tariffs. For instance, around 15% of U.S. apparel imports from the NAFTA region in 2017 did not claim the NAFTA duty free benefits, largely because of the strict yarn-forward rules of origin.

Sources

1. Lu, Sheng. "USITC Economic Assessment Report on USMCA, Textile and Apparel Sector Summary)". Accessed September 3, 2019. https://shenglufashion.com/tag/nafta/
2. "Nafta Revisiosn". Accessed September 7, 2019. https://www.strtrade.com/events-NAFTA-Revisions-Textile-Apparel-111318.html
3. Platzer, Michaela. *Renegotiating NAFTA and US Textile Manufacturing* (Washington, DC: Congressional Research Service, 2017).
4. https://www.cbp.gov/

Free Trade Zones

Free Trade Zones also known in the U.S. as Foreign Trade Zones (FTZ) work in tandem with trade agreements. This is usually a port or a designated area in the country that allows duty-free entry of selected goods that could then be stored, used for manufacturing and finally exported as finished goods to another country. For example, a company can import fabric duty free to the FTZ (it would otherwise be taxed if brought to their factory outside the FTZ). The fabric could be used to produce products which are then exported to another country straight from the FTZ. And thus, the whole process happens without being taxed. FTZ exist in many countries around the world in an attempt to make local production competitive for export. They are also meant to assist developing countries to be more competitive in entering the global trade market (every state in the US may have one or more FTZ area).

Chapter Questions

1. Going global vs. international are two different strategies. In your assessment how would the challenges facing an organization differ with each approach?

2. As a manager of a young fashion business who is considering exporting your line of T-shirts to Europe and the Middle East, examine the following:

   a. What issues or measures do you need to consider regarding your product before starting the process?

   b. What steps can you take and options to consider in order to promote your product to these foreign markets?

3. You are approached by a buyer from Japan while showing your new fashion line at the MAGIC show in Las Vegas. The buyer is interested in your line of sweaters and is asking for a price quote.

   a. Explain what the terms of your offer would be.

   b. Assuming they accept your offer, list and explain the steps you both will be expected to follow once the order is confirmed, up until they receive the product and you get paid.

Case Study
CROCS: Managing Supply Chain for Global Growth

Background

In 2002, three friends from Boulder, Colorado went sailing in the Caribbean. One brought a pair of foam clog shoes made of a waterproof, lightweight substance developed by a Canadian plastics maker called Finproject. The clogs were made from a special material that did not slip on wet boat decks, was easy to wash, prevented odor, and was extremely comfortable. The three friends, Lyndon "Duke" Hanson, Scott Seamans, and George Boedecker, decided to start a business selling a new design of these Canadian shoes to sailing enthusiasts out of a leased warehouse in Florida, they initially wanted to name the shoes something that captured the amphibious nature of the product. Since "Alligator" had already been taken, they chose to name the shoes "Crocs." The shoes were an immediate success, and word of mouth expanded the customer base to a wider range of people who spent much of their day standing, such as doctors and gardeners. As the story goes, they sold 1,000 pairs in three days. In 2004, the company decided to purchase Finproject, which was renamed "Foam Creations". Crocs now owned the formula for the proprietary resin "Croslitetm" that gave the shoes their unique properties of extreme comfort and odor resistance.

In early 2006, Crocs made its debut on the Nasdaq raising $208 million. At the time, it was America's biggest footwear initial public offering. By 2007, Crocs was a national phenomenon. Annual sales surged to $847 million, up a staggering 137% from the previous year. The surprising success for the odd shaped shoes generated diverse feedback. Slate dubbed Crocs an "epidemic", The Washington Post said they made adults look like "overgrown children", The Philadelphia Inquirer was perplexed by the "aesthetically atrocious" footwear. Crocs, the footwear that everyone loved to hate (and hates to love), became a hit.

Crocs and the Traditional Footwear Supply Chain

When Crocs started, the footwear industry was traditionally oriented around two seasons, spring and fall. The standard practice was for footwear companies preparing for the upcoming fall season to take their products to shows around the world in January. Buyers would book pre-orders for fall delivery following these shows. The fall orders that were received at the beginning of the year would be planned for delivery in August, September, October, and November. These scheduled shipments drive the production plan. The manufacturers add some excess, typically about 20% of the pre-booked orders, to take advantage of potential additional orders. A very aggressive company might add 50% to the build, but all the product would be manufactured before the season began. Most shoes were commonly produced in Asia (primarily China and Vietnam), with some manufactured in South America. This production and supply model had obvious limitations. Retailers had to estimate what their customers would want well in advance of the selling season. If they underestimated, they would have empty shelves and forego potential sales. If they overestimated, they would be stuck with unsold stock at the end of the season and be forced to have clearance sales in order to get rid of this excess stock at discounted prices. Making this even more difficult was the consideration that fashion in general was subject to trends that were difficult to predict. History was of only limited value, particularly with new products that incorporated novel design elements that might either become wildly popular or fall flat.

Crocs Distribution Channel

Crocs early sales were to small retailers as these stores were willing to take more risk than the large chains, and work with a new, rapidly growing supplier that provided a high level of support and rapid shipment of product. Small stores were also willing to work with Crocs through problems such as stockouts and shipment delays whereas large retailers generally imposed financial penalties for such problems. Accordingly, Crocs saw small retailers as important to building the brand, and providing a brand presence, and it remained so even after the majority of sales went to large retailers.

After initial success of Crocs in small stores, large retailers approached the company. Since the large retailers had seen the market acceptance of the Crocs shoes, Crocs was in a much stronger negotiating position than it would have been earlier in its development. Now it could negotiate favorable terms, which did not include the financial penalties that would previously have been required. By mid-2007, about 75% of revenue came from large retailers, split approximately evenly between shoe stores, department stores, and sporting goods stores. The rest of the revenue came from a large number of small shops representing many different segments such as gift shops, bicycle retailers, specialty food retailers, health and beauty stores, surf shops, and kiosks. These small shops accounted for a much larger percentage of orders (although at much lower dollar levels) than the large retailers, thus requiring a different approach to distribution.

The Need to Rethink the Supply Chain

Crocs looked at the supply chain from a very different perspective than traditional shoe companies. Coming from their electronics contract manufacturing backgrounds, key Crocs executives were accustomed to producing what the customer needed, when it was needed, and responding rapidly to changes in demand. Thus, they decided to develop a supply chain model that provided them with a competitive advantage and focused on customer needs, so that when a customer needed more product, they would get it.

Under the Crocs model, retailers would not need to take a big risk in January by placing large orders for their fall season, instead, they could place smaller pre-booked orders, and order more when they saw how well the products sold. Crocs wanted customers to be able to get more of a product during the season in order to take advantage of unexpectedly high demand. To do that, Crocs would have to be able to make the products during the season, and ship them to customers quickly. Accordingly, the new model rolled out in three phases.

PHASE ONE: TAKING OVER PRODUCTION

One of the first moves was buying the manufacturer of Crocs shoes (Foam Creations) in June 2004, as mentioned, so that it could own the proprietary resin and control manufacturing. At that point, Crocs purchased the raw material pellets from a variety of companies in Europe and the U.S., and shipped them to a third-party compounding company in Italy. The Italian company had been part owner of Foam Creations, and had previously done the compounding, so continuing to use it for this function avoided supply chain interruptions.

PHASE TWO: GLOBAL PRODUCTION USING CONTRACT MANUFACTURERS

Crocs started production in China in early 2005, using a large contract manufacturer. The raw materials were still being sent to Italy for compounding, but the compounded pellets were now sent to both Canada and China. To meet the needs of small customers, product made in China would be shipped to the company-owned warehouse in Denver, where the orders were configured, packed, and shipped. The company's strategy was to launch worldwide and it began to enter the Asian and European markets in the spring of 2005. Thus, it decided to bring on more manufacturing capacity to support this approach by adding contract manufacturers in Florida, Mexico, and Italy.

PHASE THREE: BRINGING THE GLOBAL SUPPLY CHAIN IN-HOUSE

As the company grew globally, it realized that in order to compete it needed to be able to quickly respond to customer demands, and to increase or stop production as required which is not how the footwear industry worked. They also realized that their new model will not work by relying on the third-party manufacturers outside Asia. Asian manufacturers had proven to be both flexible and high volume. They moved quickly and where willing to take risks in buying new equipment to accommodate production needs. No manufacturers in other countries were willing to do the same and accommodate the company's supply chain model, but Asian manufacturers also preferred to be given long-term forecasts and long-term contracts. As a result, Crocs decided to develop company-owned manufacturing operations in Mexico, Italy, and Brazil. The move had other tax benefits. The footwear industry was subject to considerable duties. For instance, the U.S. imposed duties on all Crocs shoes coming from China, with tariffs ranging from 3 to 37.5% depending on the materials in the shoe. Shoes that were entirely molded had a low tariff, while those which used leather or other materials would have a high tariff. On the other hand, under the original North American Free Trade Agreement (NAFTA), Crocs paid no duty for products made in Mexico and shipped to the U.S. It also benefited from other trade agreements that allowed duty-free shipments between different countries such as no duty on Mexican shoes sold in Europe.

The Downturn

In 2009 things started to change. After sales took off in the mid-2000s, Crocs struggled to keep up with demand. When production finally caught up, it went overboard, ending up with mountains of shoes and no one to buy them just as the economic downturn of 2008 had hit. That sent the company into a tailspin, losing $185 million in 2008, which raised doubts on the company's ability to pay off its debts.

Clogs were for sale everywhere. The company was overextended, and the recession made it worse. Crocs was saddled with excess inventory and forced to liquidate it. Retailers cut back on buying some of its newer products as shoppers turned on the brand. Crocs started opening its own stores to make up for lost distribution, but that strategy missed, in part because clogs are mainly warmer weather shoes and thus the stores were a real drag to the business in colder weather months. At this point many analysts had anticipated the end of Crocs.

The Comeback

In the years to follow, Crocs pulled off a remarkable comeback and once again by focusing mainly on its supply chain model. The company started a six-year turnaround of strategic changes which included:

- Cutting nearly a third of the company's workforce

- Getting rid of the excess inventory

- Getting rid of unprofitable lines of apparel and high-end women's shoes while sticking to products such as the Crocs which accounted for nearly 50% of the company's sales

- Securing a $200 million investment by private equity giant Blackstone Group

By 2018, clog revenue grew by 12.7%, exceeding all expectations. However, in August 2019 the company made its most aggressive move that stunned many observers. It decided to turn away from its internal production policy and in May of the same year Crocs closed a factory in Mexico and moved ahead with plans to end production at its final plant in Italy, shifting production back to third parties to increase manufacturing capacity. The goal was for all production to be outsourced to third parties, primarily in China and Vietnam.

The Outcome

The strategic shift seems to have worked and Crocs has been able to stay relevant with shoppers and adapt to retail upheaval. Crocs sandals and clog sales grew getting a boost from an online musical featuring celebrity endorser Drew Barrymore.

Retailers like Journeys and Dick's Sporting Goods that left Crocs during its struggles showed more interest in selling clogs and sandals at their stores again. In addition, the higher-margin online business was also growing, driven in part by high school and college students buying clogs to wear before and after sporting events. New high-heeled clogs for girls and women, while drawing a mixed reaction on social media, still helped to create a buzz that clearly helped the company get increased PR coverage. So, it seems that at least for now, Crocs is here to stay.

Case Study Questions

1. What are the main challenges of exporting a product such as Crocs clogs to foreign markets? And how to overcome them?

2. Crocs had relied on foreign contracting, then abandoned the strategy before returning to it again. Assess the role and impact of the strategy in both cases.

Case Study Sources

1. "Crocs: No Sign of Slowing Down". Seeking Alpha. December 12, 2019. https://seeking alpha.com/article/4312226-crocs-no-signs-of-slowing-down

2. Ivanova, Irina. "Crocs Closing Manufacturing Facilities but Will Keep Making Shoes". *CBS News*. Accessed August 9, 2018. https://www.cbsnews.com/news/crocs-closing-manufacturing-facilities-but-not-going-out-of-business-will-keep-making-shoes/

3. Marks, Michael, Charles Holloway, David Hoyt, Hau Lee and Amanda Silverman. *Crocs (A): Revolutionizing an Industry's Supply Chain Model for Competitive Advantage* (Stanford: Stanford Graduate School of Business, 2007).

4. Meyersohn, Nathaniel. "How Crocs Staged a Comeback". *CNN*. August 9, 2018. https://money.cnn.com/2018/08/09/news/companies/crocs-clogs-sandals/index.html

5. "The Ugly Shoe is Back: Crocs Ready too Try on Future with Fewer Styles and Way More Clogs". *Financial Post*. April 1, 2015. https://business.financialpost.com/news/retail-marketing/the-ugly-shoe-is-back-crocs-ready-to-try-on-future-with-fewer-styles-and-way-more-clogs

6. www.crocs.com

NOTES

1. Erascu, Ana-Maria. "Fashion Data is the New Black". Questa Group. April 17, 2018. https://analytica. questiagroup.com/fashion-data-is-the-new-black/
2. Van Gelder, Sicco. *Global Brand Strategy* (London: Kogan Page, 2003), 166.
3. Chevalier, Michael and Gerard Mazzalovo. *Luxury Brand Management* (Singapore: John Wiley & Sons, 2008), 307.
4. Shoemack, Harvey R. and Patricia M. Rath. *Essentials of Exporting and Importing* (New York: Bloomsbury, 2014), 104.
5. Keller, Kevin L. *Strategic Brand Management*, 4e. (New Jersey, Pearson, 2013), 493
6. Ibid., 499.
7. "Hofstede's Cultural Dimensions". Mind Tools. Accessed November 28, 2019. https://www. mindtools.com/pages/article/newLDR_66.htm

BIBLIOGRAPHY

Books

Birnbaum, David. *Birnbaum's Global Guide to Winning the Great garment War* (New York: The Fashiondex, Inc., 2000).

Bruce, Margaret, Christopher Moore and Grete Birtwistle. *International Retail Marketing: A Case Study Approach* (Burlington: Elsevier, 2005).

Burns, Leslie D., Kathy K. Mullet and Nancy O. Bryant. *The Business of Fashion*, 4th ed. (New York: Fairchild, 2011).

Chevalier, Michel and Gerald Mazzalovo. *Luxury Brand Management: A World of Privilege* (Singapore: John Wiley and Sons (Asia), 2008).

Choi, Tsan-Ming and T.C. Edwin Cheng. *Sustainable Fashion Supply Chain Management: From Sourcing to Retailing* (Cham: Springer, 2015).

Choi, Tsan-Ming and Bin Shen. *Luxury Fashion Retail Management* (Singapore: Springer, 2017).

Corbellini, Erica and Stefania Saviolo. *Managing Fashion and Luxury Companies* (Firenze: Rizzoli ETAS, 2012).

David, Fred R. *Strategic Management: Concepts and Cases*, 13th ed. (Upper Saddle River: Pearson, 2011).

Hill, Charles W. L. and G. Tomas M. Hult. *Global Business Today* (New York: McGraw-Hill, 2016).

Jimenez, Guillermo C. and Barbara Kolsun. *Fashion Law*, 2nd ed. (New York: Fairchild, 2014).

Jin, Byoungho and Elena Cedrola. *Fashion Branding and Communication: Core Strategies of European Luxury brands* (New York: Palgrave, 2017).

Keller, Kevin L. *Strategic Brand Management*, 4th ed. (Upper Saddle River: Pearson, 2013).

Kunz, Grace I. and Myrna B. Garner. *Going Global* (New York: Fairchild, 2011).

Kunz, Grace I., Elena Karpova and Myrna B. Garner. *Going Global: The Textile and Apparel Industry*, 3rd ed. (New York: Fairchild, 2016).

Leong, Wisner T. *Principles of Supply Chain Management: A Balanced Approach*, 3rd ed. (Mason: South-Western, 2012).

Londrigan, Michael and Jacqueline M. Jenkins. *Fashion Supply Chain Management.* (New York: Fairchild, 2018).

Morden, Tony. *Principles of Strategic Management*, 3rd ed. (Hampshire: Ashgate Publishing Limited, 2007).

Reddy, Mergen, Nic Terblanche, Leyland Pitt and Michael Parent. *How Far Can Luxury Brands Travel? Avoiding the Pitfalls of Luxury Brand Extension* (Indiana: Kelley School of Business, 2009).

Robbins, Stephan P. and Mary Coulter. *Management*, 7th ed. (Upper Saddle River: Prentice Hall, 2001).

Ross, Andrew. *No Sweat: Fashion, Free Trade, and the Rights of Garment Workers* (New York: Verso, 1997).

Schramme, Annick, Turi Moerkerke and Karinna Nobbs. *Fashion Management* (Leuven: Lannoo, 2013).

Sherman, Gerald J. and Sar S. Perlman. *The Real World Guide to Fashion Selling and Management*, 2nd ed. (New York: Fairchild, 2015).

Shoemack, Harvey and Patricia M. Rath. *Essentials of Exporting and Importing: U.S. Trade Policies, Procedures, and Practices* (New York: Fairchild, 2014).

Van Gelder, Sicco. *Global Brand Strategy: Unlocking Brand Potential Across Countries, Cultures and Markets* (London: Kogan-Page, 2003).

Varley, Rosemary, Ana Roncha, Natasha Radclyffe-Thomas, and Liz Gee. *Fashion Management: A Strategic Approach* (London: Red Globe Press, 2019).

Yousaf, Nasim. *Import and Export of Apparel and Textile* (New York: Xilbris, 2001).

Other Sources

"About Foreign-Trade Zones and Contact Info: An Introduction to Foreign-Trade Zones". U.S. Customs and Border Protection. Accessed April 16, 2018. https://www.cbp.gov/border-security/ports-entry/cargo-security/cargo-control/foreign-trade-zones/about

"Connecting You to Global Markets". International Trade Administration. Accessed April 12, 2018. https://www.export.gov/article?id=Trade-Finance-Guide-Chapter-2

"Global Fashion Industry Statistics, International Apparel". Fashion United. Accessed November 1, 2019. https://fashionunited.com/global-fashion-industry-statistics/

"NAFTA Revisions Textile Apparel". Sandler, Travis and Rosenberg, P.A. Accessed May 3, 2018. https://www.strtrade.com/events-NAFTA-Revisions-Textile-Apparel-111318.html

"Seminar: Free Trade Agreements for Garments and Apparel". W2C. Accessed September 7, 2019. https://w2c.ca/en/training/seminar/seminar-free-trade-agreements-for-garments-and-apparel-i-e-nafta-cusma-cptpp-ceta/

"Textile and Apparel Products, Rule of Origin". U.S. Customs and Border Protection. Accessed April 18, 2018. https://www.cbp.gov/trade/nafta/guide-customs-procedures/provisions-specific-sectors/textiles

"Unregistered Community Designs, Could Reference to CJEU Save London Fashion Week?". Herbert Smith Freehills. October 17, 2019. https://hsfnotes.com/ip/2019/10/17/unregistered-community-designs-could-a-reference-to-cjeu-save-london-fashion-week/

"USITC Economic Assessment Report on USMCA, Textile and Apparel Sector Summary". Sheng Lu Fashion. April 19, 2019. https://shenglufashion.com/tag/nafta/

Belgium, Deborah. "Apparel Production in Mexico Will Change Slightly Under NAFTA 2.0". *Apparel News*. August 30, 2018. https://www.apparelnews.net/news/2018/aug/30/apparel-production-mexico-will-change-slightly-und/

Luhman, David. "Japan's Complex Distribution System". *Luhman*. Accessed April 12, 2017. http://luhman.org/japanese-reports/sell-to-japan/030-japans-complex-distribution-system

CHAPTER SEVEN

Ethics and Other Fashion Management Issues

LEARNING OUTCOMES

- Understand the role of ethics and its impact on management.

- Appreciate the challenges of work and labor conditions within the industry.

- Identify the scope of copyright protection in reference to the fashion product.

- Assess the impact of counterfeits on fashion and measures taken to combat them.

ISSUE 1: ETHICS AND MANAGEMENT

Ethics is a set of moral principles or values that deal with what is good and bad as well as with moral duty and obligation. Business ethics, therefore, is concerned with good and bad or right and wrong behavior and practices that take place within a business context. Today, concepts of right and wrong are being interpreted to also include the even more difficult questions of fairness, justice, and equity.

Corporate Social Responsibility (CSR) and Corporate Citizenship

Businesses have been undergoing the most intense scrutiny they have ever received from the public in terms of their role and impact in societies where they exist. This idea of social responsibility supposes that the corporation has not only economic and legal obligations, but also certain responsibilities to society which extend beyond these obligations. Hence, the birth of the term *corporate social responsibility* which could be defined as *the obligation of decision makers to take actions which protect and improve the welfare of society as a whole along with their own interests.*[1]

This definition suggests two active aspects of social responsibility: *protecting* and *improving*. To protect the welfare of society implies the avoidance of negative impacts on society such as avoiding environmental pollution. To improve the welfare of society implies the creation of positive benefits for society such as building a new community center. Accordingly, to some scholars there is a clear distinction in approach between *ethics* and *social responsibility*; while ethics may have an organizational internal focus and protective approach by focusing on preventing bad actions and harm, *social responsibility*, on the other hand, tends to have an external proactive approach aiming to doing good and establishing the organization as a good "citizen" in the society.

The social responsibility of business has grown as a concept to encompass many aspects such as: the economic, legal, ethical, and discretionary (philanthropic) expectations that society has of organizations at a given point in time. For *example:*[2]

ECONOMIC RESPONSIBILITIES

Any business has economic responsibilities. It may seem odd to call an economic responsibility a social responsibility, but, in effect, this is what it is. A business exists to be an economic institution. That is, it should be an institution whose objective is to produce goods and services that society wants and to sell them at fair prices that society thinks represent the true value of the goods and services delivered. At the same time, it would provide the business with profits adequate to ensure its survival and growth as well as to reward its investors.

LEGAL RESPONSIBILITIES

A business has legal responsibilities. It is the business's responsibility to society to comply with its established laws.

ETHICAL RESPONSIBILITIES

Because laws are essential but not adequate, ethical responsibilities are needed to embrace those activities and practices that are expected or prohibited by society even though they are not codified into law. Ethical responsibilities embody the full scope of norms, standards, values, and expectations that reflect what consumers, employees, shareholders, and the community regard as fair, just, and consistent with the protection of its stakeholders' moral rights.

PHILANTHROPIC RESPONSIBILITIES

These are the business's voluntary, discretionary, or philanthropic responsibilities. Though not responsibilities in the literal sense of the word, these are viewed as responsibilities because they reflect current expectations of business by the public. Such activities might include corporate giving, product and service donations, employee volunteerism, partnerships with local government and other organizations, and any other kind of voluntary involvement of the organization and its employees with the community or other stakeholders.

A major distinction between ethical responsibilities and philanthropic responsibilities is that the latter typically are not expected in a moral or an ethical sense. Communities desire and expect business to contribute its money, facilities, and employee time to humanitarian programs or purposes, but they do not regard firms as unethical if they do not provide these services at the desired levels.

Corporate Social Responsiveness and Corporate Social Performance

Other concepts that have evolved from CSR include *corporate social responsiveness* and *corporate social performance*.

CORPORATE SOCIAL RESPONSIVENESS

This term represents the *action* side of social responsibility. So that while social responsibility indicates some obligation the organization may have, social responsiveness represent the actual action taken by management to fulfill and respond to this obligation.

CORPORATE SOCIAL PERFORMANCE (CSP)

This term implies that what really matters is what companies are able to accomplish, the results or outcomes of their acceptance of social responsibility, and adoption of a responsiveness philosophy.

Corporate Citizenship

In recent years, the new concept of corporate citizenship became popular and widely used. While the term may commonly refer to the active involvement of an organization in the success and welfare of the society in which it is involved, and CSR addresses the full range of responsibilities towards all stakeholders making it a broader term, it is very common to see both terms used interchangeably which is an indication of the popularity of the newer and simpler term of corporate citizenship. The term *global corporate citizenship* is used when a business enterprise's (including its managers') responsibly exercises its rights and implements its duties to individuals, stakeholders, and societies within and across national and cultural borders

WHAT DRIVES COMPANIES TO EMBRACE CORPORATE CITIZENSHIP?

According to researchers, there are both internal (within the company) motivators and external pressures that drive companies toward corporate citizenship.

Internal motivators include traditions and values, reputation and image, business strategy, retaining employees, etc.

External pressures include customers, community expectations, laws and regulations, political pressures, etc.

BENEFITS OF GOOD CORPORATE CITIZENSHIP

- Improved employee relations (e.g. improve employee recruitment, retention, motivation, and productivity)

- Improved customer relationships (e.g. increases customer loyalty, stimulates consumer purchases, enhances brand image)

- Improved business performance (e.g. positively impacts bottom-line returns, increases competitive advantage, encourages cross-functional integration)

- Improved company marketing efforts (e.g. helps create a positive company image, helps a company manage its reputation, supports higher prestige pricing, and enhances government affairs activities)

Business Ethics Framework

There are four simple questions that help us frame the business ethics of any organization:[3]

1. *What is?* It forces us to identify the reality of what is actually going on in an ethical sense in business or in a specific decision or practice.

2. *What ought to be?* The "ought to be" question is often viewed in terms of what management should do (in an ethical sense) in a given situation. Examples of this question in a business setting might be: How ought we treat our aging employees whose productivity is declining? How safe ought we make this product, knowing well we cannot pass all the costs on to the consumer? or How clean an environment should we aim for?

3. *How do we get from "what is" to "what ought to be"?* This question represents the challenge of bridging the gap between where we are and where we ought to be with respect to ethical practices. It is a practical question for management. When faced with these challenges as

depicted by our "ought to be" questions, we may find that from a practical point of view we cannot achieve our ideals.

4. *What is our motivation in all this?* The question addresses the motivation for being ethical, because sometimes it reveals some manipulative or self-centered motive.

Alignment of Ethics with Organization Culture Systems

To create a consistent ethical culture message, the formal and informal systems must be aligned (work together) to support ethical behavior. Executive leaders affect culture in both formal and informal ways. Senior leaders can create, maintain, or change formal and informal cultural systems by what they say, do, or support. As well as by creating and supporting formal policies and programs with resources. Indeed, their formal communications send a powerful message about what's important in the organization. On the other hand, they also influence informal culture by role modeling, the language they use, and the norms their messages and actions appear to support.

Ethical cultures should guide individuals to take responsibility for their own behavior, question orders to behave unethically, and report misconduct or problems. A strong ethical culture incorporates a structure that emphasizes and supports individual responsibility and accountability at every level.

Organizations can formally communicate their ethics programs and standards through many channels and events such as: websites, social media, recruiting brochures, campus recruiting events, orientation meetings, newsletters, magazines, and booklets, etc.

Codes of Conduct

Most ethics programs, good or bad, have codes of conduct stated. A code of conduct is not a substitute for an ethics program; a code is only the start of an ethics effort. They vary substantially in length, content, and readability, and they're generally designed to be the main road map, the ground rules for ethical conduct within the organization.

Many organizations prefer a long code which they would divide into parts. The first part provides the broad guiding principles. These are followed by a more detailed section that includes more specific application to cases, answers to commonly asked questions, and reference to more detailed policy manuals. Some organizations create separate booklets, as supplements to a more general code, for workers in particular functions, such as purchasing or human resources management. These booklets can provide details and answers to the questions likely to arise in that particular type of job, and the individuals in that job are more likely to read those details. Code content may also vary depending on the industry and the degree to which the firm has entered the global marketplace. Accordingly, specific issues are addressed depending on the industry.

Ethics and the Supply Chain

More and more companies are realizing that the ethics programs of their vendors or contractors have a significant impact on their own operations. If a significant vendor or contractor suffers an operational loss resulting from an ethical misstep, it could harm the company's ability to produce and/or distribute their product. This is very relevant to the fashion industry indeed, where many fashion brands and manufacturers received negative publicity and societal scrutiny as a result of the malpractices of their overseas partner and contractors (e.g. Nike). As a result, numerous companies are now routinely expressing interest in the robustness of the ethics program(s) of their vendors and suppliers. They also share with them a copy of their own code of conduct requesting they adhere to it while making sure they are posted and made visible for all workers involved with their product to see.

Example: Nike's code of conduct lays out a set of minimum standards that they expect each of their supplier factories and facilities to meet. These standards are grouped under four categories:[4]

- *Respected*: Employment is voluntary, employees are age 16 or older, supplier does not discriminate, and freedom of association and collective bargaining are respected.

- *Fair*: Harassment and abuse are not tolerated, working hours are not excessive, compensation is timely paid, and regular employment is provided.

- *Safe*: The workplace is safe, dorms, canteens and childcare facilities are healthy and safe, building is fit for purpose, fire and emergency action plans are in place, and occupational health and hygiene hazards are controlled.

- *Sustainable*: Water is valued, waste is minimized and handled properly, energy and carbon are minimized, air emissions impact is minimized, and chemicals are properly managed.

Areas of Ethical Impact
ETHICS AND THE CONSUMER
Product Safety

A major ethical obligation of any organization is to produce a quality product or service. Nothing will put a company out of business faster than offering a product that is dangerous, poorly produced, or of inferior quality. Competition in the marketplace generally helps ensure that goods and services will be of a quality that is acceptable to consumers. However, sometimes a company becomes the victim of external sabotage (*e.g. deaths due to drug tampering of Johnson & Johnson's Tylenol in 1982*), and sometimes a company makes a bad decision, and the result is a product that is not safe.

Advertising

The subject of ethics in advertising is common and very relevant to the fashion and beauty industries, simply because there are varying opinions of exactly what truth is, and what responsibility is. Companies are commonly accused of marketing manipulation by exaggerating or lying about facts. After all, does a certain moisturizer really makes skin look decades younger, or is it the 20-year-old model who has a young wrinkle-free complexion? In their attempt to stand out, gain attention, or create a buzz, companies are commonly accused of crossing cultural lines through use of sex or other sensitive issues in advertising. Benetton was highly criticized for showing an AIDS victim and real men on death row in its 1980s fashion advertisements. Calvin Klein was highly criticized for his campaign promoting the "Be" fragrance. The advertisements were seen to promote "heroin chic" depicting barely legal-aged models in images reminiscent of sleazy 1970s pornographic movies. The advertisements were pulled out and Mr. Klein had to publish a full-page apology in the *New York Times*.

Conflicts of Interest

If an organization's customers or other stakeholder groups think that an organization's judgment is biased because of a relationship it has with another company or firm, a conflict could exist. Corporate or organizational conflicts are just as risky as those that exist between individuals, and they should be avoided at all costs.

ETHICS AND THE EMPLOYEES

Employee Safety

The most basic of employee rights is the right to work without being hurt or even killed on the job. Unsafe working conditions in factories contracted for fashion production in many developing countries such as Bangladesh and India, have been routinely under scrutiny after a series of fatal incidents.

Employee Downsizings

Employee downsizings or layoffs can result from many business conditions, including economic depressions, the desire to consolidate operations and decrease labor costs, increased competition, or unmet corporate objectives, etc. However, the result always involves human misery. Organizations may not have an ethical obligation to keep labor forces at a specific number. They do, however, have an obligation to hire and fire responsibly.

ETHICS AND SHAREHOLDERS

Organizations have a clear ethical obligation to shareholders and owners. This ethical obligation includes serving the interests of owners and trying to perform well in the short as well as the long terms. It also means not engaging in activities that could put the organization out of business and not making short-term decisions that might jeopardize the company's health in the future.

ETHICS AND THE COMMUNITY

A major stakeholder in business as discussed earlier must be the communities of which corporations and other organizations are a part. Examples of ways a company can affect its community are through its approach to the environment or simply through issues like internet privacy, etc.

Examples of Fashion CSR and Ethical Initiatives

The fashion and textiles industries have been criticized for poor labor working conditions, chemical waste, and water pollution, as well as marketing manipulation, etc. However, there have been indeed many positive examples of fashion organizations acting as responsible corporate citizens and contributing to the welfare of their communities and the world at large. Here are a few samples:

- Target stores established its *Target Foundation* which offers grants supporting non-profit organizations for initiatives in areas of housing, entrepreneurship, workforce development, and community empowerment, both locally and globally.

- *Zappos for Good* by Zappos works with charitable organizations to donate goods such as backpacks, shoes, books, and school supplies to those in need.

- Stella McCartney, the luxury fashion brand, is a major advocate of sustainability. Its *Adidas by Stella McCartney* line focuses on minimizing waste and repurposing leftover fabrics. The brand also uses unannounced audits to understand how their manufacturing suppliers work and identify potential risk areas. They regularly provide training to suppliers on their requirements as well as on common social sustainability challenges.

- For TOMS Shoes, sustainability plays a key role in the company's social responsibility. The brand is known for crafting shoes from sustainable and vegan materials such as hemp and organic cotton. All TOMS shoe boxes are comprised of 80% recycled post-consumer waste, and they are printed with soy ink. TOMS is also famously known for having a positive social impact through its "One for One Movement" initiative in which the company matches every pair of shoes purchased by a customer with a new pair of shoes for a child in need.

Box 7.1 LVMH CSR Strategy

LVMH owns 70 luxury houses operating in five luxury segments. Based on its workforce-related and social priorities, as well as interactions with its stakeholders, LVMH has crafted a social responsibility policy that brings its values to life. It implements this policy with the help of its brands' houses. They identified the following four priorities or pillars for their CSR:

1. *Being respectful:* focusing on preventing discrimination and respecting individuality of the work force. Examples:
   - LVMH embraces inclusion and gender equality (in 2018, 73% of total workforce were women and 42% of key positions were held by women with a 50/50 target in 2020).
   - Giving older employees a key role in passing skills and experience (e.g. Kenzo adopted a plan whereby 5% of new hires and 15% of total workforce are employees aged 50 or older).
   - Promoting employment for people with disabilities (e.g. in 2011, Moët & Chandon set up a company MHEA, whose entire workforce is made up of people with disabilities, LVMH launched the *EXCELLhanCE* program enabling people with disabilities to obtain degrees while working at the group).

2. *Passing on expertise:* attracting talents that best match its current and future needs. Examples:
   - LVMH academic partnerships to identify future talents (e.g. Inside LVMH program giving university students an opportunity to immerse in the business, share innovative ideas, and possibly get recruited).
   - In 2014, LVMH established the *Institut des Métiers d'Excellence (IME)*, a vocational training program that helps ensure its expertise in craftsmanship, design, and sales is successfully passed on to the younger generation.
   - Supporting emerging designers through its annual LVMH Prize for Young Fashion Designers.
   - The group promotes training, cross-functional skills and supports career development (e.g. In 2018, LVMH rolled out its DARE (Disrupt, Act, Risk – to be an Entrepreneur) program. This collaborative global innovation program gives employees an opportunity to work in teams on innovative ideas that are judged to possibly be implemented within LVMH.
   - LVMH aims to offer attractive compensation packages.

3. *Being supportive:* LVMH is committed to employee health and safety. Examples:
   - Well-being through work councils and therapists.
   - Adopt an on-work-life balance approach (e.g. fostering childcare, occasional remote working, etc.).
   - Encourage employees' feedback and input.

4. *Making a commitment:* playing an active role in communities. Examples:
   - LVMH's growth is a major contributor to development of local economies and communities.

- Encouraging entrepreneurship and startups (e.g. supporting women entrepreneurs through the annual Businesswoman of the Year Award).
- Promote access to education and employment for marginalized individuals (e.g. internships and sponsorships).
- Employee volunteering in poor communities, product donations, and financial aid (e.g. BVLGARI donated over $80 million to Save The Children helping over 12 million children, Fendi supports a variety of causes, including AEM, (a nonprofit helping children, mainly in Rwanda).

Sources

1. LVMH. *LVMH 2018 Social Responsibility Report.* Accessed September 26, 2019. https://r.lvmh-static.com/uploads/2019/05/2018-social-responsibility-report.pdf.

ISSUE 2: FASHION AND LABOR ISSUES

The world's population is increasingly clothed by workers in the Asia-Pacific region. Across the region, in low and middle-income countries, around 43 million people work in factories to produce garments, textiles, and footwear, where India constitutes the biggest share of these workers at 16.7 million, followed by China (6.2 million), and Bangladesh (4.9 million). Other regions include, Africa, Latin America, and the Middle East. However, it is still China (with 37.2% of the market) that commands the largest share of global clothing exports.[5] As the global fashion industry continues to grow each year it should be credited for spurring economic growth by generating tax revenue, providing valuable skills and training, and delivering crucial foreign exchange. The industry is among the most labor-intensive in the world and a significant driver of employment for groups that have been traditionally vulnerable such as women, migrants, and young people. In some cases, the industry has been a source for empowerment and a stepping stone to a better life for these individuals. All of these factors can, and often do, contribute to improving the lives of these workers and their communities. On the other hand, the industry has also become a facilitator of exploitation and an environment for malpractices in various areas. Examples of such areas are:

Living Wage

A living wage is defined as a wage that is sufficient for workers to be able to afford the basics (food, water, healthcare, clothing, electricity, and education) for themselves and their dependents. A living wage is recognized as a human right, yet most garment sector workers in many parts of the world receive wages well below this level. In Bangladesh for instance, the minimum entry level wage for a garment worker is $63 per month. Calculations by the *Global Alliance* for a living wage suggest that a fair living wage would be approximately $214 per month for the capital city Dhaka and $177 per month for satellite cities around it. In Vietnam, the minimum wage is $153 per month, nearly half that of the estimated living wage at $290 per month. Thus, for the majority of workers in the global fashion industry, wages are so low that they leave them, and their families, trapped in poverty.[6]

Working Conditions

Fashion production throughout the Asia-Pacific region and in other developing countries is marred by the presence of slavery, child labor, structural defects, and unsafe working conditions. These issues are generally inadequately addressed as seen in recent cases of fire hazards and structural disasters in places like Bangladesh that led to the deaths of dozens of workers who could not flee for safety in a burning factory.

Forced Labor

The *International Labor Organization (ILO)* and *Walk Free Organization* estimate that there are 24.9 million forced laborers in the world. Two thirds of forced labor victims are in the same regions where the majority of the world's garment production takes place in developing countries. The risk occurs at multiple points of the supply chain, with manufacturing accounting for about 15% of forced laborers, while agriculture (such as cotton fields) accounts for a further 11%. In addition, women, who make up the largest proportion of garment producers, are also more vulnerable, accounting for 57.6% of all forced laborers.[7]

GENDER

As mentioned, women represent about 80% of global garment workers. Despite this, gender-based discrimination in recruitment, and sexual harassment, are widespread in the workplace. In addition, almost all countries report a gender pay gap. The gap is most significant in countries like Pakistan (66.5%), India (35.3%), and Sri Lanka (30.3%).

CHILD LABOR

Child labor, particularly in the production of raw materials like cotton, is prevalent in fashion supply chains. The ILO reports that there are 170 million child laborers in the world. with almost every major cotton producing country being impacted such as: China, India, Brazil, Pakistan, and Turkey, among many others. But it is not just in agriculture, the *U.S. Department of Labor* reports that child labor is used in garment, textile, and footwear manufacturing in countries across the world. Children work at all stages of the supply chain in the fashion industry, from the production of cotton seeds in Benin, harvesting in Uzbekistan, yarn spinning in India, right through the different phases of putting garments together in factories across Bangladesh. They perform diverse and often hard tasks such as dyeing, sewing buttons, cutting and trimming threads, folding, moving, and packing garments. In small workshops and home sites, children are put to work on intricate tasks such as embroidering, sequinning, and smocking (making pleats). Children are seen as easy to manage, cheaper to hire, and in some cases more suited to certain jobs. Employers get away with it because the fashion supply chain is hugely complex, and it is hard for companies to control every stage of production. That makes it possible to employ children without big brands and consumers ever finding out. They are subjected to long working hours, exposure to pesticides, and they are often paid below the minimum wage, in addition to being subject to forced labor.

Many companies that sell their products in Europe and the U.S. may have no clue where the textiles come from. They may know their first supplier and there are codes of conduct in place, but further down the chain in the lower tiers it is very difficult to know where the cotton came from, for instance. Moreover, in many cases a fashion brand may have 200 or more suppliers. Thus, tackling child labor is a complicated manner especially in areas with extreme poverty where there will be children willing to work cheaply, and susceptible to being tricked into dangerous or badly paid work.

SWEATSHOPS

The *U.S. General Accounting Office* defines a sweatshop as *an employer that violates more than one federal or state labor law governing minimum wage and overtime, child labor, industrial homework, occupational safety and health, worker's compensation, or industry regulation.*[8] However, today the term is applied loosely to almost any set of conditions considered inhumane or unfair and thus, most export-oriented factories of the developing world could be labelled as sweatshops.

Sweatshops exist both internationally and domestically making it a global issue as they employ millions of people, mostly young women and immigrant workers who are desperately poor and work long hours, sometimes up to 20 hours a day, and their wages still do not total a workable wage to feed and clothe their families. The workers are often denied bathroom breaks and forced to undergo pregnancy tests and take birth control, so the companies do not have to pay maternity leave costs. They may also suffer verbal and physical abuse and struggle to complete high quotas each day.

In the U.S., the Department of Labor estimates that over 50% of sewing shops in the U.S. are sweatshops as defined by the above definition. According to a 2019 report by the New York Times,[9] investigations by the *U.S. Department of Labor* from 2016 to 2019 have found factories in Los Angeles contracted to make clothes for brands such as Nova, Forever 21, and TJ Maxx stores paying workers well below California's minimum wage, and in some cases as little as $2.77 an hour. In fact, some studies show that a high number of Los Angeles garment factories violate workplace health and safety standards by operating under conditions such as blocked fire exits, unsanitary bathrooms, and poor ventilation. The workers in Los Angeles are almost entirely undocumented immigrants making them unwilling to report these conditions, which unfortunately means, that buying *Made-in-the-USA* clothing often does not mean "sweatshop free".

Role of Economic Factors in Creating Sweatshops

Sweatshops are generally fueled by economic reasons. In a production process some costs are considered fixed costs at least for the short run (such as rent or salaries) which producers are to pay no matter the level of production. Other costs are variable, changing based on production levels (such as materials, the more you produce the more the cost of materials). When production rises, the fixed cost is spread across more units, and thus the cost of each unit drops, and the reverse is true (the basis of the *economies of scale* principle discussed earlier). Thus, when fixed costs are high the employer is motivated to structure an operation's productivity in terms of hourly output in order to avoid paying fixed salaries, and instead attempts to manipulate and reduce this variable cost it can control. Sweatshops, in return, are characterized by very low variable costs. Workers are usually paid by the piece or on an hourly basis. In addition, costs like rent, electricity, and heat which are considered fixed costs can be transferred into variable cost by passing them along to the worker through the homework system in which workers typically either lease or buy tools and equipment to work at their home and sometimes even pay for at least part of the materials.

For places where work is done on the employer's premises rent is usually the largest fixed cost and to minimize this cost the employer will seek out cheap, substandard factory housing spaces like cellars and attics into which space they cram as many workers as possible. The attempt to reduce the rent paid per worker is the chief cause of congestion in sweetshops, affecting the way in which material, inventories, supplies, equipment, and work-in progress block aisles and ventilation, unsanitary or nonexistent bathrooms, fire hazards, etc.

Interestingly, these conditions do not impact workers' productivity because as they are paid by the piece most of this effect is borne by them. If productivity drops, then the employer can simply add fresh workers. As long as any reduction in turnout does not outweigh the savings obtained by overcrowding, the employer is unlikely to care.

The Nature of Fashion and Sweatshops

One of the factors that contributes to the problem of sweatshops and low labor conditions in general is the fact that the apparel industry remains very labor intensive, as mentioned earlier. Due to the seasonality and short lifecycle of its products, styles are so unpredictable and change so rapidly that generally, they may not be profitable to produce in the long run and justify an investment in dedicated machinery. Instead garments tend to be produced in short runs, using a combination of general-purpose tools and equipment, especially the sewing machine. On the other hand, in industries with heavy capital investment or were workers earn higher hourly wages an employer has a stake in productivity. In fashion, products that tend to have long runs, such as blue jeans and underwear, justify mechanization and large invested capital by their large foreign producers which create the kinds of fixed costs that would deter sweatshops. On the other hand, garments with high fashion content are generally difficult to produce at a distance from the market because by the time the goods arrive the season is likely to be over. Thus, this fashion segment would use foreign producers to make the initial stocks in relatively long runs with a certain degree of mechanized special-purpose equipment. If the item sells well it is then reordered from local factories that produce much shorter runs quickly to restock the retail outlets before the season ends.

Initiatives and Possible Solutions to Address Sweatshops and Labor Issues

- One of the main forces reducing the sweetshop has been unionization and government regulations, including imposing a minimum hourly wage. The employer thus has an incentive to ensure that the worker's productivity exceeds the hourly minimum which is generally a sufficient inducement to move young children out of the shop and observe health and safety codes. This way employers are forced to carry a certain cost of production regardless of the worker's level of productivity.

- There have been a number of government initiatives and congressional mandates in the U.S. to encourage a sense of social responsibility and eliminate hazardous conditions to the physical and mental health of the child. However, many of them were filled with loopholes and did not eliminate garment industry sweatshops. Nevertheless, governments should not seize taking such initiatives.

- A fair payment system could be implemented by utilizing the assistance of non-profit organizations. Non-profit organizations should be closely involved in changing the industry by forming monitoring groups. Such groups will need the backing of the government in the forms of tariffs and fines to ensure that factories maintain acceptable standards. The combination of humanitarian rights groups and the U.S. government forming monitoring groups would force human rights to be a priority of the business world.

- Economists also argue that the elimination of sweatshops will boost economies by increasing personal income. As personal income rises, economies become more independent. As workers earn greater incomes, they become able to reintroduce money into the economy that was previously reinvested abroad by foreign companies.

- It is also important to make workers aware of their rights, so they know where to file a complaint if needed.

- Brands should know their manufacturers well and visit them regularly, keeping an eye for signs the factory is subcontracting without their knowledge. For instance, they should be concerned if the factory does not have enough workers for the number of t-shirts it needs to produce.

Although most clothing brands don't own their own factories, they do have a lot of influence. Companies can adjust their purchasing practices to ensure the factories they have inspected fulfil their orders. For example, Reebok is known to have been able to effectively monitor its factories without suffering a loss of profit. Companies can also take other initiatives to address the problem. For instance, Nike has been a leader in trying to achieve best practices within their industry, which can be attributed to the criticism they faced in regard to labor practices in their supply chain in the 1990s. Nike currently audits and provides rankings for more than 785 contract factory locations on labor issues, including minimum age requirements, compensation practices, fire safety management, and worker hours. On the other hand, companies such as Walmart Stores and Gap have set out to improve working conditions in facilities located in Bangladesh. They achieved this by setting up a voluntary safety standards organization known as the Alliance for Bangladesh Worker Safety with about $42 million in funds in order to improve factories' access to capital for safety upgrades.

Box 7.2 Nike Corporate Social Responsibility and Sustainable Innovation

In the past, Nike faced several controversies related to child labor and ethics in its supply chain. However, in recent years, it has invested a lot in CSR, sustainability and reducing its environmental impact. Nike claims to focus on creating a better future for the world and the communities in which it operates through sustainable innovation.

In Nike's CSR and Sustainability Strategy the main points include:

- *Commitment to reducing the carbon footprint.*
- *Innovative manufacturing.*
- *Keeping human voice at the heart of everything it does from manufacturing to marketing.*
- *Develop a new palette of sustainable materials.*
- *Moving to complete renewable energy.*
- *Diverse workplace and inclusive culture that becomes a catalyst for innovation.*
- *Investing and encouraging employees to invest in communities where Nike operates.*

Nike is concerned about its carbon footprint and the effect it has on the environment thus it had worked to reduce it by investing in innovative products and operations. It has also set ambitious targets for itself in the near future. The brand has set a target of reaching 100% renewable energy by the year 2025. In its innovative manufacturing model, the brand has kept workers and their voices at the center while improving their role to grow their participation and engagement. The brand is also investing in innovative technology in its supply chain and manufacturing units. It has set a code of conduct for its suppliers and keeps only those who are compliant with rules and regulations.

Most of the environmental impact of Nike shoes comes from the material used to make them. It is why Nike has formed coalitions with others like Sustainable Apparel Coalition and LAUNCH for making innovative material to be used in its products. Nike is focusing on creating material with low environmental impact to move towards a high-performance closed-loop model where it can use reclaimed material from the start (*e.g. developing new recycled polyester and leather alternatives*). Nike is innovating its manufacturing processes and supply chain so it can reuse the waste material generated in its production and supply chain. Its designers have already assembled a palette of 29 high-performance materials collected from waste. Right now, the waste material left from Nike's shoes is being used in tennis courts, athletic tracks, and Nike shoes. It is also using better cotton, recycled polyester, environmentally preferred rubber, and certified leather to further lower its environmental impact.

Nike has focused heavily on its employees' welfare, developing a strong culture and an inclusive workforce that helps maximize its efficiency and impact. It is attracting and developing a highly diverse workforce. Nike is also investing in community-based initiatives and inspiring its employees to engage with their communities and supports their giving of expertise, time, and money (*e.g. Nike raised $9.8 million in donations made through Employee Matching Gift schemes*). The company is also reaching kids in various parts of the world, including China, to make them physically active from a young age. In 2015, it invested 1.9% of pre-tax income, about $78.2 million, into community initiatives.

Nike still has a set of goals that it is committed to achieving such as: Global Pay Equity, 100% renewable energy use, 100% use of sustainable cotton and materials, at least a 20% reduction in freshwater use in textile dyeing and finishing, as well as an overall reduction in waste.

Sources

1. Nisen, Max. "How Nike Solved Its Sweatshop Problem". *Business Insider.* Accessed October 17, 2019. https://www.businessinsider.in/How-Nike-Solved-Its-Sweatshop-Problem/articleshow/21122639.cms
2. Pretap, Abhijeet. "Nike Corporate Social Responsibility and Sustainable Innovation". *Notesmatic.* Accessed January 22, 2020. https://notesmatic.com/2018/02/nike-csr-and-sustainability/
3. www.nike.com

ISSUE 3: INTELLECTUAL PROPERTY AND COPYRIGHTS

Intellectual property (IP) protection is the concern of any manager or business owner. IP in the fashion industry is not a simple issue. In the fashion industry, IP takes various forms whereby a single garment may be covered by several forms of legal protection at the same time. For example, a dress or t-shirt with a screen print photograph on it and a logo on the front as well as a label with the brand name would be protected as follows:[10]

- The logo and brand name could be protected as *trademarks.*

- The photographic image could be protected by *copyright.*

- If the garment is made out of an innovative microfiber developed exclusively by the company then this textile could be protected by a utility *patent.*

- However, the garment design itself (the garment as whole) is generally not protected under U.S. law (while it may be in the EU and some other countries).

This is why in the U.S. it is usually safe and mostly *legal* to copy fashion designs with few exceptions. Unfortunately copying and knock offs are very common practices in fashion and, yet surprisingly, they did not kill creativity. Copying is indeed cheaper than creating and it allows copiers to offer copies at cheaper and competitive prices as well as lower quality. Knock offs could be either designs inspired by others and modified or simply exact copies. Thus, it is important to distinguish between copying a whole garment or copying a design feature such as a lapel shape, a pocket design, or a cut, etc. While both types of copying exist in the industry the majority seem to belong to the second type which makes it even harder to protect. Copying does not only differ in scope but also in time. Some items are copied the same season while others at later times. And in some cases, even before the original design hits the stores.

An Old Dilemma

Copying and protection have been a long-running topic and discussion in the fashion industry. In the 1940s fashion designer Maurice Rentner called for legal amendments to protect garment designs from copying and since then the calls have continued. Lately, with the rise of fast fashion there seemed to have been a renewal for these calls. In 2006 the Design Piracy Prohibition Act (DPPA) was introduced in the U.S. Congress. In 2009 representative Bill Delahunt of Massachusetts introduced another bill to protect the industry from copying. However, not much has happened and the impact of these initiatives is almost nil.

Forms of Intellectual Property (IP)

There are various forms of IP in the fashion industry such as:

A. Trademark

B. Copyright

C. Patent

TRADEMARK

A trademark is anything that is used, or intended to be used, to identify the goods of one manufacturer from the goods of others. It is the brand name and identity. It could include words, names, symbols, and logos. Anything that distinctly identifies your company can be a trademark, provided that it is for goods. The Polo name, the Nike Swoosh, or the Burberry Plaid are all considered trademarks.

Designer names, e.g. Calvin Klein or Ralph Lauren can be used as the brand name and can be protected as trademarks only if the designer can establish that the public has come to recognize the designer's name as identifying the source of the designer's products, which takes several years of significant advertising and promotional efforts. If a designer decides to leave a company which was using their name (with their permission) for its own line, they may not be totally free to make use of their own name in their new endeavor because it could create confusion in the marketplace. And while courts are generally reluctant to forbid someone from using his/her name they will do so to avoid any confusion in the marketplace. Indeed, *confusion* is the keyword for the protection of intellectual property under the U.S. laws, meaning, that the main criteria here is whether the copied item would create confusion in the consumer's mind about the origin of the product or its source.

Trademarks are also important from a branding perspective for brands in all segments, especially for luxury and prestige brands. Thus, trademarks are useful for what is known as *trade dress* which is the distinctive packaging of a brand such as the Tiffany box as we will examine later.

A certain minimal level of trademark protection can be obtained simply by placing the trademark on products and selling those products to consumers even if the trademark has not been registered at the state or federal level. This is known as *common law trademark*. However, the scope of protection offered by this form is generally narrow as they provide protection only in the geographical area in which the goods are sold. Thus, most serious businesses will prefer to register their trademark by filing a trademark application in the U.S. Patent and Trademark Office (PTO). A federally registered trademark confers more benefits than common law trademark. For example, the mark will receive nationwide protection. In addition, federally registered marks can be recorded with the U.S. customs service so that customs can be enlisted in the prevention of importation of infringing or counterfeit products. These marks would also be presumed valid in trademark infringement litigations.

From a legal perspective, there are some necessary guidelines to protect a trademark:

1. The trademark must be available, it must neither duplicate nor be confusingly similar to an existing trademark for the given type of products. Hence, conducting research is advisable. Even if the

trademark is available, it may still not be advisable from a legal point of view based on the hierarchy classification (from *weak* to *strong*) to be eligible for protection as follows:

- *Strongest: Arbitrary or fanciful trademarks* – these are trademarks that are surprising in the context in which they are used and have a fanciful meaning. They are made-up words. An example of an arbitrary mark is XOXO, BEBE, or UNIQLO.

- *Next strongest: Suggestive trademarks* – these evoke images and an imaginative leap to suggest the nature of the goods or services (but do not straightforwardly describe it). An example of a suggestive mark is Dri-Foot (antiperspirant for feet) or KitchenAid. Suggestive trademarks are generally strong.

- *Relatively strong: Descriptive trademarks* (could be strong or weak based on circumstances) – these are trademarks that describe a characteristic of a good or service and give the customer an immediate idea of what the name entails. An example could be: Cotton:on or geographically descriptive such as Brooklyn Cloth or American Apparel. The distinction between suggestive and descriptive trademarks may be a bit blurry at times however, while descriptive are straightforward, suggestive trademarks require some imagination to interpret. For example, the fictional mark SUNSTOP would likely be considered merely descriptive of sun block preparations, while SOLAR GOO is considered suggestive when used for the same type of product.[11]

  The main problem with descriptive marks is that they are not entitled to strong protection until they acquire a secondary meaning, which refers to the recognition by the public that the mark is used on particular products sold by a specific provider (e.g. the *Cloth* in Brooklyn Cloth).

- *Weak: Generic trademark* – a generic mark is one which the proposed trademark consists of the same commonly used term by which the product is known to the general public. For example, the *Denim Pants* trademark for a jeans line or a sneakers line called *Athletic Shoes* will not be acceptable by the PTO. The rationale is that no one should be able to restrict everyday usage of a common term.

There are cases where a trademark has become so successful that it became generic and thus protection was no longer afforded, such as *Aspirin* and *Escalator*, and as a result the original trademark owner lost the right to prevent others from using those marks.

2. It is also important to note that the PTO will not register the following: immoral or scandalous marks, deceptive and disparaging marks, nor marks that falsely suggest a connection with a person, institution, or national symbols, as well as geographic indications if the mark misleadingly identifies a place other than the actual origin of the good.

3. In addition, a name, portrait, or signature of a person cannot be registered without that individual's consent. A trademark will also be refused if it consists merely of a surname.

4. Finally, any mark that conflicts with an already registered mark cannot be registered.

Brands need to check the Trademark Electronic Search System (TESS) on the PTO site to determine whether the mark is already being used in connection with similar goods and/or service or not. If a search reveals that the same mark is used but for a different category or product a lawyer's legal advice may be advisable at this stage.

While common law trademarks are effective as soon as they are actually used on a product and shipped to a customer, a trademark registration will generally be issued by the PTO about 13 months after the application is filed. Once the trademark is in use or has been registered a company can prevent a competitor from using the same or similar mark on the same or similar good by promptly sending that competitor a cease and desist letter. Thus, the main advantage of trademark registration is that it offers strong legal protection against infringing activity anywhere in the U.S. However, one limitation is that a competitor's use of a similar trademark can be stopped only when used in connection with similar goods or services. Also, trademark protection usually extends only to a particular product category or closely related categories. So, for instance if a company registered a trademark for clothing it may not be able to use it for bottled water, etc. Trademark protection can last forever, however, proof of continued usage must be periodically filed with the PTO compared to copyright and patent protection which lasts for only a finite number of years, as we will see.

Trade Dress

Trade dress is intellectual property in the characteristic appearance or packaging of a product including its shape, size, color combinations, texture, graphics, packaging, labeling, or other elements of its overall look. To be protected, the trade dress must be inherently distinctive or have achieved secondary meaning (i.e. be widely recognized by the public as identifying the company that is the source of the product). The blue Tiffany box and Hermes Birkin bag shape are examples of trade dress in fashion.

Like copyright, trade dress is limited to nonfunctional design elements. Additionally, the design must signify the garment's source or producer to the consumer. In other words, the trade dress must essentially function as a label. When a consumer sees the design, the consumer must recognize it as the work of a particular producer, which rarely happens. An important limitation is that trade dress protects only nonfunctional elements, or those elements of a product design that are primarily aesthetic. A product element is considered functional when the product would not work properly without that element. Thus, trade dress is deemed functional if it is essential to the use or purpose of the article or if it affects the cost or quality of the article. Thus, to check if trade dress is protectable courts look at functionality and distinctiveness.

In some instances, a trade dress can be registered with the PTO as a trademark (e.g. Hermes Birkin bag shape). If it is not distinctive, the owner must prove that consumers associate its trade dress with its company which could be through a written article, sales success, or affidavits from experts and competitors, etc. The distinctive Tiffany blue color seen on all its packaging has been registered as a color trademark since 1998. In general trade dress can be the most difficult form of IP protection. It may be easy for large companies like Tiffany but hard for new companies. Thus, it may not be advisable to go for it unless there is no other form of protection available.

International Trademark Protection

Trademark rights are territorial, meaning that trademark protection must be obtained on a country by country basis, although in the case of the EU it is possible to obtain it for all EU members. It is also important to know that some countries have a trademark use requirement. If a company does not use its trademark in that country, it can lose its rights. In other cases, if the company is licensing trademark rights to a third party in some countries, they may need to record that license agreement with the national trademark office there as well.

Seeking trademark protection in every country may not be financially feasible, thus it should be mainly done in countries where the company sells or plans to sell its products and where the company's products are manufactured. On the other hand, it is obviously also advisable to register trademarks as an internet domain name.

COPYRIGHT

The Copyright Act of 1790 granted 14 years of protection (with a possible 14-year renewal). However, over the years Congress has extended the copyright term (today it is protected for the life of the author + 70 years) and extended the scope of subject matter as well as removed most of the formalities that once were barriers to protection. Yet, in spite of this, much of fashion remains outside of the scope of copyright protection.

The reason fashion is not protected stems from the general feature of the American copyright laws. It relates to the *functionality* and *usefulness* of the item. Indeed, while *confusion* is the buzz word for trademark protection, *usefulness* (and *functionality*) are the buzz words for copyrights. According to the law, *useful* (or functional) items can be copied freely. So, items like fashion (and furniture, etc.), where creativity is also complemented by functionality, can be copied. On the other hand, a painting or piece of music, while creative, are not functional in nature and have no functional use, thus can be protected. Accordingly, copyright laws aim at the art works that either have no function or have minimal functional attributes. As in the case of jewelry, for instance, it can be protected because it is considered ornamental and not useful as opposed to a dress (similar to protection of IP granted to other authors of original creative works). Based on this argument, a 2D sketch of the dress can be protected as a drawing but the dress itself (*the 3D form of the same sketch*) cannot. On the other hand, a dress or sweater with a jeweled appliqué, the appliqué can be protected because it can be removed but the sweater itself cannot. So, parts of the garments can be protected while the whole garment cannot because the argument goes that the appliqué itself does not directly contribute to the functionality of the sweater. The sweater will keep us warm with or without it. However, not all designs have an appliqué that could be separated and as such it is hard to protect them separately.

Prints

A printed fabric can be protected but the garment made from it cannot. As a matter of fact, textile patterns displaying a minimal level of originality are eligible for copyright, in addition to lace and decorative weaves of sweaters. As the law states, work may be *original* even if it is not *novel* as long as the work:

- Originates with the author who is claiming protection

- Possess at least some minimal degree of creativity

Having said that, in an industry full of copied work, most lawsuits aiming to protect such works tend to fail due to the lack of originality, insufficient similarity with the accused design, or other reasons. It is also an expensive process that most parties prefer to settle such disputes outside courts.

Photos

Original images placed on fashion apparel are protectable, e.g. image appliqués on a children's sweater may be protectable while the sweater itself is not. However, the more commonplace the image, the least likely the courts will support the protection. Thus, it is important to remember the *physical separability* as a decisive factor for a court's ruling in such a matter. For example, Kohl's stores were sued by a shoe designer who claimed copyright protection for a stylized line-based ornamentation on the sides of its shoes. However, the court ruled that the design was not copyrightable since physical separability did not apply because "*removing the strap, stitching, or sole of a shoe would to some degree adversely impact a wearer's ability to locomote by foot and because the design elements once removed could not be separately sold or exist as an independent work of art.*"[12] In other words, the design features of the shoe do not represent independent artistic expression as would an image displayed on the shoe's surface. Thus, because it was functional, it was not protected.

Ornaments and Sculptural Components

Ornaments such as belt buckles are protectable as they could be seen as a sculptural work with independent aesthetic value and not as an integral element of the belt's functionality. Thus, in a way it is protected as a work of art. On the other hand, costume elements such as hats are not protectable because of their utility and functionality.

International Copyright Protection

Very few countries in the world offer copyright offices and issue copyright certificate protection.

About 177 countries, including the U.S., are members of a treaty known as the *Berne Convention* which recognizes the rights of copyright owners in member countries and offer same protection to national citizens. And thus, one advantage of obtaining U.S. copyright registration (if possible) is to take advantage of the Berne Convention provisions to enforce copyright in other countries.

PATENTS

A patent mainly deals with functional inventions and new designs and thus it is applicable to fashion at least in theory. Patents offer 14 years protection. Design patents could be relatively expensive and slow to obtain (around ten to 20 months after the application has been filed with the PTO), but once obtained, design patents yield a strong protection over their 14-year term. However, they are rarely used in fashion because they are meant for truly new designs and not reworks or reinterpretations, as are common in fashion. In most cases companies seek this type of patent when copyright protection is not appropriate or helpful. In addition to being hard to obtain, expensive, and have a lengthy waiting time, the outcome for getting one is uncertain. And given the seasonality of the fashion item the wait does not make sense due to the slow process. Thus, patents have been more common in items that have a longer life span and slower turnover such as bags and shoes.

Types of Patents

In the U.S. there are two types of patents: design patents and utility patents.

1. *Design Patents.* These protect the original and ornamental design of an article of manufacture. Design patents have been called *picture patents* meaning they are used to protect ornamental appearance of an object component. They are available to any person who *invents a new, original and ornamental design for an article of manufacture.*[13] Typical objects that might be protected as design patents are eyeglasses, handbags, footwear, and tabletop items such as dishes, cutlery, and place mats, as well as perfume bottles and jewelry.

   Design patents can also protect a component of a product, for example in a watch, the watch face, the hour and minute hands, and the band might all be protected by separate design patents. The advantage of such separate patents is that if a competitor copies one and not all components there is solid protection for the one component. The inventor of a design patent is always the individual/s who have made a material contribution to the design thus a company or corporation cannot be an inventor.

   A design patent application must satisfy the following requirements:

   • The design must be new.

   • The design must be nonobvious compared to prior known designs in the marketplace or in prior patents.

   • The design must be ornamental and not solely functional, as in the case of a patent on jewelry or a handbag. For example, bag clasps possess both ornamental and functional aspects, thus the ornamental aspect might be protected under a design patent but not the functionality.

   Patent applications usually include drawings. No actual model of the product is needed which is in contrast to trademark applications. Thus, these drawings are extremely important not only because they picture the design but also because they define it. The patent covers the pictured design and nothing else. Thus, the drawings should be carefully chosen and discussed by the designer and the patent professional or lawyer. It is also important to note that design patent applications cannot be renewed but by the time it expires the company usually would have moved on to new designs.

However, it must be filed within one year of the object's first public availability or it will be invalid. A product should be marked *Patent Pending* while the application is pending and then be marked "*Design Patent No. --*" after a patent has been issued.

2. *Utility Patents.* These protect new functionality or utilitarian aspects and do not cover any aesthetic elements that design patents protect. Thus, a utility patent could protect a new hinge mechanism on a pair of eyeglasses or a new clasp device on a handbag. It can also protect processes and techniques such as the making of a type of fabric. Chemical processes such as a new method of washing jeans to achieve unusual effects are a typical example of the application of utility patent protection in the fashion industry. The patented product or service must not only be new and original, it must also be *nonobvious*. *Nonobvious* means that your invention must not only be a departure from what has been previously registered with the PTO, but must also be not immediately apparent (or obvious) by someone who has some basic skills and knowledge of the field in which your invention might be used. For example, if your invention involved a new computer processor that could run without taxing the laptop's battery as much as existing processors. This invention might be "new" in the sense that existing laptops do not use it. However, if it is widely known by the relevant audience – computer engineers or mechanical engineers – but perhaps rejected because the proposed design causes overheating or slow speeds, then it would not be patentable. It would be seen as obvious to people with "ordinary skill in the art."[14] Thus, if a fashion company or designer invents a new zipper or a new sneaker, a utility patent will protect only the nonobvious differences between the invention and prior zippers and sneakers. The comparable historical record of technical knowledge evidenced by all the patent and publications is referred to as *prior art*. Thus, to be patented, the innovation must represent a significant step beyond the prior art. Trivial differences are not patentable. It is clear that this requirement is rather subjective and open to interpretations.

Utility patents must also be filed within one year of the object's first public availability. The marking for utility patents is the same as design patents. First, *Patent Pending* and then *Patent No.* utility patents protection lasts a maximum of 20 years from the filing date of the application and cannot be renewed beyond this 20-year term.

Trade Secrets

Unlike other forms of IP, trade secrets cannot be registered. However, they could be protected through patents. Trade secrets are defined as confidential business information that is kept private and guarded within the company such as formulas, customer lists, computer software, etc. In fashion this may include perfume formulas, factory sources for the production of goods, special manufacturing techniques, and color blends, etc. Trade secrets protection is indefinite as long as the information is kept confidential within the company. This is why these secrets are also protected by confidentiality agreements signed by all employees and vendors as well.

Box 7.3 The Battle of the Gs: Gucci vs. Guess

One of the most famous battles over trademark infringements in recent years was between fashion brands Gucci and Guess. Gucci, the Italian luxury brand known for its leather goods and sexy and romantic fashion styles had sued U.S. brand Guess, known for its sportswear and denim offerings in 2009, for selling items that are "studied imitations of the Gucci trademarks." More specifically, the claims referred to the green and red stripe design, a square "G", the designer's name in script and a diamond pattern consisting of repetitive interlocking Gs. Consequently, the claim put $221 million worth of Guess products in question. Louis Ederer, Gucci's lawyer stated it was "a massive, complicated scheme to knock off Gucci's best-known and iconic designs." Guess's rebuttal, as noted by its lawyer, Daniel Petrocelli, was that out of the 1,495 Guess products in question, 99% of them "could never be confused with Gucci." Furthermore, Gucci's infringement claims were without merit because the company "sat on its rights" for at least seven years before suing. And finally, Gucci also failed to prove how consumers were misled by the designs.

After a highly publicized trial, the U.S. courts awarded Gucci a permanent injunction against Guess's use of three of the four challenged designs at issue but awarded Gucci only a fraction ($4.58 million) of the $221 million damages award it was seeking. Gucci wasted no time filing lawsuits against Guess on the same grounds in Italy, Australia, China, and France, and initiated proceedings with the European Union Intellectual Property Office.

In 2013, a Milan court ruled against Gucci, holding that Guess's Quattro G-diamond pattern is not related to Gucci's iconic interlocking G pattern. The judge declared that not only was Guess not infringing Gucci's trademarks but that a number of Gucci's trademarks, including its diamond-patterned G logo and Flora pattern trademarks, previously registered by Gucci in Italy and the European Union, were not valid.

Gucci subsequently appealed the decision, prompting the Milan Court of Appeals to uphold the decision, in part, and overturn it in other regards. For instance, the appeals court held that Guess had, in fact, committed an act of unfair competition in accordance with the Italian Civil Code by copying a number of Gucci products. However, the court agreed that Gucci's trademarks covering "the letter G with dots" and "the letter G with dots serially repeated" are "devoid of any distinctive character", and that the Flora pattern mark also is not a valid trademark, as its decorative nature does not indicate a specific commercial source. The court also sided with Guess in terms of Gucci's claim that Guess copied its green-red-green stripe, the "Gucci" logo in italics with underline, the italicized "G" logo and of the "serial squared G". The court held that Guess was using a different color combination and the signs in question were deemed "sufficiently different from a visual and aural standpoint".

In 2015, a court in Paris overruled every trademark infringement claim asserted by Gucci against Guess in the parties' French fight. The Tribunal de Grande Instance found that Guess did not engage in trademark infringement, counterfeiting, or unfair competition. Instead, the panel invalidated Gucci's "G" community registrations, meaning that Gucci could no longer claim exclusive rights in those marks. In December 2016, the EU General Court, held that "the average consumer normally perceives a mark as a whole and does not analyze its various details, only rarely having a chance to compare marks directly, and so having to rely on an imperfect recollection." As such, it found that Guess's interlocking Gs logo was dissimilar to an array of Gucci's logos and therefore, could not be blocked by the Italian design house.

Meanwhile, in Asia, the Nanjing Intermediate People's Court of China sided with Gucci on the dispute in China. Interestingly, the court held that infringement cases hinge on whether the marks look subjectively similar, not whether consumers are likely to be confused, which is the key element for trademark infringement matters in the U.S. and most other jurisdictions, and thus ruled in favor of Gucci, prompting Guess to appeal (Figure 7.1).

GUESS vs. GUCCI

Figure 7.1 Gucci vs. Guess.

Sources

1. "Almost 10 Years Later, Gucci and Guess Make Peace in Global Legal War". The Fashion Law. Accessed September 26, 2018. https://www.thefashionlaw.com/almost-10-years-later-gucci-and-guess-make-peace-in-global-legal-war/
2. "Battle of the Brands: Gucci vs. Guess". Forbes. Accessed September 4, 2018. https://www.forbes.com/pictures/ehlm45glee/gucci-vs-guess/#781ba3ba794b
3. "Gucci vs. Guess Lawsuit Decision: Gucci Wins $4.66 Million, Ban on Knock-offs". Huff Post. Accessed September 1, 2018. https://www.huffpost.com/entry/gucci-lawsuit-gucci-wins-_n_1534491
4. "Guess Versus Gucci – Gucci Versus Guess". JBCStyle. Accessed September 16, 2018. https://jbcstyle.com/guess-versus-gucci-gucci-versus-guess/
5. Kalinauskas, Nadine. "Gucci vs. Guess: A Trademark Lawsuit Over the Letter G". Accessed September 1, 2018. https://ca.style.yahoo.com/blogs/shine-on/gucci-vs-guess-trademark-lawsuit-over-letter-g-185526028.html

Examples of IP Protection Around the World

EUROPEAN UNION (EU)

The EU offers fashion designers an exclusive and independent right against design copying. *The European Community Design Protection Regulation* came into force on March 6, 2002. The regulation provides designers with exclusive rights to use their designs in commerce, to enforce those rights against infringers and to claim damages. Unlike the U.S. IP law, the European *Community Design Regulation* automatically protects designs, without the need for any formal registration or filing, once they have been disclosed in the relevant territory through, for example, first sell, online commercialization, etc. It represents a clear advantage for fashion designers who decide to enter the EU market, as they will not be limited to trademark or copyright law, having the option to opt for the three year protection of unregistered EU design tool.

This unregistered protection, known as *Unregistered Community Designs* (UCD), perfectly matches the seasonal nature of clothing designs as there will be no need to undertake a registration process (which can imply some time and costs). The *UCD* protection is limited in time (only three years from disclosure and cannot be renewed) and scope (it only protects against identical copies). If the designer wishes a longer (up to 25 years) and stronger (also against similar products) protection, there is still the option to obtain a *Registered Community Design (RCD)*, which will be quickly granted by the *European Union IP Office (EUIPO)* without any substantial examination and at a very affordable price. In all cases, the design must be new and possess individual character in order to qualify for protection. Design is defined as *the appearance of the whole or part of the product resulting from its features and in particular the lines contours, colors, shape, texture, and/or both its ornamentation and materials of the product itself.* A design is considered new if no identical design has been made available to the public. Thus, individual character is assessed by whether the overall impression the design produces on the informed user differs from the overall impression produced by any publicly available design. If a design is found to have infringed an RCD or UCD, the court will issue an injunction prohibiting infringing acts, a seizure order for the infringing products or any materials used to manufacture such products, and any other sanctions deemed appropriate. UCDs that are in existence at the time the UK leaves the EU will be replaced in the UK by a right called *Continuing Unregistered Community Design*, which will continue for the remainder of the term.

Copyright Protection vs. UCD

Both EU UCD and U.S. copyright do not require any formalities, yet these two rights are quite different and the protection criteria for each are very distinct. While a design must be new and have individual character in both, the work protected by a copyright must be *original*, which is a condition of protection classically defined as reflecting the *personality of the author*. Moreover, copyright protection enjoys two significant advantages compared to the UCD: it has a protection period of 70 years after the death of the author, and is independent of disclosure (meaning copyright can be claimed on an original work, even if it remains secret, as long as the date of creation can be proved). Theoretically, the same product may fulfil all the criteria and therefore benefit from both protections.

NATIONAL COPYRIGHT PROTECTION: FRANCE, ITALY, UNITED KINGDOM

EU design rights can also be protected under national copyright laws, but the conditions to obtaining copyright protection, including the level of originality required, would be determined by each member state. For example:

France

France's copyright system has historically protected fashion designs. The *French Intellectual Property Code (IPC)* protects original works of the mind including those that *reflect the personality of their author* and it lists *the creations of the seasonal industries of dress and articles* as a protected work of the mind. The challenge faced by design owners is showing the original character of their designs, because fashion designs usually follow the current trends and therefore may lack originality.

The design is granted protection on the date of creation, regardless of registration. The French courts tend to adhere more strictly to the originality requirement for designs and typically will deny copyright protection over a design that could be considered commonplace. Thus, new fashion designs in France can be protected not only under national copyright laws, but also under the EU as discussed above.

Italy

Like France, Italy protects fashion designs under its national copyright system. *The Italian Copyright Law (LDA)* protects *works of the mind having a creative character and belonging to literature, music, figurative arts, architecture, theater, or cinematography, whatever their mode or form of expression,* and extends to other works that *have creative character or inherent artistic character.*[15] Copyright protection does not depend on registration; under the LDA, fashion designers can seek an *ex parte interim* injunction to seize any copy of their designs that have creative and artistic value from the Italian courts and then ask for a permanent injunction and damages for unregistered works. A designer's copyright lasts the life of the designer plus seventy years after the designer's death.

In addition, fashion designs can also be protected under *Italian Industrial Property Code (CPI)* which protects designs that are registered with the *Italian Patent and Trademark Office* (IPTO) and any applicable international design registrations.

UK

In the United Kingdom, copyright law is governed under the *Copyright, Designs, and Patents Act of 1988* (CDPA). Original *artistic works* obtain automatic copyright protection in the United Kingdom. These are defined as *a graphic work, photograph, sculpture, or collage, irrespective of artistic quality, a work of architecture being a building or a model for a building or works of artistic craftsmanship.*[16] Fashion designs fall under the category of *works of artistic craftsmanship.* However, experience demonstrates that there is a high threshold to show that a work is of artistic craftsmanship, making it difficult to assert fashion design protection under copyright. Under the CDPA, if a work is considered *commonplace in the design field in question at the time of its creation,* it is not considered *original* for the purpose of the design right.

Final Note

The copyright protections granted under the national laws of France, Italy, and UK are separate and distinct from the design rights designated under the EU. But dual protection (copyright and design protection over a fashion design) may sometimes confuse courts as they try to adhere to both the novelty requirement for design protection and the originality requirement for copyrights at the same time. For example, a French Supreme Court decision had once rejected the protection of a shoe because it had the same characteristics as a preexisting model but upheld the design rights because the models were not identical!

ISSUE 4: COUNTERFEITS
....

Trademark counterfeiting is *the act of manufacturing or distributing a product or service bearing a mark that is identical to or substantially indistinguishable from a registered trademark.*[17] The market for counterfeit clothing, textiles, footwear, handbags, cosmetics, and watches alone, amounted to about $450 billion in 2017. It is very ironic that the more copied and counterfeited the brand is, the more it is considered as a manifestation of its popularity and prestige. Counterfeiting is indeed a global problem; counterfeit products can still be seen on the streets of New York as well as in the alleys and markets of many developing countries. For example, the documentary series titled *Counterfeit Culture* by *Highsnobiety* indicates how South Korea's capital Seoul, considered the fifth wealthiest city in the world, is a very lucrative market for counterfeit products. Seoul's younger generation seems to be obsessed with street culture and streetwear global trends. But covetable brands like Supreme, Stüssy, and Champion are almost impossible to buy in South Korea, a situation that has started a subculture of widely available *copycat* brands. Fake Supreme hoodies can be acquired for the equivalent of $25 on the sidewalk, while a shopping mall store may carry an exact replica of an embroidered Saint Laurent jacket, once worn by Justin Bieber. The only difference is that the label of the jacket would read *Classic Fashion* instead of *Saint Laurent.* This example demonstrates the global impact of the counterfeit problem even within developed countries.

What Counts as a Counterfeit?

It is essential at this point to understand that the term counterfeit is not interchangeable with other terms such as *knock offs* or copyright *infringement* as they are not the same (Figure 7.2):

Figure 7.2 Counterfeit Luxury Bags.

Knock Off: Refers to a fashion item of clothing that looks similar to the original design but does not necessarily utilize the original designer's name, logo, original print, etc., whereas a counterfeit product is designed to so closely resemble the original product as to be virtually identical to it. Accordingly, all counterfeits are knock offs but not all knock offs are counterfeits.

Copy Infringement: Refers to one party using the trademark of another thus creating confusion, deception, or mistake about the source of the item. Counterfeits usually include copy infringement.

There are few elements that define what a counterfeit is, such as:

• As stated above, in order for a product to be considered a counterfeit, it must include another party's *federally registered trademark* (with the U.S. Patent and Trademark Office) or one that is *substantially indistinguishable* from the other party's trademark.

• A counterfeiter must be knowingly and deliberately using another party's trademark without the authorization to do so. This use is almost always paired with the counterfeiter's intent to deceive the consumer by presenting itself as the trademark holder by way of the fake logo, fake tag, etc.

• The goods that the counterfeiter is making/selling must be of the type that are covered by the trademark holder's registrations; trademarks are registered by *class of goods or services*. Clothing and footwear, for instance, are included in Class 25.

• The use of the counterfeit trademark must be likely to cause confusion, to cause the mistake, or to deceive the average consumer in terms of the source of the product.

It is thus clear that counterfeits have serious and drastic impacts on the copied trademark/brand and the economy in general. Examples of such effects are:

- It represents a serious decline in revenue and loss of income for the original brand.

- May have a severe impact on brand status and may result in a dilution of prestige and image as they decrease the value (financial and emotional) of the authentic product in the marketplace by making otherwise exclusive products appear to be available for mass-market prices.

- It is important to remember that most counterfeits are not produced in established factories but rather by low-wage workers in sweatshops.

- Possible physical danger. Counterfeits are generally made of poor-quality products with no abiding to health guidelines or international standards when needed (e.g. flammable or toxic material or dyes, sunglasses with no ultraviolet ray protection, etc.).

- According to some government reports, counterfeit operations play an important role in funding organized crime and terrorist organizations.

- Internet purchase of counterfeit may represent increased concerns because it could not be detected. In many cases, unlike buying a fake bag in a flea market or off the street, online customers may be unaware that they are buying one for which they paid top dollar and thus being subject to clear fraud, which could also indirectly deter them from buying the same brand even from a trusted site just for security.

- Since most counterfeit operations are all cash-based operations in order to avoid keeping records or paying taxes, they are usually very hard to track down and investigate.

Attempts to Combat Counterfeits

While some counterfeits are easy to identify as counterfeit handbags purchased off the streets of Chinatown in New York City or flea markets around the world, others are sophisticated enough that they are harder to identify. Because of the difficulty of spotting counterfeits these days, companies are developing new methods to trace and detect them. Some companies have developed innovative product security devices in packaging or inside the product itself such as holograms in hang tags, while others label their products with security codes that allow the company to detect and track authentic versus imitation goods. Together with legal actions, these measures attempt to combat the problem and minimize its effects. Let us take a closer look at some of these measures:

Legal Measures

Law makers and legislatures around the world having recognized the harmful effects of counterfeits and especially their possible links to organized crime and terrorism have put a number of laws to address this issue. In the U.S. there are a number of federal acts to combat and punish counterfeit practices such as the Stop Counterfeiting in Manufactured Goods Act, 18 U.S.C2320, which establishes prison terms for up to 20 years and fines up to $15 million for the trafficking and sales of counterfeit goods. And the Trafficking in counterfeit goods and services Anticounterfeiting Consumer Protection Act of 1996, 18 U.S.C. 2320, which also imposes fines and prison terms.

Authentication Technology

Technology for product or packaging authentication is used to determine whether a product is in fact what it is declared to be or sold where it is intended to. Such technologies can be categorized as covert (hidden and invisible) or overt (visible to the naked eyes).

Covert devices enable the producer or the brand owner to identify counterfeited products. Covert technology is controlled, and only those who have administrative responsibility have access to the details. Customers are neither able to detect nor verify covert devices' presence. The advantages of covert technology include low implementation costs, no need for regulatory approval, easy upgrading or addition, and flexible implementation by either the device supplier or the manufacturer. The potential downsides of covert technology include easy imitation if widely applied, increasing cost if more security options are required, and risk of compromise if the device is solely administered by component suppliers.

On the other hand, *overt technology* which can be visible to the naked eye and includes holograms, embossed optical film, and sequential product numbering etc. that are visible to the naked eye (e.g. watermarks used in a $100 bill) making it easy for users to authenticate products. This type of authentication technology remains, to a great degree, within the packaging technology rather than within the product. For example, there are a variety of hologram products integrated into anti-counterfeiting efforts in the supply chain, such as hologram foils, hologram stickers, hologram labels, and holographic films. These packaging labels offer great protection against counterfeits through high-security holograms and invisible ultra-violet (UV) printing, which is another covert technology. Color-shifting ink changes color depending on the angle at which the package is viewed. Usually, consumers will notice this effect as a change of color when shifting the viewing angle. Watermarks technology has been integrated to combat fake products as well. Packaging images created by watermarks are visible when the packages are held up to light. Optically variable devices (OVDs) display two distinct colors depending on the angle at which the printing is viewed. OVDs serve as an ideal authentication solution because they cannot be scanned or reproduced, nor can they be imitated or replicated. By their nature, OVDs are overt and are thus known as first level security features. In general, the possible downsides of overt technology include the need for user training, potential imitation and reuse, and possible false assurance. Moreover, overt devices require high security commitment on the supplier side and appropriate disposal procedures on the user side to avoid unauthorized use or reuse. As such, overt technology can increase the cost of production. Additionally, genuine overt features can be faked by counterfeiters to confuse average customers.

Technology for tracing and tracking products includes technologies like *electronic product codes* (EPCs) and *radio frequency identification* (RFID) which are wireless technologies meant to follow products as they move through supply chains. Anti-counterfeiting technologies can be used to identify authentic goods from phony items. At present, a range of anti-counterfeiting technologies, including watermarks, holograms, color-shifting ink, security thread, micro-printing, anti-forgery ink, barcode technology, holographic technology, physical security technology, packaging protective technology, biological anti-counterfeiting technology, and latent image decrypt anti-counterfeiting technology, exist to protect product authentication. For example, starting 2010, Italian fashion house Fendi started using, in addition to a 16 or 17-digit serial number, a Fendi RFID tag with eight embroidered digits in all its bags. The tag contains a wireless Fendi RFID chip inside holding the bag's information such as the model, serial number, color, manufacturing details as well as the bag's history. It is the same technology used in ID cards commonly used in business offices or gated communities to gain entry access. The technology allows Fendi to track down its products and where they are sold in an effort to combat grey markets.

Chapter Questions

1. While *Ethics* has an internal focus and a protective nature, *Social Responsibility* has an external focus with a proactive approach. Explain this statement giving examples.

2. Examine the following two real-life court cases:

   a. *Case 1: Kieselstein-Cord vs. Accessories by Pearl, Inc.* In determining whether a designer belt buckle could receive copyright protection. The court ruled in favor of protection.

b. *Case 2: Carol Barnhart Inc. vs. Economy Cover Corp.* In determining whether mannequins of the human torso with hollowed backs could receive copyright protection. The court ruled against granting copyright protection.

Based on what is discussed in this chapter what are the bases of both court decisions to grant or deny protection?

3. Research examples of measures taken by famous fashion brands in order to combat child labor and enhance labor working conditions in factories located overseas. Give at least two examples.

Case Study
Brunello Cucinelli: The Humanistic Capitalist

Background

Brunello Cucinelli has been described in many ways throughout his long career in the fashion industry. He is the *King of Cashmere*, the *Philosopher-Designer* and a *Part Businessman, Part Philosopher, and Part Monk* given his philosophical approach to business and his keen interest in the welfare of his employees and community. Cucinelli had a very humble beginning, born in Castel Rigone in central Italy in 1953 to an uneducated farmer, and grew up in a rural community outside the city of Perugia. At the age of 24 he dropped out of engineering school and developed a great interest in philosophy instead. In 1978 he got engaged to his wife Frederica who ran a small clothing shop in the village of Solomeo. It was then that he considered venturing into the knitwear business. Cucinelli explained that he wanted to have a specialty or niche given that the nearby city of Perugia was already one of the main manufacturing centers. He noticed that there was no colored cashmere for women in the market, instead, most of the offerings were basic and bland. So, with the help of a bank loan and a friend, Cucinelli bought a small amount of cashmere and had it made into half a dozen sweaters which he took to a famous local dye expert in the area and asked him to dye the sweaters in bright colors such as orange. Cucinelli took his three round-neck and three V-neck sweaters to northern Italy where a retailer placed an order for fifty-three pieces. He eventually sold 400 pieces in the first three months. He later bought out his friend and expanded the business to Germany then to the U.S. And so, the Brunello Cucinelli company was basically created in 1978 in the small village of Solomeo with just the equivalent of $550.

Over the next 15–20 years, and in its pursuit for perfection, Cucinelli remained entirely focused on one product category which is its innovative cashmeres. He was the Cashmere King. Womenswear was the first step and then around the 1990s the company introduced a knitwear line for men. By 1998–99 sales reached 200,000 sweaters a year, despite the fact the label operated only one small store. In 2000, following requests from American buyers for a complete Brunello Cucinelli look, the brand expanded its product offering. Over a period of six years, during which the brand annually rolled out four or five stores globally, Brunello Cucinelli established his namesake brand's aesthetic. Cucinelli took his business public in the Milan Bourse's only IPO in 2012, becoming a billionaire in the process. In 2013, the company generated $444 million in revenue. Today, Cucinelli is the chief executive and designer of a global luxury lifestyle brand with a market capitalization of more than $1.5 billion.

Humanistic Capitalism

Cucinelli believes in what he calls a *humanistic enterprise* where a business should comply in the noblest manner with all the rules of ethics that man has devised over the centuries. He dreams about a form of humanistic modern capitalism where profit is made without harm or offence to anyone, and part of it is set aside for any initiative that can really improve the condition of human life: services, schools, places of worship, and cultural heritage. And thus, *Humanistic Capitalism* as penned and defined by Cucinelli is a business philosophy that is:

1. Built on fairness and strikes a balance between profit and giving back; donating to the world as guardians of creation, leaving to those coming after us not the very same world we found, but a more amiable one.

2. Aiming on making profit with ethics, dignity, and morals. Making profit without harming mankind in the process, or as little as possible.

In the Cucinelli organization the focal point is the common good. "Cucinelli is convinced that human dignity is restored solely through the rediscovery of the conscience and that work elevates human dignity and the emotional ties that derive from it," as stated on the company's website. And thus, people remain at the very center of every action and production process with the quality of the workplace of the utmost importance. According to Cucinelli, humanistic capitalism starts by carefully choosing a location for one's premises and working to disseminate a great corporate culture and citizenship; that's what capitalism is all about in his view. With quality of workplace comes fair working hours where there is a time for work and a time for the soul in every worker's life. Fair work should never steal people's souls. Showing esteem and appreciation for someone's work is important because it increases responsibility and creativity.

Humanistic Capitalism in the Cucinelli Organization

Cucinelli built his company with a deep respect for his employees, his community, and the human impact of his business. He has transformed his hometown of Castel Rigone and Solomeo by building factories, a theater, a library, a soccer stadium, and a tuition-free arts school to teach traditional skills like gardening and, of course tailoring, in addition to an ever-growing list of projects, many of which are overseen by Brunello himself and the Federica Cucinelli Foundation. And while in recent years many Italian clothing manufacturers have increasingly sought cheaper labor in countries such as India and China, Cucinelli has remained committed to keeping his business local. All his clothes are made in Italy, with 80% in and around Solomeo where he met his wife and started his business almost 40 years ago. 720 employees work in Solomeo and, on average, are paid about 20% more than they would make elsewhere.

Every day at 1 P.M., at Cucinelli's palatial HQ in Solomeo, the entire staff is invited to the cafeteria for a family-style lunch complete with several courses, wine, and views of the Umbrian hills. The gathering is seen by observers as a way of physical and spiritual nourishment. Cucinelli expects discipline among his employees, discipline that is indeed expected rather than imposed. For instance, workers are not asked to clock in or out. He sends his staff home at 5:30 P.M., when the power goes off. No after-hours e-mails are allowed. To Cucinelli, being away from work is an important part of being better at work. Again, it's the concept of a time for work and a time for the soul.

When the financial crisis hit in the fall of 2008, Cucinelli called his employees together and assured them that he would not lay anyone off for eighteen months; in return, he asked them to be more creative in their thinking. One example of his employees' input was a cleaning lady, who being inspired by the collection of autographed soccer balls that Cucinelli had artfully arranged in a cashmere-lined suitcase in his office, advised him to make a soccer ball from cashmere. Several were produced, as promotional items. Cucinelli's general approach towards his employees is best summed up by one of them who said: "We're treated like humans, and in other places we are treated more like machines. We get respect for what we do with our hands. It doesn't seem like a lot, but we appreciate it." Shortly, after the crisis, Cucinelli turned a profit, and hired new people into the company.

Cucinelli also looks to do good works for people not on his payroll. He donates 2% of the company's annual profits for charity or "for humanity" as he puts it. For example, he underwrote the construction of a hospital in the African nation of Malawi, after one of his two daughters took a trip to the country.

Cucinelli's integration of high-end manufacturing with a higher purpose is widely admired among his colleagues in the fashion industry. Bob Mitchell, a retailer based in Connecticut who has been selling Cucinelli's clothes for more than a decade described how he saw the people around Solomeo to be happy and content, asserting that it is something that takes time to achieve. Ron Frasch, the former president of Saks Fifth Avenue, wrote to Cucinelli once to say that he felt lucky to have his company as a close partner and in the fall of 2009 the store dedicated its windows to Cucinelli and hosted an event in his honor. Cucinelli had also received countless honors and awards for his work. He strongly believes that while most people respond to his famous suits, knits, outerwear, and accessories as symbols of effortless luxury, it is the conscience of the company that is the real star and remains to be the highlight of his operation.

Case Study Questions

1. How would you assess the "Humanistic Capitalism" initiative from an ethics and CSR perspectives? Explain.

2. As a manager of a small fashion organization located in your hometown, inspired by Brunello Cucinelli, how can you positively impact the lives of your employees outside the organization as well as that of the whole community?

Sources

1. "Brunello Cucinelli". Business of Fashion. Accessed July 12, 2017. https://www.businessof fashion.com/community/people/brunello-cucinelli

2. Vaccaro, Antonino and Gianmichele Potito. *Brunello Cucinelli: Ethical Luxury, the Luxury of Ethics or What?* (Barcelona: IESE Business School, University of Navarra, 2016).

3. http://www.brunellocucinelli.com

4. Mead, Rebecca. "The Prince of Solomeo". March 29, 2010. https://www.newyorker.com/ magazine/2010/03/29/the-prince-of-solomeo

5. Victorine, Jacob. "Brunello Cucinelli: Philosopher King or Steward of Small-Town Life? November 9, 2017. https://www.grailed.com/drycleanonly/brunello-cucinelli-history

6. Williams, Michael. "Why Brunello Cucinelli is Worth the Price". September 18, 2017. https://www.gq.com/story/brunello-cucinelli-buying-for-value

Notes

1. Sison, Alejo J. *Corporate Governance and Ethics: An Aristotelian Perspective* (Cheltenham: Edward Elgar Publishing Limited, 2010), 71.
2. Carrol, Archie B. and Ann K. Buchholtz. *Business & Society: Ethics and Stakeholder Management*, 7th ed. (Mason: South-Western, 2009), 40.
3. Ibid., 250.
4. "Code of Conduct". https://purpose.nike.com/code-of-conduct.

5. Nimbalker, Gershon, Jasmin Mawson, Claire Harris, Meredith Rynan, Libby Sanders, Claire Hart, and Megan Shove. *The 2018 Ethical Fashion Report*. Baptist World Aid, 9.
6. Ibid., 15.
7. Ibid., 11.
8. "What is a Sweatshops". FastFashion, Accessed October 23, 2018. http://fastfashion.weebly.com/unethical-production.html.
9. Bain, Marc. "There Are Clothing Sweatshops in the US, Too". Quartz. December 16, 2019. https://qz.com/1769309/fashion-nova-accused-of-using-los-angeles-sweatshops/.
10. Jimenez, Guillermo and Barbara Kolsun. *Fashion Law*, 2nd ed. (New York: Fairchild, 2014), 26.
11. "Connecting the DOTBLOG: Is Your Trademark Descriptive or Suggestive?". JDSUPRA. January 25, 2017. https://www.jdsupra.com/legalnews/connecting-the-dotblog-is-your-71201/.
12. Jimenez, 49
13. Ibid., 55.
14. Farkas, Brian. "How Do I Know if My Invention Is "Nonobvious" When Applying for a Patent?". NOLO. Accessed February 11, 2020. https://www.nolo.com/legal-encyclopedia/how-do-i-know-if-my-invention-is- nonobvious-when-applying-for-a-patent.html
15. Witzburg, Francesca M. "Protecting Fashion: A Comparative Analysis of Fashion Design Protection in the United States and Europe". Cardozo AELJ. December 1, 2016. http://www.cardozoaelj.com/2016/12/01/protecting-fashion-comparative-analysis-fashion-design-protection-united-states-europe/.
16. Ibid.
17. Jimenez, 139.

BIBLIOGRAPHY

Books

Anguelov, Nikolay. *The Dirty Side of the Garment Industry: Fast Fashion and Its Negative Impact on Environment and Society* (Boca Raton: CRC Press, 2016).

Ballard, Marcella, Stephanie Sheridan, Paolo Strino, Jonathan Goins, Roxanne Elings, Nathaniel St. Clair and Charles Klein. *Navigating Fashion Law, 2016 edition: Leading Lawyers on Exploring the Trends, Cases, and Strategies of Fashion Law* (Eagan: Aspatore, 2016).

Birnbaum, David. *Birnbaum's Global Guide to Winning the Great garment War* (New York: Fashiondex, Inc., 2000).

Brooks, Andrew. *Clothing Poverty: The Hidden World of Fast Fashion and Second-Hand Clothes* (London: Zed Books, 2015).

Bruce, Margaret, Christopher Moore and Grete Birtwistle. *International Retail Marketing: A Case Study Approach* (Burlington: Elsevier, 2005).

Burns, Leslie D., Kathy K. Mullet and Nancy O. Bryant. *The Business of Fashion*, 4th ed. (New York: Fairchild, 2011).

Carrol, Archie B. and Ann K. Buchholtz. *Business & Society: Ethics and Stakeholder Management*, 7th ed. (Mason: South-Western, 2009).

Chevalier, Michel and Gerald Mazzalovo. *Luxury Brand Management: A World of Privilege* (Singapore: John Wiley and Sons (Asia), 2008).

Choi, Tsan-Ming. *Fashion Retail Supply Chain Management: A Systems Optimization Approach* (London: Taylor and Francis Group, 2014).

Choi, Tsan-Ming and T.C. Edwin Cheng. *Sustainable Fashion Supply Chain Management: From Sourcing to Retailing* (Cham: Springer, 2015).

Choi, Tsan-Ming and Bin Shen. *Luxury Fashion Retail Management* (Singapore: Springer, 2017).

Hameide, Kaled. *Fashion Branding Unraveled* (New York: Fairchild, 2011).

Hill, Charles W. L. and G. Tomas M. Hult. *Global Business Today* (New York: McGraw-Hill, 2016).

Jimenez, Guillermo C. and Barbara Kolsun. *Fashion Law*, 2th ed. (New York: Fairchild, 2014).

Jin, Byoungho and Elena Cedrola. *Fashion Branding and Communication: Core Strategies of European Luxury Brands* (New York: Palgrave, 2017).

Keller, Kevin L. *Strategic Brand Management*, 4th ed. (Upper Saddle River: Pearson, 2013).

Kunz, Grace I. and Myrna B. Garner. *Going Global* (New York: Fairchild, 2011).

Kunz, Grace I., Elena Karpova and Myrna B. Garner. *Going Global: The Textile and Apparel Industry*, 3rd ed. (New York: Fairchild, 2016).

Large, Joanna. *The Consumption of Counterfeit Fashion* (Bristol: Palgrave, 2019).

Leong, Wisner T. *Principles of Supply Chain Management: A Balanced Approach*, 3rd ed. (Mason: South-Western, 2012).

Londrigan, Michael and Jacqueline M. Jenkins. *Fashion Supply Chain Management* (New York: Fairchild, 2018).

Mele, Domenec. *Management Ethics: Placing Ethics at the Core of Good Management* (New York: Palgrave, 2012).

Reddy, Mergen, Nic Terblanche, Leyland Pitt and Michael Parent. *How Far Can Luxury Brands Travel? Avoiding the Pitfalls of Luxury Brand Extension* (Indiana: Kelley School of Business, 2009).

Ross, Andrew. *No Sweat: Fashion, Free Trade, and the Rights of Garment Workers* (New York: Verso, 1997).

Sherman, Gerald J. and Sar S. Perlman. *The Real World Guide to Fashion Selling and Management*, 2nd ed. (New York: Fairchild, 2015).

Shoemack, Harvey and Patricia M. Rath. *Essentials of Exporting and Importing: U.S. Trade Policies, Procedures, and Practices* (New York: Fairchild, 2014).

Trevino, Linda K. and Katherine A. Nelson. *Managing Business Ethics; Straight Talk About How to Do It Right*, 5th ed. (Hoboken: John Wiley and Sons, Inc., 2011).

Van Gelder, Sicco. *Global Brand Strategy: Unlocking Brand Potential Across Countries, Cultures and Markets* (London: Kogan-Page, 2003).

Wheelen, Thomas L. and J. David Hunger. *Strategic Management and Business Policy: Toward Global Sustainability*, 3rd ed. (Upper Saddle River: Pearson, 2012).

White, Nicola and Ian Griffiths. *The Fashion Business: Theory, Practice, Image* (New York: Berg, 2000).

Wong, W.K. and Z.X. Guo. *Fashion Supply Chain Management Using Radio Frequency Identification (RFID) Technologies* (Kidlington: Woodhead Publishing, 2014).

Yousaf, Nasim. *Import and Export of Apparel and Textile* (New York: Xilbris, 2001).

Other Sources

"Almost 10 years Later, Gucci and Guess Make Peace in Global Legal War". The Fashion Law. April 18, 2018. https://www.thefashionlaw.com/home/almost-10-years-later-gucci-and-guess-make-peace-in-global-legal-war

"Brunello Cucinelli". Business of Fashion. Accessed August 30, 2019. https://www.businessoffashion.com/community/people/brunello-cucinelli

"Design Protection". Europe. Updated September 3, 2020. https://europa.eu/youreurope/business/running-business/intellectual-property/design-protection/index_en.htm

"Ethical Fashion". Victoria and Albert Museum. Accessed May 18, 2018. http://www.vam.ac.uk/content/articles/w/what-is-ethical-fashion/

'Ethical Fashion and the Sweatshop Issue, Why Should We Care?". Cock and Bull. Accessed May 16, 2018. https://www.cockandbullmenswear.co.uk/ethical-fashion-and-sustainable-menswear-the-sweatshop-issue--why--we-should-care

"Fashion Design Protection: US vs. EU". IP Wisely. June 21, 2018. https://www.ipwisely.com/blog/fashion-design-protection-us-vs-eu

"Feminists Against Sweatshops" Feminist Majority. Accessed May 14, 2018. http://feminist.org/other/sweatshops/sweatfaq.html

"Fendi Authentication Guide: Real or Fake Fendi Handbag". Monalisalikes. Accessed July 23, 2018. https://monalisalikes.com/fendi-bags-authentication/

"Gucci vs. Guess Lawsuit Decision: Gucci Wins $4.66 Million, Ban on Knock-Offs". Huffpost. May 21, 2012. https://www.huffpost.com/entry/gucci-lawsuit-gucci-wins-_n_1534491

"Guess Versus Gucci, Gucci Versus Guess". JBC Style. April 2, 2012. https://jbcstyle.com/guess-versus-gucci-gucci-versus-guess/

"Louis Vuitton Sues Counterfeit Online Sellers in China". Business of Fashion. Accessed August 26, 2019. https://www.businessoffashion.com/articles/news-analysis/louis-vuitton-sues-counterfeit-online-sellers-in-china

"LVMH Social Responsibility Report 2018". LVMH. Accessed October 3, 2019. https://r.lvmh-static.com/uploads/2019/05/2018-social-responsibility-report.pdf

'Safe Workplaces". Bangladesh Accord. Accessed March 3, 2019. https://bangladeshaccord.org/

"The Counterfeit Report: The Big Business of Fakes". The fashion Law. October 11, 2018. https://www.thefashionlaw.com/home/the-counterfeit-report-the-impact-on-the-fashion-industry

"The Origins". Brunello Cucinelli. Accessed August 5, 2019. https://www.brunellocucinelli.com/en/the-origins.html

"Trademark Basics". U.S. Patent and Trademark Office. Accessed April 24, 2018. https://www.uspto.gov/trademarks-getting-started/trademark-basics

"TruLens Micro-Optic Label Series". Brad Brand Protection. Accessed May 16, 2018. http://www.bradybrandprotection.com/en/product-authentication/overt-technologies/trulens-micro-optic-label-series

'What is an EP&L?". Kering. Accessed October 11, 2019. https://www.kering.com/en/sustainability/environmental-profit-loss/what-is-an-ep-l/

Abrams, Rachel. "Retailers Like H&M and Walmart Fall Short Pledges to Overseas Workers". NY Times. May 13, 2016. https://www.nytimes.com/2016/05/31/business/international/top-retailers-fall-short-of-commitments-to-overseas-workers.html

Bain, Marc. "There are Clothing Sweatshops in the US, Too". Quartz. December 16, 2019. https://qz.com/1769309/fashion-nova-accused-of-using-los-angeles-sweatshops/

Blanchard, Tamsin. "Did You Know Sweatshops Exist in the UK?" Vogue. August 23, 2017. https://www.vogue.co.uk/article/sweatshops-exist-in-the-uk-leicester

Eror, Aleks. "Is Counterfeiting Actually Good for fashion?" Highsobriety. August 28, 2017. https://www.highsnobiety.com/2017/08/28/counterfeit-fashion-brands/

Farkas, Brian. "How Do I Know if My Invention is "Nonobvious" When Applying for a Patent?". Nolo. Accessed November 23, 2019. https://www.nolo.com/legal-encyclopedia/how-do-i-know-if-my-invention-is-nonobvious-when-applying-for-a-patent.html

Fischer, Fridolin. "Design Law in the European Fashion Sector". World Intellectual Property Organization. Accessed February 15, 2019. https://www.wipo.int/wipo_magazine/en/2008/01/article_0006.html https://www.wipo.int/portal/en/

Kitroeff, Natalie. "Fashion Nova's Secret: Underpaid Workers in Los Angeles Factories". NY Times. December 16, 2109. https://www.nytimes.com/2019/12/16/business/fashion-nova-underpaid-workers.html

Moulds, Josephine. "Child Labour in the Fashion Supply Chain". The Guardian. Accessed September 14, 2019. https://labs.theguardian.com/unicef-child-labour/

Nisen, Max. "How Nike Solved Its Sweatshop Problem". Business Insider. May 10, 2013. https://www.businessinsider.in/How-Nike-Solved-Its-Sweatshop-Problem/articleshow/21122639.cms

Pratap, Abhijeet. "Nike Corporate Social Responsibility and Sustainable Innovation". Notesmatic. January 19, 2020. https://notesmatic.com/2018/02/nike-csr-and-sustainability/

Prentice Nancy, K. "All of the Retail Technology to Rock Your Sales". Mr. Magzaine. January 10, 2019. https://mr-mag.com/all-of-the-retail-technology-to-rock-your-sales/

Segran, Elizabeth. 'Did a Slave Make Your Sneaker? The Answer is: Probably". Fast Company. December 14, 2018. https://www.fastcompany.com/90279693/did-a-slave-make-your-sneakers-the-answer-is-probably

Silverman, Iona. "Copyright and Fashion: A UK Perspective". World Intellectual Property Organization. Accessed February 20, 2019. https://www.wipo.int/wipo_magazine/en/2014/03/article_0007.html

Sperry, Isabel. "5 Fashion Companies Leading the Sustainability Movement". Vault. September 22, 2016. https://www.vault.com/blogs/in-good-company-vaults-csr-blog/5-fashion-companies-leading-the-sustainability-movement

Williams, Michael. "Why Brunello Cucinelli is Worth the Price (Hint: It's Not Just the Cashmere)". GQ. September 18, 2017. https://www.gq.com/story/brunello-cucinelli-buying-for-value

Witzburg, Francesca M. "Protecting Fashion: A Comparative Analysis of Fashion Design Protection in the United States and Europe". Cardozo Aelj. December 1, 2016. http://www.cardozoaelj.com/2016/12/01/protecting-fashion-comparative-analysis-fashion-design-protection-united-states-europe/

Index

Page numbers in **bold reference tables.

4Ps of Growth 122

Aaker, David 86
accessible luxury, Longchamp 110
AD (Advertising Directors) 37
ad valorem 209
Adidas 39
Adidas by Stella McCartney 223
advertising: ethics 222; franchising agreement 170; licensing agreement 155–6
Advertising Directors (AD) 37
advised LC 198
advising banks 198
affiliate links 102
agency agreements 145–6
aided awareness 89
airway bills 196
alignment: brands 85–6; of ethics with organization culture 221
Alliance for Bangladesh Worker Safety 229
Amazon 81
Ansoff's product/market expansion grid 117–18
Apparel Sourcing 193
Apple Watch 84
arbitrary trademarks 232
area franchises 162
artists, textile mills 51
the Athlete 11
attitude 88
audit rights, licensing agreement 156
authentication technology 242–3
autocratic leaders 23
auxiliaries 55–6

BA (banker's acceptance) 202
backward vertical integration 104
Balenciaga 106
Balenciaga, Cristobal 106
Banana Republic 69
Bangladesh 229
banker's acceptance (BA) 202

banks: confirming banks 198; LC (letter of credit) transactions 197
BAV (Brand/Asset Valuator) model 92–4
BCG (Boston Matrix) 118–20
behavior 88
behavioral-oriented methods, brand valuation 92–4
Benetton 173–6
Benetton, Giuliana 173
Benetton, Luciano 173
Berne Convention 235
better segment 52
bill of exchange 200
bill of lading (BL) 196, 200
BIS (Bureau of Industry and Security) 204
BL (bill of lading) 196, 200
BMM (Brand Marketing Manager) 36
Boedecker, George 212
Boston Matrix (BCG Matrix) 118–20
boutiques 54
brand adjacency 125
brand advocate 85
brand alignment 85–6
brand ambassadorship 101
brand amnesia 81–2
brand associations 90
brand audits 103–4
brand awareness 89–90, 92
brand believers 86
brand communication 100
brand creation 117
brand decision 96–7
brand ego 81–2
brand equity 86; brand loyalty 86–8; checkpoints for 90–1; measuring 86
brand extensions 115, 123; advantages of 128–9; brand adjacency 125; categories of 123–5; challenges 129–30; equity and 131; guidelines for implementing 127–8; licensing 133; managers 133–4; naming strategies 133
Brand Finance 91–2

brand identity 82–3
brand image 92
brand knowledge 92
brand loyalty 86–8; relationship marketing 89
brand market value 91
Brand Marketing Manager (BMM) 36
brand mentions 102
brand positioning 84
brand preference 88
brand proposals 183–4
brand providers 86
brand relevance 81–2, 125
brand reviews, influencer marketing 101
brand stature 93
brand strength 93
brand valuation 86, 91; behavioral-oriented methods 92–4; combined methods 94–5; financial-oriented methods 91–2
brand valuation methods **92**
brand value 80–1
brand visionaries 85
Brand/Asset Valuator (BAV) model 92–4
branding 84, 86, 96; brand decision 96–7; co-branding 102–3; influencer marketing 100–2; positioning map 99; positioning statement 98; positioning strategy 97–8; trademarks 231
brands 78–80; disruptive positioning 84–5; evaluation 103–4; growth strategies 104; lifestyle brands 117; positioning and alignment 85–6; re-launching 104–6; repositioning 104–5; revitalization of 104–6; store experiences 83–4
Brand's Dynamic Pyramid 87
brand-specific values 81
breakaway brands 85
bridge segment 53
Brown, Millward 87
Brunello Cucinelli 244
budget segment 52
Burberry 69
Bureau of Industry and Security (BIS) 204
business development 22
business ethics 218; *see also* ethics
business ethics framework 220–1
business management, VCM (value chain management) 61
business policy 26

Calvin Klein 69, 105–7; advertising, ethics 222; brands **125**; licensing 149–50; licensing partners **150**
cancellation policies, franchising agreement 170
cannibalization, franchising 164
CAPRI 64
Capsule Show 192

Cardin, Pierre 125–6
case studies: Under Armour 38–43; Benetton 173–6; Crocs 212–15; Cucinelli, Brunello 244–6; Longchamp 108–12; Uniqlo 71–5
cash in advance, terms of payment by importers 197
Cassegrain, Jean 108
categories of brand extensions 123–5
category conventions 185
category extensions 124–5
category killers 54
CDPA (Copyright, Designs, and Patents Act), United Kingdom 240
celebrity influencers 101
centralization, versus decentralization 14
chain of command 14
Chanel 81
check payments, terms of payment by importers 197
child labor 226
Chung, Alexa 112
CIF (cost, insurance and freight) 195
CMT (Cut, Make, and Trim) 59
Coach 110
co-branding 102–3
codes of conduct 221
coercive power 23
collectivism 208
color, brand identity 82–3
co-marketing 102–3
combatting counterfeits 242
combined financial/behavioral methods, brand valuation 94–5
combined tariffs 209
commercial banks, financing exports 202
commercial invoices 196
commitment, stages of 87
committed buyers 87
common law trademark 231
communication, brand communication 100
communication strategy, global marketing programs 205
communities, ethics and 223
companies, brand decision 96–7
comparing, control process 25
compensation, licensing agreement 157–8
competitive advantage 31–2
complaint limitations, franchising agreement 168
complementary category extensions 125
compliance risks 136
Comrade 11
concentric diversification 122
confirmed irrevocable LC 198–9
confirmed LC 198
confirming banks 198

conflicts of interest, ethics 222
conglomerate diversification 122
consideration set 90
consignment, terms of payment by
    importers 201–2
consular invoices 196
consumers: brand decision 97; impact of
    ethics 222
consumption categories, versus investments 147
contemporary segment 53
contributions, VCM (value chain management) 60
control 2
control process 24–5
control risks 136
controlling risk 137–8
conventional corporate culture 12
converters 50–1
copying fashion 229–30
copyright 233–5; licensing 147; national copyright
    protection 239–40; UCD (Unregistered
    Community Designs) 239
Copyright, Designs, and Patents Act (1988),
    United Kingdom 240
Copyright Act of 1790 233
copyright infringement 240–1
core competency 30–1
core values, brands 81
corporate citizenship 218, 220
corporate culture 10–11
corporate governance 28
corporate social performance (CSP) 219
corporate social responsibility (CSR) 218;
    LVMH (Louis Vuitton Moet Hennessy) 224–5;
    Nike 229–30
corporate social responsiveness 219
cost, franchising 166
cost leadership strategy 33
cost-based methods 91
The COTERIE 192
Coty, Inc. 149
counterfeits 240–3
credibility, franchising 166
credit cards, terms of payment by importers 197
credits, licensing agreement 156–7
Crocs 212–15
CSP (corporate social performance) 219
CSR (corporate social responsibility) 218;
    LVMH (Louis Vuitton Moet Hennessy) 224–5;
    Nike 229–30
Cucinelli, Brunello 244–6
cultural conventions 185
Cultural Dimensions theory 208
culture: brand decision 97; corporate culture
    10–11; ethics 221; global environment and 208;
    leadership and 24; organizational culture 11–12

Customer Insight Team, Uniqlo 75
customer retention 86
customization, versus standardization 205
Cut, Make, and Trim (CMT) 59

damages, franchising agreement 168
date draft 201
decentralization, versus centralization 14
decision-making process 7–8
defaults, franchising agreement 168
Delafontaine, Sophie 108–10
Delahunt, Bill 231
delivery, licensing agreement 156
democratic leadership style 23
department stores 54
departmentalization 13
departments within fashion organizations
    21–2
descriptive trademarks 232
design, licensing agreement 154
design and development 21
design directors, jobbers 51
design patents 235
Design Piracy Prohibition Act (DPPA) 231
designer segment 53
desired points-of-difference 131
developing markets, versus developed markets
    204–5
DFC (U.S. International Development Finance
    Corporation) 204
DFS group 190
Diesel 131–2
differentiation strategy 33
Digital Marketing Manager (DMM) 37
directional plans, versus specific plans 10
Director of Product Development (DPD) 36
discount stores 54
dispute resolution, franchising agreement 169
disruptive positioning, brands 84–5
distribution: Crocs 213; licensing agreement
    154–5
distribution strategy, global marketing programs
    205–6
Diversification Strategy 122
Divisional Merchandising Manager (DMM) 37
divisional structures, organizational design 15–16
DKNY 133
DMM (Digital Marketing Manager) 37
DMM (Divisional Merchandising Manager) 37
Dockers 130
documents, export documents 196
Donna Karan 133
Downing, Ken 70
DPD (Director of Product Development) 36
DPPA (Design Piracy Prohibition Act) 231

duration: franchising agreement 168; licensing agreement 153–4
duty free outlets 189–90

economic responsibilities 219
economic value, brands 80
economies of scale 33, 64, 122, 182, 191, 206
Ederer, Louis 237
EEI (electronic export information filing) 196
effectiveness, management 2
efficiency, management 2
electronic export information filing (EEI) 196
electronic product codes (EPCs) 243
elite corporate culture 11
EMC (Export Management Company) 203
employee downsizings, ethics 223
employee safety, ethics 223
employees, ethics and 223
enterprises, acquiring in foreign markets 189
entities, brands 79
environmental risks 136
environments, global environment 208
EPCs (electronic product codes) 243
EPZ (export processing zones) 59
equity: brand extensions 131; brands 80
Esmark Inc. 139
Estée Lauder 134
e-tailing 54
ETC (Export Trading Company) 203
ETF (electronic transfer of funds), terms of payment by importers 197
ethical responsibilities 219
ethics: alignment with organization culture systems 221; communities and 223; CSR (corporate social responsibility) 218; employees and 223; impact on consumers 222; labor issues 225–30; management and 218–25; shareholders and 223; supply chains 221–2
EU (European Union), IP (intellectual property) 238–9
European Community Design Protection Regulation 238
European Union (EU), IP (intellectual property) 238–9
evaluation, brands 103–4
event coverage, influencer marketing 102
EX Works 194–5
exclusivity, licensing agreement 153
EXIM (Export-Import Bank) 204
exit strategies, franchising agreement 170
expert power 23
export decision 190–3
export documents 196
export intermediaries 202–3
export licenses 196

export management companies 202–3
export packing lists 196
export price quotes 194–5
export process 193–5
export processing zones (EPZ) 59
export trading companies 202–3
exporters, considerations for 204–9
Export-Import Bank (EXIM) 204
exporting: advantages of 191; challenges 192; export decision 190–3; foreign markets 190
exports, financing exports 202–4
external analysis 185
external risks 136
external sources 8

facilities, franchising 165
factoring, financing exports 203
factors, financing exports 203
factory outlets 54
fanciful trademarks 232
fashion conglomerates 63–4
fashion design, manufacturing and 52–4
fashion director (FD) 34
fashion industry, SCM (supply chain management) 59
fashion merchandising 21; retailing 55
fashion retailers 54–5
fashion shows 56
fashion trade fairs 192–3
"Fashion Weeks" 56
fast fashion model 64–5
Fast Retailing (FR) 74
FD (fashion director) 34
femininity 208
Fendi 243
FF (freight forwarder) 200
finance and accounting 21
financial controls, franchising 165
financial risks 135
financial versus strategic goals 9
financial-oriented methods, brand valuation 91–2
financing exports 202–4
Finproject 212
flagship stores 54
flat organization, organizational design 16
FOB (Free on Board + name of port of shipment) 194–5
focus strategy 33
forced labor 226
Ford, Tom 69, 105, 134–5
foreign markets 185–90; export documents 196; export process 193–5; financing exports 202–4; terms of payment by importers 196–202
forfaiting, financing exports 203

formal versus informal planning 8
formalization 14
forward vertical integration 104
FR (Fast Retailing) 74
France, copyright 239
franchise categories 162
franchise fee/investment, franchising agreement 171
franchisees 164–6
franchising 160–6; foreign markets 190
Franchising 2.0 174
franchising agreements 166–72
franchisors 162–4
franchisor's right of first refusal, franchising agreement 169
the Free Spirit 11–12
free trade zones (FTZ) 211
freight forwarder (FF) 200
French Intellectual Property Code (IPC) 239
FTZ (free trade zones) 211
fully owned subsidiaries 187–9
fully vertically integrated 104
functional organizational structures 15

Gap Inc. 72, 229; hybrid organizational structure 17; influencer marketing 102
gender, labor issues 226
General Merchandising Manager (GMM) 37
generic trademarks 232
G-III Apparel Group, Ltd. 149
Giorgio Armani 125
global environment, culture and 208
global expansion 116, 182; brand proposals 183–4; Crocs 212–15; exporting 190–3; external analysis 185; internal analysis 183–5; see also foreign markets
global market 181
global marketing programs 205–7
global presence 182
global trade barriers 209
GMM (General Merchandising Manager) 37
goal setting 5–6; SMART goals 6–7; strategic versus financial goals 9
granting of rights, licensing agreement 153
greenfield ventures 188
griege 49
growth: global expansion 182; reasons for 115; risk management and 135–7; Smart Growth 122–3
growth matrix 117
growth strategies 115–16; brand extensions see brand extensions; brands 104; Diversification Strategy 122; existing customers 116; Market Development Strategy 120–1; Market Penetration Strategy 117; new users and

situations 116–17; PEST analysis 121; Product Development Strategy 121–2
Gucci 105–6, 134, 236–8
guerrilla marketing 170
Guess 236–8

H&M 72
habitual buyers 87
Halston 138–40
Halston Heritage 140
Halston III 139
Hanson, Lydon "Duke" 212
Harley Davidson Cologne 81–2
haute couture 53
hazard risk 136
Hess, Edward 122
High Fashion 53
Hofstede, Geert 208
holacracy organization structure, Zappos 18–19
horizontal corporate culture 11–12
horizontal diversification 122
horizontal integration 104
horizontal organization 16
human resources (HR) 22
Humanistic Capitalism 244–5
humanistic enterprise 244
hybrid organizational structure 17
hyper-stores 54

identity, brands 80, 82–3
identity symbols 82–3
ILO (International Labor Organization) 226
images, brands 92
indemnification: franchising agreement 169; licensing agreement 157
Inditex 72
individual franchises 162
individualism 208
indulgence 208
influencer marketing, branding 100–2
Influencer Marketing Hub 100
informal versus formal planning 8
innovation: brands 80; growth 116
in-store boutiques (shops-in-shops) 54
insurance: franchising agreement 169; licensing agreement 157
intellectual property 229; copyright 233–5; franchising agreement 168; patents 235–8; protections for 238–9; trademarks 231–3
Interbrand 86
internal analysis 183–5
internal risks 135
internal sources 8
international copyright protection 235
International Labor Organization (ILO) 226

international licensing, Ralph Lauren 160
international presence 181
international trademark protection 233
investments: versus consumption categories 147; franchising agreement 171
investor relations 22
IP (intellectual property) 229; copyright 233–5; patents 235–8; protections for 238–9; trademarks 231–3
IPC (French Intellectual Property Code) 239
irrevocable LC 198
IT (information technology) 22
Italian Copyright Law (LDA) 239
Italy, copyright 239–40
items, brand identity 83

Jacobs, Marc 140
JCPenney: Halston III 139; positioning statement 98
Jenner, Kendall 112
JIT (just-in-time) 65–6
jobbers 51
joint ventures (JV) 186–7
just-in-time (JIT) 65–6
JV (joint ventures) 186–7

Kate Spade 69
Keller, Kevin 131
KERING 63–4
key opinion leaders (KOLs) 101
knock offs 229, 240–1
Kohl's 234
KOLs (key opinion leaders) 101
Krogh, Astrid 111

labor issues 225–30
laissez-fair leaders 23
layoffs, ethics 223
LC (letter of credit, terms of payment by importers 197–200
LD (licensing director) 34
LDA (Italian Copyright Law) 239
Le Pliage, Longchamp 108
leaders: versus managers 22–3; sources of power 23
leadership, culture and 24
leadership styles 23
leading 2
lean manufacturing 66
leasing, financing exports 203
legal responsibilities 219
legitimate power 23
letter of credit (LC), terms of payment by importers 197–200
levels of management 3–5

Levi's 130
licensed products, licensing agreement 151
licensed property, licensing agreement 151
licensee 150–1
licensing 129, 144–5; advantages for licensor 147–8; advantages of for licensee 150; brand extensions 133; Calvin Klein 149–50; copyright 147; disadvantages to licensee 150–1; disadvantages to licensor 148–9; foreign markets 190; versus franchising 161; registered designs 147; trademarks 146; unregistered designs 147
licensing agents 145–6
licensing agreements 151–60
licensing director (LD) 34
The Licensing King 126
licensing partners, Calvin Klein **150**
licensing valuation method 91–2
licensor 147–8
lifestyle brands 117
LifeWear, Uniqlo 71–5
line extensions 123–4
living wage 225
local distributors, foreign markets 186
location, franchising agreement 166
logos: brand identity 83; franchising agreement 170
London Textile Fair 193
Longchamp 108–12
long-term orientation 208
long-term risks 136
Louis Vuitton 69; brand value 86
Louis Vuitton Moët Hennessy (LVMH) 63; CSR (corporate social responsibility) 224–5; DFS group 190
low-level managers 4–5
loyalty, brand loyalty 86–8
Loyalty Matrix 88–9
luxury segment 53
luxury side 20–1
LVMH (Louis Vuitton Moët Hennessy) 63; CSR (corporate social responsibility) 224–5; DFS group 190

macro influencers 101
Macy's Inc. 104
Magic 192
Maglificio di Ponzano Veneto dei Fratelli Benetton 173
management 1–2; business policy 26; corporate governance 28; ethics and 218–25; global expansion 183–4; levels of 3–5; strategic management see strategic management
Management by Objectives (MBO) 8–9
management positions in fashion industry 34–7

management process: controlling 24–5; leading 22–4; organizing *see* organizing; planning *see* planning

managerial action, control process 25

managers 2–3; brand extension opportunities 133–4; versus leaders 22–3; low-level managers 4–5; mid-level managers 4; top-level managers 3–4

managing risk *see* risk management

manufacturing segment 52–4

Marcolin Group 134

Market Development Strategy 120–1

Market Penetration Strategy 117

market valuation 86

marketability, franchising 165

marketing 55–6; export marketing plans 194; franchising agreement 170; global marketing programs *see* global marketing programs; guerrilla marketing 170; Longchamp 111

Marketing Director (MD) 36

marketing mix, internal analysis 184–5

masculinity 208

mass merchants 54

mass-market 20, 52–3

master franchises 162

Mastige (Mass+Prestige) 53

matrix organizational structure 16–17

MBO (Management by Objectives) 8–9

McKinsey Consultant group 90

MD (Marketing Director) 36

MDBs (Multilateral Development Banks) 204

measuring: brand equity 86; control process 24–5

Mediakis 100

medium-term risks 136

membership clubs 54

Merch. M (Merchandising Managers) 37

merchandising 55

Merchandising Managers (Merch. M) 37

Michael Kors 69

micro influencers 101

mid-level managers 4

Milano Moda Donna 193

Milano Moda Uomo 193

mills 49

minimum order quantity (MOQ) 73

mission statements 10

Missoni, competitive advantage 31

mixed system, franchising 161

Mizrahi, Isaac 130

MODA 193

model prototypes, franchising 165

moderate segment 52

modern organization 17

The Momad Metropolis 193

MOQ (minimum order quantity) 73

Moss, Kate 108

Mulberry 69

Multilateral Development Banks (MDBs) 204

multiple unit franchises 162

NAFTA 2.0 210–11

names, brand identity 82

naming strategies, brand extensions 133

nano influencers 101

narratives, culture 13

national copyright protection 239–40

needs conventions 185

net present value (NPV) 86

network organization 17

Nike 39–40; brand value 86; code of conduct 222; CSR (corporate social responsibility) 229–30; growth through innovation 116; mission statements 10; SWOT analysis 29–30; vision statements 10

Nomad 12

non-competition covenant, franchising agreement 169

Nordstrom 81

Norton Simon 139

notices, licensing agreement 156–7

NPV (net present value) 86

obligations, franchising agreement 168

OBM (original brand manufacturing) 60

ODM (original design manufacturing) 59–60

OEM (original equipment manufacturing) 59

off-price discounters 54

Oliver, Shayne 132

"One for One Movement," TOMS Shoes 223–4

ongoing fees, franchising agreement 171

online shopping 54

open accounts 201

operation management, SCM (supply chain management) 61

operational plans, versus strategic plans 9

operational risks 135

opportunities, global expansion 209

Opportunities (O) 29

opportunity risks 136

oral reports 25

organizational culture 11–12

organizational design: elements of 13–14; types of 14–17

organizations: alignment of ethics and culture 221; internal analysis 183–5

organizing 1, 13; departments within fashion organizations 21–2; elements of organizational design 13–14; luxury side 20–1; mass-market 20; types of organizational design 14–17

original brand manufacturing (OBM) 60

original design manufacturing (ODM) 59–60
original equipment manufacturing (OEM) 59
ornaments, copyright 234
overt technology 243

packing, brand identity 83
Pantene, positioning statement 98
Pareto, Vilfredo 89
Pareto's 80/20 theory 89
Parker, Sarah Jessica 140
participative leaders 23
Patent and Trademark Office (PTO) 231
patents 235–8; franchising agreement 170
pattern makers 53
patterns, brand identity 83
payments, licensing agreement 158–9
people, culture 13
personal observation 24
personality, brand identity 83
personnel, franchising 165
PEST analysis 121
philanthropic responsibilities 219
Phillips-Van Heusen Corporation 64
photos, copyright 234
physical separability 234
picture patents 235
Pitti Immagine Bimbo 193
Pitti Immagine Uomo 193
place, culture 13
Plank, Kevin 38
planning 1, 5; culture 11–13; decision-making
    process 7–8; formal versus informal 8;
    Management by Objectives (MBO) 8–9;
    mission versus vision statements 10; setting
    goals 5–6; SMART goals 6–7; specific versus
    directional plans 10; strategic versus financial
    goals 9; strategic versus operational plans 9
plant managers 35
Plato's Closet 171–2
PM (product manager) 34–5
points of parity 131
policy 26; versus strategy 27
pop-up stores 54
Porenza Schouler 69
Porter's Model of Five Forces of Competition
    32–3; Under Armour 40
Porter's value chain analysis model 61–3
positioning, brands 80, 84–6
positioning map, branding 99
positioning statement, brands 98
positioning strategy, branding 97–8
power distance 208
PPM (Product Marketing Manager) 36
PR (Public Relations) 37
practices, culture 13

Prada 64, 69, 128
preferential programs, trade agreements 209–11
Première Vision Designs 192
premium segment 53
price-oriented methods 91
pricing strategy, global marketing programs 206
prints, copyright 234
pro forma invoices 196
process, management 1
Prod. M (production manager) 35
Product Development Strategy 121–2
product licensing, Ralph Lauren 159–60
product manager (PM) 34–5
Product Marketing Manager (PPM) 36
product safety, ethics 222
product strategy, global marketing programs 205
product-based brands 97
production manager 35
profitability, franchising 165
profit-based methods 91
progressive corporate culture 12
Project 192
protection of proprietary information, franchising
    agreement 168
protections for, intellectual property 238–9
PTO (Patent and Trademark Office) 231
Public Relations (PR) 37
PVH Corp. 64, 149

QC (quality control): franchising agreement 168;
    licensing agreement 154
QM (quality control manager) 35–6
QR (quick response) 65–6
quality control manager (QM) 35–6
quality control (QC): franchising agreement 168;
    licensing agreement 154
quick response (QR) 65–6

radio frequency identification (RFID) 243
Ralph Lauren 69, 81; licensing 159–60
RCD (Registered Community Design) 239
Rebecca Minkoff (RM), SNBN (see now, buy now)
    69–70
recognition, brand awareness 89–90
referent power 23
Registered Community Design (RCD) 239
registered designs, licensing 147
relationship marketing, brand loyalty 89
relationships between parties, franchising
    agreement 169
re-launching, brands 104–6
relevance, brands 81–2, 125
renewal rights, franchising agreement 170
Rentner, Maurice 229
repositioning brands 104–5

restraint 208
restrictions on consumers, licensing agreement 156
retail categories 54–5
retail licensing 160–1
retailing, fashion merchandising 55
revitalization: of brands 104–6; of Calvin Klein 106–7
Revlon 140
revocable LC 198
revolving LC 198
reward power 23
RFID (radio frequency identification) 243
RICHEMONT 64
risk management, growth and 135–6
Robertson, Brian 18
Role Marketplace, Zappos 18–19
roles: of licensing agents 145–6; of managers 2
Rolex 81
RoO (rules of origin) 210
Rosso, Renzo 131
royalties: franchising 160; franchising agreements 171; licensing agreements 157–8
Royalty Relief Method 91
Rubchinskiy, Gosha 132

sales after termination, licensing agreements 157
sales and marketing 21
sales efforts, licensing agreements 155
sample makers 53
SBA (U.S. Small Business Association) 204
SCM (supply chain management) 56–60; versus VCM (value chain management) 61
sculptural components, copyright 234
Seamans, Scott 212
secured financing 202
see now, buy now (SNBN) 66–7
segment-specific values 81
service-based brands 98
shareholders, ethics and 223
short-term orientation 208
short-term risks 136
sight drafts 200–1
signage, franchising agreement 170
Simon, Hermann 206
Simons, Raf 105–7
simple structure, organizational design 14
skills, of managers 2–3
SMART goals 6–7
Smart Growth 122–3
SNBN (see now, buy now) 66–70
social responsibility 218
Sole, Domenico de 134
Soto, Tatiana 91
sources of power, leaders 23

sourcing and production 22
span of control, organizing 14
specialty stores 54
specific plans, versus directional plans 10
Sperry, influencer marketing 102
sponsorships, influencers 101
Srivastava, Rajendra K. 85
stages of commitment 87
standardization, versus customization 205
statements, licensing agreement 158–9
Stella McCartney 223
Stop Counterfeiting in Manufactured Goods Act 242
store experiences 83–4
strategic category extensions 125
strategic decisions 27–8
strategic management 28; SWOT analysis 28–9
strategic plans, versus operational plans 9
strategic risks 135
strategic versus financial goals 9
strategy 26–7; versus policy 27
strength-opportunity strategies 29
Strengths (S) 28
strength-threat strategies 29
Styld.by campaign, Gap Inc. 102
stylists 51
sub-franchising 162
sublicensing 156
subsidiaries 187–9
suggestive trademarks 232
supply chain management (SCM) 56–60
supply chains 49; ethics 221–2; SNBN (see now, buy now) 67; Uniqlo 73–4
support services, franchising agreement 168
sustainable innovation, Nike 229–30
Swatch 84
sweatshops 226–9
switchers 87
SWOT analysis 28–9; Under Armour 40–1; Nike 29–30; versus Porter's Model 33

Tajimi, Hana 74
Takeuchi, Hirotaka 74
Target 130
Target Foundation 223
tariffs 209
teachability, franchising 165
team-first corporate culture 11
tech packs 21
termination: franchising agreements 170; licensing agreements 157
terms of payment by importers 196–202
territorial franchises 162
territory, franchising agreement 166
TESS (Trademark Electronic Search System) 232
textile converters 50–1

textile segment 49–52
textile trade shows 192–3
Texworld Paris 193
Texworld USA 192
Thakoon 69–70
Thomas, Gregory 85
Threats (T) 29
time drafts 201
timing in textile industry 51–2
Tom Ford 69, 134–5
TOMS Shoes 223–4
top-level managers 3–4
Toray 73
trade, free trade zones 211
trade agreements 209–11
trade barriers 209
trade dress 233
trade secrets, patents 236
trademark counterfeiting 240
Trademark Electronic Search System
    (TESS) 232
trademarks 231–3; franchising agreement 170;
    licensing 146
traditional/hierarchical structure, organizational
    design 14–16
traditionalist 12
training, franchising agreement 168
transactional leadership 23
transfers, franchising agreement 169
transformational leadership 23
trend responsive 64
triple transformation 210
typography, brand identity 83

UCD (Unregistered Community Designs) 238;
    copyright protection 239
UK (United Kingdom), copyright law 240
unaided awareness 90
uncertainty avoidance 208
Under Armour 38–43
Uniqlo 71–5
United Colors of Benetton 174
United Kingdom (UK), copyright law 240
United States Commercial Service (USCS) 204
Unregistered Community Designs (UCD) 238
unregistered designs, licensing 147
unsecured financing 202

U.S. International Development Finance
    Corporation (DFC) 204
U.S. Small Business Administration (SBA) 204
USCS (United States Commercial Service) 204
USMCA (U.S.-Mexico-Canada Agreement) 210–11
utility patents 236

value, brands 79–81
value chain management (VCM) 60–3
value chain (VC) 60–1
value creation 60
values, culture 12–13
VC (value chain) 60–1
VCM (value chain management) 60–3; versus
    SCM (supply chain management) 61
vertical brand extensions 124
vertical integration 104
VF Corporation 64
virtual organization 17
vision, culture 12
vision statements 10

Wachner, Linda 149
Walk Free Organization 226
Walker Consulting, Loyalty Matrix 88–9
Walmart 229; brand value 80–1; value
    chains 61
Warnaco Group 149
Weaknesses (W) 29
weakness-opportunity strategies 29
weakness-threats strategies 29
wholesale 22
wholly owned subsidiaries 188
Winmark Corporation, Plato's Closet 171–2
wire transfers, terms of payment by
    importers 197
work specialization 13
working conditions 225–6

Y&R (Young and Rubicam) 92
Yanai, Tadashi 71
yarn-forward rules of origin (RoO) 210
Young and Rubicam (Y&R) 92

Zappos 18–19; culture 11
Zappos for Good 223
Zara 72; competitive advantage 31